THE VICTORIAN KITCHEN *Book of* PASTRIES AND PUDDINGS

THE VICTORIAN KITCHEN *Book of* PASTRIES AND PUDDINGS

ISLAND BOOKS
PRODUCED FOR S. WEBB & SON

The Victorian Kitchen Book Collection

Designed, written and edited by
THE BRIDGEWATER BOOK COMPANY LTD

Text Amelia Swann
Art Director Annie Moss
Designer Jane Lanaway
Managing Editor Anna Clarkson
Page make-up Chris Lanaway
Photographer Trevor Wood
Hand-coloured plates Lorraine Harrison
Food preparation and styling Jon Higgins

CLB 4189

This edition published by S. Webb & Son

Colour separation by Sussex Repro, England
Printed and bound in Singapore

ISBN 1-85833-455-1

CONTENTS

INTRODUCTION

I think I could eat one of Bellamy's veal pies.

Alleged last words of *William Pitt the Younger (1759–1806)*

BEFORE THE DAYS of cars and central heating, before labour saving devices and mechanisation released most people from a daily grind of hard physical work, well-filled pastries and good, substantial puddings that really lined the stomach were a vital source of heat and energy. These days, it may not be advisable to consume such calorie-laden goodies on a daily basis, but they are unbeatable as an occasional treat or for a special celebration.

The recipes in this book represent only a fraction of the huge and imaginative range of baked, steamed and boiled puddings and pies, tarts and pastries made by Victorian cooks. All the recipes are based on authentic recipes of the period, but have been carefully adapted to suit the smaller families and less heroic appetites of today.

MRS BEETON'S

PASTRY HINTS

Here are Mrs Beeton's main commandments, rendered into modern English.

1 Touch the pastry as little as possible.
2 Work with cool hands on a cool surface such as a marble slab.
3 Add liquids gradually and work them in with a flat blade.
4 Work as fast as possible to keep the pastry light.

BOILED PUDDING HINTS

1 Simmer custard-based puddings rather than boiling them fiercely, or they will be honeycombed with air holes.
2 Always fill the pudding mould up completely.
3 Keep the water in the boiling saucepan topped up.
4 Stand the pudding to rest for five minutes when it is cooked to let out the steam.

Variety in the ingredients, we think, is held only of secondary consideration with the great body of people, provided that the whole is agreeable and of sufficient abundance.

Mrs Beeton on Puddings

PREPARING THE MOULDS

Make sure all moulds, basins or dishes are clean and dry. For substantial puddings, be generous when you butter the moulds. For lighter puddings, brush the moulds with clarified butter.

CRUSTS AND PASTES

The Victorian cook enjoyed an impressive repertoire of pastry (which was called crust or paste) aside from shortcrust in its varying degrees of richness or sweetness. Suet and butter crust were used for puddings; cream crust, French crust, today called pâté brisée, and puff paste were used for sweet and savoury pies and tarts.

Suet for Pastry

Suet is obtained from hard animal fat. The fat from beef and veal is preferred, and the best comes from the fatty cushion that protects the animals' kidneys. It must be carefully chopped to remove all trace of meat fibre, then minced very finely before use.

Pastry is one of the most important branches of culinary science. It increasingly occupies itself with ministering pleasure to the sight as well as the taste.

MRS BEETON

A PANTRY FULL OF AUTHENTIC VICTORIAN PASTRIES AND PUDDINGS

Bakewell Pudding, a truly delicious classic dish

Lady Shaftesbury's Pudding

EMILY SHAFTESBURY (1810–1872), wife to the philanthropic Lord Shaftesbury, kept a recipe book. Among other dishes and household hints, there is a recipe for Bakewell Pudding with a meringue topping.

This pudding is famous not only in Derbyshire, but in several of our northern counties, where it is usually served on all holiday occasions.

ELIZA ACTON

BAKEWELL PUDDING

This is a truly delicious classic dish, based on Mrs Beeton's recipe; she describes it as "very rich". It should always be called a pudding, not a tart. Eliza Acton's recipe incorporated candied peel in the jam, but she herself regarded this as "unrefined".

INGREDIENTS

4oz/125g Puff Pastry
Jam
5 Fresh Eggs
6oz/175g Caster Sugar
4oz/125g Melted Butter
1oz/25g Ground Almonds

METHOD

❦ Roll the puff pastry out thinly and line a 9in/22cm flan ring. Over the base, spread a good thick layer of jam, preferably homemade strawberry.

❦ Into a mixing bowl place the yolks of four eggs and the yolk and white of the fifth and beat thoroughly. Add the sugar, melted butter and almonds and mix until well incorporated. Pour the mixture over the jam and spread out evenly.

❦ Bake at 180°C/350°F/gas mark 4 for about 30 minutes until the crust has turned a beautiful golden brown.

Windsor Castle Staff Carrot Pudding

In Queen Victoria's day, the army of staff that ran her palaces took a lot of feeding. One of their favourite dishes was carrot pudding. It was essentially the same as Mrs Beeton's recipe, but made with industrial amounts of carrots, flour, suet and dried fruit; three cupfuls of orange peel were added as well as some baking powder to lift the load. It took five hours to boil.

CARROT PUDDING, A FAVOURITE WITH CHILDREN

A Sweet Vegetable

Carrots contain a lot of sugar and 19th-century cooks in France, Italy and England used them for all manner of delicious sweet tarts, cakes and puddings. There was even a carrot jam, made in southwest France; it was imaginatively named Cheveux d'Ange, or Angel's Hair.

CARROT PUDDING

This is based on a Mrs Beeton recipe; the natural sweetness of carrots makes a filling, wholesome pudding suitable for hungry children. Serve it with custard sauce.

INGREDIENTS

12oz/350g Fresh Carrots
3 Eggs
8oz/225g Fresh Breadcrumbs
4oz/125g Suet
4oz/125g Raisins
4oz/125g Currants
3oz/75g Caster Sugar
Milk
Icing Sugar

METHOD

- Peel the carrots and place in a pan of fresh water to boil until soft. Remove from the heat and drain. Put the carrots in a large mixing bowl and mash down to a purée.
- Stir in the eggs and the remaining dry ingredients along with sufficient milk to make a thick batter-like mix. Pour into a well-greased pie dish.
- Cook for one hour at 180°C/350°F/gas mark 4 until it is well risen and the crust has browned nicely. Dust well with sifted icing sugar before serving.

PLUM PUDDING OF FRESH FRUIT

Mrs Beeton considered that raw plums, although refreshing, lacked nourishment. Her reservations did not extend to cooked fruit "which even the invalid may eat in moderation". This is one of the most delicious ways to eat cooked plums.

INGREDIENTS

12oz/350g Suet Crust Pastry
1lb 8oz/700g Fresh Plums
4oz/125g Moist Brown Sugar

METHOD

- Roll the suet pastry out to roughly ½in/13mm thickness and line a pudding basin, reserving some pastry for the lid. Thoroughly wash the plums and cut in half removing all the stones. Fill the lined basin with the fruit, sprinkling in the sugar between layers.
- Roll out the reserved pastry and make a lid for the basin, pinching the edges together tightly to prevent any juices leaking. Dust a pudding cloth with a little flour, tie tightly over the top of the basin and place the pudding in a saucepan of boiling water to cook for two hours.
- When ready lift the pudding from the water and remove the covering. Serve with a custard sauce.

Eliza Acton's Vegetarian Plum Pudding

This economical recipe used mashed potatoes, carrots, flour, currants, sugar, suet, nutmeg and salt. She points out that the "cost of the ingredients does not exceed half a crown (12½ pence) and the pudding is of sufficient size for a party of 16 persons".

Life's a pudding full of plums.
W. S. GILBERT

COOK'S TIP

When the pudding has been taken out of the water, allow to stand for a few minutes to cool slightly and "shrink away" from the sides of the basin. This will allow you to turn it out on to a serving dish more easily.

I'm not so think as you drunk I am.

Sir John Squire,
Ballade of Soporific Absorption

Tipsy Puddings, just the thing for a frivolous lunchtime interlude

Tipsy Puddings

These gorgeous rum-soaked puddings are based on a Mrs Beeton recipe. They are quick and easy to make, just right for an impromptu celebration. Try them with champagne.

INGREDIENTS

2 Eggs
3oz/75g Caster Sugar
4oz/125g Plain Flour
3–4 tbsp/50ml Dark Rum
Desiccated Coconut to Decorate

METHOD

❦ Break the eggs into a bowl and beat together with the sugar until the mixture is smooth. Lightly fold in the flour until it is all incorporated, taking care to keep the mixture light.

❦ Grease six small moulds suitable for the oven with a little butter and sprinkle lots of caster sugar into them. Fill them three-quarters full with the mixture and bake at 180°C/350°F/gas mark 4 until they are well risen and firm to the touch (about 20 minutes).

❦ Remove from the oven and soak each pudding with some of the dark rum. Sprinkle with a little coconut before serving.

CHAMPAGNE CHARLIE

Champagne Charlie is my name
Champagne drinking is my game
There's no drink so good as
fizz, fizz, fizz
I drink every drop there is, is, is.
All around town they know
my name
By pop! pop! pop! I rose to fame
I'm the idol of the barmaids
And Champagne Charlie is
my name.

GEORGE LEYBOURNE AND ALFRED LEE

A Large Tipsy Pudding

You can also make a single, large tipsy pudding for an after dinner dessert. According to one traditional Victorian recipe, you make the pudding in one mould, turn it out and then pour over "as much warm Madeira as it will imbibe". Mask the, by now, tipsy pudding with apricot jam and decorate with slivers of blanched almonds.

CHRISTMAS PUDDING

Every Victorian cook had her own closely-guarded recipe for Christmas Pudding. This is just one of Mrs Beeton's selection and she called it "very good". She also offered a Rich Christmas Pudding, an inexpensive one and a Fruitarian Pudding which omits the suet.

INGREDIENTS

1lb/450g Plain Flour
8oz/225g Fresh Breadcrumbs
1lb/450g Shredded Suet
1lb/450g Raisins
12oz/350g Currants
4oz/125g Chopped Mixed Peel
4oz/125g Soft Brown Sugar
2oz/50g Chopped Blanched Almonds
1oz/25g Ground Mixed Spice
Good Pinch of Salt
6 Eggs
⅓pt/225ml Milk
2floz/50ml Brandy

METHOD

❦ In a large bowl mix together all the dry ingredients; to ensure that everything is thoroughly incorporated, it is best to use your hands for this.

❦ Lightly beat the eggs and stir into the mixture, then add the milk and brandy and stir until the pudding has a soft consistency. Pack the mixture into a buttered basin, pressing down well, and tie a layer of greaseproof paper over the top. Finish off with a pudding cloth tied tightly over the greaseproof.

❦ Place in a saucepan of boiling water that comes about two thirds of the way up the side of the basin and boil for about 6 hours. When cooked, remove the cloth and greaseproof paper and turn out on to a serving dish.

CHRISTMAS PUDDING, THE UNDISPUTED STAR OF THE LAVISH VICTORIAN CHRISTMAS

Heap on more wood! The wind is chill;
But let it whistle as it will
We'll keep a merry Christmas still.

SIR WALTER SCOTT

Buckingham Palace Plum Pudding

Each Christmas, 150 small plum puddings were made for the Royal Household. The recipe called for 60lb of flour, 30lb of sugar, 40lb each of raisins and currants, 30lb of candied peel, 50lb of beef suet, 150 eggs, 4 gallons of strong ale, 1lb of mixed spice and a bottle apiece of rum and brandy.

COOK'S TIP

For an even richer pudding, you can substitute cream for the milk, add an extra egg, and sprinkle candied peel in among the sultanas.

BREAD AND BUTTER PUDDING, EATEN IN NURSERIES AND GENTLEMEN'S CLUBS WITH EQUAL RELISH.

BREAD AND BUTTER PUDDING

Bread and Butter Pudding, the mainstay of the Victorian schoolroom and Gentlemen's Clubs, can be as plain or as rich as you like. This recipe is based on Mrs Beeton's Baked Bread and Butter Pudding.

INGREDIENTS

8 Slices of Stale, Buttered White Bread
3oz/75g Sultanas
3 Eggs
2oz/50g Caster Sugar
1pt/600ml Fresh Milk
¼pt/150ml Double Cream
Zest of 1 Lemon

METHOD

❦ Cut the bread into triangles and layer it in a lightly greased pie dish with a sprinkling of sultanas and a little lemon zest between each layer.

❦ Lightly beat the eggs and caster sugar in a mixing bowl and add the milk and cream, stiring to combine all the ingredients. Strain the mixture over the bread and allow to stand for one hour so that the milk can soak into the bread.

❦ Bake at 180°C/350°F/gas mark 4 until the egg custard is firm to the touch and the top layer of bread is golden brown.

BAKED APRICOT PUDDING, WARM AND GOLDEN, AND DELICIOUS WITH CREAM

METHOD

❦ Cut the apricots in half and remove the stones. Place the fruit in a saucepan with a little water and boil until the flesh has become soft. Pass the apricot pulp through a sieve to remove the skins and put the purée to one side.

❦ Bring the milk to the boil and pour over the breadcrumbs, mix well and allow to cool a little. Lightly whisk the egg yolks and add to the milk mixture along with the sugar, sherry and prepared fruit.

❦ Roll out the pastry and line the rim of an ovenproof dish, and fill with the mixture. Bake in a moderate oven 180°C/350°F/gas mark 4 until firm to the touch.

COOK'S TIPS

For a more intense flavour, crush some of the apricot kernels and add them to the fruit purée.

If apricots are not in season, use well-drained tinned or preserved fruit. Add a tablespoon of flaked almonds to make up for the missing apricot kernels.

BAKED APRICOT PUDDING

This is based on a recipe from Mrs Beeton. For a dressier dessert, take the dish out of the oven as soon as the pudding has set, add a layer of meringue spangled with crystallized apricot and return to a low oven for the meringue to cook.

INGREDIENTS

12 Apricots
1pt/600ml Milk
6oz/175g Fresh Breadcrumbs
4 Egg Yolks
3oz/75g Caster Sugar
5tbsp/75ml Sherry
4oz/125g Shortcrust Pastry

ROLY POLY PUDDING

The delight of schoolboys of all ages, this rib-sticking pudding is traditionally served with custard. Any cook worth her salt would have a recipe for the pudding; this is based on Mrs Beeton's.

INGREDIENTS

12oz/350g Suet Pastry
12oz/350g Your Favourite Homemade Jam

METHOD

❦ Roll out the pastry into a large rectangle about ½in/13mm thick. Evenly spread the jam over the pastry to within 1in/25mm of the edge all round. Carefully roll the pudding up and seal the end with a little water.

❦ Place on a greased baking sheet and cook in a fairly hot oven, 200°C/400°F/gas mark 4 for about 30 minutes or until nicely brown on top.

Roly Poly Pudding,
a sweet reward after a hard day's play

As for the Roly-Poly, it was too good.

William Thackeray,
The Book of Snobs

COOK'S TIP

You can make an excellent pudding using marmalade or mincemeat instead of jam.

BACHELOR'S PUDDING

This simple yet tasty pudding is based on Mrs Beeton's recipe for A Bachelor's Pudding. It has an austere, masculine air about it, but tastes very good with sweet butter sauce.

INGREDIENTS

4oz/125g Apple, Peeled and Cored
4oz/125g Fresh Breadcrumbs
4oz/125g Currants
2oz/50g Soft Brown Sugar
3 Eggs, Whisked
Rind of 1 Lemon
Freshly Grated Nutmeg

METHOD

❦ Chop the apples finely and mix together thoroughly with the rest of the ingredients. Allow to stand for 30 minutes.

❦ Pack into a well-greased pudding basin. Add a drop of milk if the mixture appears a little stiff.

❦ Cover tightly with foil and place in a saucepan two-thirds full of water to boil for about 3 hours.

❦ When cooked, gently turn the pudding out on to a dish and serve immediately.

Two old bachelors
were living in
one house,
One caught a Muffin,
the other caught
a Mouse.

EDWARD LEAR

BACHELOR'S PUDDING, ORIGINALLY MADE AS HOME COMFORTS FOR HARD-WORKING SCHOLARS

FIG PUDDING

A very dignified pudding based on a Mrs Beeton recipe. Figs, like rhubarb, appealed to the valetudinarian leanings of the Victorians, although there is no medicinal taste about this sticky, delicious pudding.

INGREDIENTS

16oz/450g Dried Figs
8oz/225g Chopped Suet
8oz/225g Flour
8oz/225g Fresh Breadcrumbs
1 Egg, Beaten
Milk

METHOD

❦ Chop the figs into small pieces and place in a large bowl along with the suet, flour and breadcrumbs. Mix together well with the egg and sufficient milk to form a stiff mixture and pack firmly into a well-greased pudding basin.

❦ Cover tightly with a piece of foil and a pudding cloth and place in a saucepan two-thirds full of water to boil for three hours. When cooked, carefully turn the pudding out of the mould and serve with Wine Sauce.

Train up a fig tree in the way it should go and when you are old sit under the shade of it.

CAPTAIN CUTTLE IN *Dombey and Son*,
CHARLES DICKENS

RIPE FIGS FOR A MOUTH-WATERING FIGGY PUDDING

Cabinet Pudding frequently graced the high tables of the Victorian Establishment.

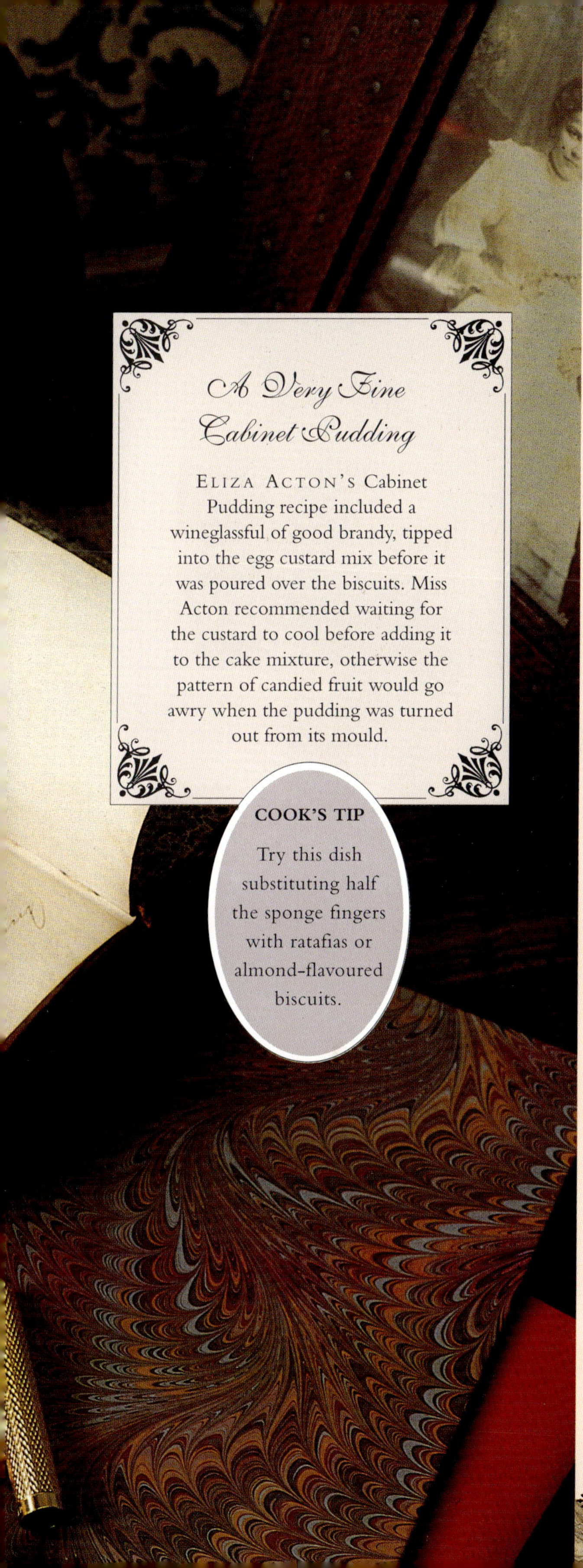

A Very Fine Cabinet Pudding

ELIZA ACTON'S Cabinet Pudding recipe included a wineglassful of good brandy, tipped into the egg custard mix before it was poured over the biscuits. Miss Acton recommended waiting for the custard to cool before adding it to the cake mixture, otherwise the pattern of candied fruit would go awry when the pudding was turned out from its mould.

COOK'S TIP

Try this dish substituting half the sponge fingers with ratafias or almond-flavoured biscuits.

CABINET PUDDING

This solid, manly pudding is based on Mrs Beeton's recipe; she also calls it Chancellor's Pudding. It should be served with a sweet sauce or, according to Eliza Acton, a "well-made wine sauce".

INGREDIENTS

2oz/50g Chopped Candied Peel
4oz/125g Currants
4oz/124g Sultanas
Sponge Fingers, Sliced
Melted Butter
4 Eggs
2oz/50g Caster Sugar
Rind of 1 Lemon
1pt/600ml Milk

METHOD

❦ Thoroughly grease a pudding basin with a little butter and place the chopped peel and a few currants and sultanas in the bottom of the basin. Cover the fruit with a layer of sponge finger slices and brush with the melted butter. Continue building up layers with the fruit and sponge fingers until the basin is nearly full.

❦ Break the eggs into a bowl and beat well. Add the sugar, lemon rind and milk and beating again until all the ingredients are thoroughly mixed.

❦ Strain the mixture over the prepared pudding and allow to stand for one hour to soak into the sponge. Bake at 180°C/350°F/gas mark 4 until the egg custard is firm. This takes about 30 minutes.

Suet Crust Pastry

"This crust is so much lighter, and more wholesome, than that which is made with butter, we cannot refrain from recommending it in preference to our readers." Thus Eliza Acton eulogised suet crust pastry, giving several recipes for it. Mrs Beeton also considered it suitable for children and recommended that it be made by mixing 6oz/175g finely chopped beef suet to every 1lb/450g flour and making it into a paste with ½pt/300ml water.

APPLES FROM THE WINTER STORE FOR WHOLESOME FAMILY FARE

Coleridge holds that a man cannot have a pure mind who refuses apple-dumplings.

CHARLES LAMB

BAKED APPLE DUMPLINGS

These dumplings, simple yet delicious, are based on Mrs Beeton's recipe. She calls them "a plain family dish".

INGREDIENTS

6 Medium Apples
Sugar
12oz/350g Suet Crust Pastry
Icing Sugar to Decorate

COOK'S TIP

Use puff pastry instead of suet crust for richer dumplings.

METHOD

- Carefully peel and core the apples, taking care not to damage the fruit, and liberally sprinkle each one with sugar.
- Roll out the pastry and wrap each apple individually, taking care to join the pastry edges neatly so that round balls are formed.
- Place the dumplings on a baking sheet and cook at 180°C/350°F/gas mark 4 for 30 minutes. When cooked, remove from the oven and dust well with icing sugar.

FASHIONABLE DUMPLINGS

Eliza Acton gives a fascinating recipe entitled "Fashionable Apple Dumplings"; the dumplings are boiled in little knitted snoods to give a "pretty effect".

PUBLISHER'S PUDDING

This is an adaptation of Eliza Acton's recipe. She observed, rather drily, that "this pudding can scarcely be made too rich". Presumably, she devised it for the delectation of her publisher's taste buds. Her Modern Cookery for Private Families *was published in 1845. The pudding is light, though rich; she recommends that it is served with German Sauce, a thick, creamy custard flavoured with vanilla and cinnamon.*

INGREDIENTS

4oz/125g Ground Almonds
2oz/50g Fresh Breadcrumbs
½pt/300ml Double Cream
4oz/125g Macaroons, Crushed
8oz/225g Beef Suet
4oz/125g Flour
6oz/175g Caster Sugar
4oz/125g Glacé Cherries
4oz/125g Raisins
4oz/125g Candied Peel
6 Egg Yolks
Grated Rind of 1 Lemon
3–4 tbsp/50ml Brandy
Good Pinch of Salt

METHOD

❦ Put the ground almonds and breadcrumbs into a large mixing bowl and pour over the cream which has been brought to the boil. Put to one side and allow to cool.

❦ Add the rest of the ingredients one by one, mixing thoroughly until all are fully incorporated. Pour the mixture into a well-greased pudding basin, filling it to the top.

❦ Cover tightly with foil and a pudding cloth and place in a saucepan of water to boil for four hours. When cooked, allow the pudding to stand for several minutes before turning out on to a serving dish.

PUBLISHER'S PUDDING, EXCELLENT WITH A GOOD BOOK

I'll publish right or wrong.
Fools are my theme, let satire be my song.

LORD GEORGE BYRON

PARADISE PUDDING

This heavenly mixture of brandied apple and light pudding is based on a recipe from Mrs Beeton. Presumably, its name alludes to the prominence of apples in Paradise.

> *All Paradise opens! Let me die eating ortolans to the sound of soft music.*
>
> BENJAMIN DISRAELI

INGREDIENTS

1lb/450g Apples
4oz/125g Fresh Breadcrumbs
3oz/75g Caster Sugar
3oz/75g Raisins
Rind of 1 Lemon, Grated
3 Eggs
3–4 tbsp/50ml Brandy

METHOD

❦ Peel and core the apples and chop them into small pieces. Place them in a mixing bowl with the remaining dry ingredients and combine thoroughly.

❦ Beat the eggs and add them to the bowl along with the brandy, and stir until well mixed. Pour the mixture into a well-buttered basin and cover with a pudding cloth. Place in a saucepan of water and boil for $1\frac{1}{2}$ hours. Serve with a sweet sauce.

CANARY PUDDING,
PERFECT FOR A LADIES' LUNCH

Canary Pudding

This is based on a recipe from Mrs Beeton. The light, lemony, delicious pudding turns out a beautiful yellow colour, hence the name.

INGREDIENTS

6oz/175g Butter
6oz/175g Caster Sugar
Rind of 1 Lemon, Grated
4oz/125g Flour
3 Eggs

METHOD

❦ Melt the butter in a saucepan and stir in the caster sugar and lemon rind. Slowly sieve in the flour, continually stirring until it is fully incorporated.

❦ Whisk the eggs and add to the mixture; beat thoroughly. Pour the pudding into a buttered basin, cover with foil and tie over a pudding cloth.

❦ Place in a saucepan of water and boil for 2 hours. Serve with a sweet sauce.

COOK'S TIP

Mrs Beeton suggests that you add two tablespoons of raspberry jam to the ingredients to convert it into Washington Pudding.

BREAD PUDDING

This is based on Mrs Beeton's recipe for Queen of Bread Puddings and would grace any formal dinner table. Her more everyday versions were frugal exercises involving stale bread crumbs, dried fruit and chopped suet.

INGREDIENTS

1pt/600ml Milk
10oz/275g Breadcrumbs
1oz/25g Butter
1oz/25g Caster Sugar
Rind of 1 Lemon, Grated
2 Eggs
Homemade Jam of Your Choice

METHOD

- Bring the milk to the boil and pour over the breadcrumbs, butter, sugar and lemon rind in a mixing bowl. Put to one side and allow to cool.
- Separate the eggs. Beat the yolks and add to the cooling mixture stirring thoroughly. Grease an 8in/20cm pie dish and pile the mixture into it. Bake at 200°C/400°F/gas mark 6 for about 10 minutes until the pudding sets.
- Remove from the oven and spread a good, thick layer of jam over the pudding. Top off with the egg whites that have been beaten until very stiff. Sift over lots of caster sugar and return to the oven for the meringue to cook and take on a little colour (about 40 minutes).

THE HUMBLE BREAD PUDDING MAKES A FORMAL APPEARANCE AT THE TABLE, TOPPED WITH A LAYER OF MERINGUE

A Plain Receipt

Eliza Acton's recipe, which omits the meringue topping, is very similar, but Miss Acton considered it "quite a plain receipt". She advocated the addition of a small glass of brandy, a handful of candied peel and some currants; then "a very excellent pudding will be obtained".

They lived at the bottom of a well
They lived on treacle.
It was a treacle well.

LEWIS CARROLL,
ALICE IN WONDERLAND

TREACLE PUDDING, A WINTER WARMER FOR THE COLDEST OF DAYS

Treacle Pudding

This melting, multi-layered pudding is based on a recipe from Mrs Beeton. It's very filling and even more delicious served with a custard sauce.

INGREDIENTS

8oz/225g Plain Flour
4oz/125g Chopped Suet
½oz/12g Baking Powder
Pinch of Salt
A Little Cold Water
Treacle
1oz/25g Breadcrumbs
Rind of 1 Lemon, Grated

METHOD

❦ In a bowl mix together the flour, suet, baking powder and salt and add sufficient cold water to make a firm pastry. Split the pastry into two halves and use one half to line a pudding basin. Spread a thin layer of treacle over the bottom of the lined basin and sprinkle over plenty of breadcrumbs and a little lemon rind.

❦ Roll out the remaining half of the pastry thinly and cut a circle to completely cover the first layer of treacle. Dampen the edges lightly and press into place, ensuring it seals to the pastry lining. Repeat the process of layering the treacle and pastry until the basin is full.

❦ Cover with a layer of foil and steam in a double boiler for approximately 2½ hours. Let is stand for 5 minutes before turning out, then serve immediately.

Georgie Porgie, Pudding and Pie
Kissed the girls and made them cry
When the boys came out to play
Georgie Porgie ran away.

Traditional Nursery Rhyme

STRAWBERRIES, RASPBERRIES AND CHOCOLATE MAKE LUSCIOUS TARTLETS FOR TEATIME INDULGENCE

CHOCOLATE TARTLETS

A chocoholic's dream, these tartlets are based on a Mrs Beeton recipe. They are delicious with morning coffee.

INGREDIENTS

2 Eggs
3oz/75g Caster Sugar
2oz/50g Plain Chocolate, Grated
4oz/125g Cake Crumbs
½oz/12g Cornflour
2oz/50g Melted Butter
8oz/225g Shortcrust Pastry
Chocolate Icing for Decoration

METHOD

❦ Separate the eggs and cream the yolks and caster sugar together. Stir in the grated chocolate, cake crumbs, cornflour and melted butter and ensure it is all mixed together well.

❦ In a clean bowl, whisk the egg whites until they form stiff peaks and gently fold into the filling mixture. Roll out the pastry thinly and line some patty tins.

❦ Spoon in the chocolate filling and cook at 180°C/350°F/gas mark 4 for 20 minutes. When cool, spread with chocolate icing.

Doubtless God could have made a better berry (than the strawberry) but doubtless God never did.

WILLIAM BUTLER

STRAWBERRY TARTLETS

These delicious pink summer tartlets are based on an Eliza Acton recipe. She pronounced them "good". You could also make them using fresh raspberries instead.

INGREDIENTS

10oz/275g Fresh Strawberries
2oz/50g Icing Sugar
4 Eggs, Whisked
8oz/225g Shortcrust Pastry

METHOD

❦ Thoroughly wash the strawberries and remove any remaining stalks, then mash the fruit down to a fine pulp. Stir in the sugar until well mixed and slowly add the eggs a little at a time until all are incorporated.

❦ Roll out the shortcrust pastry thinly and, using pastry cutters, cut out discs to line some small patty tins. Fill each pastry about two-thirds full with the strawberry mixture and bake at 200°C/400°F/gas mark 6 for 10 minutes.

The Queen of Hearts
She made some tarts
All on a Summer's day;
The Knave of Hearts
He stole the tarts
And took them clean away.

NURSERY RHYME

RHUBARB PIE, A TASTY TEATIME TREAT FOR HARD WORKERS

And spectral dance, before the dawn
A hundred vicars down the lawn;
Curates, long dust, will come and go
On lissom, clerical, printless toe;
And oft betweeen the boughs unseen
The sly shade of a Rural Dean.

RUPERT BROOKE,
THE OLD VICARAGE, GRANTCHESTER

CURATE'S PUDDING

A frugal, filling pudding constructed from simple kitchen ingredients and one of the less exciting fruits from the kitchen garden; just the thing to satisfy a curate without tempting him to indulgence, unless you serve it with cream. This is based on a recipe from Eliza Acton.

INGREDIENTS

2lb/900g Fresh Rhubarb
6oz/175g Caster Sugar
8 Thin Slices of Bread
3oz/75g Fresh Breadcrumbs
2oz/50g Butter

METHOD

❦ Wash the rhubarb and cut into 1in/25mm lengths. Spread a layer of the fruit over the bottom of a deep pie dish and sprinkle with a third of the caster sugar.

❦ Remove the crusts from the sliced bread and use half of them to cover the fruit over completely. Continue building up the pudding with alternating layers of rhubarb and sugar and bread. Top the final layer of rhubarb with the remaining sugar and breadcrumbs mixed together.

❦ Melt the butter and pass it through a clean muslin cloth to clarify. Pour over the pudding and cook at 200°C/400°F/gas mark 6 for about 30 minutes.

COOK'S TIP

According to Eliza Acton, apples or blackcurrants, sweetened and flavoured with nutmeg and lemon rind also "make an excellent pudding of this kind"; if you use apples, butter the slices of bread.

RHUBARB PIE

This recipe is based on one of Mrs Beeton's who considered rhubarb to be "one of the most useful of all garden productions that are put into pies or puddings".

INGREDIENTS

8oz/225g Puff Pastry
2lb/900g Fresh Rhubarb
4oz/125g Caster Sugar

METHOD

❦ Roll out the puff pastry thinly and line a deep pie dish. Wash and dry the rhubarb and cut into small pieces roughly 1in/25mm in length. Pile the prepared fruit into the lined dish and sprinkle over the sugar; do not worry if the fruit is higher than the top of the dish as it will reduce during cooking.

❦ Roll out some more pastry and cover the tart with a lid. Brush the top with a little beaten egg and sprinkle generously with caster sugar.

❦ Cook at 200°C/400°F/gas mark 6 for 30 to 45 minutes or until the pastry has risen and turned a golden brown.

BEEFSTEAK PUDDING

This savoury batter pudding is based on Mrs Beeton's recipe for Baked Beefsteak Pudding. It makes a refreshing change from the more familiar steamed suet variety.

INGREDIENTS

6oz/175g Plain Flour
2 Eggs
Scant pint/525ml Fresh Milk
1lb 8oz/700g Rump Steak, Cubed
8oz/225g Kidney, Cubed
Salt and Pepper

METHOD

❦ Sieve the flour and a pinch of salt into a large mixing bowl and make a well in the centre. Break the eggs into the well and add a little of the milk. Stirring with a wooden spoon, gradually incorporate the flour into the egg mixture and slowly pour in the rest of the milk until you have a smooth, thick batter.

❦ Pour a little of the batter into the bottom of a pie dish and add the cubed steak and kidney. Season well with pepper and salt and pour over the remaining batter.

❦ Place in hot oven and cook at 210°C/425°F/gas mark 7 for 1 hour or until the batter has risen and turned a deep brown.

Dr Johnson's morality was as English an article as a beefsteak.

NATHANIEL HAWTHORNE

Ruth Pinch's Celebrated Pudding

In Charles Dickens' *Martin Chuzzlewit*, Ruth, the pretty sister of the saintly Tom Pinch, makes a beefsteak pudding for her brother to celebrate their setting up home together. Eliza Acton quotes the recipe in her *Modern Cookery for Private Families*, published in 1845, just a year after Dickens' novel. Ruth used a very rich butter crust, moistened with egg yolks. Her pudding was also called Beefsteak Pudding a la Dickens.

Beefsteak Pudding for a hearty lunch to satisfy the most Dickensian of appetites.

COOK'S TIP

Boil the pudding in a long loaf shape; slice it just before dinner is served and brown the slices in the meat juices of the roasting pan.

Take care to top up the saucepan with extra boiling water if needed.

PEASE PUDDING, A TRADITIONAL SAVOURY PUDDING TO ACCOMPANY BOILED BACON.

PEASE PUDDING

Recipes for pease pudding are among the oldest in England, as pease pudding with bacon is one of the oldest dishes. Serve this pudding, based on a Mrs Beeton recipe, with boiled bacon and onion sauce. It's very filling, you will not need potatoes.

INGREDIENTS

1½lb/700g Dried Split Peas
2oz/50g Butter
2 Eggs
Salt and Pepper
Handful Fresh Mint, Finely Chopped

METHOD

❦ Put the peas in a bowl, cover with water and allow to soak overnight. The following day, drain off the soaking water and put the peas in a saucepan and cover with fresh cold water. Bring to the boil then reduce to a simmer and cook for 1½ hours until the peas are soft.

❦ When cooked drain them well and press them through a sieve. Add the remaining ingredients and mix together until all are thoroughly incorporated. Spoon the prepared pudding into a well-greased pudding basin and cover tightly with a piece of foil.

❦ Place it in a saucepan half-full of water and boil for 45 to 60 minutes until the pudding is firm.

Pease Porridge

Pease porridge hot
Pease porridge cold
Pease porridge in the pot
Nine days old.

ANON

An Economical Plan

This is Mrs Beeton's artful suggestion for frugal living. "Where there is a large family of children, and the means of keeping them are limited, it is a most economical plan to serve up the pudding before the meat as, in this case, consumption of the latter article will be much smaller than it otherwise would be."

KENTISH SUET PUDDING

Eliza Acton's recipe, which she called Kentish Suet Pudding, adds an egg to the basic recipe. Miss Acton maintains that it is "very good sliced and broiled or browned in a Dutch oven, after having become quite cold".

SUET PUDDING TO EAT WITH BEEF

This traditional and very tasty accompaniment to the Sunday roast is based on Mrs Beeton's recipe for Suet Pudding to Eat with Roast Meat.

INGREDIENTS

1lb/450g Plain Flour
6oz/175g Chopped Beef Suet
½pt/300ml Fresh Milk
Good Pinch of Salt and Pepper

METHOD

❦ Place the flour and suet in a mixing bowl along with the seasoning and mix well. Slowly stir in the milk until a smooth paste is formed.

❦ Pour the prepared pudding into a buttered basin, cover with foil and stand in a saucepan half-full of water to boil for 2½ hours.

GAME PIE

This is based on Mrs Beeton's recipe for Raised Game Pie, an elaborate and complicated affair involving a raised pie crust and marrow-bone jelly. Game pies should be eaten cold and are excellent for picnics; in Victorian times they would have been sent out for shooting-party luncheons.

INGREDIENTS

1 Large Fowl or 2 Pheasants
8oz/225g Brown Breadcrumbs
3oz/75g Shredded Beef Suet
2oz/50g Fresh Chopped Parsley
1 Egg
1lb/450g Shortcrust Pastry
8oz/225g Good Sliced Ham
Salt and Pepper
Cornflour
Egg for Glazing

METHOD

❦ Prepare and clean the birds and cut into portions. Put them in a pan with sufficient water just to cover them and bring to the boil. Reduce to a simmer and cook until the flesh comes away from the bone. Remove the meat from the pan and cut into chunks, reserve the cooking stock.

❦ Prepare the forcemeat by mixing together the breadcrumbs, suet and parsley and adding the beaten egg to bind it all together. Roll out the pastry and line a deep pie dish reserving enough to make a lid. Build the pie up in alternating layers of cooked game, forcemeat and sliced ham with a little seasoning between each.

❦ Once the pie dish is full, reduce the reserved stock and thicken with a little cornflour dissolved in water. Pour the sauce over the prepared pie. Roll out a lid using the reserved pastry; to ensure it seals well brush the edges with cold water. Brush the top of the pie with a beaten egg and cook at 200°C/400°F/gas mark 6 for 30 minutes, until the crust is golden.

LITTLE RAISED PORK PIES

These delicious little pies, just right for a picnic or a lunch box, are based on a traditional Victorian recipe. Mrs Beeton also gives a recipe, but for so large a number that she must have been catering for a house party.

INGREDIENTS

4oz/125g Butter
1lb/450g Plain Flour
4oz/125g Shredded Beef Suet
2lb/900g Lean Pork, Minced
Salt and Pepper
1 Egg, Beaten

MAKES ABOUT 10 LITTLE PIES

METHOD

❦ Place the butter in a saucepan and gently melt over a low heat, add the flour, suet and a good pinch of salt and mix into a stiff paste. Taking small pieces of the warm paste, form into little pots, remembering to leave sufficient pastry for the lids.

❦ Fill the pots with the minced pork and add a pinch of seasoning before covering with the lids and brushing thoroughly with beaten egg. Cook at 180°C/350°F/gas mark 4 until the pastry has turned a deep brown colour.

RAISED PORK PIES AND GAMES PIES, TRADITIONAL FARE FOR PICNICS ANDS SHOOTING PARTIES

COOK'S TIP

Mrs Beeton suggested that you "Clean three of the pigeon feet and place them in a hole made in the crust at the top; this shows the kind of pie it is"

Promises and pie crusts are made to be broken.

JONATHAN SWIFT

PIGEON PIE

This is based on a Beeton recipe called Epsom Grandstand Recipe. Before she married, Mrs Beeton actually lived in the Grandstand at Epsom where her stepfather, Henry Dorling, was Clerk of the Course. Isabella helped to run the extended household; Pigeon Pie must have been a regular on the menu.

INGREDIENTS

2 Pigeons, Prepared
Salt and Pepper
2oz/50g Butter
1lb/450g Fresh Rump Steak
½pt/300ml Chicken Stock
8oz/225g Puff Pastry
1 Egg Yolk

METHOD

❦ With a sharp knife cut the pigeons in half lengthways. Season well with salt and pepper. Heat the butter in a pan and quickly brown the birds on all sides. Remove from the heat and put to one side.

❦ Line the bottom of a pie dish with the rump steak cut into cubes and lay the pieces of pigeon on top. Bring the stock to the boil, adjust the seasoning and pour into the pie dish. Roll out the pastry to make the lid, but line the rim of the dish with a strip of pastry first. This will ensure the lid stays firmly in place during cooking.

❦ Brush the top of the pie with beaten egg yolk and cook at 180°C/350°F/gas mark 4 for about an hour until the pastry has risen and turned golden brown.

GROUSE PIE

A hearty pie based on Mrs Beeton's recipe. In England and Scotland, grouse is only in season between glorious August the twelfth and the end of December, so this is a treat to be savoured.

INGREDIENTS

1lb/450g Fresh Rump Steak
A Brace of Grouse, Plucked and Drawn
Cayenne Pepper
Salt and Pepper
½pt/300ml Chicken Stock
8oz/225g Puff Pastry
1 Egg Yolk

METHOD

❦ Cut the rump steak into cubes and line the bottom of a pie dish. Joint the grouse, season well with cayenne, salt and black pepper and lay in the dish on top of the meat. Pour over the stock.

❦ Roll out the puff pastry evenly and line the rim of the dish with a pastry strip before covering the pie with its pastry lid.

❦ Beat the egg yolk and brush over the pie before cooking at 180°C/350°F/gas mark 4 for 45 minutes.

GROUSE PIE *with hare in the middle is fare*
Which duly concocted with science and care
Doctor Kitchener says is beyond all compare
And tenderer leveret Robin had never ate.

INGOLDSBY LEGENDS

PIGEON AND GROUSE PIES, RELISHED IN GRAND DINING ROOMS AND POACHER'S COTTAGES ALIKE

RICH RABBIT PIE

Rabbit pie is an ancient country dish relished by poachers and gamekeepers alike. Many recipes for it abound, but this is based on Mrs Beeton's version.

INGREDIENTS

1 Rabbit, Skinned and Jointed
4oz/125g Bacon
4 Hard Boiled Eggs
8oz/225g White Breadcrumbs
3oz/75g Shredded Suet
2oz/50g Fresh Chopped Parsley
1 Egg, Beaten
Salt and Pepper
⅕pt/125ml Fresh Cold Water
8oz/225g Puff Pastry
Egg Yolk for Glaze

METHOD

❦ Bone the rabbit pieces and cut the flesh into slices. Place the bones in a saucepan and cover with water. Bring to the boil then simmer gently until well reduced. Strain off and reserve the stock. Place the rabbit meat in a pie dish along with the bacon cut into strips and the hard boiled eggs cut into quarters.

❦ Mix the breadcrumbs, suet and chopped parsley in a bowl and bind together with the beaten egg. Form this forcemeat into little balls and add to the pie dish. Season the pie well with salt and pepper, pour in the cold water and cover with a puff pastry lid. Make a hole in the centre of the lid with a knife and brush the top thoroughly with the beaten egg yolk.

❦ Cook at 200°C/400°F/gas mark 6 for about an hour. Reduce the reserved stock made from the bones and pour it through the hole in the lid.

COOK'S TIP

You can leave the pie to cool so that the stock turns to jelly. Then the pie can be eaten cold for picnics or summer luncheon parties.

RICH RABBIT PIE, A SUBSTANTIAL SUPPER DISH

Bye Baby Bunting
Daddy's gone a hunting
Gone to get a rabbit skin
To wrap the Baby Bunting in
Bye Baby Bunting.

NURSERY RHYME

COOK'S TIP

If the pastry begins to brown too much, cover with a sheet of greaseproof paper for the remainder of the cooking time.

INDEX

Back Page United

A CENTURY OF NEWSPAPER COVERAGE

MANCHESTER UNITED

For Kevin
And United supporters everywhere

Back Page United

A CENTURY OF NEWSPAPER COVERAGE
MANCHESTER UNITED

STEPHEN F. KELLY

Aurora Publishing

A QUEEN ANNE PRESS BOOK
forAurora Publishing

First published in Great Britain in 1990
by Queen Anne Press, a division of
Lennard Associates Limited
Mackerye End
Harpenden
Hertfordshire AL5 5DR

Revised Edition 1994

ISBN 1 85926 043 8

British Library Cataloguing in Publication Data is available

Cover photographs
Front: Ryan Giggs (right) and the Manchester team after winning the FA Cup at Wembley to complete the double in 1994. (Colorsport)
Back: Matt Busby and Bobby Charlton after Manchester United had beaten Benfica to win the European Cup in 1968. (Sport & General)

Printed and bound in Spain

CONTENTS

INTRODUCTION

Manchester United is a glamour club. Its name conjures up magic wherever football is played. Liverpool may have won countless league championships and Nottingham Forest may have captured the European Cup, but there is still only one Man United. No club gains more headlines, fills more column-inches and boasts more photographs on the back pages than Manchester United.

The magic created by their name is almost inexplicable, but it is a fact that wherever you travel in the footballing world, the first British football club that trips off the foreign tongue is Manchester United. For many years, they have been the best supported club in the Football League, and even when they were relegated in 1974 they could still command gates of over 40,000. Wherever they play, crowds flock to watch them and they can boast active supporters' clubs from London to Malta, from the Midlands to Australia and from Glasgow to Vancouver. Few other clubs can claim to attract the loyalty and enthusiasm that is part of the United baggage.

Of course, it was not always so. There was a time when United were just another football club. Before they captured their first league championship in 1908 they were an ordinary, run-of-the-mill side, playing on one of the most atrocious pitches in the country. They offered little in the way of excitement or entertainment. But winning two championships and the FA Cup in the space of four seasons, plus a move to what was, and probably still is, the finest ground in the Football League, put United's name firmly on the map.

Sadly, it did not last. Times became difficult, their charismatic manager was tempted to Manchester City, and Old Trafford soon echoed to the sound of lone voices. And then war intervened. When United picked up the threads again in 1919, they were about to embark on the most miserable period in their history. For the next 20 years, the trophy room lay bare as United were relegated and promoted on three occasions. The nadir came when they almost crashed into the third division north at one point, saved only by a surprise victory at Millwall. There were no signs then of the glamour that was to accompany them in later years.

But, as peace returned to bomb-shelled Old Trafford at the end of the second world war, United made a signing that was to change their fortunes when Matt Busby agreed to become their new manager. Over the next six seasons they won the league title, the FA Cup and were league runners-up on four occasions. The scribes did battle to use the most hyperbole to describe the lovable side of Carey, Rowley, Pearson and Mitten. As if that were not enough, Busby then created another team – the Busby Babes – to succeed the ageing men of post-war United. Into their boots stepped teenagers Duncan Edwards, Roger Byrne, Tommy Taylor and Bobby Charlton, boys who soon stormed to two league titles, an FA Cup final and a rousing, innovative venture into Europe.

Yet, even then, the press regarded United as just another club, fit, perhaps, to rank alongside the likes of Arsenal, Huddersfield Town, Everton and Aston Villa with their glorious triumphs and celebrated histories. The United of the Busby Babes captured acres of headlines with their goalscoring feats and triumphs, but the event that turned the great club into a legend was the disaster at Munich. A nation was stunned. It was, as the writer H E Bates later commented, 'the cruellest day in English sporting history'. A team of prodigies had been destroyed and we would never discover their true potential. That moment, in its ghastly awfulness, transformed United into the most famous football club in Britain. Like the assassination of President Kennedy, those who were alive at the time can recall precisely where they were when they first heard the chilling news from Munich. And, when Matt Busby returned to the helm to lead a new side towards the European Cup, it merely added more emotion to the story. And to do it with the precocious skills and flair of George Best, Bobby Charlton and Denis Law, fuelled the legend, bringing the crowds flocking to see them wherever they played. Since then the press have usually continued singing their praises.

Headlines about Manchester United, like those about soap opera stars, sell newspapers, even though the Reds may not have captured the coveted league title for more than a generation. When Michael Knighton made his abortive bid to take over the club, it was front page news for days from the *Manchester Evening News* to the *Financial Times*. What other club could provoke such interest among so wide an audience?

So, from those days when United was just another football club with modest success and triumphs, they have today become a multi-million-pound business and a centre of footballing excellence. Their name still evokes memories of the Busby Babes and of Law, Best and Charlton. They were what every team aspires to be – exhilarating, inventive, and skilful.

Living up to the legend is almost impossible and, doubtless, the press will strive to make it doubly difficult. This then is the history of Manchester United as seen through the eyes of the newspapers and as written by the countless journalists who have chronicled its fate. Beginning with its early years, when only the local Manchester papers took much notice of its fortunes, to more recent events when national papers even turned over their front pages to its concerns, it is a story not just of triumphs, but of scandals as well. It may go just a small way to explaining why Manchester United has become the most glamorous club in British football.

ACKNOWLEDGEMENTS

The history of Manchester United has already been well documented, although I would hope that I have perhaps made a few new additions to it here and there. Therefore, I would like to thank first those who had trodden this path before me: writers such as Geoffrey Green, David Meek, Tom Tyrrell, Ian Morrison and Alan Shury who have told the story and compiled the statistics in previous volumes. Their beavering has made my job that much easier. I am also most grateful to the staff of Manchester Central Library, who, over a period of many months, dragged newspapers from the vaults or searched diligently for a new roll of microfilm. They never complained at my incessant demands and always took an interest in the project. I am indebted as well to the staff of the British Newspaper Library at Colindale for providing photocopies of all the various newspaper cuttings. I would also like to thank the staff and players of Manchester United Football Club who have helped wherever they could with anecdotes and facts. And a special vote of thanks is owed to Cliff Butler, who read and checked the manuscript but is in no way responsible for any mistakes which might have crept in.

I am also indebted to my publishers, Queen Anne Press, and especially my editor Ian Marshall, himself a Manchester United fan, for whom I hope this book has been a labour of love rather than a laborious occupation. Picture editor Donna Thynne should also be mentioned for her painstaking efforts to unearth new photographs from the early years of the club where so few exist. My appreciation goes to designer Glynis Edwards, Celia Kent and finally to Alan Samson of Macdonalds who helped conceive and encourage the idea.

I am also grateful to many others, including the Association of Football Statisticians, the Football Association, the Football League and my agent John Pawsey whose help has been much appreciated. A special mention also to life-long United supporter Kevin McAleny whose devotion to United has been pressed on me for more than 30 years. Thanks also to the lads of the Chorlton five-a-side football team whose interest in the book and occasional kicks on the shin every Friday night kept me going throughout the months of work. Finally, thanks to my wife Judith, an unswerving Liverpool supporter, who has had to put up with non-stop talk of Manchester United this past year, and Nicholas whose first word, uttered during the course of writing this book, was 'Kenny'.

Stephen F Kelly
Manchester 1990

1892

BLACKBURN ROVERS v. NEWTON HEATH.—At Blackburn. A rainstorm made the ground heavy. Newton Heath kicked off, but the Rovers first became dangerous. Clements relieved, and clever play by Stewart carried the game into the Rovers' quarters, but Forrest sent the ball back, and Southworth worked through the "Heathens'" back division and scored a splendid goal for the Rovers. The game continued in favour of the Rovers, and immediately afterwards Hall scored for the home team. Newton Heath were still kept to their quarter. At the end of fifteen minutes' play Chippendale secured the ball on the line, and made a tricky pass to Hall, who placed the Rovers three goals ahead. The visitors then played up in much better style, and were able to reach the Rovers' goal, Donaldson finishing a nice piece of work by shooting a goal. The game became much more even, and at length the visitors made several efforts to lower the Rovers' colours, and shortly before the interval Couper scored another goal for the visitors. Nothing further was done before half-time, when the Rovers led by three goals to two. The game was of a more even character in the second half, but after a fine shot by Mathieson, Newton Heath pressed. The Rovers afterwards worked hard and obtained a good position, but Southworth was brought to the ground several times when about to shoot. A severe charge was made on the "Heathens'" goal, and Chippendale scored. Ten minutes later Farman scored for the visitors. Final:—Blackburn Rovers, four goals; Newton Heath, three. Teams:—Blackburn Rovers: Pennington, goal; Murray and Forbes, backs; Almond, Dewar, and Forrest, half backs; Chippendale and Walton, right wing; Southworth, centre; Hall and Bowdler, left wing. Newton Heath: Warner, goal; Clements and Brown, backs; Perrins, Stewart, and Errentz, half backs; Farman and Coupar, right wing; Donaldson, centre; Carson and Mathieson, left wing.

Guardian, 5 September 1892

IN SEPTEMBER 1892 Queen Victoria was in the 55th year of her reign. William Gladstone, her Prime Minister and himself now aged 83 and deaf, had just won a fourth general election. His Liberal Party ruled over the House of Commons and the Labour Party had yet to be formed. Away from the political life of the capital, a terrifying explosion at the Park Slip Colliery in South Wales had left 140 dead, while in Manchester there was concern about cholera, with a cluster of cases reported around Liverpool. It was a time when one could still voyage by liner from Manchester to almost any port in the world. The *Manchester Evening News* advertised regular sailings to China, Japan and Calcutta while at Liverpool you could board a Royal Mail steamer bound for Brazil or the River Plate. Manchester Grammar School was advertising for pupils at four guineas a term and there were plenty of jobs listed for servants and washerwomen. But it was also an age of increasing leisure. In the sporting world, W G Grace was still playing for his beloved Gloucestershire and league football was just about to arrive in the great northern city that had fostered the Industrial Revolution. Of course, the game had been played there for many years but not until 1892 could Manchester boast a Football League team.

The League had been formed in 1888, but, although a team at Newton Heath had been playing since 1878, it had not been initially invited to join the dozen clubs that kicked off the new league. The club had been founded by a group of railway workers employed at the carriage and wagon department of the Lancashire and Yorkshire Railways at Newton Heath. They adopted the name Newton Heath (LYR) and took possession of a small ground in North Road, Monsall Road, Newton Heath. It was from these unpromising roots that Manchester United would later flower.

Newton Heath, or the Heathens as they quickly became nicknamed, were a resounding success, beating all opposition. They were soon obliged to look further afield than Manchester for new, tougher competition. In 1885 they turned professional and four years later were admitted to the Football Alliance after an attempt to join the Football League failed miserably when they secured just one vote. For the next three seasons they battled determinedly to impress the footballing authorities, applying to join the League each year. Eventually they succeeded in the summer of 1892, when division one was enlarged from 14 to 16 clubs and a second division added. And, as luck would have it, they were duly elected to join the enlarged first division. Neighbours Ardwick, later to become Manchester City, found themselves elected to the second division, giving Manchester the added luxury of a second league club.

Newton Heath's inaugural league fixture took place on Saturday, 3 September 1892 against the mighty Blackburn Rovers at Ewood Park. Blackburn were probably the most famous club in football. Founder-members of the League, they had won the FA Cup on no fewer than five occasions. They boasted a team overflowing with internationals, including the famous England centre forward Jack Southworth. United's opening fixture was a baptism of fire.

The game kicked off at 4pm with 8,000 spectators braving a torrential rainstorm, and within minutes the Heathens were a goal down as Jack

The Newton Heath team for 1892/93 which struggled in its first season in the Football League. Curiously, there is no goalkeeper in the line-up.

Southworth exploited their early nerves. The Rovers soon capitalised further and, with Newton Heath looking overawed by the occasion, they swept into a three-goal lead. By half time, however, Newton had scored twice with Robert Donaldson privileged to score the first league goal for Manchester United. Coupar had added the second but, following the interval, Blackburn regained control, taking a 4–2 lead, and held on comfortably, although Farman struck a third for Newton Heath to give a final scoreline of 4–3 to Blackburn Rovers.

Robert Donaldson, the proud scorer of United's first league goal, also struck the club's first league hat trick when he hit three goals against Wolverhampton Wanderers a month later in a 10–1 win that still stands as a record today. The centre forward had been with the club since the opening of the 1891/92 season and had been the leading goalscorer with 20 goals during the side's final season in the Football Alliance when they had finished as runners-up to Nottingham Forest. In his first league season he netted 16 goals, but the following year he could manage only seven. The Scot remained at United just one more season and signed for Luton Town before ending his playing days with Glossop North End.

It had been a gruelling first hurdle for Newton Heath, but at least they had not been humiliated and had shown that they were capable of rolling up their sleeves and battling when the odds were stacked against them. By the end of the season they would need all the fighting spirit they could muster.

1893

UNITED'S FIRST SEASON in the league almost ended in disaster and only a surprise victory in the relegation/promotion play-offs saved them from a humiliating drop into the lower division. Having lost to Blackburn in their opening fixture, they then went a further six games without a win. Burnley were the visitors for North Road's inaugural league match and a 1–1 draw gave the Heathens their first league point. Some heavy defeats followed, with Everton putting six past them while Burnley and West Brom managed four each. Then came a sensational triumph as they thrashed Wolverhampton Wanderers 10–1 at North Road to notch up a record victory. Donaldson and Stewart both struck hat tricks. But success was short-lived. More defeats followed, though in their final game of 1892 they trounced Derby 7–1, only to lose 7–1 at Stoke in their first game of 1893. The remainder of the campaign was abysmal, with six consecutive defeats. So, by the end of the season, they were in 16th place, propping up the rest of the division, having conceded 85 goals and collected just 18 points.

Strange as it may seem, the Football League had not worked out the question of relegation and promotion and no automatic promotion from the second to the first division had been agreed. So, instead, the bottom three teams from the first were forced into a play-off with the top three from the second division in what became known as the Test Matches. The Heathens found themselves drawn against Small Heath – later to become Birmingham City – who had topped the second division. Small Heath were odds-on favourites, having lost only three matches all season and scored 90 goals.

The game took place at Stoke on Saturday, 22 April 1893. More than 4,000 turned up in the warm sunshine for the crucial clash. Small Heath won the toss, but Newton soon surprised the Midlanders when Farman met a Cassidy cross to shoot them into the lead. Small Heath responded with some vigorous, slick attacking but at half time Newton were still clinging to their slender advantage. However, it seemed only a matter of time before the Midlanders would draw level and, sure enough, shortly into the second half, they equalised. Nevertheless, the Heathens held on and after 90 minutes the two teams were still all square.

NEWTON HEATH v. SMALL HEATH.—These teams met at Stoke. There were four thousand spectators, and the heat of a brilliant sun was tempered by a stiff breeze which blew across the goound. Small Heath won tha toss, and elected to take advantage of the wind. The Birmingham forwards, by quick close passing, almost immediately became dangerous, and Mitchell smartly returned a quick shot from the foot of Mobley. Newton Heath retaliated, and Cassidy looked extremely dangerous, but the Small Heath backs were in grand form, and defended strongly. Play ruled fast and very even, but the wind often upset the calculations of the players. The Small Heath forwards were playing a most scientific game, but the rushes of Newton Heath were often very dangerous. From a pretty rush down the Birmingham right, Hallam put in a splendid shot, which Davies saved well, and Charsley effected a brilliant save at the other end almost immediately afterwards. The game was at this period of a most exciting character, both teams being warmly cheered by their supporters, who were present in strong force. Splendid play by Farman, in which he tricked three or four opponents in masterly fashion, almost resulted in the downfall of the Birmingham goal, but he was badly supported, and Pumfrey relieved. Cassidy then ran down the left and put in a splendid cross, which Farman met, and scored the first goal for Newton Heath with a splendid oblique shot. This reverse took a lot of the dash out of the Birmingham team, and for a considerable time Newton Heath attacked persistently, Charsley and the backs showing fine defence. Recovering from this temporary slackness Small Heath played with more spirit, and the Manchester goal had a series of narrow escapes, splendid shots being put in by Jenkyns, Hallam, and Mobley. Small Heath had slightly the best of the game to the interval, but Davies and his backs offered a very stubborn resistance. Half-time arrived with Newton Heath leading by a goal to none. The second half opened at a great pace, the Small Heath forwards showing brilliant form. Newton Heath, however, offered very strong defence, repelling repeated attacks in grand fashion. After brilliant work by the whole of the Small Heath forwards, Wheldon equalised the score with a grand shot. A series of exciting tussles round each goal ensued, but the defence on each side showed good form, and a splendidly contested game ended in a draw—one goal each. The teams were as follow:—Small Heath: Charsley, Bagley Pumfrey, Ollis, Jenkyns, Short, Hallam, Walton, Mobley, Wheldon, and Hands. Newton Heath: Davies, Mitchell, Clements, Perrins, Stewart, Brentz, Farman, Coupar, Donaldson, Fitzsimmons, and Cassidy.

Guardian, 24 April 1893

The Football League, of course, had not anticipated a draw but it was agreed that there should be a replay and, the following Thursday, the two teams met again, in Sheffield. This time there was a slight fancy for Newton, given that they had already held the Midlanders once and it was reckoned that Sheffield was their lucky city. But with just six minutes gone they were a goal behind and the second division seemed to be beckoning. However, luck was on their side and, within minutes, they were awarded a penalty. Farman slammed home the opportunity and at half time the scores stood level. The second half turned into one of the most exciting tussles of the season, with Small Heath edging into a 2–1 lead. Cassidy quickly replied and then, for the first time in the contest, Coupar put them ahead. Suddenly Small Heath were looking weary while the Heathens were living up to their first division status. Farman added two more and at the final whistle Newton Heath had won by the surprising scoreline of 5–2.

Farman, seated on the left, scored a hat trick in the replayed Test Match to keep Newton Heath in the first division.

That victory meant there would be first division football again, although this time it would not be at Newton. Their old ground at North Road was a disgrace. The pitch was a mud bath and hardly conducive to league football. The dressing rooms were half a mile down the road in the Three Crowns pub and visiting teams were beginning to complain about the appalling facilities as well as the pitch. So, in September 1893, they moved across the city to Clayton. Although their new ground at Bank Street was three miles away, the directors hoped that the improved conditions and bigger ground would attract more supporters. They still clung on to their old name although even this would, in time, cause problems. Unfortunately, Bank Street proved to be little better than North Road. A bellowing chemical works stood alongside the ground and, although there was more accommodation for spectators, they now had to contend with dreadful toxic fumes when the breeze blew in their direction. The pitch also turned out to be just as bad and soon there were plans to move yet again.

1894

AFTER A MISERABLE inaugural season in the Football League, which ended with the Heathens clinging on to their first division status by the skin of their teeth, they found themselves in virtually the same position the following season. They finished bottom of the league again, this time with even fewer points and only six wins in 30 games. The previous season they had escaped the big drop by surprisingly winning their Test Match play-off, but this time there was no such respite and they probably got what they deserved – relegation to the second division.

The play-off took place at Blackburn against Liverpool, who had only been in existence for two seasons. But, in their first season in the Football League, they had topped the second division without losing one match. The odds were always against the Heathens and, true to form, Liverpool swept into a two-goal lead long before half time. The Heathens had a couple of chances but Liverpool were by far the superior side and few among the 6,000 crowd could complain at the outcome.

The backbone of the Newton Heath team in those days was Fred Erentz, a tall, robust Scot who could play almost anywhere in defence. More often than not he was to be found at full back but he was equally at home as a wing half or centre half. He had joined United in 1892 and over the next 10 years went on to play more than 300 games for the club. His career spanned the league days of Newton Heath. He played his final game in April 1902, just before the club changed its name to Manchester United. His brother Harry also played for the Heathens before moving on to Tottenham Hotspur where he won a Cup-winners' medal in 1901.

ASSOCIATION.

THE FOOTBALL LEAGUE TEST MATCHES.

LIVERPOOL v. NEWTON HEATH.—At Blackburn, before 6,000 spectators. There was not a breath of wind to affect play, which was of an even and exciting kind during the first quarter of an hour, both sets of backs doing an enormous amount of work. Then from a free kick in midfield M'Lean, with a huge kick, sent the ball right under the crossbar, and Gordon headed through. In the next minute M'Cartney struck one of the posts with a terrific shot, and Liverpool proceeded to press. Falls saved splendidly from a bully, but a judicious centre by Gordon gave M'Queen an opening, and he scored with a lightning-like shot. After this Newton Heath had a couple of chances, which were spoiled by bad shooting. At half time the score stood:—Liverpool, two goals; Newton Heath, none. On resuming, Liverpool attacked determinedly, their play being much superior to that of their opponents. At length Newton Heath forged ahead, and gained a couple of free kicks for "hands" close to the Liverpool goal; but the danger was cleared. The excitement which had previously been manifested subsided, and though Liverpool continued to have the best of matters the play on both sides was but moderate, the players suffering from excitement. Towards the finish Newton Heath made an effort to score, and Donaldson had a clear run, but preferred to shoot, and sent the ball wide of the posts. On the play Liverpool deserved their victory, showing greater smartness all round and a far superior combination. Result:—Liverpool, two goals; Newton Heath, none. Teams:—Liverpool: M. M'Queen, goal; Hannah and M'Lean, backs; M'Cartney, M'Que, and M'Bride, half backs; Gordon, M'Vean, Henderson, Bradshaw, and H. M'Queen, forwards. Newton Heath: Falls, goal; Mitchell and Erentz, backs; Perrins, M'Naught, and Davidson, half backs; Clarkin, Farman, Donaldson, Hood, and Peden, forwards. Referee: Mr. Lewis, of Blackburn.

Guardian, 30 April 1894

Fred Erentz, seated third from the right, was a key figure in the side for 10 years.

MANCHESTER'S FIRST league derby was played on Saturday, 3 November 1894 under the shadow of the railway arches at Ardwick, home of Manchester City. It was not the first time the two clubs had met; they had often faced each other in the Manchester Cup,

Smith, seated second from the right, scored four goals in the first league derby as the Heathens ran out 5–2 winners. No other United player has ever hit four against the local rivals in a league match, though two have managed a hat trick. By the end of 1989/90, United were 41–32 up in the series.

1894

the Football Alliance and even the FA Cup, but this first league meeting was their most important encounter to date and it turned out to be a memorable occasion for the recently relegated Heathens.

The game drew an estimated 15,000 to Hyde Road in dull and threatening weather. It was one of the biggest crowds Manchester had ever seen for a football match, with possibly only the 1893 Cup final at Fallowfield drawing more supporters. Although extensive improvements had been carried out at Hyde Road it was still a makeshift ground barely capable of holding 15,000. The occasion marked the home debut of a young Welshman in the City side called Billy Meredith. He had made his debut the previous week in a 5–4 defeat at Newcastle and, although nobody present at that first Manchester league derby could have known it, Meredith would go on to play as crucial a role in the story of Manchester United and Manchester City as any player in history.

The Heathens began well and, in the 13th minute, Smith gave them the edge with a well-taken goal. By half time he had added another and, with City reduced to 10 men for much of the second half, United forged ahead. Clarkin contributed a third and then Smith struck the fourth and fifth. Meredith, regularly breaking down the right, pulled one back for City and in the closing minutes Sharples converted a Meredith cross to make it 5–2 to Newton Heath. First

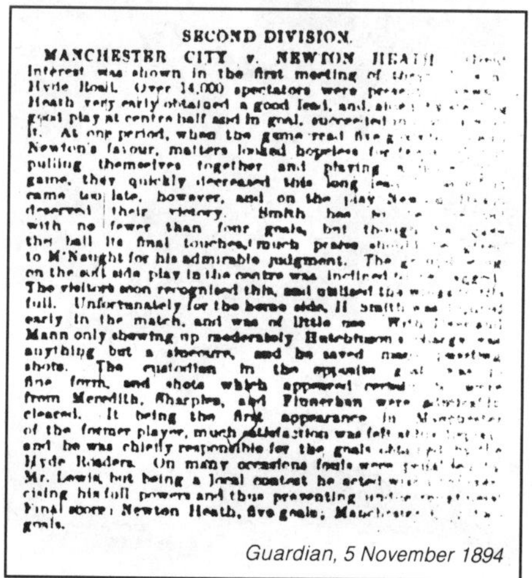

SECOND DIVISION.

MANCHESTER CITY v. NEWTON HEATH. [illegible] interest was shown in the first meeting of [illegible] Hyde Road. Over 14,000 spectators were pres[illegible] Heath very early obtained a good lead, and, [illegible] good play at centre half and in goal, succeeded [illegible] it. At one period, when the game read five g[illegible] Newton's favour, matters looked hopeless for [illegible] pulling themselves together and playing [illegible] game, they quickly decreased this long [illegible] came too late, however, and on the play New[illegible] deserved their victory. Smith has [illegible] with no fewer than four goals, but though [illegible] the ball its final touches, much praise should [illegible] to M'Naught for his admirable judgment. The [illegible] on the and side play in the centre was inclined [illegible] The visitors soon recognised this, and utilised the w[illegible] full. Unfortunately for the home side, H. Smith was [illegible] early in the match, and was of little use. With [illegible] Mann only showing up moderately Hutchinson's charge was anything but a sinecure, and he saved many [illegible] shots. The custodian in the opposite goal was [illegible] fine form, and shots which appeared certain [illegible] from Meredith, Sharples, and Finnerhan were [illegible] cleared. It being the first appearance in Manchester of the former player, much satisfaction was felt at [illegible] and he was chiefly responsible for the goals [illegible] Hyde Roaders. On many occasions fouls were [illegible] Mr. Lewis, but being a local contest he acted wi[illegible] cising his full powers and thus preventing [illegible] Final score: Newton Heath, five goals; Manchester [illegible] goals.

Guardian, 5 November 1894

blood to United and in the return fixture later that season United swept them away again with a 4–1 victory.

1895

IT WAS THE game that never happened; the day United hit a record 14 goals only to have the match frustratingly declared null and void by the Football League. It took place on Saturday, 9 March 1895 when Walsall Town Swifts were the visitors for a second division fixture. The Heathens had been playing at Bank Street since leaving the atrocious mud of North Road in September 1893. There was still precious little grass and far too much sand, so visiting clubs regularly complained about the playing surface.

When Walsall arrived for their first visit to Bank Street they took one look at the state of the pitch and immediately lodged a complaint. It was not even fit for schoolboys to play on, they grumbled. But there was little Newton could do except throw down another layer of sand and so the fixture took place as arranged.

Robert Donaldson and Joe Cassidy were both among the goals in Newton's two home games against Walsall when 23 were scored.

THE LEAGUE.—Second Division.

Results up to date :—

	Pld.	Won.	Lost	Drn.	Goals For	Goals Agst.	Pts.
Bury	24	20	3	1	69	27	41
Newton Heath..	23	13	4	6	68	30	32
Notts County ..	25	14	7	4	62	36	32
Darwen	23	14	6	3	60	27	31
Grimsby Town..	23	15	8	0	74	42	30
Leicester Fosse..	24	10	7	7	62	49	27
Woolwch Arsenal	25	11	9	5	58	53	27
Burton Wand'rs	23	10	8	5	40	32	25
Manchester City	23	11	10	2	60	57	24
N'castle United.	24	10	11	3	65	60	23
Burton Swifts ..	24	9	12	3	45	60	21
Rotherham Town	26	9	15	2	47	55	20
Lincoln City....	23	5	15	6	39	64	16
Walsall	22	6	16	0	30	80	12
B'sl'm P'rt Vale	25	3	18	4	20	73	10
Crewe Al'xandra	23	3	17	3	22	79	9

Newton Heath v. Walsall.—At Clayton, on a fearfully heavy ground, before about 4000 onlookers. Each team played as advertised, Cassidy, late of the Celtic, figuring in the centre for the Heathens. The home players monopolised practically the whole of the opening play, and Hawkins and his backs did extremely well to keep out some splendid efforts by the Heathens, especially one mighty rush after a lofty kick by McNaught. Cassidy, well fed by Peters and Smith, made some fine runs, and at length the new centre passed to Donaldson, who beat Hawkins in good style. After this the Walsall men, led on by Devey and Holmes, made several dashing runs, but not being united, they were easily sent back, Douglas only once touching the ball. Newton Heath then resumed their aggressive tactics, and after a time Smith scored from a pass by Donaldson, whilst a little later Smith notched the third point after Cassidy had put in a tremendous shot. The Heathens continued to have all the play, the forwards being in rare trim, and only the sloppy nature of the ground, together with the good defence, of Hawkins in particular, kept them out. Towards the interval, a miss by McCartney let in the visitors, and Cox called upon Douglas, who saved, and at half-time Newton Heath led by 3 goals to nil. On resuming, play hovered round Hawkins, and in two minutes Cassidy sent in a shot which, it may safely be said, was out of the power of anyone to keep out, the ball travelling at a terrific rate and going through just under the crossbar. A miskick then gave the visitors a superb chance, but Devey when clear of the backs shot at Douglas, who nevertheless saved well. The Heathens again pressed hotly, the fine shooting of Cassidy being a feature. Eventually Smith notched the fifth point, and after an abortive free kick in the Walsall goal and some disjointed breakaway by the visitors, Smith added the sixth point. The Heathens were irresistible, and, after a run by the visitors, Devey being prominent, but whom Erentz repulsed, Peters notched the seventh point, Smith the eighth, and Cassedy the ninth. The score was made into double figures by a cross by Perrins to Smith, who headed through. The visitors made one or two ragged efforts; once Devey being ruled offside when about to shoot, and soon Clarkin put on the 11th and Cassidy the 12th goal, both being the result of high shots. M'Cartney (full back) afterwards scored the 13th and Cassidy the 14th. Walsall, it was understood, handed in a protest before the match as to the condition of the ground. Final :—

NEWTON HEATH .... 14 goals
WALSALL .... Nil

The Umpire, 10 March 1895

It is hard to say whether the Walsall players were as dispirited at the state of the pitch as their manager and it is equally impossible to know whether the state of the pitch played a part in the result. Perhaps the Walsall players did feel annoyed at having to play in a mud bath, but the Heathens also had to cope with the same conditions. And, judging by the eventual outcome, it is probably reasonable to assume that Walsall – second from bottom in the league – were simply a poor side.

The Heathens attacked from the whistle, with centre forward Joe Cassidy playing only his fifth game for the club. By half time Newton held a comfortable 3–0 lead thanks to a couple of goals from Smith and one from Robert Donaldson. But, in the second half, Newton, to the delight of the 4,000 crowd, ran riot, hitting a further 11 goals. At the end of 90 minutes they had notched up a record 14–0 victory. Smith had hit an astonishing six goals while Cassidy had struck four himself.

The Football League, however, were not impressed by Newton's mammoth score and sided with Walsall who, they pointed out, had actually complained before the match and not afterwards. The referee, Mr Jeffries, had also backed the Walsall case and so the result was cancelled and a replay ordered. The Heathens were bitterly disappointed, but there was little they could do except repeat the exercise. Four weeks later on Wednesday, 3 April in pleasanter weather the two teams met again at Clayton. This time the pitch was a little drier although Walsall, with three of their key players missing, must have been more than apprehensive. By half time they appeared to be faring somewhat better, having conceded only one goal, but in the second half they collapsed and the Heathens piled on the agony. Eight goals went thundering past the Midlanders and, but for some agile goalkeeping as well as poor shooting by the Heathens, it might have been 14–0 again instead of 9–0. This time the goals were shared by Cassidy, Donaldson, Smith and Peters, with a couple each, and Clarkin. In the two matches against Walsall the Heathens had hit 23 goals.

Joe Cassidy had joined Newton Heath from Glasgow Celtic in 1893. He managed four games towards the end of the 1892/93 season but then had to wait until March 1895 before reappearing in the line-up. He was supposedly a winger but was converted to centre forward, serving the club admirably in that position, and was leading scorer on four occasions. He remained at Clayton until 1899 when he joined Manchester City, by which time he had made 174 appearances and scored 100 goals.

The Association Football Cup

SECOND ROUND.

NEWTON HEATH MAKE A PLUCKY FIGHT.

[By Harricus.]

Newton Heath have not been pleasing their supporters by their recent displays, and though their tie with Derby County was looked upon as a rare opportunity of swelling the club's coffers, there was not much hope of them pulling it off. Preparations had been made for coping with the crowd, which numbered something like 18,000 strong, the gate receipts totting up to £508. Newton Heath had protested against Stevenson, on the ground that he had taken part in a match during the close season, but this was considered frivolous, in fact, the County took no notice whatever of the objection. The Derby club is the most fortunate one in the League with regard to their players, for not only have they got a good eleven together, but they are able to play them week after week without any alteration, which in itself is a strong point, but the same cannot be said of Newton Heath, for they are always changing.

Athletic News, 17 February 1896

1896

UNITED'S FA CUP performances were hardly spectacular. In the seven seasons they had entered the competition they had never progressed beyond the second round. Although 1896 proved no exception, at least they were eliminated by one of the finest sides to grace the era. The prospect of Derby County visiting Clayton was keenly awaited but few gave second division Newton much chance against the first division giants who ended that season as runners-up. But a big gate would at least help solve some of the Heathens' financial problems. In the event 18,000 turned up and the £500 they paid went some distance in keeping the bailiff away. In the first round United had made heavy weather of eliminating non-league Kettering, but Derby County were a far different proposition.

For a start, Derby boasted a team oozing with talent. In goal was Jack Robinson who would soon become the regular England keeper, while upfront there was John Goodall the England centre forward and at inside right the splendid Steve Bloomer, a new recruit to the England team. In the years to follow, the magnificent Bloomer was capped 23 times and led Derby County to three Cup finals. There were few teams in the country that could compare with Derby.

The game was played on Saturday, 15 February 1896 with a low-lying fog hanging around the touchline. Derby began furiously, their freescoring forwards repeatedly peppering the United goal with long-range shots. But United struggled on, playing, as the *Athletic News* reported, 'go-ahead football' leaving the 'pretty game to their rivals'. But, with 15 minutes to the interval, John Goodall chipped a speculative ball into the United goalmouth and, in the scrimmage that followed, Bloomer poked the ball into the net. At half time the score was still 1–0 to Derby, but after the restart United took control, though not before County had almost scored. But as the half progressed the Derby forwards slowly lost their way, perhaps exhausted by the muddy conditions or dispirited by United's stubbornness. They had given their best but the United defence had clung on, with goalkeeper Ridgway defiantly holding Bloomer and Goodall at bay. Without a doubt United deserved their equaliser which arrived courtesy of Kennedy who strained to reach a Peters centre. They might even have gone on to win the game, having had one goal disallowed, and finished by far the better side. But it was not to be and the two teams traipsed wearily off the field to fight another day.

The *Athletic News* waxed lyrically about United's performance calling it 'a great and glorious contribution to Manchester's football history', yet the replay the following Wednesday at the Baseball Ground turned out to be a mere formality as Derby romped home 5–1. But United did have excuses. Ridgway broke a finger and had to leave the field for a time while Carlin was also injured, so at one point United were down to nine men. But they had fought bravely and could count their draw against Derby as one of their best Cup performances to date.

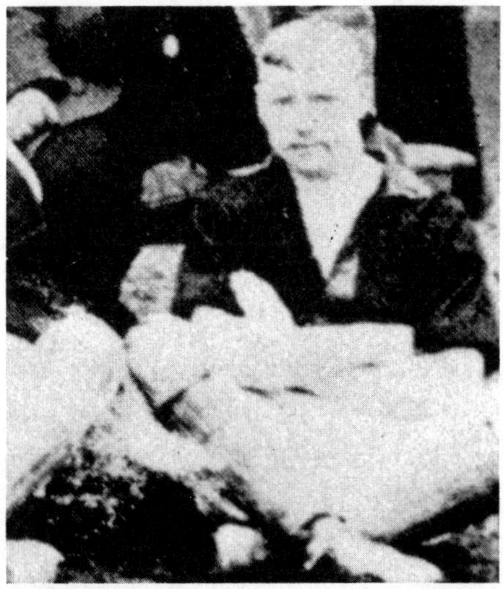

Clarkin (left) and Peters (right) were two of the Heathens' battling heroes in the Cup against Derby.

1897

FOOTBALL.

THE ASSOCIATION GAME.

LEAGUE TEST MATCHES.

SUNDERLAND v. NEWTON-HEATH.—At Sunderland last night in splendid weather, before 6,000 spectators. Newton Heath had the same team as on Saturday. On the home side M'Allister took Boyle's place at half-back, while Morgan went centre and Campbell on the wing. Sunderland faced the sun during the first half. The home side pressed determinedly from the start, but beyond two corners could not get through. Fifteen minutes from starting Gillespie headed through a splendid goal amid ringing cheers

Sporting Chronicle, 27 April 1897

FOR THE FOURTH TIME in five years Newton Heath found themselves facing the end-of-season play-offs. Their record was miserable; only on the first occasion had they been successful. Along with them in the play-offs were Sunderland and Burnley, the bottom two clubs in the first division, and Notts County, champions of the second division.

Newton Heath had ended the season in second spot, three points behind Notts County, and had wound up their campaign in fine style. They may have lost their final fixture at Loughborough but it had been their first defeat since New Year's Day and they remained undefeated at Clayton, having conceded only 10 goals. Newton Heath may not have entered the play-offs as favourites but there was every hope that they might make it back to the upper division.

Their first play-off was away to Burnley, who had finished bottom of the first division, four points adrift of Sunderland, but against the Heathens they managed a 2–0 win. Right back Harry Stafford had been injured and old stalwart Roger Doughty had to be recalled, while centre forward Boyd also missed the game through injury. By all accounts, it was a match they should never have lost and they were reckoned to have outclassed Burnley. Nevertheless, the Heathens took their revenge a few days later at Clayton, winning 2–0 with goals from Boyd and Jenkyns, and then faced Sunderland at Bank Street on Saturday, 24 April.

More than 18,000 turned up to watch Sunderland, who had been league champions in 1892, 1893 and 1895. The Wearsiders had temporarily fallen on hard times, although it would not be for long. This time Newton Heath took the field without the normally dependable Walter Cartwright, while the injured Bryant bravely limped on. The game ended in a 1–1 draw with Boyd scoring for Newton. This left the play-off table finely poised as the Heathens travelled to Wearside with Notts County on four points, Newton Heath on three and Burnley and Sunderland on two each. At best Newton needed a win to secure first division football but a draw might be sufficient. Sunderland, on the other hand, desperately needed both points if they were to remain in the first division.

Stafford was still missing from the line-up as the two teams faced each other in front of 6,000 at Roker Park on Monday, 26 April. But from the kick-off Sunderland were the better team and strode into a 15-minute lead. The score miraculously remained 1–0 at half time with the Heathens under continual bombardment and, not surprisingly, 10 minutes from the end the Wearsiders made it 2–0. Newton Heath wound up in third place and had to face yet another season in the lower division.

The Heathens line up in their new kit: white shirts and blue shorts.

THE ATHLETIC NEWS,
MONDAY, DECEMBER 26 1898.

THE RACE IN THE SECOND DIVISION

CLIMBING THE GOLDEN STAIRS.

Athletic News, 26 December 1898

1898

AS 1898 DREW to a close Newton Heath and rivals Manchester City were jockeying for the top spot in division two. The *Athletic News*, itself a Manchester-based newspaper, marked the occasion with a suitable cartoon. After 16 games City were just two points ahead at the top of the table, with the Heathens in second place and New Brighton Tower lying third. That Christmas weekend Newton Heath thrashed Darwen 9–0 at Clayton while City had won 4–2 at Blackpool. Joe Cassidy and Bryant both hit hat tricks for the Heathens in what turned out to be their biggest win of the season. Following the Darwen game the two Manchester clubs faced each other in a crucial Boxing Day clash at Ardwick. The Heathens lost 4–0 and, although they ended the year with a 6–1 hammering of Gainsborough Trinity, the defeat by City severely dented their promotion hopes. City went on to capture the second division championship comfortably, six points ahead of runners-up Glossop North End and nine points ahead of Newton in fourth place.

The Heathens battled to the end, finishing their season with a run of seven games undefeated. Cassidy was the club's top scorer, with 18, for the second time in three years and he did not miss a match all season. Bryant was the only other player to reach double figures. It was he who achieved the rare feat of scoring a hat trick – against Tottenham in the FA Cup – and still ending up on the losing side.

Indeed, the season was a frustrating one for the club. Once more they had challenged for promotion only to fall by the wayside. In five seasons in the second division they had never finished lower than sixth.

Sadly, City knocked Newton Heath down the stairs in their Boxing Day match.

1899

WE TEND TO assume that trouble on and off the football field is something new to the game but, on the contrary, it is as old as the sport itself. Before the turn of the century fans had rioted at Goodison Park after the referee had abandoned a match and, in 1909, in the replayed Scottish Cup final between Rangers and Celtic, so-called supporters tried to burn the ground down, setting light to turnstiles and ripping down goal-posts. For three hours, more than 200 police battled with rival fans through the streets of Glasgow and 81 policemen were treated in hospital. Manchester United may not have experienced anything quite so dramatic in its early years (although a trip to the Continent in 1908 would bring its problems), but the club nevertheless experienced some difficulties both with players and fans.

In March 1899 the *Athletic News* reported that the club had placed two players on the transfer list and suspended a third following an investigation into their extracurricular activities. Quite what these were was never explained but there were enough hints to surmise that the three had been drinking. 'If men who are paid good wages don't think it worth their while to keep themselves in condition they are better out of the team', roared the *Athletic News*. 'The directors are to be congratulated for dealing with the offenders in a firm manner.'

The two players suspended and placed on the transfer list were Boyd, who the paper described as a 'most capricious individual', and Cunningham. Little is known about either except that Boyd was something of a prolific goalscorer, hitting 35 goals in only 62 appearances for the club. He had joined Newton Heath in 1896 as a centre forward and made his league debut in the 6–0 win over Loughborough in February 1897 when he also scored. His final match was against Grimsby Town just prior to the suspension. He was the club's top scorer in the 1897/98 season and had established a more than useful partnership with Joe Cassidy. Cunningham, an inside forward, had joined the Heathens in 1898 and was a regular choice, having made his debut on 5 November that year. Seventeen games and four months later he was suspended and never played again for Newton. The other player involved was Gillespie, also an inside forward, but he apologised for 'certain indiscretions' and was forgiven by the club, though not before serving a suspension. Gillespie had made his league debut for the Heathens in November 1896 and remained a regular first-teamer until the 1900 close season, making 89 appearances in all and scoring 21 goals.

MANCUNIAN MURMURINGS.

[BY NIBBES.]

Friendly matches have long ago lost their attractions, and one was not a bit surprised that the game between Newton Heath and West Bromwich at Clayton on Saturday was only witnessed by some 4,000 spectators, notwithstanding most delightful weather. The match can be summed up in a few words. It was not exciting, brilliant, or entertaining. It was as good as "friendlies" go, however, and it had one redeeming feature. It was wound up in a most exciting fashion. The two elevens struggled vainly until about five minutes from time without scoring. Then Bryant got hold, and before the whistle blew put the ball past Reader twice. The incident quite roused the spectators, and it must be said that the two points were really capital ones.

The Newton Heath team was much changed, and only Cassidy and Bryant of the first team were included in the front rank. Erentz was absent at back, and his place was efficiently filled by Turner. Roberts was again given a trial on the left wing, and I think that the Newton Heath directors will have a difficulty in leaving him off the team. Morgan and Cartwright again gave a fine exhibition at half-back. The former is playing splendidly at present, and so is Stafford. As for the visitors, they shone mostly at back. But truth to tell they rarely exerted themselves.

During the week the directors of Newton Heath have been forced to take strong measures with some of their players. Boyd, who seems to be a most capricious individual, has been placed on the transfer list, and so has Cunningham I suppose we have heard the last of these players, as far as Newton Heath is concerned, and it is as well. If men who are paid good wages don't think it worth their while to keep themselves in condition they are better out of any team. The directors are to be congratulated for dealing with the offenders in a firm manner. Gillespie, who has also been suspended, has, I understand, apologised for certain indiscretions, and he has been forgiven. It is exceedingly unfortunate that the club should be troubled with its players at the most critical part of the season. The officials had no alternative but to deal with the players as they have done, and I am sure every Manchester enthusiast wishes Newton Heath well out of their difficulties.

Athletic News, 13 March 1899

A week after this incident the *Athletic News* reported yet more trouble at Clayton. This time it was the fans who were causing problems. Following a 2–1 defeat by New Brighton Tower in front of a huge gate of 20,000, which seriously dented Newton Heath's hopes of promotion, a group of supporters took unilateral action against the referee. By all

Boyd and Gillespie in happier times. In front of them is the Lancashire Senior Cup, which the Heathens won for the first time in 1897/98, beating Blackburn Rovers 2–1 in the final. Boyd, a scorer on that day, was soon on his way.

accounts the game had been badly handled, with the referee ignoring his linesman on at least one vital occasion and making a number of other questionable decisions. As the referee walked off the field 'a crowd of hot-headed youths got round him and jeered and booed him', reported the *Athletic News*. But help, fortunately, was at hand as 'officials of the club together with several policemen prevented anything approaching mobbing'. Nevertheless the whole incident was severely frowned-upon by the newspaper, even though it was prepared to admit that the youths had been provoked by some dubious refereeing. At the end of the season the two points hardly mattered, although arguably a win might just have spurred them on to sustain a serious challenge.

NEWTON HEATH v. BOLTON WANDERERS.

This return match was played at Clayton, before 5,000 people. Rain fell steadily and spoiled what would have been a most attractive game. Not many minutes had elapsed when Cartwright was rather seriously injured and had to leave the field. Despite his absence the "Heathens" played vigorously, and Sutcliffe, on three occasions, had to defend. At length the Wanderers assumed the aggressive, and Barrett was beaten by a good shot from the left wing about ten minutes after the start. Although playing with ten men, the "Heathens" retaliated, and Somerville and Hadley had to defend. After a few minutes absence Cartwright returned, but for a short time the Wanderers were the better team. Barrett was tested on three occasions before the "Heathens" fairly got into their opponents' quarters. Griffiths played grandly in centre half, and repeatedly broke up the opposing combination. After repeated attempts to equalise, Newton Heath were successful. Bryant started a splendid run, and after a fine passing bout Parkinson headed through. Half-time - Newton Heath 1; Bolton Wanderers 1. The second half opened with Newton Heath strongly pressing. Sutcliffe saved a very large number of splendid shots from the home forwards. Cassidy was particularly prominent with grand shooting, and Parkinson, Bryant, and Clark also tested the Wanderers' custodian. Then Newton Heath became the masters of the situation, and it was only the superb defence of Sutcliffe which prevented further scoring. Jack and Morgan occasionally broke away, but Stafford and Erentz, with the able assistance of the half-backs, kept them away from Barrett. Jack and Morgan occasionally broke away, and the former was very near after a good run. Cassidy and Bryant caused Sutcliffe further trouble, but again the custodian saved splendidly. After pressing for nearly the greater part of the second half Barrett made a great mistake, and let the ball through the goal, thus giving the Wanderers the lead. There was nothing further scored, and the game ended: –

BOLTON WANDERERS 2
NEWTON HEATH 1

Sunday Chronicle, 7 January 1900

NEWTON HEATH kicked off the 20th century with a league fixture at Clayton against Lancashire rivals Bolton Wanderers. But it was not a portentous initiation to the new age as they lost 2–1. Bolton were later promoted, while the Heathens once more finished in fourth place and again missed out on promotion. After eight years in the Football League they had achieved little and were now languishing in the shadow of their close neighbours Manchester City, recently promoted to the first division. It would eventually improve but, unfortunately, not before it got worse.

There were few notable changes in the line-up. Frank Barrett remained in goal with Harry Stafford and Fred Erentz shielding him. Morgan, Griffiths and Cartwright were automatic choices for the half back line while up front Bryant, Jackson and Cassidy were the regulars. Centre half William Griffiths was a local lad who took over the role after James McNaught had left for Tottenham Hotspur in 1898. Griffiths went on to play more than 150 league games for the club and was joint top scorer with 11 goals in the 1903/04 season. Walter Cartwright was another loyal member of that team, playing throughout those difficult years without complaints or demands. A left-sided player, he had arrived from Crewe in 1895 and made more than 250 appearances for the club.

The closing years of the 19th century had seen Newton Heath wave goodbye to two fine players in James McNaught and John Peden. Both came from Linfield in Ireland and Peden was already an international when he arrived in Manchester, winning an astonishing 24 caps between 1887 and 1899. He stayed for just one season, 1893/94, before moving on to Sheffield United. He eventually returned to Ireland, joining Distillery, before finishing his days with his former club, Linfield. He was an outside left, dubbed by some as the first George Best, and was said to delight in weaving his way down the wing and, by all accounts, was just as temperamental and awkward as his successor.

The club had also forged strong links with Wales and by 1900 could boast seven Welsh internationals on their books at various times, many of them coming to find work on the Lancashire and Yorkshire Railway. Most, like Tom Burke, Jos Davies, Gary Owen and Jack Powell, had played with the club in its pre-league days, but there were others who won honours when the club was a league member. They included the two Doughty brothers, Jack and Roger. Both had been with the Druids prior to joining Newton Heath and had appeared in Welsh Cup finals. Jack won a total of seven caps while Roger won three in all. Between them they once scored six goals as Wales thrashed Ireland 11–0. There was also Caesar Jenkins, a centre half who joined the Heathens via Small Heath and Woolwich Arsenal. He won just one cap in his single season at Newton but boasted eight by the end of his career.

There were no England players prior to 1900, but Billy Bryant did play for the Football League against the Irish League in 1897. Scotland was hardly represented, although goalkeeper Frank Barrett had won two Scottish caps while still with Dundee. One signing in 1900 proved to be inspired: Liverpudlian Alf Schofield, who came from Everton where he had played only a handful of games. He remained with United until 1907, when, after 179 games, he was succeeded on the right wing by Billy Meredith.

1900

Billy Bryant and Joe Cassidy started the 20th century by causing the Bolton goalkeeper 'further trouble', but failed to score and the game was lost when Barrett conceded a soft goal.

1901

NEWTON HEATH at the turn of the century were little more than an average second division side. After almost a decade in the Football League they had little to show for their endeavours – two years in the first division and in both of those years they had ended up in bottom place. Since then they had shuffled along fairly comfortably in the second division, initially challenging for promotion but at the end of the 1900/01 season they finished 10th, their worst-ever position. But, just as their fortunes seemed at the lowest ebb, a fairy godmother turned up and with the wave of a magic wand (or, in this case, a bundle of money) their luck began to change.

NEWTON HEATH FOOTBALL CLUB.

BAZAAR IN ST. JAMES'S HALL.
OPENING BY SIR J. FERGUSSON.

Manchester Evening News, 27 February 1901

The fairy godmother was John Henry Davies, the managing director of Manchester Breweries. His involvement with United arose out of a chance meeting in 1901 which revolved around a bazaar organised by the club to raise funds. The club's lowly position was causing alarm among its members and the only solution was to raise £1,000 in order to buy new players. And so they hit upon the idea of a bazaar to raise the money. It was held from Wednesday, 27 February for four days at the St James Hall. 'Judging by the programme it should be one of the best bazaars ever held', reported the *Manchester Evening News*, announcing that the Northern Military and The Besses-o'th-Barn brass band would be playing. The bazaar was formally opened by Sir James Fergusson, the Conservative MP for Manchester North East who told those assembled that 'the members of the club have come to the conclusion that they must collect a handsome sum to enable them to engage a team which will be capable of securing and holding a place in the first league'. Secretary James West moved a vote of thanks and the audience was left to wander around the various exhibits which included scenes depicting the splendours of India, Italy and the Mediterranean. The bazaar ended on the Saturday evening, but the proceeds turned out to be far less than expected. When the cost of hiring the hall had been deducted there was barely any profit. But a fortuitous meeting as a result of the bazaar reaped large dividends.

Strangely, it was a dog which was to play a part in setting up that meeting. The dog was a St Bernard which belonged to the Newton Heath captain Harry Stafford. Stafford had loaned the dog to the bazaar and each day it wandered about the hall with a collecting box hung around its neck. But one evening the dog escaped and was later found roaming the streets by the licensee of a pub owned by Manchester Breweries who also happened to be a friend of John Davies. He showed the dog to Davies who took a fancy to it and bought it from him. Feeling guilty, Davies decided to trace the dog's owner and soon discovered that it belonged to Harry Stafford. The two men met, whereupon Stafford told Davies how the dog had disappeared from the hall and how the bazaar had been organised to raise funds for the club. Davies seemed genuinely concerned at their difficulties and, as a gesture of goodwill, made a contribution, also promising to help further in the future.

Stafford did not forget that promise. Within a year results had gone from bad to worse and the financial plight of the club had hit rock bottom. It was time to call upon Davies again.

The most important dog in United's history with his team-mates.

1902

BY JANUARY 1902 Newton Heath were in serious trouble, but as the New Year dawned nobody guessed that the club was on the verge of extinction. The Heathens owed money left, right and centre and on 9 January one of its creditors, William Healey, who also happened to be the president of the club, appeared before the Ashton-under-Lyne County Court where an application was made for the compulsory winding-up of the Newton Heath Football Club Company Limited. It was that serious.

Healey was owed £242 17s 10d, a not inconsiderable sum in those days. Even when the club appeared before the court they were still unable to pay their debt, leaving the judge with little option but to initiate bankruptcy proceedings. The *Manchester Evening News* reckoned Healey had been a little impatient, especially as he was president of the club, and pointed out that the directors had gone to some lengths to come to terms with him. But the truth was that Newton Heath were more than £2,600 in debt and that it was only going to get worse before it got any better.

The bankruptcy of one of football's leading clubs caused a sensation. Nevertheless, the directors put on a brave public face, insisting that it did not mean the end of the club. A few good gates might solve the problems, they argued, as long as the creditors did not press too hard. Under immediate threat was Saturday's fixture against Middlesbrough at Clayton. There were assurances that the game would go ahead as planned and even on the Friday evening the *Manchester Evening News* informed its readers that the match was on. Unfortunately, the Football League and the official receiver intervened and, in an unprecedented step, closed the ground and postponed the fixture.

In the meantime captain Harry Stafford began a campaign to raise money. Their next fixture, away to Bristol City, was threatened and if the money could not be raised for travelling expenses then that game too would be called off. Quite where that would have left the club is anyone's guess, but it is fair to assume that two postponed fixtures would have meant the end of Newton Heath. The club was probably within 24 hours of extinction. But the money did come in, not in vast quantities, but enough to keep them going. With the doors of the Clayton ground locked there was also a pressing problem over the reserve team's next fixture, and poor Harry Stafford found himself scouring the playing fields of Manchester looking for someone to lend them a ground. In the end they found accommodation in Harpurhey.

For some months the club staggered on in this fashion, never knowing from one week to another whether they would survive, and it was largely thanks to

FOOTBALL.

THE AFFAIRS OF THE NEWTON HEATH CLUB.

WINDING-UP ORDER GRANTED.

At the Ashton-under-Lyne County Court, this afternoon, Dr. Bradley, barrister, instructed by Messrs. Brett, Hamilton, and Tarbolton, solicitors, of Manchester, applied to the Judge on behalf of Mr. W. J. Healey, of Salford, for a compulsory winding-up order against the Newton Heath Football Club Company, Limited. There was no appearance to the petition.

Dr. Bradley explained that the petition was brought on account of an unsatisfied debt of £242. 17s. 10d. due to Mr. Healey, who was at one time a director of the club, and who brought these proceedings with very great reluctance. Mr. Healey had filed an affidavit in which it was stated that the club was incorporated in 1892, and that the registered offices were at Clayton. The capital of the company was 2,000 shares of £1 each, and the amount paid was £766. 3s. 6d. The object for which the company was established was to carry on business as a football club. The club was indebted to Mr. Healey for the amount mentioned.

NO OPPOSITION PRESENT.

His Honour: Is there any opposition present?

Dr. Bradley: No.

His Honour: What is a football club, limited? How do they carry on business? Do they make money?

Dr. Bradley said the club engaged professional players to play matches and took the gate receipts. He did not suppose that a company of this kind was formed with the object of gain. It was formed with the object of ascertaining the liabilities and seeing that they did not exceed a certain amount. According to what the receipts were they paid the players.

A MODIFIED SUCCESS.

His Honour: Was it a success?

Dr. Bradley: At first it was, but lately it has not been.

His Honour: Has it paid any dividends?

Dr. Bradley: I don't think so. I think I may safely say it never has paid any, the object being not to pay dividends but to play football. The club is in the second division of the League.

His Honour: Are all the proceedings regular?

Dr. Bradley: The application has been advertised.

His Honour: Have you received any notice of opposition?

Dr. Bradley: No; the latest time for opposition to be lodged was six o'clock last night, but none had been received at eleven o'clock this morning.

His Honour: Is there no correspondence, no answer from the secretary?

Dr. Bradley: No. Negotiations have, however, taken place for a settlement of the debt, but they have not come to anything.

His Honour: Your debt is not disputed?

Dr. Bradley: No. We have had an offer of 10s. in the pound after the proceedings were commenced. We agreed to accept the offer, and they did not pay.

His Honour: You seem to be entitled to your order. The proceedings are regular, and the order will be made, with costs.

THE POSITION OF THE CLUB.

NO QUESTION OF EXTINCTION.

The decision arrived at this morning in the Ashton County Court, though serious from a financial point of view to many of those connected with the club, does not mean the death of Newton Heath as a playing club and a member of the Second Division. No one who has the slightest interest in such an old club could contemplate this fate with equanimity, and it is certain that when the immediate stress of financial resources has been removed a big effort will be made to put the club on a much sounder basis than it has been for the past few years. Many clubs in this country are propped up by one or two men of means, but the withdrawal of these financial supporters would not, of course, involve the complete downfall of the clubs. It is possible for a club to be absolutely insolvent one month and to be in a comparatively flourishing position the next. This fact is realised, and for the most part the gentlemen who have advanced money to the club are content to wait until the change of fortune comes. Mr. Healey is doubtless quite justified in taking steps to recover his money, though it might fairly be expected of such an excellent and liberal supporter of the game that he would have shown a little more patience. However, Mr. Healey's claim will have to be met in some way or other, and providing other creditors do not press their claims, there ought to be no difficulty in making an arrangement. One or two really good "gates" would soon improve matters, and rather than there should be any fear of the club not being able to meet its League engagements the thousands of footballers who have long followed the fortunes of Newton Heath will doubtless be prepared to make some special effort in the near future. There is, of course, nothing to prevent other clubs from coming to the assistance of Newton Heath, temporarily or otherwise. This has been done in other cases where the club has had no such record to boast as the old Manchester organisation.

Originally formed in connection with the Lancashire and Yorkshire Railway carriage works, the club became a member of the old Alliance in the days when the League was formed. In 1892 they gained a place in the First Division but fell to the bottom of the table, with the result that they had to take part in the test match. This gave them another lease in the premier combination, but in April, 1894, they were defeated in the final test and disappeared from the First Division. Since then they have existed in the Second Division with varying fortunes, last season being the worst they ever had from a playing point of view. Bad luck rather than bad management is responsible for their present plight, for both last season and this season they have had many attractive matches ruined by the weather from a financial point of view.

THE FUTURE OF THE CLUB.

SATURDAY'S MATCH TO BE PLAYED.

The Newton Heath Football Club, although the pioneer of Association football in Manchester, has lately fallen upon evil days, and even the bazaar held in the St. James's Hall last year failed to clear the club financially. It was hoped that things would be put right this season, but the weather has been all against large gates at the important home matches, and the crisis has at length arrived. One of the directors told our reporter this afternoon that they had done their best to come to terms with Mr. Healey with regard to the money he had advanced, and they much regretted that the matter had had to go into court. He emphatically denied that the granting of the winding-up order would mean the extinction of the club, and said the match arranged with Middlesbrough on Saturday next would certainly take place at Clayton, indeed the team is to be selected this evening. The directors confidently believe that, given fine weather, there should be a big gate at the match, and if this should be the case and the supporters of the club will turn up in force, they are sure that the present great difficulty will be overcome. The directors meet to-night to discuss the situation.

Manchester Evening News, 9 January 1902

NEWTON HEATH FOOTBALL CLUB.

ITS POSITION AND PROSPECTS.

HANDSOME OFFER OF SUPPORT.

One of the most enthusiastic meetings ever held in connection with the Newton Heath Football Club took place last evening in the New Islington Hall. Mr. F. Palmer, who presided over a crowded attendance, explained that the supporters of the club had not been called together earlier, because the Football Association did not give consent for the reforming of the club until about 10 days ago. The Association, he added, were satisfied that the directors were not to be blamed for the club being landed in the bankruptcy court. The players had stood by the club in the most loyal manner, and he appealed to the public to render all the support possible. The present executive could not be expected to run any further risks, and the question to be solved was how the club was to be carried on in the future. There was a prospect of the Hyde Road team being in the Second Division next season, and that would to a certain extent improve the finances of Newton Heath.

Mr. James West, secretary, said the receipts at the matches since the winding-up proceedings was £402. 3s. 8d., and they had contracted no tradesmen's debts. They, however, owed the players £181. 10s. 6d. Each director had done his utmost, but bad luck had persistently dogged the steps of the officials.

Mr. H. Smith, a sixteen years supporter of the team, and Mr. James Robinson, a director, both made a strong appeal to the supporters to stand by "the old club."

A GENEROUS OFFER.

At this point Mr. Harry Stafford, the captain of the team, asked what amount would be required to set the club on a sound financial basis, and the Chairman replied that when it was formed into a limited liability company a sum of £2,000 was asked for, but he did not suppose that amount would be requisite now, seeing they had a well-equipped ground. Mr. Stafford thereupon stated that he would give the names of five gentlemen who were each willing to give £200 each, and pay the money into the bank at once if need be. Loud cheering greeted this announcement, and the large audience would not be satisfied until Mr. Stafford ascended the platform. He said the names of the individuals were Mr. Davies, Old Trafford; Mr. Taylor, Sale; Mr. Bown, Denton; Mr. Jones, Manchester; and himself. (Renewed cheering.)

The Chairman said it was no use discussing the matter till the gentlemen mentioned by Mr. Stafford had been seen by the present officials, and the meeting was accordingly adjourned.

Before the meeting broke up, one old supporter suggested that the name of the club should be changed to "Manchester United," but this did not meet with much favour.

THE POSITION OF STAFFORD.

We are in a position to say that at the end of the season it is the intention of Stafford to ask the Football Association to allow of his being reinstated as an amateur. The Newton Heath officials are indeed fortunate in having such a player as Stafford. Ever since he joined the team he has been a tireless worker in its interests, both on and off the field, and it is questionable if any club ever possessed such a thorough sportsman. By the winding up proceedings he lost considerably, but fortunately for him he has been in a position for some time to play football for the love of the game, and if the efforts which he is now making are accepted in the proper spirit there is a chance of the team being placed on a better footing than it has been before.

Manchester Evening News, 19 March 1902

John Davies, along with Harry Stafford, helped save the club from bankruptcy.

Harry Stafford that the club did continue. A right back, he had joined Newton Heath from Crewe in 1895 and played throughout the difficult years, often sacrificing his training in order to devote time to keeping the club afloat. He played 200 games for Newton Heath, scoring just one goal, and played his last match in March 1903. It was Stafford and his St Bernard dog who introduced John Davies to Newton Heath and Stafford who dug into his own pocket to help save the Heathens. Without him Newton Heath would almost certainly have gone under. His loyalty was rewarded when he was made a director, but in 1911 he left Manchester due to ill health and went to live abroad. United gave him £50, which hardly seems much recompense for the great debt they owed him.

In March 1902, Stafford again came to the rescue of the club when the members met to discuss the financial crisis. The meeting took place on Tuesday, 18 March at the New Islington Hall in Ancoats with Mr Palmer presiding. He informed members of the bankruptcy proceedings and secretary James West added that since then they had receipts of £402 and had incurred no further debts other than to the players who were owed £181 10s 6d in wages.

Harry Stafford immediately rose and asked how much the club would need to solve its problems. 'Two thousand pounds' came the reply. 'Well, I know five men who will each give two hundred pounds', announced Stafford. 'Tell us their names', yelled the audience. 'A Mr Davies of Salford, Mr Brown of Denton, Mr Deakin of Manchester, Mr Taylor of Sale and myself', he answered. There was an enormous cheer. Stafford had saved the day and he was ushered on to the platform to take the applause. But there were conditions: in return for their investment the five men wanted control of the club and the meeting was adjourned so that the directors could meet with them to discuss their proposal. The directors had little option but to hand over control and it was not long before John Henry Davies found himself installed as president of Newton Heath Football Club. Stafford's St Bernard meanwhile had installed itself in the Davies household. It seemed a fair exchange.

1902

THE NAME Newton Heath was not to the liking of everyone. After all, it had been nine years since the club had left its home in Newton Heath for Bank Street, Clayton. The club had been formed in 1878, 10 years before the birth of the Football League, when some of the workers employed by the Lancashire and Yorkshire Railway at the Newton Heath depot decided to set up a football team. They were given permission to use land owned by the railway company which was almost adjacent to their depot. And so, not unnaturally, they adopted the name Newton Heath and soon became known as the 'Heathens'. Once they had joined the Football League in 1892, visitors began to arrive from as far afield as London and the Midlands. There was confusion. Where exactly was Newton Heath? Did the club actually play there? On at least one occasion the visiting team turned up at the old Newton Heath ground only to find a dilapidated and empty pitch, and had then to dash across the city to Bank Street, arriving with just minutes to spare before kick-off.

Above: Louis Rocca, the man who thought of the name 'Manchester United'.

Following the reorganisation of the club in 1902 it was also decided that it should be renamed. There were a number of suggestions, although all seemed agreed that the name Manchester should appear somewhere in the title. Someone put forward the name Manchester Central, but that sounded too much like a railway station. Another suggested Manchester Celtic, but then Louis Rocca, a man destined to play a major part in the history of the club, hit upon the name Manchester United. All were agreed that this was by far the best suggestion. Oddly enough, at the famous March meeting to discuss the club's financial plight someone had suggested changing the club's name to Manchester United but it had, according to the *Manchester Evening News,* received 'little favour'.

On Saturday, 26 April 1902 the *Manchester Evening News* publicly revealed the club's new name for the first time and commended it to its readers. 'There is no doubt it is a step in the right direction', said the *News.* 'Visiting teams and supporters have many times been led astray by the name of the club and have journeyed either by car or train to Newton Heath only to find that they were miles away from the home of the club.'

> The proposal to change the name of the Newton Heath club to Manchester United will not be received with favour in certain quarters, but there is no doubt it is a step in the right direction. Visiting teams and their supporters have many times been led astray by the name of the club, and have journeyed either by car or train to Newton Heath only to find that they were miles away from the home of the club. A mistake of this kind not very long ago put a team in a very awkward position. They reached the old ground in North Road, and then found it a difficult matter to procure conveyances to take them across to Clayton. The result was that the players reached the ground within five minutes of the fixed time for starting the game. We should imagine that the League clubs generally will support the change.
>
> *Manchester Evening News, 26 April 1902*

The club staff line up below their new name emblazoned on the Bank Street stand.

1903

FOOTBALL MANAGERS have always faced pressure, particularly at Manchester United where results matter so much. And the first United manager to feel the cold stare of the board and fans was James West. West had been at United since 1900, arriving from Lincoln as the club floundered through its various financial crises, and, over the next few years, he did much to help United overcome its debts. Yet, although West may have put the club on a firm administrative footing, it was results on the football field which really counted and United were still a second division side, as promotion continued to elude the club.

They had begun the 1903/04 season with a draw and two defeats and, although they then trounced Glossop 5–0 and Bradford City 3–1, the writing was on the wall. On Monday, 28 September 1903 James West handed in his resignation. 'I am not unmindful', he wrote to the board, 'that my name may be associated with the failure of several of the newer members of the club to sustain the high reputations they had previously gained in first-class football; and solely with a view to relieving the executive of the club from embarrassment I have decided to place the resignation of the secretaryship in the hands of the members of the board.' Was he pushed or did he jump? We may never know, but at least he took the honourable course. The *Manchester Evening News* felt some sympathy for him when it reported that 'Mr West, like other football secretaries, has been blamed for mistakes for which he was not really responsible'. Nothing changes.

> FOOTBALL.
>
> MANCHESTER UNITED.
>
> APPOINTMENT OF SECRETARY.
>
> Owing to the resignation of Mr. James West, the secretary of the Manchester United Football Club, the directors have been negotiating for a successor. They have now secured the services of Mr. J. E. Mangnall, of Burnley. Mr. Mangnall is a gentleman well versed in football matters, and has for some time been the secretary of the Burnley Club. Mr. West will not terminate his engagement with the United Club until this week-end.
>
> *Manchester Evening News, 30 September 1903*

But at least the resignation of West allowed United to cast a new net. Nor did they have to throw it too far, for only two days later, on 30 September, they were able to announce that they had secured the services of the Burnley secretary, Ernest Mangnall – 'a man well versed in football matters'. Mangnall had recently helped Burnley through a difficult financial period and chairman JJ Bentley recommended him to the board as just the man to guide United. Bentley had known Mangnall for some years, having played Lancashire County football with the one-time goalkeeper. It was inspired advice, for over the next decade Mangnall would lead United out of the doldrums of the second division and to the top of the first. He would transform them from a mediocre Lancashire team into the finest side in the land. Only Matt Busby would ever have as much influence as Mangnall and, when he left the club to join Manchester City in 1912, he took with him his inspiration and knowledge. United's loss would be City's gain, as he built a new stadium at Maine Road to compare with the one he had just built at Old Trafford. Meanwhile, United began to slip back to their old, indifferent ways.

A Bolton man, he had been educated at Bolton Grammar School where he played inside right for the school team and then the Old Boys. He was also a keen cyclist and during his youth cycled from Land's End to John O' Groats. It was a pastime he always enjoyed and even in his later years it was not uncommon to spot him on his bike near Old Trafford. Not unnaturally, he became a supporter of Bolton Wanderers and before long was elected a director of the club, eventually becoming secretary before moving on to try his hand at Burnley in 1900.

Ernest Mangnall, one of United's greatest managers. Although the club did not win promotion until his third season, once in the top flight honours came swiftly, providing the income to build Old Trafford. Manchester United had been transformed in a few years.

Mangnall's skill was in spotting talent. He was a shrewd businessman who bought wisely and often cheaply, although even in those days United were not averse to spending big money when necessary. He brought goalkeeper Harry Moger to Clayton, along with Alex Bell, Dick Duckworth and that most elegant of centre halves, Charlie Roberts. But his greatest coup was in signing Billy Meredith and the other Manchester City renegades, Herbert Burgess, Sandy Turnbull and Jimmy Bannister. He left no stone unturned in his determination to sign players and if it meant some underhand tactics, then why not? He preferred to call it out-manœuvring. Above all he searched for skill and in Meredith and Roberts he acquired the two most talented players in the land who set the standards for others to emulate and bought United the success they so richly deserved.

1904

BANK STREET, Clayton was not a particularly attractive site for a football ground. It stood next to a chemical plant which belched out smoke across the ground, choking players and spectators alike with its pungent fumes. United had moved there in 1893 when the cost and mud of North Road, their first ground, proved prohibitive. Bank Street was considerably cheaper, but there was little else to commend it. The pitch was almost as bad and spectators now had further to travel, but at least there were changing rooms and a thousand-seater stand had been erected. Crowds at Bank Street were generally poor in the early years, averaging less than 10,000, although they did increase substantially as the fortunes of United climbed and touched the 30–40,000 mark at times.

That Bank Street should have been chosen as the venue for a major international fixture was perhaps surprising, but the Football League probably felt that, as the nation's second city, Manchester was deserving of another representative match. City's ground at Hyde Road had hosted a fixture between the Football League and the Irish League in 1897 and the city was long overdue another fixture. This time it was United's turn and so on Monday, 4 April 1904 the English League met the Scottish League in an afternoon fixture at Clayton.

The *Manchester Evening News* estimated that 40,000 turned up when only 20,000 had been expected, making it one of the largest attendances on record for Bank Street. Inevitably, it had been raining and, as usual, the pitch was a mud bath, so that for some hours before kick-off the game was in doubt. But, fortunately, a stiff breeze blew away the rain clouds and allowed the pitch to dry out for a few hours. The game was a prelude to the annual England/Scotland fixture which was scheduled to take place in Glasgow the following weekend and many of the players chosen for that game were also on display at Bank Street. There were no United players on show that day, although City did boast Herbert Burgess (later to become a United player) and Frost in the League side. Captaining the English team was Bob Crompton, the famous Blackburn Rovers defender, while Steve Bloomer of Derby County and Sam Raybould of Liverpool were in attack. Scotland went into an early lead when Robertson scored in the 13th minute and, although the Scots held out until half time, they succumbed to a Sam Raybould equaliser eight minutes into the second half. Eventually, Steve Bloomer netted England's winner later in the half to give them a well-deserved 2–1 victory.

On the same day as the great international United and City met in the semi-final of the Manchester Senior Cup at Hyde Road, giving the city of Manchester two outstanding games on the same day. That game resulted in a 1–1 draw and, even though both clubs fielded their reserve teams, because of so many commitments, it still attracted a gate of 10,000. The two matches had drawn an audience of over 50,000, demonstrating that the city of Manchester was more than eager for top-class football.

The muddy Bank Street ground was not ideal for a club with ambition.

LEAGUE INTERNATIONAL.

ENGLAND v. SCOTLAND.

A GREAT CROWD AT CLAYTON.

The match of the season so far as Manchester football is concerned took place at Clayton this afternoon, when the representatives of the English and Scotch Leaguers opposed each other on the ground of the Manchester United Club. Fortunately the weather though boisterous was fine, and there was an enormous gathering, though the ground was by no means tested to its fullest capacity. The gates were opened about one o'clock, and the spectators immediately began to flock into the enclosure, and by two o'clock it was estimated that there would be 20,000 people present. Car loads of people were still being conveyed to the ground, and right up to the kick-off the gates were besieged by would-be spectators. Shortly before the time for the commencement the ground presented an animated appearance, the whole of the stand accommodation being utilised, the enclosure being surrounded by living banks. The playing piece was without a vestige of grass and resembled more than anything else a tide-washed shore. Under the influence of a strong drying wind and the grateful warmth of the sun it had dried rapidly, and though still soft and somewhat treacherous in places it was in fairly good condition for a fast game.

THE TEAMS.

Almost up to the last moment it was doubtful whether or not Burgess, who strained his side badly against Newcastle, would be able to play. The little back himself was very anxious to turn out and take part in the match, and having had his injured side well wrapped up, he declared himself fit for play, and consequently Vincent Hayes, who was spoken of as a possible substitute, was not called upon. Consequently there was only one alteration in the England eleven, Bache being replaced by Shearman, of Nottingham Forest. The Scots played the team originally selected, and the sides were therefore:—

English League: Baddeley (Wolverhampton Wanderers), goal; Crompton (Blackburn Rovers) and Burgess (Manchester City), backs; Frost (Manchester City), Greenhalgh (Bolton Wanderers), and Abbott (Everton), half backs; Rutherford (Newcastle), Bloomer (Derby County), Raybould (Liverpool), Shearman (Notts Forest), and Cox (Liverpool), forwards.

Scottish League: Rennie (Hibernians), goals; Jackson and Cameron (St Mirren), backs; Young (Celtic), Thomson (Heart of Midlothian), and Robertson (Glasgow Rangers), half backs; J. Walker (Glasgow Rangers), R. Walker (Heart of Midlothian), R. Hamilton (Glasgow Rangers), Macfarlane (Dundee), and Quinn (Celtic), forwards.

Referee: Mr. W. Sunnerly, of Wrexham.

Manchester Evening News, 4 April 1904

1904

WHEN UNITEDS MEET.

The game at Clayton, where Manchester United and Burton United met, was a very moderate sort of an affair, and the only really satisfactory feature was that Manchester won by 2—0. The Burton weakness lay in the attack. The backs were distinctly good, Messrs. Ashby and Kirkland being gluttons for work. They never relaxed their efforts, and time and again they cleared their goal when points seemed certain. Bromage, too, was decidedly good, and in the opposite goal Moger was never at fault. The home eleven included two men who had not previously appeared in their ranks. These were Lyons, late of Black Lane Temperance, at inside right, and Roberts, who left Grimsby on the previous evening, at centre half. The forward has a useful turn of speed and knowledge of the game, but Roberts was almost the best man on the field. His presence certainly strengthened the line, and he may safely be looked to as a player who will give a satisfactory account of himself in the future. Sandy Robertson and Grassam scored the goals for the winners.

Athletic News, 25 April 1904

IN APRIL 1904 United made what was to be one of the most important deals in their early history when they signed a young half back from Grimsby by the name of Charlie Roberts. His transfer on the evening of Friday, 22 April was largely overshadowed by Manchester City's appearance in the Cup final the following day and passed unmentioned in both the local and national press. And even when he made his debut the following day in a second division fixture against Burton United at Clayton it went almost unnoticed. The *Manchester Evening News*, however, in its match report commented that 'Roberts gave a capital display, and his sound play was all the more remarkable when it is remembered that he had made the long journey from Grimsby that morning'. But it was the *Athletic News* whose astute reporter realised that in Roberts United had made an important purchase when he wrote that 'Roberts was almost the best man on the field. His presence certainly strengthened the line, and he may be safely looked to as a player who will give a satisfactory account of himself in the future'.

United won that game against Burton 2–0 to end the season in third position just one point behind Woolwich Arsenal. It may have been a disappointment to have missed out on promotion, but in Roberts United had sowed the seeds that would reap dividends in the years ahead. Born in Darlington, Roberts was only 20 when United signed him from Grimsby for £400 having played for just one season with the Yorkshire club after joining them from Bishop Auckland. He was a sturdily built, fast centre half who was said to be able to run 100 yards in 11 seconds at a time when the world record stood at 9.6 seconds. He soon became United's captain and within five years had led them to their first league championship and FA Cup victory.

Roberts was the epitome of the modern centre half, always using his strength and speed to good effect. Vittorio Pozzo, who coached the Italian national side to a famous World Cup victory in 1934, styled his team around the influence of the man he had so admired when he was a regular spectator at Clayton. Pozzo took back to Italy the lasting memory of Roberts and created a side that was to become one of the finest pre-war teams in Europe and which would retain the World Cup in 1938. Roberts may have been admired by the Italians, but he was not always so admired by his own Football Association. He insisted on wearing short shorts when the FA ruled that shorts should cover the knees. He was also a pioneer of the Players' Union, becoming its chairman and later played a leading role in the Outcasts. Consequently he won only three England caps. Perhaps Roberts was simply years ahead of his time but if England were to ignore his talents, United certainly did not. Over the years they would owe him a great debt as one of the creators of the modern Manchester United.

In all he played 299 League and FA Cup games for the club, scoring 23 goals. His skill, combined with his charisma, earned the respect of the players. Indeed, as late as 1930, he was still a powerful voice during the boycott controversy, urging support for the team.

Charlie Roberts won his first cap within a year of joining United and was the first player from the club to be selected for England. However, Jack Powell was the side's first international, playing for Wales in 1887. Sadly, Roberts did not remain in favour with the selectors.

1904

The rivalry between Liverpool and United stretches back to the club's earliest days, when Liverpool relegated Newton Heath in the 1894 Test Match. Even in 1904 the press followed the tie closely. Williams, Roberts and Arkesden were the scorers in United's 3–1 triumph.

THE TRADITIONAL Christmas holiday tussles between United and Liverpool can be traced back as far as the early days of the 20th century. One of the first, and most memorable for United, was on Boxing Day 1904 when the Merseysiders were on the wrong end of a 3–1 defeat. The two teams had met only twice in the league, with Liverpool trouncing them 7–1 in their first meeting in 1895. In the return fixture United ran out 5–2 winners. The two clubs had also met in a relegation/promotion Test Match in 1894 which Liverpool won 2–0, consigning United to the second division. So, when the two teams met on a bitterly cold December day in 1904, United had much to play for. Liverpool, recently relegated to the second division, were already looking likely favourites for a quick return to the first and were currently lying in second place with United close on their heels.

Athletic News, 26 December 1904

Although it was only a second division fixture, the *Athletic News* rated it the game of the day, highlighting it on the front page with a cartoon. Photography was in its infancy, with action shots yet to be perfected, and newspapers still had to overcome the difficulties of reproduction. So, instead of using photographs, many papers like the *Athletic News* employed artists to record the events and capture the action on the field. It was one of the first times United had featured in the front page cartoon of *Athletic News* and it commemorated a fine United victory which shot them into second spot, one place ahead of Liverpool. Forty thousand turned up at Clayton for the fixture, one of the highest gates United had ever attracted, and they were treated to a fine display from the home side. Charlie Roberts was United's outstanding player with only the Scotland goalkeeper Ned Doig saving Liverpool from a severe hammering. However, United's joy was to be short-lived. Liverpool took their revenge four months later with a 4–0 win at Anfield and ended the season at the top of the table five points ahead of United, who were lying in third position and just out of the promotion places.

1905

IN EARLY January 1905 United welcomed unusual visitors to Clayton in the shape of Fulham for an FA Cup tie. The London club were members of the Southern League and the Cup was the only opportunity the northern clubs usually had to size up their southern opponents. And it had been some years since a Southern League club last visited Clayton for an important fixture.

Although United were still a second division side they began as favourites against a Fulham team hovering in the middle of their league. The tie was considered so attractive that the *Athletic News* featured it as their front page cartoon. Both teams took the tie seriously enough to spend a week training on the Lancashire coast and actually found themselves lodging within half a dozen miles of each other. But, despite the attraction of the fixture, only a small crowd of around 16,000 turned up at Bank Street to witness the clash of north and south.

United almost shot into an early lead when they were awarded a penalty, but Tom Arkesden contrived to blast his shot wide. After half an hour Fulham unexpectedly went ahead, but, three minutes from half time, Mackie converted a Williams cross to make it 1–1. United's second goal came almost from the restart when Arkesden made up for his earlier miss, but Fulham fought back and grabbed a late equaliser to give them a crack at United on their own Craven Cottage ground. However, the replay two days later turned out to be a goalless draw and the two teams were forced to meet again on the neutral ground of Villa Park the following week where United went down 1–0 and, once again, their Cup run came to an early end.

United's FA Cup jinx continued in 1905. However, their first round tie against Fulham was an epic, only decided in the second replay.

Athletic News, 16 January 1905

1906

After their splendid victory over Villa, United met Arsenal in the fourth round.

SATURDAY, 24 FEBRUARY 1906 saw United achieve one of the finest results in their early history when they routed the previous season's Cup-winners, Aston Villa, in a thrilling third round Cup tie at Clayton.

Villa were unquestionably one of the leading teams of the day. League champions in 1894, 1896, 1897, 1899 and 1900, they had also won the Cup in 1887, 1895, 1897 and 1905. No one doubted their pedigree and, having beaten Newcastle to win the Cup the previous season, they began as hot favourites against second division United.

United's Cup run had begun back in January with a 7–2 thrashing of Staple Hill in front of distinguished politicians Winston Churchill and J R Clynes. In the second round they were drawn at Clayton again, this time against Norwich City of the Southern League. They won that game comfortably, 3–0, and then found themselves facing the mighty Midlanders in the tie of the round.

A near-record crowd of 40,000 turned up, paying £1,460 in receipts. It was a typical Manchester day, dull with a hint of rain in the air, but Villa looked fully prepared for their battle after a week's training on the North Wales coast. Yet after only 10 minutes the first division side were in for a rude awakening when United shot into a one-goal lead. It was not long, however, before Villa equalised, but in the 35th minute United stormed back and began to take control.

At half time the score stood at 2–1. In the second half, as the infamous Clayton pitch began to cut up, Villa lost their way and three more goals were added – United had beaten the Cup favourites 5–1. Three of the goals had come from John Picken with Charlie Sagar adding the other two. Never before had any Cup-holders received such a drubbing, reported the *Athletic News* under the headline 'Extraordinary Doings At Clayton'. It was one of the biggest Cup upsets in years.

Although Villa might have argued that the Clayton pitch was a disgrace, there was no doubting the superiority of United on the day. Peddie and Picken had been exceptional, repeatedly outsmarting the Villa offside trap and spearheading United's sensational victory. John Picken, or Jack as he preferred to be called, had joined United that season after spells with Bolton and Plymouth. The Scottish inside forward scored 25 goals in his first season and, although he was never as prolific again, he served United until 1911 when they captured their second league title. John Peddie, another Scot, was also a former Plymouth player, joining United for the second time in 1904 after only one season with the Southern League club. He had originally joined United in 1902 from Newcastle but after just one season left for Plymouth. A year later he was back and soon became top scorer at Clayton, hitting a total of 58 goals in 121 appearances. He eventually returned to his native Scotland, joining Hearts in 1907.

EXTRAORDINARY DOINGS AT CLAYTON.

[BY SPRINTER.]

LOOKED at from every point of view—and the game, in each of its phases, was cinematograph enough in all conscience—the battle at Clayton produced a crop of extraordinary happenings. Hours before the kick-off some superstitious folk—and I, for once, can class myself in that category—felt that something was going to happen; that there would be an upheaval; or that somebody's feelings were going to be hurt.

And all those somethings, and much more, did happen. Let me attempt to tell some of the incidents—the huge gate; the fights for entry to the ground; the swarms of people from all over the North and Midlands, who battled for what they were worth to gain admittance; the slamming together of the doors in some places 45 minutes before the start; the thousands of disappointed people clamouring outside the turnstiles and at every possible hole in the hoardings; and still more, the countless hundreds approaching the district from all points of the compass, long after kick-off. An overflow match at Hyde-road, or a tussle 'twixt the sides' reserves there, would not have been a bad idea.

A MEMORABLE MEETING.

The match has made history, I think, for I do not recall any previous Cup-holders who have received such a drubbing in the third round series of the next campaign as the Villa did on Saturday. How is it to be accounted for? Was it a case of styles failing to blend, or of a team of sloggers, mud-larkers, or what you will, overcoming a polished, finished, extremely artistic—perhaps too much so—combination? Was it that the state of the turf was against the development of the artistry of the Villa? There is something in each query, but those questions do not answer themselves, as some do.

Athletic News, 16 February 1906

United's triumph over Villa was short-lived. In the next round, the quarter-finals, they faced first division Woolwich Arsenal at home and although they put up a magnificent fight the Londoners sneaked away from Clayton with a 3–2 victory. United had reached the last eight of the Cup for the first time since 1897, but it was probably just as well they were eliminated as it left them fresh to concentrate on the more important battle of getting back into the first division.

1906

Downie Mogar Bonthron
Mangnall (*Secretary*) Picken Sagar Blackstock Peddie
Beddow Roberts Bell Arkesden

MANCHESTER UNITED

Mangnall's revived United look forward to success in the first division – but the squad still needed to be strengthened if it was to succeed.

AFTER 12 UNHAPPY seasons lingering in the second division, United eventually climbed back to their rightful spot at the end of the 1905/06 season. They had narrowly missed out in the previous two seasons, finishing in third place, but in 1906 they managed one better and ended in second spot four points behind Bristol City but nine points ahead of third placed Chelsea. It had been a magnificent season with a Cup run that had taken them to the quarter-finals. They had also thrashed the Cup-holders Aston Villa, as well as playing before their biggest crowd ever (more than 60,000 at Stamford Bridge), and now they had won promotion.

Bristol City were the outstanding team of the division, although one would hardly have guessed it given that United opened their campaign with a 5–1 victory over the West Country side. However, City quickly improved, losing only one more game all season. The remaining promotion place was always a contest between United and Chelsea and, when United clung on for a 1–1 draw at Stamford Bridge before that enormous Easter crowd, it was clear that they would wind up in second spot.

Promotion was virtually clinched with a 3–1 victory at Leeds City on 21 April, but, four days later, they made sure by winning 3–2 at Lincoln. In the remaining game of the season United returned to Clayton and gave a 16,000 crowd something extra to cheer when they trounced second from bottom Burton United 6–0. Even that score was said not to reflect United's superiority. As for Burton, they survived only one more year in the Football League. On the scoresheet that day was George Wall, a tough little winger from Barnsley who had joined the club that year. Between then and the outbreak of war he played over 300 games for United, helping them to two league titles and the FA Cup, and scored almost a century of goals as well as winning seven England caps.

When the final whistle blew, the Clayton pitch was invaded and the team was carried shoulder-high from the field. Chairman J H Davies and secretary Ernest Mangnall addressed the cheering crowd that had remained and gathered in front of the stand and promised that this was only the beginning.

FOOTBALL.

IN THE PREMIER DIVISION.

Manchester United's Prospects.

Although this afternoon will end the season at Clayton from a playing standpoint, the work of Mr. J. E. Mangnall and that of Mr. J. H. Davies, along with Messrs. Bentley, Lawton, Taylor, and Bown, is far from being over. Having obtained his ambition in reaching the premier division Mr. Davies is determined to get together an eleven that will be able to do honour to the city, and negotiations are already in progress with a view to strengthening the team. It is, of course, impossible at this point to mention any names, but the football loving public may take it for granted that when September comes round the club will be represented by one of the best sides in the country.

Manchester Evening News, 28 April 1906

1906

FOOTBALL.

Sensational Transfer.

MEREDITH SIGNS FOR MANCHESTER UNITED.

As we indicated a fortnight ago Meredith, the well-known outside right, has been signed by Manchester United. For reasons which are known to all followers of the game, Meredith did not take part in football last season, and quite a flutter was caused recently when it was announced that the Manchester City Executive had put him on the transfer list, placing the fee for his transfer at the large sum of £500.

Many clubs have been desirous of securing his services, but Meredith, for business and other reasons, was not desirous of leaving Manchester. The probabilities are that the player would have signed before now but for the fact that the findings in what has become known as the "Meredith case" have not yet been made known.

Yesterday the famous winger had a long consultation with the Manchester United officials, which resulted in him signing the necessary forms, but owing to various little details having to be fixed up, we were not then in a position to announce the fact. These have been complied with to-day, and Meredith is now a member of the Manchester United club.

Although Meredith has been playing football for over ten years, he has still few, if any, superiors at outside right, and he should prove a valuable acquisition to the Clayton club. The outside right position last season was one of the weak spots in the team, but next season it should be exceptionally strong, for the names of Meredith and Peddie look like forming a very strong wing.

Manchester Evening News, 16 May 1906

NO PLAYER features larger in the early years of United's history than Billy Meredith. The Welsh Wizard, as he was known, helped transform United into one of the land's leading sides. He did not, of course, do it single-handedly. Others, like Charlie Roberts and the guiding influence of Ernest Mangnall, were vital but Meredith provided the spark of genius that set United apart from other clubs and established a tradition for players of the highest quality and skill. He was the George Best of the Edwardian era – rebellious, skilled and popular.

By 1906 Meredith was already a legend. A Manchester City player since 1894, he had helped the Hyde Road club not only to first division status but to an FA Cup victory in 1904 and the runners-up spot in the league during the same season. In 339 appearances for City the enigmatic right winger had scored 146 goals. Then, in August 1905, Meredith was sensationally suspended by the Football Association for the alleged bribery of an Aston Villa player in an important end-of-season fixture. The affair uncovered much more, including illegal payments by City to players supposed to be on the £4 a week maximum wage. Instead City had been paying £6 or £7 a week. The FA were furious and severely rebuked the club, dismissing five of its directors and banning 17 of its players from ever appearing for them again. It was a catastrophic blow for City that destroyed their Cup-winning team. Meredith himself was lucky to escape a lifetime ban from the game and eventually had his suspension reduced until 31 December 1906.

Events across the city did not go unnoticed at Clayton. City had to unload the bulk of their Cup-winning side and virtually an entire football team was up for sale. The jewel in the crown

Billy Meredith, the most exciting player of United's early years turns yet another opponent. He inspired the side to two league titles and an FA Cup triumph within five years of his arrival.

The Welsh Wizard remained with United for 15 years, making 333 league and cup appearances in that time. He was capped on 48 occasions for Wales between 1895 and 1920, scoring 11 goals.

was Meredith but United could not afford to wait for any auction and, quick off the mark, they made an early approach to the Welsh international. Meredith was only too glad of United's interest. He was reluctant to leave the area because of his sports shop in St Peter's Square and enthusiastically agreed to join the newly-promoted first division club. There were formal consultations between Meredith and United secretary Ernest Mangnall on Tuesday, 15 May 1906, with the details completed the following morning, and that afternoon the Welsh Wizard duly signed for United. The *Manchester Evening News* scooped Fleet Street on the transfer story of the season. Not surprisingly it caused a further sensation in the already astonishing life of Billy Meredith. But that was not the end of the tale either, for there were still a number of other fine City players of interest to United.

An auction of all the City players had been arranged at the Queens Hotel in Manchester for November and interested clubs were invited to attend. But United could hardly afford the likely asking prices that such an auction would generate. There was only one thing for it – a secret approach. And so, Ernest Mangnall privately met a number of the players and secretly negotiated their transfer to United. When the other clubs found out they were furious. Everton, favourites to sign full back Herbert Burgess, complained bitterly to the FA about United's underhand tactics. But the FA were not interested and the deal stood. At the end of the day, United had signed not only Meredith but inside forward Sandy Turnbull and centre forward Jimmy Bannister, as well as the England full back Herbert Burgess. It was a major coup for United that would pay handsome dividends over the next few years. All they had to do now was wait until the 31 December deadline so that they could field their new contingent.

1907

NEW YEAR'S DAY 1907 marked the beginning of a dynamic era for Manchester United Football Club. It was the day new recruits Billy Meredith, Sandy Turnbull, Herbert Burgess and Jimmy Bannister all made their debuts for the Bank Street side. The four former Manchester City players, suspended over illegal payments and attempted bribery, had signed for United during 1906 but could not make their debuts until their lengthy suspension ended at midnight on 31 December of that year. It had been an agonising wait but now, just hours after the deadline passed, their first opportunity to pull on the red shirt of United came in a home fixture against third-placed Aston Villa. The fixture list had cunningly contrived to provide United with a real test.

The Clayton ground was bursting at the seams with more than 40,000 eager fans crammed around the piled-up snow and giving what the *Manchester Evening News* described as 'one of the most enthusiastic welcomes ever accorded a football team'. But it was Meredith they had really come to see and the vast crowd repeatedly called out his name. With the Welsh Wizard taking his place on the right wing, United now boasted a prize team which possessed the quality to lead a determined attack on the first division championship.

In goal was the reliable Harry Moger who had joined United from Southampton in 1903 with a reputation as the safest keeper in the south. In front of him was the new recruit and experienced England international Herbert Burgess who was partnered by the former Dundee full back Robert Bonthron. They played behind one of the most elegant half-back lines in United's history – Roberts, Bell and Duckworth. Alex Bell was a South African, born of Scottish parents, who went on to win an international cap for Scotland, while alongside him was the highly regarded Dick Duckworth. Born locally, he was a one-club man, who played more than 250 games for United before his retirement in 1914. Captain Charlie Roberts was probably at his peak in 1907, with three England appearances under his belt, and was the most respected name in the game. In attack United now fielded as exciting a forward line as any in the first division. On the wings a young George Wall (later to be capped seven times by England) partnered the Welsh international Billy Meredith, while Sandy Turnbull and Jimmy Bannister were the men who turned their running into goals.

The only issue which remained in doubt as the two teams lined up that snowy New Year's afternoon was whether the long lay-off, particularly for Meredith, would have had any effects. The question was soon answered as the Welshman sprinted and darted about, teasing the Villa defence. Turnbull soon showed his old goalscoring knack when he slammed home a Meredith cross to give United a 1–0 victory. Bank Street was ecstatic. The snow and the bitterly cold weather were quickly forgotten and the 40,000 crowd left eagerly awaiting the next home fixture.

It was a result which promised much, taking United, during their first season back in division one, into the middle of the table. By the end of the season United had climbed into eighth spot and were ready to make their challenge for the championship.

NEW YEAR'S GIFT.

GREAT CROWD AT CLAYTON

UNITED DEFEAT ASTON VILLA.

A FINE GAME.

MEREDITH AT HIS BEST.

Manchester Evening News, 1 January 1907

Sandy Turnbull (left) and Herbert Burgess (right) were two of United's recruits from City who made their debuts on New Year's Day 1907.

1908

AFTER FINISHING eighth in the table during their first season back in division one, Ernest Mangnall had brought together a team now capable of challenging for the championship. With the new recruits from Manchester City and the elegant half-back line of Bell, Roberts and Duckworth, United boasted one of the finest sides in the land. But they now had to prove that they could go one better than their neighbours City and finally bring the league title to Manchester.

The season began in earnest style with a 4–1 hammering of Aston Villa, a 4–0 victory against Liverpool and a 2–1 win over Middlesbrough. They then lost the return fixture with Middlesbrough but proceeded to win the next 10 games. Fourteen games played and only two points dropped – there was no need to say where United stood in the table. They had hit six goals at Newcastle, five at Blackburn and four against Everton, Arsenal and Birmingham. They then lost against Sheffield Wednesday in late November and rounded off the year with three wins and a couple of draws. United were the talk of the footballing press. Not for them the aerial game but instead the elegant passing skills that stemmed from their half-back line coupled with the tireless running of Meredith and Wall.

It had been a magnificent opening half to their campaign and, although the second half of the season never quite lived up to the first, there was never really any doubt that the title would come to United. They lost seven more games that season, including an embarrassing 7–4 defeat at Anfield, and goals were not so easily come by. Both Jimmy Turnbull and Sandy Turnbull missed games through injury and the goalscoring exploits of the earlier part of the season evaporated. There was also a dispiriting 2–1 defeat by Fulham in the fourth round of the Cup from which they never really recovered. In the end the title was clinched by other teams losing; United won only one of their last six fixtures. That victory was against Preston North End at Clayton where United needed just two points to better Newcastle's 51-point record. It took an own goal to give United a 2–1 victory that day but it was well deserved and set a new league record. They had scored 82 league goals with Sandy Turnbull hitting 25, George Wall 19 and Jimmy Turnbull 10.

United owed much to the two Turnbulls, who had collected 35 goals between them. Alex 'Sandy' Turnbull, the former Manchester City inside forward, remained with United until 1915 when he was banned from football for taking part in a notorious bribery scandal. He subsequently enlisted with the Manchester Regiment but was sadly killed in action on 3 May 1917 at Arras. He had played 245 games for the Reds, scoring 100 goals, collecting two league championship medals and scoring the winning goal in the 1909 Cup final.

Although they were not related, Jimmy Turnbull (sometimes known as 'Trunky') was another Scot who arrived at United from the Southern League side, Clapton Orient, in May 1907. During the next three years he played 76

Moger makes a save during United's 4–1 victory over Chelsea at Stamford bridge in September 1907. As so often, he was rarely troubled.

Action from United's FA Cup defeat at Fulham. The huge crowd was treated to an action-packed game with the Fulham goalkeeper, Skene (left), much involved. Meredith (centre) is foiled heading for goal. However, the team battled away (right) to the end.

games for United, scoring a remarkable 42 goals before leaving to join Bradford Park Avenue. Although both men were Scots, surprisingly neither was honoured by their home country. Charlie Roberts was also largely ignored by his country, although he continued to lead United by example and endeavour, and it was fitting that at the end of the season he should be handed the league trophy.

UNITED'S GREAT FEAT.

Manchester City's Ambition Not Realised.

VILLA FINISH SECOND.

GAME EFFORT BY NOTTS.

BRISTOL'S BIG SCORE.

(By "RARA AVIS.")

The League programme has almost run its course, but there is still one important little matter to be decided, and that is the settling of the question as to whether Bolton Wanderers or Notts County shall go down into the Second Division. Notts County made a superb effort at Bolton yesterday in a game which was big with fate for both clubs, and it is to the great credit of the Midlanders that they managed to win. They have to win the match at Chelsea on the 29th inst., before they can again claim membership of the First Division, but at the same time their fate is in their own hands, and they may be relied upon to leave nothing to chance when the fateful match is decided. Bolton have now to stand idly by, as it were, and await their fate. It is not a pleasant mode of passing the time.

Manchester United have won the League Championship, and in the process created a record in the number of points scored, the 52 they have earned just beating the previous best by Newcastle United and Liverpool respectively. But it has not been given to the City to finish second to their Clayton friends and rivals. Although they drew at Blackburn, Aston Villa went one better by winning at Chelsea, with the result that the famous "Clarets" have finished as runners-up. The progress made by the Villa has been remarkable, bearing in mind that it is not so long ago that there were fears in Birmingham that they would lose their position owing to a succession of failures at home. On the other hand, it tends to show what comparatively little difference there is in three-parts the teams in the division.

Birmingham have concluded their programme in inglorious fashion. Bristol City who have only during the past few days made their position safe—to be accurate, on Tuesday evening last, when they drew at Hyde-road—making holes in the Brummagem defence at St. Andrew's. Birmingham's fate has been known for some time past, but, as previously stated, the future must be left to decide whether Bolton Wanderers or Notts County must accompany the old Small Heath club into the Second Division. There is nothing further of interest in the competition.

* * *

NEW LEAGUE RECORD.

Manchester United Wind Up With a Win.

UNINTERESTING GAME.

(By "THE GENERAL.")

Results up to date:—

	Pld.	Won	Lost	Drn.	Goals For	Goals Agst.	Pts.
Manchester United	38	23	9	6	81	48	52
Aston Villa	38	17	12	9	77	59	43
Manchester City	38	16	11	11	62	54	43
Newcastle United	38	15	11	12	65	54	42
Sheffield Wednesday	38	19	15	4	73	64	42
Middlesbrough	38	17	14	7	54	45	41
Bury	37	14	12	11	57	59	39
Nottingham Forest	38	13	14	11	59	62	37
Liverpool	37	15	16	6	66	60	36
Bristol City	38	12	14	12	58	61	36
Everton	38	15	17	6	58	64	36
Preston North End	38	12	14	12	47	53	36
Chelsea	37	14	15	8	52	60	36
Blackburn Rovers	38	12	14	12	51	63	36
Woolwich Arsenal	38	12	14	12	51	63	36
Sunderland	38	16	19	3	78	73	35
Sheffield United	38	12	15	11	52	58	35
Bolton Wanderers	38	14	19	5	52	58	33
Notts County	37	12	17	8	37	50	32
Birmingham	38	9	17	12	40	60	30

* * *

YESTERDAY'S RESULTS.

Bury .... 2 *Nottingham Forest. 1
(Did not meet last season.)

*Blackburn Rovers.. 0 Manchester City ... 0
(Blackburn won last season 4—0.)

Bristol City .... 4 *Birmingham 0
(Last season's game was drawn 2—2.)

*Manchester United. 2 Preston North End.. 1
(United won last season 3—0.)

*Everton .... 0 Sheffield Wednesday. 0
(Everton won last season 2—0.)

Notts County ..... 1 *Bolton Wanderers . 0
(Last season's game was drawn 0—0.)

Aston Villa .... 3 *Chelsea 1
(Did not meet last season.)

*Denotes home club.

* * *

GOAL SCORERS.

Manchester United, Meredith and Halse; Preston North End, Lyon; Notts Forest, Woodlands; Bury, Hibbert and Pearson; Notts County, Cantrill; Bristol, Burton (2), Rippon, and Kearns (Birmingham); Chelsea, Birnie; Aston Villa, Hall (2) and Bache.

* * *

The Umpire, 26 April 1908

1908

Half back Alex Bell was one of the two players to suffer head injuries when Hungarian fans rioted.

FOLLOWING THEIR league triumph the United board rewarded the team with an adventurous close season tour of the Austro-Hungarian Empire. It was the first international tour the club had undertaken and it turned out to be far more adventurous than anyone had presupposed.

The tour began in May with a game in Vienna against a combined XI from the two crack Austrian teams – Vienna Sport and Vienna FC. United won comfortably by 4–0 and then travelled by rail, via Prague where they played another game, to Budapest for a couple of fixtures against Ferencvaros Si Torna Klub. It was here that United discovered a new meaning to the word 'friendly'. United won their first match against Ferencvaros 6–2 and then faced the same Budapest team for a return clash a few days later on Sunday, 24 May. It was probably the first time United had ever played a match on a Sunday and they were soon longing for the more peaceful repose of a Manchester sabbath.

United, the English league champions, were a star attraction in Hungary where football was just taking root. Ferencvaros themselves had only been formed in 1901 but had already won the Hungarian championship four times and were, without doubt, the finest team in their country. More than 11,000 turned up for the return fixture and they were soon applauding as United swept into an early lead. But the applause gradually turned sour as United struck more goals against the Hungarians' favourites.

What sparked off a minor diplomatic incident was not United's continuing dominance but poor refereeing. Perhaps the Hungarian referee was not too well acquainted with the rules – after all, the game was only seven years old in Hungary. At the centre of the dispute was Thomson, the United reserve centre half who was penalised for fouling one of the Hungarians. Thomson protested vigorously; perhaps a little too vigorously, for he caught hold of the referee's arm in an attempt to explain what had happened. The referee, unable to speak English, misinterpreted Thomson's gesture and assumed that he was about to be assaulted. Hands were raised and players rushed towards the referee and in the chaos that followed three United players, including Thomson and Duckworth, were ordered off the field.

By now the spectators in the cheap seats bordering the touchline were on their feet and angry scenes ensued. The United players steadfastly refused to leave the field and at one point it looked as if the game might be abandoned. Meanwhile interpreters were summoned and for 15 minutes the arguments raged. The game eventually resumed with United at full strength and they added a further goal to give them an easy 7–0 victory.

But the worst of the trouble was yet to come. As the final whistle blew and the players trudged from the field, stones were hurled from the terraces, players were spat at and sticks were waved angrily at the United team. Fearing a riot, the Hungarian police drew swords and rushed the crowd, dispersing them in a dozen directions.

That was not the end of the incident. As the United team left the ground for their Budapest hotel, 5,000 spectators jeered them on their way. Guarded by the police, the team safely negotiated the mob. Hardly had they gone a couple of miles, however, when a crowd lying in wait charged their open-top coach, hurling more stones. The *Athletic News* correspondent was hit on the head while Alex Bell and John Picken also suffered head wounds. The police again drew swords and charged the demonstrators, making scores of arrests, before the United party could return safely to the quiet of their hotel. The Hungarian authorities apologised profusely and that evening the two teams dined together amicably. United diplomatically shrugged off the incident and promised to return to Budapest the following year. But when Ernest Mangnall finally arrived back in Britain he vowed he would never go back to Hungary. United's first taste of Continental opposition had not been a happy one.

MANCHESTER UNITED STONED.

Hostile Crowd in Hungary.

Reuter's correspondent at Buda-Pesth, the capital of Hungary, telegraphed yesterday the following message:—

The team of the Manchester United Football Club to-day played a match against the Ferencvaro si Torna Klub. The visitors were victorious by seven goals to nil. A large crowd witnessed the play. Considerable uproar arose during the match, the onlookers alleging that the Englishmen had infringed the rules of the game. The referee also found fault with the Englishmen's play, but he subsequently withdrew his remarks on the visitors pointing out that they were keeping within the rules of the game as played in England. The crowd pelted the visitors with stones, but only one of the team was hit, sustaining a small bruise on the head. It was only owing to the intervention of the police that the Englishmen were able to leave the ground without further molestation.

Manchester Evening News, 25 May 1908

THE LEAGUE AND THE SOUTHERN LEAGUE.

MANCHESTER UNITED WIN THE CHARITY SHIELD.

(By Tityrus.)

Manchester United, 4 Queen's Park R... 0

So long as football players are merely men, and not automatic, devised by some weird, mechanical genius, there is no guarantee that the champions of one season will be the premier eleven of the next campaign. Very nearly four months have been merged in the past since Manchester United, of The League, and Queen's Park Rangers, of the Southern League, each the head club of their class, did battle in the spacious and glorious arena of Chelsea for the new silver shield, which is the charity trophy of the Football Association. Then the struggle was indecisive owing in the main to a Meredithian marvel of a goal from the cunning foot of that great outside right. But the Football Association had what Sir Francis Burnand would call a happy thought. The teams should play again. The last match cost Manchester United £50, and much effort and inconvenience. In spite of this the United responded to the call, and they travelled to Bedford on Friday evening. They reached St. Pancras about one o'clock on Saturday in the care of Mr. Ernest Mangnall, the diligent secretary-manager, and, having refreshed themselves, drove to Stamford Bridge. I never heard a murmur among the players either about being called to London a second time, or about an extra match thrust upon them on a hot day in the close season.

Their one desire was to play as champions should, and take the shield to Manchester. They took it. The Rangers watched them. Therein lies the application of my opening sentence. The superior team of one April may be the inferior of next September. In the spring the Rangers and the United were on an equality. On Saturday the United showed football justifying their title. The Royalists were not so strong as when last I saw them. But it would be ungallant and unchivalrous to draw sweeping conclusions from this one match. The London

Athletic News, 31 August 1908

1908

A CHARITY SHIELD game had been played each year since 1898, usually between a professional side and a top amateur team, but in 1908 the Football Association took charge of the fixture and decided that the Football League champions should play the Southern League champions with a new shield as the prize. And, as champions, United found themselves pitted against Queen's Park Rangers, champions of the Southern League. The Football League, although it had boasted two divisions since 1892, was still dominated by the northern and Midland clubs. Sides such as Tottenham, Portsmouth, Southampton and QPR remained in

Goalmouth action from the Charity Shield replay at Stamford Bridge.

EVE OF THE FOOTBALL SEASON.

CHARITY SHIELD.

J. TURNBULL'S "HAT TRICK."

The Umpire, 30 August 1908

Meredith, shirt outside his shorts as usual, attacks Queens Park Rangers down their left flank. In a magnificent display United won 4–0, with Jimmy Turnbull scoring a hat trick. It seemed to presage great things, but the title challenge faltered in the new year as the Reds concentrated on the FA Cup, the only major trophy still to elude the club.

a strong Southern League. QPR's record in the Southern League during the 1907/08 season was impressive, making them favourites with at least one newspaper to clinch the contest. It should be, reckoned the *Athletic News*, the outstanding game of the season.

The first match turned out almost as forecast. Played at Stamford Bridge in late April, United were held to a 1–1 draw by an attractive and combative QPR side. Indeed it was only a brilliant solo effort by Meredith which saved the day for the Manchester club. But there were excuses: United were weary after a heavy league programme and had made the trip to London reluctantly.

So, a second game was arranged for Saturday, 29 August and a more enthusiastic United made the return trip to the capital. Despite the exciting counter-attraction of the Olympic Games at the White City, more than 40,000 turned up at Stamford Bridge, considerably more than the 6,000 who had attended the first contest. From the whistle there was only one team in it – United. In the 28th minute Jimmy Turnbull headed home a Meredith centre and shortly before half time he tapped in an easy chance to make it 2–0. It continued much the same in the second half, with George Wall hitting United's third and Turnbull collecting his hat trick with another header from a Meredith cross to give United an impressive 4–0 victory. The *Athletic News* eulogised over United's performance, calling them 'brilliant', and predicted that further honours would soon fall their way. The vast crowd assured the future of the Charity Shield as a national institution.

1909

UNITED HAD COME no closer to winning the FA Cup than the last eight. Three times, in 1897, 1906 and 1908, they had stood on the brink of a semi-final only to be thwarted at the crucial moment. In 1908 their shock defeat at Fulham had sent waves of despair through the team, affecting results for the rest of the season. They might well have been dreaming of the double that year, and probably deserved to achieve it, but the Cup, as ever, had its surprises. But with the league championship finally resting in the boardroom, United hoped to make amends the following season.

Their campaign began at home to the Southern League side, Brighton. They were really no match for United but put up a stubborn struggle and only a goal from Harold Halse saved United from a long journey south. In the second round they were again drawn at home, this time against Everton. The Merseysiders, who had won the Cup in 1906 and were riding high in the league, found United in devastating form and another Halse goal helped them into the third round. Fellow Lancastrians Blackburn were the visitors for the third round and although they boasted an impressive line-up United were in a mean mood and thrashed them 6–1. This time it was the two Turnbulls who shared the spoils with three goals apiece.

After three home draws United's luck finally evaporated when they found themselves facing an away tie in the fourth round against second division Burnley. But if luck had deserted them in the draw, it returned during the game. A goal down with only 18 minutes remaining, the United jinx at the quarter-final hurdle looked to be threatening again. But lady luck was smiling on them in the form of snow. Down it came from the skies, dancing pleasantly in the breeze to begin with and then ferociously raging in a blinding storm. The referee had little alternative but to call off the tie. And, as so often happens, the replayed game turned out very differently, with United running out 3–2 winners.

United were in the semi-finals for the first time in their history but faced a difficult proposition in the previous season's Cup-winners, Newcastle, at Bramall Lane. Newcastle, like United the previous season, were chasing the double. But, like United, they also found that two competitions were too much and lost 1–0. United were in the final, thanks to a Halse goal, but there was compensation for Newcastle who marched on to clinch their third championship title.

The final took place at the Crystal Palace on Saturday, 24 April 1909 with middle-of-the-table Bristol City as United's opponents. The ground was not altogether unknown to the United players; some had played internationals there, while Meredith, Burgess and Sandy Turnbull had all appeared on the south London ground for Manchester City when they won the Cup in 1904. But now it was United's turn and the city of Manchester was gripped by Cup

A huge crowd of over 70,000 gathered on the open terraces at Crystal Palace for the 1909 FA Cup final.

L. & N.-W. RAILWAY.

FINAL TIE—ENGLISH CUP,

AT CRYSTAL PALACE, APRIL 24th,

MANCHESTER UNITED versus BRISTOL CITY.

EXCURSIONS

To LONDON (EUSTON STATION)

WILL RUN AS UNDER:—

	Friday Evening, April 23.	Friday Night, April 23.		Saturday Morning, April 24.
MANCHESTER (London Road) ....depart	8 0 p.m.	11 0 p.m.	11 25 p.m.	7 35 a.m.
STOCKPORT.. „	8 10 p.m.	11 10 p.m.	11 35 p.m.	7 45 a.m.
LONDON (Euston) ....arrive	12 0 night.	3 45 a.m.	4 20 a.m.	11 35 a.m.

PERIODS AND FARES.

FRIDAY EVENING.		FRIDAY NIGHT AND SATURDAY MORNING.	
Two Days (Return Saturday)	12/6	One Day (Return Saturday)	11/-
Three Days (Return Sunday)	16/-	Two Days (Return Sunday)	12/6
		Three Days (Return Monday)	12/6

Parties going to London for the Final Tie Match, and desirous of securing Saloon Accommodation, are invited to communicate with Mr. C. LOWNDES, District Superintendent, Exchange Station, Manchester.

Euston Station, London, April, 1909.

FRANK REE, General Manager.

Manchester Evening News, 17 April 1909

final fever. The local papers advertised excursions to London at 11 shillings for a day return and dozens of extra trains were ordered to take the vast crowd south. Ernest Mangnall decided to take his team away from the city as early as possible, travelling to Chingford during the week where they set up camp at the Royal Forest Hotel. It was a relaxed few days – a little golf, some light training and some jokes with music hall comedian George Robey. Robey, a lifelong football supporter, had been on the books of Millwall as a young man but had found fame on a different stage. Nevertheless, he remained closely associated with the game, regularly organising charity matches and playing host to famous players. He was also a member of the Manchester United club and took pride in presenting the team with a new set of shirts as well as organising the post-final entertainment. United had been forced to change their strip and instead of their usual scarlet shirts they wore white with a red V.

On the day of the final, the spring-like weather of the previous week took a sudden turn for the worse with grey skies and the threat of rain, but it did little to dispirit the thousands of United fans arriving in the capital. With their red and white umbrellas, rosettes and hand-bells, the Manchester army brought their colour and northern wit south. United preferred some peace and quiet and, after a light lunch at the Great Eastern Hotel, arrived at the ground shortly after 2pm. The only doubt in their team was Sandy Turnbull who had been nursing a knee injury. 'Let him play', urged Charlie Roberts. 'He might get a goal and if he does we can afford to carry him.' The decision was taken; Turnbull played.

More than 70,000 were inside the ground as the two teams kicked off. City, led by England international Billy Wedlock, stood higher in the league than United but a couple of key players were injured and they began as underdogs. By all accounts it was a poor game. United started brightly, creating several openings in the first 10 minutes. Then, in the 22nd minute, Harold Halse struck a shot against the crossbar and Sandy Turnbull, lurking dangerously in the six-yard box, slammed the rebound into the back of the net. It was the only goal of the game. Few other chances were created and Meredith was reckoned to be the difference between the two sides as he added a second Cup-winners' medal to his growing collection of honours.

United proudly display their first FA Cup trophy.

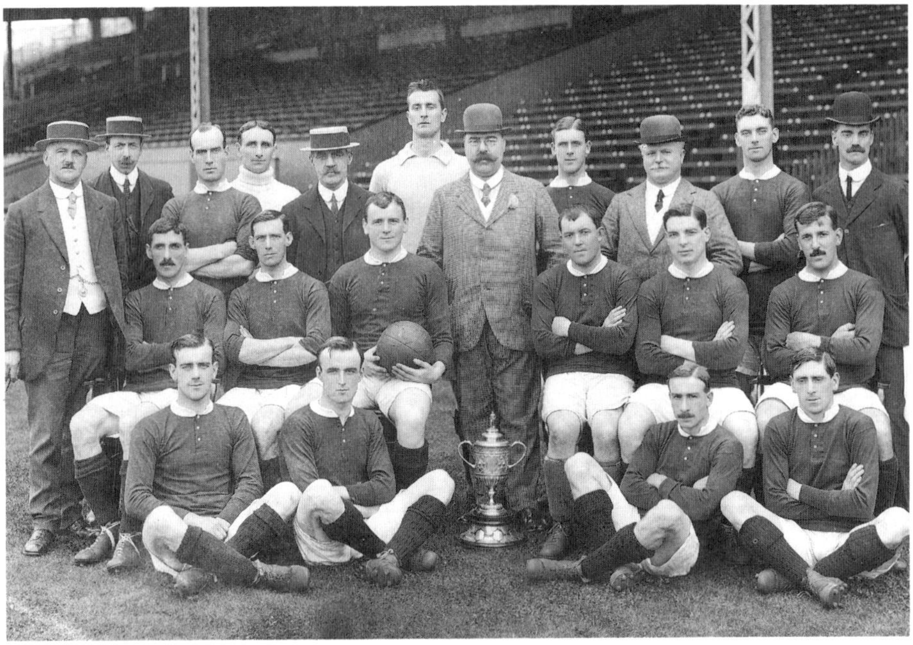

THE CUP FINAL

MANCHESTER UNITED JUST TOO GOOD FOR BRISTOL.

"SANDY" TURNBULL'S GOAL DECIDES.

The Umpire, 26 April 1909

1909

UNITED'S FA CUP victory also led to them being featured in numerous adverts – a clear sign that they were becoming one of the most famous sides in the land. It may not have been the first time they had endorsed various products, but to find themselves in such demand was certainly new. Manufacturers from Oxo to Wincarnis were keen to boast that the team had used their products in the build-up to the Cup triumph. Wincarnis was a tonic supposed to 'freshen the energies in a most exhilarating way' and 'Manchester United have found it very useful in their training for the final tie to increase their powers of endurance' read the advert. Whether or not the United players actually indulged in the tonic remains in doubt, but it is probably just as likely as today's players using Sharp electrical appliances.

As much in demand as the team for advertising was Billy Meredith. The Welsh international was the most popular footballer of his era, overwhelmingly voted the number one player by readers of the *Umpire* in 1904. He was frequently to be found in adverts, and, when Manchester City reached the FA Cup final in 1904, the Great Central Railway Company advertised their excursions to the game with a famous painting of Meredith hitting the winning goal with the accompanying line: 'Billy Meredith secures the Cup, he wants you to see the match and travel in comfort . . .' It was crystal-ball advertising: Meredith, never one to disappoint his supporters, duly obliged by actually scoring City's winning goal.

Recommended by athletes, doctors and the armed services it may have been, but Manchester United was the biggest name on the Wincarnis advert.

The Umpire, 25 April 1909

1909

AFTER THEIR magnificent Cup triumph United made their way back to London and spent the evening at the Alhambra Theatre, where they were entertained by football favourite George Robey. Accompanying United supporters in tweed caps and jackets were said to contrast starkly with the clientele of the grand circle dressed in their evening jackets and bow ties, but, when Robey asked Charlie Roberts to display the Cup, there was a loud cheer from the cheaper seats. Robey entertained them again the following day at his home in Finchley where there was an embarrassed moment when nobody could find the lid of the Cup. After a considerable search, however, it was eventually discovered in the pocket of Sandy Turnbull's jacket, having been put there by some joker. After sightseeing around the capital on the Monday the team eventually left St Pancras station on the Tuesday morning, arriving back at Central Station Manchester at 3.30pm that afternoon. And what a welcome!

Thousands had turned up to see them make the short journey to the Town Hall. As the train pulled slowly into the station a great cheer rang out, but even that was nothing to the roar that greeted the Cup when the bowler-hatted Ernest Mangnall opened the carriage door and lifted the old trophy high. Behind him came Charlie Roberts in a cloth cap, Meredith, Turnbull and the rest of the triumphant team, many of them wearing red and white hats. The band struck up 'See, the conquering hero comes', and one by one the players were hoisted on shoulders and carried towards the waiting horse-drawn wagons decked out in the colours of United. The procession seemed to take an eternity, with office workers leaning from open windows high above the streets and the crowd sweeping continuously on to the road. And in the square outside Manchester's magnificent Victorian Town Hall another vast sea of colourful supporters were awaiting them, hanging from every available vantage point. They clung from lampposts, stood on pillar boxes, balanced on shoulders and swarmed dangerously over nearby roofs. Never before had Albert Square witnessed such scenes.

Following a welcome from the Mayor they then proceeded to Bank Street where they were scheduled to kick off at 6pm against Woolwich Arsenal in the final home fixture of the season. There were crowds the entire route and inside the Clayton ground more than 30,000 had been awaiting their arrival for almost an hour. It was perhaps Clayton's most memorable night, for United had already given notice that they would soon be quitting its muddy fields for the more salubrious surroundings of a new stadium at Old Trafford. Not surprisingly the celebrations of the weekend had taken their toll and United went

The United team and management on the steps of Manchester Town Hall. Roberts holds the trophy.

The New All-Picture Morning Paper.

TREMENDOUS WELCOME OF THE CUP WINNERS IN MANCHESTER.

ENGLISH CUP FOR MANCHESTER: SCENES AT THE FINAL.

Daily Sketch, 26 April 1909

Huge crowds packed the streets to join in the celebrations for United's first FA Cup victory as the side paraded the silverware around the streets.

down to the southerners. After the game chairman J H Davies took the trophy into the Arsenal dressing room where he cracked open a bottle of champagne and invited each of the Arsenal players to drink the health of United. It had been a long, hard weekend.

1909

IN AUGUST 1909, just four months after winning the FA Cup, the entire Manchester United team was suspended. They were banned from the game not for any misdemeanours on the football field, but because they refused to renounce the trade union they had helped form.

An attempt to set up a footballers' union had been made as early as 1897 by John Bell, the Everton international, yet despite initial interest the movement had failed and there were no further attempts to resuscitate it until 1907 when Billy Meredith and John Bell again instigated meetings around the country. This time the conditions were more favourable. Trade unionism was now firmly established among the working classes and football was, after all, another activity thriving in the industrial communities. The sport had also become a business and the freedoms which professionals once enjoyed were now becoming severely restricted. A maximum wage of £4 a week had been introduced in 1901 and eight years later it remained the same. Meanwhile, football had grown in popularity, with bigger gates and more money flowing through the turnstiles. There were also grumblings about the transfer system, with some arguing that players ought to be free to move from club to club without any fees being demanded, while others felt players should receive a percentage of the transfer fee. Whatever the complaints there was clearly a groundswell of support for some organisation to represent the players' interests. After meetings in Manchester and London, it was decided to form a union.

And so, in December 1907 Billy Meredith, John Bell and others met at the Imperial Hotel in Manchester for the inaugural meeting of the new Players' Union. More than 500 players were represented and Herbert Broomfield was elected secretary. From the start the Manchester United players, led by Meredith and Charlie Roberts, were enthusiastic supporters and had it not been for their loyalty the Players' Union would probably have foundered almost before it was off the ground.

Unfortunately, the Football Association were not as keen on the new organisation and, as it began to spread, the FA took steps to curtail its influence by ruling that in any new contracts there would have to be a clause disowning the union. The new ruling effectively banned the Players' Union. As clubs issued new contracts the vast majority of players climbed down and signed up. One by one they deserted the union, leaving only the Manchester United players refusing to sign the new deal. A deadline was issued; it approached and passed, with the United players still clinging to their principles. The FA had threatened and in August 1909 they acted by suspending the entire United Cup-winning side. It was a sensation.

The United players stood firm, but they also had an eye to the new season. When official training resumed again at Old Trafford in early August they went to nearby Fallowfield and trained on their own, with Charlie Roberts leading

THE "OUTCASTS."

English Cup Winners Training at Fallowfield.

With the exception of Hayes, Stacey, and Halse, the Manchester United players, who won the English Cup, have been suspended by the Football Association because they would not desert the Union and the "outcasts," as they have styled themselves, have had to rent the ground of the Manchester Athletic Club at Fallowfield. In response to the request of Roberts the men turned up to-day for training, and right heartily they set about their work. "Sandy" Turnbull was half an hour ahead of his colleagues, and he whiled away the time by mowing the grass in the centre of the field. Livingstone was engaged for a considerable time in walking exercise, but later, along with Meredith, Moger, Burgess, Duckworth, Picken, Wall, Downie, and Roberts, he indulged in ball practice, a couple of hurdles taking the part of goalposts.

Despite the hot sun, the men stuck to their task, and to-morrow they will be joined by James Turnbull, who is assured of a warm welcome from his old clubmates. Bell was unable to turn out to-day on account of his having launched into the grocery and provision business, and Bannister is due to report himself to Roberts before the end of the week.

Fighting for Bread and Butter.

That the men have spent their summer's holidays well was evident from their condition today, and there was much truth in the remark of Roberts when he said "Boys, we could play a hard League game on Saturday and win too."

"We are fighting for our bread and butter, and we shall win too if the Newcastle and other players will only stand by us," remarked another player. Continuing, he went on to say that it had been a hard struggle for many of the team to be deprived of their summer pay, but they were fighting the battle for the whole of the professional footballers of the country, and if they won it would be worth the sacrifice.

The spirit of the United men must certainly commend itself to the public. The majority of the suspended players would, had they agreed to submit to the dictation of the Football Association, been receiving £4 per week, and this is certainly a big price for the men to have to pay for their loyalty to a Union, the policy of which they believe to be just and all for the betterment of the game.

Manchester Evening News, 10 August 1909

The Outcasts proclaim their defiance to the authorities.

AT THE ELEVENTH HOUR.

PEACE: THERE, MY LAD, PLAY AWAY!

The FA and the players only came to an agreement on the day of the first fixture.

them through their routines. They had all been deprived of their summer's pay yet they remained solid. United trainer Fred Bacon was impressed and a few days later threw in his lot with the rebels while the public turned up to voice their support. A team photograph was taken and Charlie Roberts chalked the name 'The Outcasts' on a blackboard. The name stuck.

Then, unexpectedly, they began to gain support from elsewhere. Tim Coleman of Everton walked out on his Goodison colleagues to join them while Newcastle, Sunderland and Middlesbrough all reconsidered their earlier position and agreed to side with United. They were followed by Everton and Liverpool and as more teams returned to the Union the new season looked distinctly threatened. Frantic discussions were held and eventually on the eve of kick-off the FA backed down and a compromise was agreed. The FA would recognise the Union if it would end its moves to affiliate with the General Federation of Trade Unions. It was a muddled agreement and, although the Union did eventually affiliate to the TUC, it did not win any concessions on pay or transfers for another 50 years. But it was thanks to the Manchester United players, particularly Meredith and Roberts, that the Union survived. Their unswerving loyalty in the face of determined threats from the FA was an example of which even the aristocrats of the trade union movement would have been proud.

THE FOOTBALL CRISIS.

A TRUCE DECLARED.

DRAMATIC CHANGE OF FRONT.

ALL MATCHES TO BE PLAYED.

At the eleventh hour, the Football Association have so far given way to the demands made on behalf of the players that a truce has been declared, and the programme of League matches arranged for this evening will be carried out. Though the men who have successfully agitated against the governing body are well satisfied with the course events have taken, they are loth to claim a victory or to say anything calculated to interfere with a complete settlement of the dispute. Still, the fact remains that the most vital point at issue, namely the question whether players under suspension for their adherence to the Players' Union should be deprived of the wages withheld during suspension, has been answered in favour of the players. That being so, there was nothing left to fight about, and the terms offered were, subject to the approval of the Federation of Trade Councils, accepted.

The Terms Agreed Upon.

They were, as quoted in our last edition, last evening:—

The F.A. are prepared to acknowledge the Union, and to give them the right to take cases under the Workmen's Compensation Act into Court.

With regard to all other claims the Players' Union must first place them before the F.A. and then if either party is dissatisfied, the Union shall have power to proceed in law courts.

The F.A. will remove all suspensions and allow payment of all back wages to suspended players.

The First Surprise.

The conference convened by the F.A., at Birmingham, yesterday, took an unexpected course in several respects. Firstly, it was surprising to find that players who were not loyalists were admitted, the only exception being in the case of players who were actually under suspension. This kept the Manchester United leader, Charles Roberts, out of the room. Then not only were the members of the press privileged to hear another statement of the F.A. case by the chairman, but they were, by the unanimous wish of the players, permitted to remain and hear what was a very interesting discussion, during which the F.A. officials were fairly and squarely tackled by players who were delegates on behalf of the "loyalists," but who ventured to air grievances against the governing body. The greatest surprise was reserved for the close of the meeting.

Manchester Evening News, 1 September 1909

1910

THE MOVE TO a new stadium had been agreed as far back as 1908, with plans officially revealed in the *Athletic News* in March 1909, shortly before United's Cup final appearance. Bank Street, Clayton was, to put it bluntly, a disgrace of a pitch. During the winter months it turned into a quagmire and was hardly conducive to the kind of free-flowing football Meredith, Roberts, Turnbull and Wall were capable of displaying.

The new stadium was situated close to the home of Lancashire County Cricket Club in Old Trafford and was designed by Archibald Leitch, the noted football ground architect. Over the next 30 years Leitch stamped his hallmark on football with shrines at Ibrox, Sunderland, Everton, Tottenham, Blackburn, Huddersfield and many other places. If you wanted a football stadium designed, you went to Leitch.

It was the age of expansion. Crowds were flocking to matches everywhere and soccer had firmly established itself as the nation's favourite sport. Edwardian England enjoyed more leisure time than ever before, with the five-and-a-half-day week now standard in many industries. In Manchester alone, a dozen theatres played to huge audiences nightly while fun parks at the White City and Belle Vue entertained many others. Unfortunately, most of Britain's football grounds could not cope with this new influx of spectators. They were old, dilapidated stadiums, usually with a rickety wooden stand along one side and cinder banking at both ends. Such makeshift grounds had been in existence since the early days of the Football League, but now, as more money flowed into the game, it was time to design new and grander stadiums with more seating, comfort and safety.

The Old Trafford ground was to be

MANCHESTER UNITED'S NEW HOME.

A CLASSIC GROUND.

Accommodation for One Hundred Thousand People.

THE GRAND STAND.

(By "FORERUNNER.")

Of the making of football grounds there is no end. And such has been the growth of interest in the popular winter game that the modest grounds of the 80's, when professionalism was in its infancy, would prove quite unequal to present day requirements. In almost every football centre of any moment efforts have been made in recent years to provide a ground commensurate with modern and present-day requirements. Birmingham, Newcastle, Chelsea, Liverpool, and other populous centres have kept pace with the times, but those conversant with the grounds at Clayton and Hyde-road, which never boasted of beauty of situation, surrounding or approach know how inadequately the Manchester football public have been served by our local clubs. But football grounds are not to be found anywhere. In the selection of a suitable spot there are many considerations, such as accessibility, area, proximity of population, etc., all of which may be summed up under the one word—suitability.

Admirably Situated.

Manchester United have long been dissatisfied with Clayton, and only a few of the immediate residents have urged the club to stay on at the patch which for far too long has done duty for the club. The venue selected is a happy one. Old Trafford is the classic home of sport, and has an association far wider and more important than is covered by this name of Manchester. Its reputation is to say the least of it national. The ground is admirably situated and its selection does credit to the directorate responsible for the choice. It is easily reached from the city by train or car, it is within easy reach of scores of thousands of residents in Manchester and Salford, and, in a word, it would have been impossible to find a better site.

There was a preliminary view to the Press only prior to yesterday's match, when the ground was visited from end to end, and its chief features and attractions explained. It is unnecessary to go into details, as the showman says, it must be seen to be believed. The playing pitch is completed and pronounced "A 1 at Lloyds." It looks for all the world like turning the players out to play on a beautiful green plush carpet. I know groundsmen who would weep at the mere thought of using such a perfect pitch for so reckless a game, but football knows no sentiment. And the best use to which any ground can be put is the use for which it is most needed, and Manchester wants a real good football ground badly. The appurtenances of the ground are excellent in conception, construction, and arrangement. It is wasting time to write of the capabilities of Mr. Leitch as an architect of football grounds, and when I have said that he is responsible for the design and arrangement of the ground, the public can take with all the assurance of truth every word of commendation and praise in good faith. And when you have as the responsible officials a body of gentlemen like the United directors, with Mr. J. H. Davies at the head, it may be assured that nothing will be left wanting to make the enclosure a great, tip-top, comfortable football home.

The Grand Stand..

At present there is accommodation for 60,000 people, but when the ground is complete 100,000 will be able to see in comfort. The arrangement of the entrances and passages makes it an easy matter to distribute the crowd so as to prevent overcrowding. The grand stand is the very best in the kingdom, and nowhere will the comfort of the patrons have greater consideration than at Old Trafford. The elite of football society can attend and watch the match from their plush-seated chairs in comfort and luxurious ease. There is covered accommodation for 12,000 persons. The dressing-rooms are replete with every modern convenience and contrivance. The patrons of the game, the players, and the officials are practically on velvet all the time. Every spectator will enjoy an uninterrupted view. The grand stand, with its 60 rows of seats, is considerably larger than any stand on any football ground in the kingdom, and yet the ground is so compact that, unlike the Crystal Palace and other grounds, you always seem reasonably near the playing pitch. The recreation rooms and gymnasium for the players will be so up to date and replete with every modern comfort and convenience that they will satisfy the taste and requirements of the most exacting players. The players must not forget that these appendages to a footballer's daily training have their drawbacks and dangers, and should be used only as a means to an end. Let them add to the best fraternal feeling between the players and to a good spirit between directors and players, and they answer a good purpose. The officials of the game in the provision and arrangements for their comfort will find every reasonable accommodation, and the new ground at Old Trafford should at once spring into popularity. The architect, the contractors (Humphreys, I London), and the directors are to be congratulated on the magnitude of the scheme nd the excellent manner in which the work has been done.

The First Match.

Liverpool yesterday enjoyed the honour of opening the ground and heralding a new era in connection with the history of the club. With the removal from Clayton the last association with Newton Heath has gone. The removal has proved opportune, for on Thursday last the grand stand on the old ground suffered severely, being almost swept away by the hurricane. The roof was blown across the street, alighting on the houses opposite, the hoarding at the back of the stand was blown out, and there is a mere wreck of a stand left. What a tragic ending, and how singular that it should happen at the present time. Still, the stand has done its work, and the ground answered a long and useful purpose. If it had the power to tell its life story, what a history of trials and triumphs! Clayton can boast a proud record. Manchester United is dead. Long live Manchester United! Clayton has at best been the temporary shelter, and now we welcome a new United and usher in a new era. It is a cordial good-bye and a more cordial welcome. In the completion of the ground and the new start under conditions worthy of the best traditions and aspirations of the club the directors see the fruition of their labours and hopes. Notwithstanding what some may say and others think, the great credit for the carrying through of this work belongs to Mr. J. H. Davies, the president of the club. As a business undertaking it is thoroughly sound; as an achievement in the interests of sport it is majestic and generous. By this public-spirited action the public of Manchester will be the great benefactors, and it is to be hoped that they will show their appreciation in the most popular methods by generously supporting the club.

Two Good Clubs.

The arrangement whereby City and United are at home and away alternately makes it possible to be an active supporter of both clubs, and surely the Manchester public is sufficiently sporting in character to support two good clubs. They may well thank their lucky stars they have the chance. In common with many readers, I heartily wish the club long life and success at its new home, a new home well worthy to be the battle ground of the greatest football contests that the future of the game can provide.

The Umpire, 20 February 1910

An aerial view of the magnificent Old Trafford ground taken soon after it was built to Archibald Leith's design.

the biggest and finest in the land, fit for a team that had recently won the league and Cup. It was originally designed to hold 100,000 spectators with plush facilities for the payers. Dressing rooms would have baths, there was to be a laundry, a gymnasium and even a billiards room. The site had been purchased with a £60,000 grant from chairman John Davies. However, construction work cost a further £30,000, so plans had to be scaled down, restricting the gate to around 60,000.

Clayton was sold to Manchester Corporation for £5,500 and the final game at the old ground was played in front of only 8,000 spectators on Saturday, 22 January 1910 against Spurs and ended with a 5–0 victory to United. It had been hoped that this would be the inaugural match at Old Trafford but work was incomplete and the grand opening had to be postponed. Instead, Old Trafford was opened on Saturday, 19 February 1910; Liverpool were the visitors. Two days before, a gale swept across Manchester and blew down the Bank Street stand causing extensive damage to houses in neighbouring streets. It was a fitting finale for Clayton.

Estimates of the gate at that first match vary, but at least 50,000 were reckoned to be present with 5,000 sneaking in free of charge when gatemen, unable to cope with the queues, simply opened their turnstiles. The *Guardian* reported that such a crowd had never been seen in Manchester, with hordes of people swarming up the Chester Road. Trams clattered along barely able to move under the weight of passengers, while others took to carts and even horses. Admission to the ground was six pence, with the best reserved seats costing five shillings. The pitch was said to be a remarkable, luscious green, not unlike a billiard table. Fans standing at the top of the open terraces had to tie their hats on with scarves as the stiff breeze whipped across the nearby Manchester Ship Canal.

The prestige of scoring Old Trafford's first goal deservedly went to Sandy Turnbull. But Liverpool spoilt the occasion by winning 4–3 after United had led 2–0. It had been United's first experience of the ground as well, but once they became acquainted with the new pitch there was no stopping them. They won all their remaining home league games that season and the following season lost only once. It would be 21 October 1911 before they were defeated again at Old Trafford.

Meanwhile, Old Trafford became one of the finest football stadiums in the world. In 1911 it hosted the Cup final replay and in 1966 the World Cup finals. But it was never extended to give the 100,000 capacity its architect had originally envisaged, although a record crowd of 76,962 witnessed the FA Cup semi-final between Wolves and Grimsby in 1939. Today, with its plush executive boxes and restaurants, Old Trafford can comfortably accommodate around 56,000, making it one of the largest grounds in Britain.

No sooner had Manchester United left Bank Street than the main stand collapsed in a storm, causing much damage to the surrounding houses.

1911

THE 1910/11 SEASON was one of the most exciting in the history of the Football League, with Aston Villa and Manchester United battling it out for the title until the final fixture of the season. United began their campaign with much the same side as the previous year but had added the young Nottingham Forest centre forward Enoch West to their ranks. Jimmy Turnbull had moved on but, with a forward line of Billy Meredith, Harold Halse, Enoch West, Sandy Turnbull and George Wall, United were well equipped for a second assault on the title.

By the midway stage Villa, the previous season's champions, were on top, just above United on goal average with Sunderland and Everton tucked in behind them. By the end of January, United had sneaked ahead of Villa and two months later were four points clear of the Midlanders with only six games remaining. There seemed to be little doubt that the title would go to Old Trafford but suddenly nerves got the better of United. By Easter Saturday, with just three games left to play, the

MANCHESTER UNITED CHAMPIONS.

VILLA DISAPPOINTED.

Bristol City Drop Out.

EVERTON SAVE BURY.

ROVERS WIN ON TEESSIDE.

(By "RARA AVIS.")

After much moaning and groaning, intermixed with exultation, the football season has come to a close. Rarely, indeed, have the vital issues been delayed until the very last, as they have been on this occasion, which in a way is just as it should be—at any rate, the treasurers of the League clubs will tell you so.

To win the Championship the Villa had to draw at Liverpool, though in the event of Manchester United beating Sunderland at Old Trafford by a fairly substantial margin the honours would rest with the Mancunians. As it happened, the Villa were beaten at New Anfield after a really brilliant display on the part of the Merseysiders, and though Manchester United defeated the Wearsiders by the substantial score of 5—1, as events turned out a win by the narrowest of margins would have sufficed to give the United the honour. There was, I learn, a very enthusiastic scene at the close of the match with Sunderland. Without wishing to be in the slightest degree partial, I must say that, in my opinion, the League Championship was well deserved. The United were the victims of cruel misfortune when, at a critical part of the season they had Roberts injured, while others to be on the casualty list for sustained periods were Duckworth, Halse, and Wall. When at full strength I consider them to be the best team in the country.

BRAVO, UNITED!

Sunderland Well Beaten.

GOOD WIND-UP.

(By "THE GENERAL.")

MANCHESTER UNITED 5 SUNDERLAND 1

When Manchester United won the League Championship at the close of the season 1907-8 they put up a new record in scoring fifty-two points. Yesterday they equalled that performance and the same number of points proved enough to again carry off the championship, Liverpool helping the Manchester team to this end by beating Aston Villa.

It has been a strenuous season, and I feel sure the Manchester players would have created another record in points had it not been for rank bad luck in the shape of injuries, as well as other misfortunes on the field of play. But as these accidents come to all teams and have to be counted in the game, the Manchester United players and directors will rest content that matters have ended so well, and that they can go away until next September with the knowledge that they have done their best and have pleased their many thousands of faithful followers. I hope and trust they will be as keen next season, when the club will have been formed into a limited company.

The United turned out without Hofton, Roberts, Bell, and Wall, but they had capable substitutes in Donnelly, Whalley, Hodge, and Blott. Sunderland were short of Coleman, Troughear, and Jarvis. The game was played in drizzling rain, and a stiff wind favoured the visitors, Duckworth, who acted as captain, having lost the toss.

The early play was conspicuous for a fine run by Blott, who got in a perfect centre, but saw it cleared. For some seconds the visitors did the most pressing, but the United defenders showed great form and managed to keep them out. The play was keenly contested, in spite of the fact that the elements were against good football, and Thomson tested Edmonds with a long shot which he caught and cleared. Blott and Meredith on the one side, and Mordue and Holley on the other, threatened danger, but the biggest mistake of the match was made when West was given a clean run in, but shot five yards from goal, and saw the ball pass the wrong side of the right post.

It was a bad miss on the part of West, who had the goal at his mercy. The United had terribly bad luck, for soon after this the ball was sent across the Sunderland goalmouth, and West headed into the net; but just as the centre forward was heading in the referee whistled for offside, amidst protests of both West and Turnbull, but the referee would not heed them. The game had been in progress twenty-two minutes when the visitors got

AN UNEXPECTED GOAL.

Play was going on in the Wearsiders' half, and Forster and Milton were working manfully to keep the United out, the ball being sent along the floor to Low, and in a few minutes Holley got hold and shot hard, the ball hitting the under side of the bar and dropping into the net. This was a great disappointment to the home team, who did not want to lose any goals in such a momentous game.

A free kick to United brought about the equalising goal. Meredith took it and placed the ball to Turnbull's head, and the ball was in the net. Mordue was given some opportunities of showing his speed, and he did not forget to place the ball in front of goal, but his centres were met by either Whalley or the backs, and the game was taken to the other end where a corner kick was taken by Meredith, and West headed into the net. The United had the better of the game, and there was now no stopping them, a third goal coming as the result of a shot by Halse, Worrall making a vain attempt with his foot, and in another minute or two the interval was called.

There was much excitement when the teams came out again consequent on the score from Liverpool, and when the United players heard that Villa were two goals down they showed themselves greatly pleased. The game had not been long in progress when Low got hurt and had to go off, Mordue going centre. This loss penned the visitors in their own half, and from a great run by Meredith, Halse shot into the net. The home team continued to have the game in their keeping, but Bridgett went off and nearly beat Edmonds, but he caught the shot and cleared in brilliant style.

Another corner by Meredith saw a goal come from Turnbull, Milton assisting it into the net, making the fifth. There was no mistaking the earnestness of the home side, but I must not omit to say that Tait and Low, who had been in the wars, both had to leave the game owing to injuries, and Sunderland were a well beaten side. But the remnants did their level best to attack, and Thomson, Holley, and Bridgett worked the ball towards the United goal, only to see Whalley clear. Turnbull worked his way in the centre and gave a pass to Meredith, whose shot hit the wrong side of the post and went out.

There was some danger of one of the visitors' rushes taking effect, but on the other hand the United had several chances, West, Halse, and Turnbull having the hardest of hard lines in not getting three or four more goals, and the game ended with

UNITED EASY WINNERS.

The game was full of interest, and it struck me that Sunderland did United a good turn when they scored the first goal, for it certainly made them look alive to the fact that they might let the League championship slip away from them. The goal spurred the home side on, and they took charge of the game in quick time, and made no mistake afterwards. I hasten to congratulate the substitutes, Donnelly, whom we have seen before, Whalley, Hodge, and Blott. They gave a very good display, and could not have been improved on. Donnelly rarely made a mistake. Whalley was, I thought, to blame for allowing Sunderland to score, but did all right on the whole; and Hodge was ever a thorn in the side of Mordue and Buchan.

The surprise of the day was however Blott, whose exhibition at outside left was the best seen this season. He could beat the half back, showed rare speed, and centred well.

The Umpire, 30 April 1911

The squad that took the title in 1910/11 with a record-equalling number of points, having conceded fewer goals than any other champions since the first division expanded to 20 clubs in 1905/6.

gap was down to one point. On Easter Monday, United could only draw at Sheffield Wednesday and then the following Saturday they faced Villa in the match of the season. It looked as if this would be the deciding encounter and a record crowd of 55,000 turned up at Villa Park. But it was an ill-tempered and unpleasant affair highlighted by the sending off of Enoch West. United went down 4–2 and, as they trooped miserably from the field, they must have thought their title chances had all but gone. They were now a point adrift of Villa with only one game to play. Villa were at Anfield for their final fixture and merely needed a draw to claim the title, while United entertained Sunderland at Old Trafford.

United looked to have the harder game, with Sunderland lying in third place while Liverpool were in the lower half of the table. Few would have bet on Villa losing, yet that was precisely what happened. Sunderland even went ahead at Old Trafford, but United's heads did not drop. Instead, Meredith rolled up his sleeves and rallied his troops. Minutes later, they were back in contention as Turnbull headed home the Welsh international's cross. Meredith was playing out of his skin, weaving one way and then dodging another and before much longer Enoch West had headed another Meredith cross into the net. Halse then added a third and as the teams reached the dressing room at the interval the news came over that Liverpool were two goals ahead at Anfield. A great roar went up from the crowd and if ever United needed any incentive this was it.

They reappeared for the second half determined to seize their opportunity. Meredith continued his jinxing down the right and after another burst he centred for Halse to score his second of the game. And, not surprisingly, it was a Meredith corner which produced their fifth. As the final whistle blew everyone waited expectantly for the result from Anfield. The Sunderland players returned wearily to their dressing room while the United players hovered nervously around the pitch. Meredith chewed on his toothpick and the crowd fidgeted. Then a silence fell as the score from Anfield was relayed on the telegraph board. Liverpool 3 Aston Villa 1. United were champions.

Not only were they champions but they had equalled their own points-scoring record. Their goals had come primarily from Enoch West with 19 and Sandy Turnbull with 18. West had proved to be an inspired signing – one of the last ever made by secretary Ernest Mangnall. Born in Nottinghamshire, West had automatically signed for Forest, where he scored almost 100 goals in his five years with them and was the first division's top scorer in 1907/08. During his five seasons at United he hit 80 goals in 181 appearances. But such was the wealth of talent in the England team that he never had the chance to represent his country. Shortly before war brought league soccer to a standstill, West was accused with two other United players of fixing a game with Liverpool. He was found guilty and banned from football for life, although the FA eventually lifted the ban in 1945.

1911

SWINDON OUTPLAYED.

Manchester United Win F.A. Charity Shield Match by 8 Goals to 4.

After an extraordinarily fast and quite sporting game Manchester United defeated Swindon Town at Stamford Bridge for the Football Association Charity Shield by 8 goals to 4. Such scoring between teams of this class is quite extraordinary. It would seem to show slackness to the man who merely read, but did not watch.

There was not, however, the slightest sign of lack of keenness from beginning to end. The forwards of both sides played with a wonderful control of the light ball, played with great dash, speed and cleverness, and shot brilliantly.

The pace set by Manchester, especially, made the Swindon attack look weak and half-hearted in front of goal: and yet Swindon's defence is known to be pretty strong.

After six minutes' play, fine work on the left by Lamb and Bown ended in a perfect centre from the latter, which Fleming headed through. Roberts, by the way, was off the field at the moment, but returned immediately.

A couple of minutes later Halse fogged the Swindon defence, and gave Turnbull an easy chance to score. Swindon then pressed, but, after a couple of corners, Halse broke away on his own. Skiller ran out, but half-heartedly, and Halse scored easily.

A BRILLIANT SAVE.

Three minutes later Bown looked certain to score for Swindon, but Edmonds rushed out and threw himself at the ball, as a full-back will go down to a rush at Rugby. A terrific shot by Halse was just saved at the expense of a corner. Swindon failed to clear cleanly, and after some exciting work Hamill scored easily. Swindon had themselves to blame for this goal: for, instead of playing to the whistle, they stood around shouting to the referee for a free kick.

Then Fleming got away at a great pace, and passed out beautifully to the right. Jefferson took the ball up and centred perfectly, and Wheatcroft headed through. Two minutes afterwards, however, Halse went through and scored again, the Swindon defence, apparently, having another misunderstanding among themselves. Just before half-time a penalty was given against Hofton for fouling Wheatcroft, and Tout scored with a fast low shot, making the score only 4—3 at half-time in favour of the United.

After eighteen minutes in the second half Halse scored again, and it was a pretty goal. He used the feint of the body, that looks like a dribble, which G. O. Smith was so famous for: the charging back went for the body, missed Halse entirely, and left him a good chance which he took promptly.

An extraordinary screw kick from Halse made it 5—3, and the issue certain. And once again, thank you, Mr. Halse: again the body wriggle and Halse scored his fifth goal against Swindon, a feat which won't be duplicated again this year, anyway.

Five minutes from the finish Wall scored the eighth goal for the United, but Swindon stuck to it, and Jefferson got through for them just on time.

At the conclusion of the match Sir Charles Wakefield presented the shield and medals to Manchester United.

F. B. WILSON.

Daily Mirror, 26 September 1911

AS LEAGUE CHAMPIONS United were once again invited to take part in the Charity Shield. This time their opponents were Swindon Town, winners of the Southern League, and Stamford Bridge was the venue. The game, played in late September, attracted a gate of only 8,000. This was a shame because United and Swindon served up a 12-goal thriller that had the few reporters present ecstatic over United's performance. But few would have guessed the size of United's victory as the Southern Leaguers shot into an early lead. Minutes later, however, Sandy Turnbull scored an equaliser that began the rout of Swindon. Harold Halse added a second and then a third to make it 3–1. Swindon then pulled a goal back before Halse completed his hat trick. A penalty late in the first half gave Swindon some hope and at the interval the scoreline stood at 4–3 to United.

The few fans present had certainly had their money's worth (gate receipts, incidentally, were £229) and would no doubt have been content had the second half remained goalless. But there was little chance of that. Within 18 minutes Halse had made it 5–3 and he then added two more to give him a hat trick in each half. George Wall added United's eighth shortly before the whistle and Swindon scored a consolation goal almost on time to give an amazing final scoreline of 8–4.

Harold Halse's six goals turned out to be one of the finest individual goalscoring feats in United's history. He had joined the club in 1908 after spells with Clapton Orient and Southend and over the next five seasons netted 50 goals in 124 appearances. He was not a prolific goal-scorer but was an able partner to Sandy Turnbull, providing the Scottish centre forward with so many of his chances. Although he was only a slender man, standing just 5 feet $5\frac{1}{2}$ inches and weighing $10\frac{1}{2}$ stone, he was a nippy, scheming inside right and, above all, an opportunist. It was his shot rebounding off the crossbar in the 1909 Cup final that led to Turnbull scoring the only goal of the game. He won a league championship medal with United in 1911 and an England cap in 1909, scoring twice during England's 8–1 win over Austria. Yet surprisingly, he was never chosen to represent his country again. At the end of the 1911/12 season he moved to Aston Villa where he won another Cup-winners' medal in 1913. A month later he returned south, joining Chelsea, and appeared in the 1915 Cup final at Old Trafford, this time on the losing side.

Before the match, Swindon were seen very much as the underdogs – and so it proved. United won 8–4.

THE HOPE OF THE SOUTH.

Time! Gentlemen.

1912

Only Matt Busby has been more successful as United manager than Ernest Mangnall.

FOOTBALL.

THE MANCHESTER CITY SECRETARYSHIP.

The Position of Mr. J. E. Mangnall.

Although the Manchester United officials have declined the offer of Blackburn Rovers of £1,200 for the services of West, and the sum of £1,500 for the transfer of Roberts to the Manchester City club, it is just possible that they may lose the help of Mr. J. E. Mangnall, who for many seasons has acted as secretary and manager of the club. It is, of course, well known that Manchester City are in search of such an official, and last week the Hyde Road directorate reduced the number of applicants from 107 to three. They are naturally anxious to secure the services of a gentleman with a good record, and we understand that Mr. Mangnall has been offered the post.

Whether the Manchester United officials would care to liberate him is, of course, a very different matter, and a special meeting of the Old Trafford Executive is to be held this evening, when the question will be under discussion. The committee of the City club will meet to-morrow evening, when it is expected that the final choice will be made.

The Manchester United officials are faced with a very difficult problem, for they must recognise that in Mr. Mangnall they have an official who has done yeoman service. When he came to the club from Burnley the organisation was a struggling one, but under his management the club won its way into the First Division of the League, has once carried off the English Cup, and has twice won the championship of the English League. He obtained at a cheap figure the services of Meredith, Bannister, Turnbull, Burgess, and Livingstone from the Manchester City club, and there has been other notable captures, but Mr. Mangnall was, perhaps, fortunate in serving under a generous board of directors. It is perhaps not generally known that Mr. Mangnall was really the founder of the Central League, and his knowledge of footballers and his acquaintance with football officials have been of the greatest service to the club.

If Mr. Mangnall decides to go to the rival organisation the Old Trafford officials will have a difficult task in finding his successor. It is understood that the post may be offered to a player attached to a northern club, whose name is a household word in football circles. This gentleman, whose name is still on the list of half backs, would, of course, not be expected to take any further part in the game if he comes to Manchester.

A Manchester United official, when spoken to on the subject to-day, said it was quite true that the board were meeting this evening to discuss the situation, but he could not, of course, say what would happen. Mr. Mangnall had had a long and honourable connection with the club, and if he should decide to leave them he would take with him the good wishes of all concerned. It was true, added this gentleman, that in view of the possible retirement of Mr. Mangnall, a certain well-known half back had been approached in the matter.

Manchester Evening News, 19 August 1912

WHEN BILLY MEREDITH crossed the city of Manchester to join United in 1906, it had caused a sensation among Mancunians. But, six years later, the Hyde Road club took sweet revenge when United's manager, Ernest Mangnall, left Old Trafford for Manchester City. How could Mangnall desert a club that had just won two league titles and the FA Cup?

City had received 107 applications for the job of secretary but only three applicants had been shortlisted. Mangnall was always the favourite with the City board, even though in that same week he had turned down their £1,500 offer for Charlie Roberts. Mangnall was duly interviewed and on Monday 19 August 1912 the *Manchester Evening News* speculated that he was about to become the new City manager. That evening the United board held an emergency meeting to discuss Mangnall's position, but there was little they could do to change his mind. Indeed, they seemed almost too happy for the Havana-smoking secretary to depart and the following day Mangnall was formally appointed secretary/manager of Manchester City. For United it was the end of an era.

Just 18 months later, City were top of both the first division and the Central League while United were struggling next to bottom. Unfortunately, war intervened and the rebuilding work he had done at City was interrupted. Nevertheless, he took City through a difficult financial period, taking them to the runners-up spot in 1921 and instigated the construction of a new stadium at Maine Road. He left City in 1924, when his contract was not renewed, and died eight years later in September 1932.

His achievements at United can never be underestimated. Not only did he steer them to two league championships and the FA Cup but he bought players of the calibre of Meredith, Roberts, West, Turnbull, Bell, Wall and Duckworth to give United a stamp of class. And, to top it all, he had built the finest stadium in the land at Old Trafford to accommodate all this talent. It took United 40 years to recover fully from the loss of Mangnall.

1913

Roberts (left) with Colin Veitch during a Players' Union gala match at Newcastle.

IF THE DEPARTURE of Ernest Mangnall caused something of a sensation, then the transfer of the United captain Charlie Roberts sent shock waves around Old Trafford. Roberts had been with United since his £400 transfer from Grimsby in April 1904. During the next nine years he led the club to two league championships and an FA Cup victory. It was his leadership on the field, his enthusiasm and his determination that had been the key to United's success. But, on the Saturday evening of 23 August 1913, Roberts signed for neighbouring Oldham Athletic. Oldham were not the only team interested in acquiring his services. Manchester City, Newcastle and Blackburn Rovers had all made firm offers but had been turned down, and it took a record £1,500 fee from Athletic to persuade United to part with their jewel. Record fee or not, the Oldham manager, David Ashworth, reckoned he had a bargain.

United were in dire financial difficulties following the building of Old Trafford and were, no doubt, persuaded by the huge fee. Roberts had also requested a second benefit match and this had been refused by the board on the grounds that another benefit would deprive younger players of any. With a weekly maximum wage of £5, the only opportunity for a player to earn any substantial payment was through a benefit match. Roberts himself had already made £900 from a benefit against Sheffield Wednesday and was branded as greedy in demanding a second one. In retrospect, with war just a year away and with his career past its peak, his transfer had little consequence and could well be viewed as a shrewd slice of business.

Mangnall's departure had marked the beginning of the end for United and Roberts' transfer was merely another nail in the coffin. His half back partner Alex Bell had just been sold to Blackburn Rovers for £1,000 after also being refused a second benefit, while Dick Duckworth was in dispute with the club over his benefit as well. Goalkeeper Harry Moger had moved on and Herbert Burgess had left in 1910 – the outstanding United team of the period had all but broken apart.

FOOTBALL SURPRISE.

Roberts Transferred to Oldham Athletic.

Manchester Evening News, 25 August 1913

Roberts had made 299 appearances for United, scoring 23 goals, and was the club's regular centre half throughout his nine full seasons, rarely missing a game. Within 18 months his combative, calming influence would be sorely missed as United struggled at the foot of the table, while Oldham, now captained by Roberts, topped the league. Athletic in fact missed out on the title by just one point. Roberts remained with Oldham until war disrupted league football when he decided to retire. He was persuaded out of retirement and returned to Boundary Park in 1921 as manager, only to quit 18 months later for more peaceful activities – running a tobacconist's shop. During his career he made three appearances for England, represented the Football League XI on seven occasions and was chairman of the Players' Union. He died, aged 56, a month before the outbreak of the second world war.

1914

FOOTBALL NOT TO STOP.

But Internationals Abandoned.

"GAME NOT A HINDRANCE TO RECRUITING."

Official Statement.

A meeting unique in the history of football was held at the offices of the Football Association, Russell Square, London, yesterday, when decisions were arrived at upon momentous issues affecting the future of the game. The gathering took the form of a conference, called at the instigation of the Scottish Football Association, of the four governing bodies comprised in the British Isles, and after protracted deliberations the following resolutions were issued to the press:

1. It was decided to recommend to each national association that the international matches for this season be abandoned.

2. There is no evidence in fact that the playing of football has hindered, or is hindering, recruiting. On the contrary, there is good reason to conclude that football has encouraged and assisted recruiting.

In these circumstances, this meeting recommends that, except as regards international matches, it is not right that football should be stopped or suspended. Further, this meeting is of opinion that to deprive the working people of our country of their Saturday afternoon recreation would be unfair and very mischievous.

Manchester Evening News, 4 December 1914

ON A WINDSWEPT boulevard in Sarajevo in June 1914 a young Serbian student pulled a gun from his jacket and fired three fatal bullets into Archduke Ferdinand of Austria. It was an act that would spark off a war costing millions of lives and untold damage. The daily life of the nation was disrupted for four years. Nothing was ever quite the same again.

As war swept across Europe, however, Edwardian England carried on regardless. After all, the politicians and generals believed it would last only a matter of months. The fighting was hundreds of miles away and was unlikely ever to affect mainland Britain, so it was decided to proceed as normal to boost morale. And so, football continued despite some objections.

War was declared on 4 August 1914, but the new soccer season went ahead as planned after representatives of the four footballing associations met to discuss the crisis. For the time being, they could see no reason for calling a halt but promised to review the situation intermittently.

Initially, there was little effect on the game. Clubs encouraged their players to enlist, there were collections for the war effort and adverts in programmes urged supporters to join Lord Kitchener's mighty army. It was only when news of the fighting at Ypres filtered through in November 1914 that the full horror of the war was realised. Thousands of men were dying every day, more were being recruited for the battle while factories and shipyards worked overtime to provide the munitions for the front. It was not long before attendances began to fall at games and eventually the public lost its appetite for fun. United ended the 1914/15 season in 18th place, avoiding relegation by the skin of their teeth. The war marked the end of the careers of many outstanding United players. George Wall, the tough little Barnsley winger who had been at the club since 1906, never played for United again. He had helped them to two championships and the FA Cup as well as winning seven England caps. Centre forward Enoch West and full back George Stacey, another former Barnsley player, had both enjoyed exciting triumphs with United but would never play for them again. But perhaps the most tragic of all was Sandy Turnbull who was killed in action in France on 3 May 1917.

The 'Khaki Cup final' held at Old Trafford in 1915 was one of the last major matches played during the war. Sheffield United won 3–0.

1914

John Robson, seen here during his Brighton days, took over at a bad time.

AFTER THE SURPRISE departure of Ernest Mangnall, the secretary/manager's job was taken on by JJ Bentley. Bentley had been at United since 1902, serving as a director and chairman, and had also been president of the Football League between 1894 and 1910. Prior to United he had been a player with Bolton Wanderers before he became secretary/manager at the same club, leading them to the 1894 Cup final. He also had experience as a referee. He seemed well qualified for the job and hopes were high.

Bentley was keen to have a crack at managing United and was even thought to have been interested in the Manchester City job. So, for a brief spell, he took over the reigns of management but was not altogether successful. There were disputes over pay and a serious dressing room argument with Sandy Turnbull that led to the latter's suspension and a players' revolt. It was an uneasy period that also took its toll on Bentley's health. The great team of Mangnall was past its peak and beginning to disintegrate. Faced with all these difficulties it was agreed to seek a new manager – a man who would be involved solely with the playing side – leaving Bentley to continue as secretary. And so, after some careful searching, United announced shortly before Christmas 1914 that John Robson of Brighton had been appointed to the new post.

United had attempted to recruit Robson at the beginning of the season but had failed. This time, however, they were successful. Robson who had previously been connected with Middlesbrough and Crystal Palace remained at the helm until 1921. But, if Bentley had experienced troubled times, Robson was to suffer even worse. As the war effort grew, the league structure was disbanded, players marched off to the front and the Old Trafford debt became crippling.

New Manager for Manchester United.

The news that Manchester United have appointed a team manager will occasion little surprise, as for some time the officials have recognised that they were asking Mr. J. J. Bentley to do too much. Mr. Bentley has not been in the best of health for many months, and unfortunately the members of the board of directors were not able to give the help that gentlemen in similar positions with other clubs are able to give. It was hoped to get the aid of Mr. J. Robson, of Brighton and Hove, at the opening of the season, but the effort then failed, and Mr. Bentley has had to struggle on. However, Mr. Robson has now been secured, and he will take over his new duties in about a week's time.

It should be understood that the new appointment will in no way interfere with the duty of Mr. Bentley, who will continue to fill the role of club secretary. Mr. Robson is a gentleman with a thorough knowledge of football and its management. He was for some years connected with the Middlesbrough club, and afterwards went to the Crystal Palace club.

Manchester Evening News, 21 December 1914

1915

ON GOOD FRIDAY 1915 United faced Liverpool at Old Trafford in what was a vital game for the home club. Struggling in the relegation zone, United desperately needed the points if they were to stave off a humiliating drop into the second division. Liverpool, on the other hand, were comfortably placed in the middle of the table with no chance of relegation or championship honours. It was a game United needed to win … and a game which in fact they did win – 2–0.

The fixture might have passed almost unremarked upon had it not been for some strange happenings in the betting world. The referee reckoned it was a peculiar match and one or two newspapers commented on Liverpool's lackadaisical approach, but there was little else to draw the attention of football's administrators. There had been plenty of jeering at the game and Liverpool had missed a penalty, but United had won and there was nothing particularly unusual in that, given Liverpool's equally poor form.

However, a couple of weeks later handbills were being circulated in the Manchester area offering a £50 reward for any information to substantiate an allegation that the match had been squared. By the end of April, the sporting press were on the scent and had alerted the soccer world to a possible scandal. The handbill had been published by a firm of bookmakers known as the 'Football Kings' who alleged that an unusual number of bets, involving considerable amounts of money, had been laid at 7–1 on a winning scoreline of 2–0 to United. It was certainly not unusual to bet on football in those days, but it was unusual to bet on the scoreline.

Sandy Turnbull was in trouble again – this time over allegations of match-fixing.

EN PASSANT.

THE GRAVE SCANDAL.

A PLOT to cheat the public, to sell to the faithful followers of football a sham instead of the genuine article, to rob bookmakers by criminal fraud, and to conspire for the suppression of the truth has been revealed. For the moment the game of Association football, as played by professionals, staggers under the grave scandal that the League match between Manchester United and Liverpool last spring was a complete and deliberate fake. Hitherto any irregularities proved have been in the main offences against the rules and regulations of football, but this alleged contest amounts to a breach of the criminal law of England. It is not an offence to bet, but it is a crime to make wages and obtain money by false pretence.

The Findings of the Commission.

The report issued by the joint commission of these governing authorities reads as follows:—

MANCHESTER UNITED v. LIVERPOOL, APRIL 2, 1915.

The Commissions appointed first by the Football League, and afterwards by the Football Association, have fully investigated the rumours and allegations largely circulated in several districts during and immediately after the above match, to the effect that the result was pre-arranged for the purpose of betting and winning money thereby. A mass of information was received.

The allegation of squaring the match carried with it a charge of conspiracy by some of the players, and as a result of long and searching investigations we are satisfied that a number of them were party to an arrangement to do so, and joined together to obtain money by betting on the actual result of the match.

It is proved that a considerable sum of money changed hands by betting on the match and that some of the players profited thereby.

"Every opportunity has been given to the players to tell the truth, but although they were warned that we were in possession of the facts some have persistently refused to do so, thus revealing a conspiracy to keep back the truth.

Athletic News, 27 December 1915

Enoch West, who had scored 71 goals in 167 league games for United, was not forgiven until 1945 for his part in the scandal of April 1915.

The Football League immediately launched an investigation which began in Manchester on 10 May and continued until mid-December when their findings were published. They had unearthed clear evidence of a conspiracy to fix the result. The report caused a sensation and the finger was firmly pointed at three United players, four Liverpool players and a Chester player. As a result all eight players were suspended from the game for life.

The United players involved were Sandy Turnbull, Enoch West and Arthur Whalley, although West was the only one to have actually played in the match. It transpired that the Liverpool player Jackie Sheldon, who was a former United player, had acted as the go-between. He had introduced some of the participants to each other in a Manchester pub a week before the match, where it was agreed to fix the result at 2–0 to United. Bets were laid with bookmakers around the country so as to make a quick killing. With the nation already at war and the Football League about to be suspended they had decided to supplement their meagre wages with a few extra pounds to carry them over the difficult period ahead.

The Liverpool culprits were Sheldon, Tommy Miller, Tom Fairfoul and Bob Purcell. Enoch West always maintained his innocence and even instigated a libel action which was heard in open court. Unfortunately, it uncovered little new evidence and West lost his case. With league football about to come to an abrupt end the suspensions made little difference and, in an act of magnanimity, the authorities lifted the ban at the end of the war on all players except West. He continued to maintain his innocence, however, but was not forgiven until 1945, by which time he was a bitter and disillusioned man who had shunned football since that eventful day.

There has always been doubt about how much the other United players knew of the conspiracy. Meredith insisted he had no knowledge, although he soon guessed something was up once the game was under way. The players had ostensibly agreed it, not to help United avoid relegation, but for personal profit. Yet, ironically, it was United who benefited most from the result, avoiding relegation at the end of the season by just two points.

The Manchester United-Liverpool "Match."

Permanent Suspension of Celebrated Players.

Robbery!

We have great sympathy with some of those who will have to live under a cloud in that they participated in this hippodrome hocus-pocus and this nefarious contrivance to rob bookmakers who had no chance of preserving their own property.

We have not a scrap of compassion for those who have been punished for, not only devising the result of the "match," but for taking money from the pockets of bookmakers, who are as much entitled to the protection of the law as other men. Some people don't approve of their business, but the majority of them are at least as honourable in their payments as those engaged in ordinary trading.

Indeed, had it not been for the bookmakers, corroborated in a most emphatic and extraordinary manner, the collusion between the culprits in the rival camps could not have been proved.

There was a carefully worked out plan by which the bookmakers in whole districts were filched at such odds as seven and eight to one against the actual result. Places so far apart as Liverpool, Manchester, Nottingham, and London came within the sphere of operations.

In one or two instances the suspicion of the bookmaker was aroused by the insistence upon betting on the actual result and the amount of money tendered. Generally speaking, the bookmakers paid their clients, although they discovered that they had been "rooked," but a few refused to disgorge. That is not our business.

What Was the Temptation?

It may be urged that these footballers succumbed to temptation because of the reductions in wages that they had suffered and because there was no probability of any salaries during the summer months as have been customary. This cannot be justly urged in mitigation of their crime, for many other people have lost their earning capacity during this war, but they have not lost their honesty.

Presumably these men connived to "make a bit" so that they would not feel the pinch of poverty. There must have been some personal motive. We do not believe that there was any cause for their action other than personal aggrandisement.

Does not this exposure indirectly suggest the wisdom of insisting upon a law that the man who plays football for money must at the same time work for his livelihood? Wages from football should be supplementary and not the sole support of any man. It is quite probable that had these players been engaged in skilled handicrafts, or even in situations where trained eyes and hands are not essential, they would not have succumbed to this temptation.

They saw their income disappearing, and had ample time to work out their deep-laid designs. That, however, is merely a consideration, and is not even a palliation of their diabolical machinations. The money they have handled will pollute their lives, for they have enriched themselves in a manner which not only disgusts the public and defrauds bookmakers, but threatens the very existence of the game to which hundreds of other professionals have honestly devoted themselves for legitimate and, in scores of cases, ambitious and honourable purposes.

Power Justly Used.

But there are aspects, even of this affair, which should assure the public. The decision of the joint commission of The League and the Football Association proves that those who govern the game are determined that the spectacular sport as presented by professionals shall be honest and pure. Rather let the whole fabric, so laboriously built up, collapse like a house of cards than that such venal practices should be permitted.

The moment that rumours were reported to the President of The League, he appointed a commission to investigate. There was no hesitation, even though his own club was concerned. The commissioners scoured the country for information. They forwarded the result of their minute searchings in all kinds of nooks and corners to the Football Association, who then came on the scene. Taking no imputation for fact the Association joined hands. There came a time when there was a deadlock. The authorities were convinced that the match was unreal, but that the offence could be brought home to one man only.

At this juncture there was a sudden revelation from one quarter, and proof was piled on proof. The authorities were impartial. They did not screen their eyes or stop their ears. They have punished drastically. Said a great writer: "Justice discards party, friendship, kindred."

Athletic News, 27 December 1915

1916

FOOTBALL WAS finally suspended at the end of the 1914/15 season. By then, news from the war meant that nobody was in the mood for taking sport too seriously. In place of the familiar Football League a variety of divisions on a regional basis were established. To begin with, United joined forces with Everton, Liverpool, Manchester City and Stockport County to form a Lancashire league southern section but, in time, the country was simply split into a northern and southern league. The rules governing professional players were also relaxed and as more players were called up to join the forces a guesting system was introduced.

It was a low period for United. Their magnificent ground at Old Trafford stood empty and silent and, even when the opposition was Liverpool or City, attendances were low. The ground had created a crippling burden of debt before the war; now it was soaking up all the club's resources. Most of the players had enlisted and were either training at home or seeing action in Europe. Some, like Arthur Whalley, were wounded, while centre forward Sandy Turnbull was tragically killed in action in France during May 1917. Turnbull had been one of the most outstanding centre forwards of his day. A former Manchester City player, he had joined United in the exodus from City after the illegal payments scandal in 1906. His former partner at both City and United, Billy Meredith, returned to Manchester City as a wartime guest and there were few remaining members of the famous league- and Cup-winning side. It was a strange and largely unknown United team which took the field during those grim years with their unfamiliarity showing in the results. Stockport, Oldham and Rochdale regularly had the better of them and, in March 1916, United could attract barely 500 spectators to Boundary Park, albeit in dismal weather, and went down by a single goal. It was now City who were the pride of Manchester while United slumped to the bottom of even their short league.

(SOUTHERN DIVISION.)

DEFEATING THE ELEMENTS.

Oldham Athletic...1 Manchester United.0

[BY HARRICUS.]

UNDER normal conditions the visit of Manchester United to Oldham would have aroused great interest, but on Saturday there were not 500 spectators to welcome them to Boundary Park, and the wonder is that so many attended on what must be regarded as one of the most exposed grounds in the country. There were none so foolhardly as to disdain the shelter of the stands, for the wind blew with cutting bitterness from goal to goal, and the side facing the blizzard were fighting Nature as well as opponents. Singularly, whilst the Oldham captain lost the toss, his team played far better against the beating snow than did the United, who were supposed to have an advantage in being almost blown into their opponents' quarters.

There is no doubt about it, the Athletic made a fine fight, and it is a fact that they secured the only goal of the match when battling against the elements. This occurred about eight minutes from the interval. Lucas had just previously kicked the ball away as it appeared to be passing into goal, but it was never really clear of danger ere Wolstenholme, who was close up, put the ball low and sure into the net. There were many interesting movements in the first half, which on the whole was very enjoyable, but the second portion of the game was void of any really live incidents. Possibly the Athletic thought that a goal was good enough to be going on with, and certainly they were not so virile as in the first half.

At any rate they were quite good enough to retain the lead, and to send the United home without so much the consolation of a goal. The Athletic had quite a good side in the field, though Roberts is still unable to appear, and they were disappointed in Crawshaw, of Accrington Stanley, being unable to lead the attack, as was anticipated would be the case. On the other hand, the United were quite an unknown quantity, and the only players I could recognise were Halligan and Woodcock. Certainly a better stamp of men will be required when the League competition is resumed. But after all, Saturday was really no fit day to judge the merits of any player.

OLDHAM'S SOLID DEFENCE.

There were many capable exponents engaged, however, and the defence of Matthews, Hodson, and Goodwin was excellent. Matthews was like a cat in goal, and once more Goodwin greatly impressed me. He has certainly come to stay in first-class football, for he possesses all the traits of a high-grade exponent. Hodson defended bravely, though apparently he on several occasions urged the referee to stop the game. I have seen the Oldham half-backs to greater advantage, Wilson being easily the best of the trio, and he made some capital attempts to score.

The forwards were good and bad in turns, with Cashmore the best of the bunch. He was full of fire, and had Donnachie displayed the same enthusiasm the United defenders would have had a worrying time. Douglas never struck me as a real leader of the attack, and Wolstenholme might be regarded as the second best forward. Knight evidently prefers a dry pitch. Whilst not so solid, in a double sense, as the Athletic trio, the play of the United defenders was very satisfactory. Swann made many good saves, and he was clearly unsighted when he was beaten by Wolstenholme.

Lucas, of Eccles Borough, was making his first appearance with the club at right full-back, and his debut was an eminently satisfactory one. And, by the way, all three defenders were ex-Eccles Borough players in addition to Walker, the centre half-back, and Mr. R. Tomlinson, the Eccles secretary, was present at the match to lend his moral support as it were. He would certainly be satisfied with the display of Lucas, and Barlow is a greatly improved defender.

Athletic News, 13 March 1916

Arthur Whalley (front, second left) and Sandy Turnbull (middle, third left) were war casualties.

1918

Bentley (seated, centre) with the rest of the Football League Management Committee in 1903. He was one of the most influential men in football.

MR. J. J. BENTLEY.

DEATH OF A PROMINENT FOOTBALL LEGISLATOR.

A Great Authority on the Game.

Manchester Evening News, 2 September 1918

ON 2 SEPTEMBER 1918 one of Manchester United's – and the Football League's – outstanding administrators died. Possibly more than any other man, John James Bentley was responsible for the spread of football in Lancashire. Born in 1860 at Turton, the home of Lancashire football, he took up playing as a 16-year-old when Turton found themselves a player short. And so began a long and distinguished association with the game. Within two seasons he had won his county cap and had become secretary and treasurer of the Turton club. He later joined the Bolton Association club but in 1884, when his playing career was cut short by an accident, he moved into administration. He took over as secretary of Bolton Wanderers, a post he held, save for a short break, until 1897.

When William McGregor had mooted the idea of a Football League, Bentley's Bolton had been one of the first teams to respond positively. It was therefore fitting that when McGregor retired as president of the League in 1893 he should be succeeded by his disciple. Bentley held the post until 1910, leading the Football League out of its Victorian amateur ways and into the age of professionalism.

Bentley first became associated with Manchester United in 1902 when John Davies took control of the club after it had been reformed following its financial collapse. Davies needed someone at the helm who understood football and who better than the president of the League itself? Consequently, Bentley was offered the chairmanship of United, a post he continued to hold until 1908. During that period he recommended his old friend, Ernest Mangnall, to the board as secretary and helped straighten out the financial plight of the club.

With Mangnall's departure to Manchester City in 1912 Bentley took over the job of secretary/manager. But he was not altogether successful. There were dressing room rows and arguments over benefit matches, as well as the controversial transfers of Charlie Roberts and Alex Bell. Results were poor and the stress affected Bentley's health, so he stepped down from team management in 1914, handing the job on to John Robson. He continued as secretary, however, until his resignation in 1916.

Bentley was also a journalist and contributed a regular column to the *Bolton Evening News* during the 1880s. He later wrote for the *Athletic News* and joined its staff, becoming editor between 1892 and 1900. He was a referee as well and the founder of inter-league matches, refereeing the first ever inter-league game between the Football League and the Scottish League. On occasion, he was also known to have written up match reports for the *Athletic News* of games he had actually refereed, though in those days reporters always had pseudonyms. As president of the Football League, chairman of one of its leading clubs, editor of the biggest-selling sports newspaper and a league referee, Bentley wielded considerable influence throughout the many avenues of the game.

In the history of our national sport, Bentley is a much forgotten figure, often overshadowed by the League founder William McGregor and the longest serving president, John McKenna of Liverpool. Nevertheless, his contribution to the birth and spread of the game was equally outstanding and his association with Manchester United of paramount importance during those difficult early years of the 20th century when the club stood on the brink of collapse. He was a quiet, unassuming man and a good listener who usually got his way through charm and tact rather than aggression. 'If you wish to successfully handle a league team,' he once said, 'never show any favouritism; treat the players as men first and professional footballers afterwards.'

1919

ON SATURDAY, 30 August 1919 league football finally resumed after its four-year disruption. The war had already been over for several months, but its conclusion had come too late for the authorities to organise a new season, and so the reintroduction of league soccer had to wait.

It began precisely as it would had the 1915/16 season commenced with the same teams in the same leagues. United remained in the first division and kicked off against Derby County who had won promotion just as hostilities brought an end to the game. But it was a very different United who travelled to the Baseball Ground that summer's day. Gone were many of the stars who had shot them to fame. George Wall had signed for Oldham Athletic, O'Connell had gone to Dumbarton, Hunter to Portsmouth and Robert Beale to Gillingham, while Sandy Turnbull had been killed in action, Enoch West had been banned and Billy Meredith was in dispute over his transfer. The only remaining names from the pre-war period were John Mew, Arthur Whalley, Montgomery and Woodcock, all of whom were now four years older.

In place of their lost stars, manager John Robson had been grooming a brood of young players such as Clarence Hilditch, Charlie Moore and John Silcock. Centre half Hilditch had arrived at Old Trafford from Altrincham in 1916 and immediately went into the first team when league football resumed. He remained there, almost a permanent fixture, until 1932 and made 322 appearances. Charlie Moore had also arrived from non-league soccer, joining United in 1919 from Hednesford Town. Over the next 11 years his full back partnership with John Silcock was regarded as one of the surest in the league. He played just over 300 games for the club yet never managed to get on the scoresheet. John Silcock played even more games – 449 – and scored a couple of goals over the next 15 years and won three England caps.

On the first day of peacetime football, huge crowds gathered everywhere, with 258,000 spectators at the 11 first division games alone and half a million watching all three divisions, despite the fact that admission had doubled from six pence to one shilling. There were 40,000 at Highbury, 35,000 at Everton but, sadly, only 12,000 at Derby. Before the war this fixture might have been a clash of the giants, attracting many more spectators as the two masters of the game, Billy Meredith of United and Steve Bloomer of Derby, faced each other. But they were no more.

United opened the scoring after half an hour through Woodcock and held out nervously until eight minutes from time when Derby equalised. It was a frantic final period; the United goal was under constant bombardment and, by all accounts, United were lucky to survive. But survive they did and although they never challenged for title or Cup they ended the season in a respectable 12th place.

The United team that played during the first peacetime season in 1919. There were many new faces in the side.

The Real League Football Resumed.

Athletic News, 1 September 1919

1920

In the years after the first world war, football attendances were extremely high as pent-up demand for 'real' soccer, combined with greater leisure time, meant that the crowds came flocking back to football grounds. Few places could compare with the attractions of Old Trafford.

RECORD CROWDS AT THE HOLIDAY GAMES.

VILLA'S TRIUMPH.

72,000 SPECTATORS.

Manchester United Home Failure.

Sporting Chronicle, 28 December 1920

THE YEARS IMMEDIATELY following the war saw a massive increase in football attendances. Suddenly everyone was free to indulge in leisure without the burden of guilt that had accompanied soccer during the 1914–18 period. The nation returned to peacetime work and, although unemployment was a feature of the 1920s, the economy built up a head of steam as it returned to manufacturing the goods that were so desperately needed. For those in work this meant they had higher wages, overtime bonuses and greater purchasing power. In many industries the five-and-a-half-day week was common while cheap rail excursions and more extensive coverage in newspapers all helped popularise the game.

The average gate at any first division match was around 22,000 shortly after the war while even second division fixtures attracted average crowds of 12,000. Not surprisingly, Old Trafford reflected the nation's growing interest in the sport. Gates of 40–50,000 were not unusual, although the average was nearer 30,000. It came as only a mild surprise then that at Christmas 1920 there were the largest ever crowds for a weekend football programme, with the gate at Old Trafford the highest of all.

On 27 December, 70,504 spectators paid to see United play Aston Villa in the first division – a record attendance to watch United at Old Trafford which still stands today. The *Sporting Chronicle* put the figure even higher, at 72,000, but the official record has since downgraded the figure. It is not the highest attendance at an Old Trafford game, that remains for the FA Cup semi-final between Wolves and Grimsby in 1939 when 76,962 were crammed into every available nook and cranny in Old Trafford. Ironically, the day following the great crowd against Villa, United played the Corinthians in a friendly and, although they fielded their first team, only 3,000 turned up. There could hardly have been a greater contrast between the two games, with the vast empty spaces of Old Trafford echoing to the players' shouts.

For the record United were squarely beaten 3–1 by Villa. The Midlanders led by a single goal at half time, though United might have pulled themselves back into the game had they not unluckily struck the bar on a couple of occasions. But, after 27 minutes of the second half, Villa made it 2–0. When Harrison pulled one back for United it must have been greeted with the mightiest roar Old Trafford had ever heard but Villa quickly stepped up a gear and added a third to give them a deserved victory. As the crowds spilled out of the ground the club realised how fortunate it was that it had had the foresight to build such a large stadium. Although it had been something of a white elephant for many years, leading to heavy debts, it was about to pay its way handsomely and give United a secure financial footing for the immediate years ahead.

A FAMOUS INTERNATIONAL IN A NEW ROLE.

Athletic News, 8 August 1921

1921

Above: Billy Meredith was still the focus of attention over 30 years after he had left the club. Matt Busby and Johnny Carey are among his audience.

Below: The Welsh Wizard displays his collection of awards.

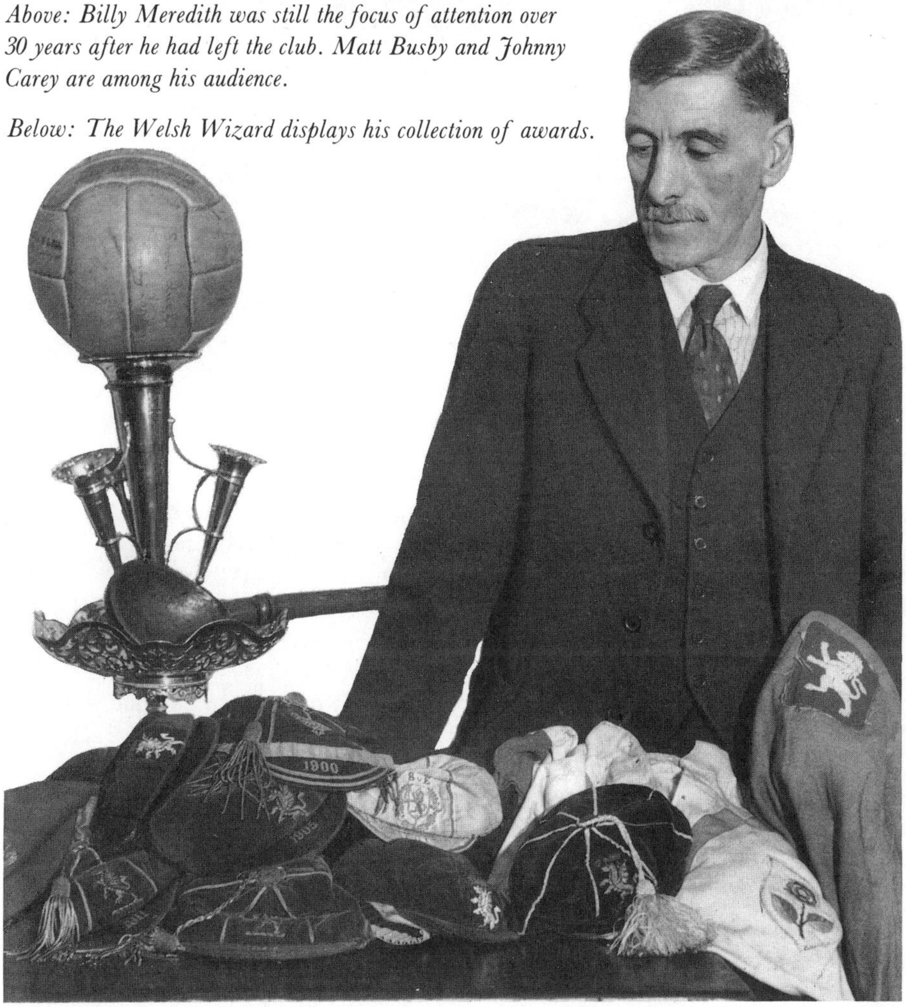

UNITED'S TIES with an Edwardian era that had brought them league and Cup glory were finally severed during the 1921 close season when the incomparable Billy Meredith signed for rivals Manchester City. Meredith had sensationally crossed the city in 1906, joining United from the Hyde Road club. Now, he was on his way back after 332 games in United's colours to become City's new player-coach. Surprisingly, he had scored only 35 goals in his 14 years at United yet the goals he had created with his dazzling runs and razor-sharp crosses were too many to count.

Meredith had been guesting for City during the war and had sought a transfer when hostilities ceased. United, however, had demanded a fee for the Welsh international, but Meredith, as principled and belligerent as ever, refused to move if any payments were made, arguing that they were not pieces of merchandise to be sold to the highest bidder. So, he remained on United's books for an unhappy period, reluctantly making 21 appearances in the first season after the war and then 14 appearances the next season. Eventually, United relented and their most famous player was on his way back to Manchester City where he would end his days, playing his final game at the grand old age of 50.

In all he made 670 appearances for the two Manchester clubs and scored 181 goals. He was capped 48 times by Wales and scored 11 goals for his country. He had been a founding member of the Players' Union and a continual thorn in the side of the footballing authorities. He was both enigmatic and contradictory, yet as a player he had few equals. He stood for fairness, demanding that players be treated like decent human beings, yet found himself at the centre of at least one bribery scandal. He was perhaps not always as innocent as he seemed and at times could be unnecessarily awkward and demanding. He was never cowardly and was always eager to test his skills against combative full backs, always prepared to push the ball past opponents and beat them in the sprint. On the field, he was unmistakable with his shrew-like physique, his well-groomed moustache and distinctive toothpick gripped between his teeth. He may have caused a few problems for the management but the crowds at Old Trafford loved him and sorely missed their favourite in the years ahead.

1921

Chapman makes his point to one of his best signings – Frank Barson.

SINCE THE END of the first world war United had wound up in 12th and 13th spot in the first division and had shown little appetite for the FA Cup. The new season, 1921/22, began with a sequence of poor results. They were thrashed 5–0 at Everton and then lost 3–2 to West Brom, though they recovered sufficiently to beat the Merseysiders 2–1 in the return at Old Trafford a week later. Three consecutive goalless draws then followed before they lost at Preston. They had just five points from seven games and had already sunk into the relegation zone. Manager John Robson was ill and, although he was soldiering on admirably, the burden of responsibility was doing neither him nor the club much good. So it was agreed that he should step down to play a less taxing role in the club's affairs and a new manager took over.

The man appointed to the hot seat was John Chapman, a Scot who had been in charge at Airdrieonians for the past 15 years and turned them into one of the foremost clubs in Scotland. It was ironic that one of Chapman's final acts at Airdrie was to sign a young Lanarkshire lad called Hughie Gallacher who, over the next few years, led Airdrie to the Scottish Cup and the runners-up spot in the Scottish league. Chapman had himself played as an amateur with Glasgow Rangers, but had had a largely undistinguished playing career. At United he was given a five-year contract and a four-figure salary plus a house, while John Robson agreed to take on the less arduous task as his assistant.

But Chapman could not turn the tide. The deterioration continued and by the end of the season United could boast just eight victories and finished in bottom place with 28 points. Gates slumped, with only a couple of fixtures attracting more than 30,000 fans to Old Trafford. Perhaps Chapman wished he had stayed north of the border, as Airdrie prepared to take the Scottish first division by storm while United faced the forthcoming season in the second division.

Manchester United's Manager.

John Chapman, who takes up his duties as manager of Manchester United, on November 1, has been in charge of the Airdrieonians' club for the past fifteen years. To them he has been more than manager—he has been guide, philosopher, and friend. In an unostentatious way, he has done much to make the Airdrieonians one of the foremost clubs in the Scottish League.

J. Chapman, Airdrie.
Photo, E. Hulton & Co., Ltd.

He is a shrewd judge of a player, for he was one himself, having signed an amateur form for the Rangers during the period when the Ibrox forward line contained such famous men as R. C. Hamilton and Finlay Speedie. He was an outside right.

His engagement with the United is for five years, and his salary runs into four figures, in addition to which the club will provide him with a house.

These are generous terms, but those who know John Chapman believe that the club will have no reason to regret the bargain if he is not interfered with.

John Robson, having done a very great deal to put Manchester United in such a position that the club has a prospect, for the first time since the laying out of the Old Trafford ground, has been made the assistant-manager.

During his tenure of office John Robson has discovered many fine players such as Silcock, the international, and Clarence Hilditch, the Inter-League half-back, besides others—and he has, at little cost, built up a team capable of earning a profit, so it is stated, of £29,591 in the last two seasons.

Wherever John Robson has been he has proved himself a rare schemer in extricating clubs from difficulties, and he has always declared that he would make way for somebody else as soon as Manchester United was on the way to prosperity.

To a large extent the road has been cleared for John Chapman, who will not have the financial worries of the past years.

Athletic News, 10 October 1921

1922

DESPITE THEIR new manager the slide continued. Chapman worked doggedly but he could not find a winning formula. Indeed, they had almost fared better before he arrived. After 1 November, when he took charge, they won only one game in the next three months. City thrashed them 4–1, Middlesbrough 5–3 and Burnley 4–2. United were bottom of the league and seemed glued to their ignominious position. The defence was leaking goals and the attack could not find its shooting boots. On only three occasions under Chapman did they manage to score more than two goals in a game. At the end of the season Joe Spence was the leading marksman with a mere 15 goals, followed by Sapsford with nine.

UNITED'S FAREWELL.

Pugh Makes a Promising Start at Old Trafford.

Manchester U.....1 Cardiff City.......1

[BY JACQUES.]

FOR a season at least the curtain rung down at Old Trafford on Saturday on First Division football. The result, a draw of one goal each was very fair, for with a strong breeze blowing down the ground each side had their period of supremacy. Mid-week accidents in a Welsh charity match robbed the United of the services of Silcock and M'Bain, so that Pugh, from Abertillery, entered First Division football as the left-back, while Harris reappeared in the home half-back line at centre-half.

Cardiff City had Evans at outside left and Kneeshaw in goal. The United had the wind with them in the first half, and they played better football than they had shown for most of the season. They were powerful in defence, and Hilditch at right half-back played a perfect game, while Harrison, doubled, ran, and centred like the Harrison of years ago. The tragedy of it, for the 18,000 spectators, was that the whole thing did not matter so far as the relegation business was concerned.

Athletic News, 1 May 1922

Generally, it was a dismal performance all round and, by Christmas, it was obvious that United were doomed for the second division. Results did not pick up in the New Year either and their final 10 games of the season brought just one win, seven defeats and two draws. It was little wonder they finished bottom with only 28 points.

LEAGUE, DIV. 1.

TOO LATE.

Old Trafford Men Surprise the Athletic.

RADFORD SUPREME.

Oldham Athletic...1 Manchester U......1

[BY JACQUES.]

PLAYING the best football they had shown for weeks, Manchester United won a point at Oldham on Saturday. A week previous, at Old Trafford, the Athletic had played the United almost to a standstill, and prior to the start on Saturday, the position was that the Athletic needed two points to give them absolute security, whereas the foe were a doomed club.

Athletic News, 24 April 1922

Joe Spence, a Northumbrian, had joined United in March 1919 from Scotswood and remained at Old Trafford until June 1933, when he signed for Bradford City. During that time he made 510 appearances for the club, a record which stood until bettered 40 years later by Billy Foulkes. Although the goals did not come often during the 1921/22 season, he was top scorer or joint top scorer on seven occasions, hitting 24 goals during the 1927/28 season. He was always adaptable, not just slotting into the centre forward role, but often playing on the wing where he would delight the Old Trafford faithful with his adventurous, carefree runs.

Spence was one of United's greatest servants, scoring 168 goals in all. Despite this, he was capped only twice by England.

1923

NOTTS COLLAPSE.

Goldthorpe in Great Scoring Mood.

*Manchester U.....6 *Notts County....1*

[By Jacques.]

ONE of the sensations of the season was provided by Manchester United on Saturday, when at Meadow-lane, Nottingham, they routed the forces of the leaders of the Second Division by such a score as six goals to one. Notts County had Flint at right half-back for Kemp, and the United played Thomas, their reserve outside left, on the extreme right wing—a daring experiment which, it may at once be said, was quite successful.

Athletic News, 12 February 1923

WHEN MANCHESTER UNITED visited Notts County on 12 February 1923, County were riding high at the top of the second division, while United were in sixth place finding their first season back in the division more difficult than they had anticipated. It had been a tough opening half to the season, with too many points sloppily thrown away against teams of mediocre calibre. But suddenly, with what the *Athletic News* called 'one of the sensations of the season', United turned on the style everyone knew they were capable of as they thrashed the league leaders 6–1.

In Albert Iremonger, County boasted not only one of the greatest goalkeeping names of the day but, at 6 feet 6 inches, the tallest player in the league. He was now getting on in years and his experience could be said to far outmatch his agility. And, that afternoon at the County Ground, he was forced to scramble six times in the back of his net to retrieve the ball; rarely had he been so humiliated. Yet we should not detract from United's outstanding victory by blaming it on Iremonger. United were simply superb that day and Iremonger could be faulted for only one goal.

Oddly enough, it was County who shot into the lead in the seventh minute and their 10,000 supporters must have reckoned they were in for another fine County win. But it was not to turn out that way. Two minutes later Goldthorne levelled the scoring and United began to recover from the early shock. In the 22nd minute Myerscough shot them into the lead and then added a third before half time. In the second half the rout continued with Goldthorne hitting a hat trick between the 62nd and 66th minute. It was a truly incredible result.

The man of the match had been Frank Barson, a Sheffield man who had been a blacksmith before turning professional footballer. He had started his career with Barnsley and then moved to Aston Villa where he won a Cup-winners' medal in 1920. United signed him two years later for £5,000 with the added promise of the proprietary of a public house should United be promoted within three years. They were, but the story goes that when Frank opened the doors of his new pub he was swamped in the rush and decided there and then that running a pub was not the life for him. During his five years at Old Trafford he made 152 appearances at centre half before moving to Watford. A typical no-nonsense Yorkshireman, his career was blemished by regular suspension after numerous sendings-off. He was always a little too quick to retaliate and was once said to have threatened his manager at Aston Villa with a gun. All of this may well account for the fact that in spite of being a fine centre half he won only one England cap. And, to show that age does not necessarily mellow one, he was even sent off in the last game of his professional career.

United's victory that chilly February day began a sequence of good fortune that helped them to make rapid progress up the league. But, just when they needed a little more help to carry them over the threshold, their luck deserted them. They lost to both Blackpool and Leicester as the season wound to its climax and, instead of promotion, they finished in fourth place and had to face another year in the lower reaches. Notts County meanwhile were promoted to the first division as champions.

Frank Barson, although smiling here, was a fiery customer on the pitch but his talent cannot be denied.

1924

Although already aged 32 when he joined Manchester United in 1923, Frank Mann was to be a regular player in the side until his last league game in November 1929. His experience was vital to a side which struggled to maintain its position in the first division. To strengthen the midfield, he dropped back from his more usual position of inside forward. The season after he left, United were relegated.

AFTER A SEASON as a second division outfit United quickly had the chance to test their talents against a first division side when they drew Huddersfield Town out of the hat for the second round of the FA Cup. The tie attracted enormous attention and was billed as the match of the round.

It was a Huddersfield Town team that was being talked about wherever it travelled. They were managed by Herbert Chapman who, until 1920, had been the manager of Leeds City. In the short time that he had been at Huddersfield his team had already won the Cup, beating Preston in the 1922 final, and had been third in the league the previous season. When the two teams met at Old Trafford in early February 1924 Huddersfield were lying in fourth place in the first division while United were struggling halfway up the second. In the United line-up that day was a former Huddersfield player, Frank Mann, who had been part of the team that had won the 1922 FA Cup. Mann was what the modern game would call a midfielder but was reckoned by many to be past his best when he signed for United at the age of 32. But he had a few more years' service to provide and went on to make almost 200 appearances for United. Yet, at the end of his career, he must have reflected on whether his move to Old Trafford was a wise one considering the honours which were about to befall Huddersfield.

Much was expected of Town in the 1923/24 season and they did not disappoint. In time, Chapman became the finest manager of all, as his Huddersfield, and later Arsenal, sides each completed a hat trick of championship victories. Their arrival at Old Trafford drew a vast crowd of 66,678, the largest of the day, all eager to see the side that was setting the first division alight. Nobody was disgruntled by what they saw and even diehard United supporters had to applaud the quality of their Yorkshire visitors.

After a fiercely fought victory over Plymouth Argyle at Old Trafford in the first round, United fans reckoned they were ready to create a major upset. But there was little chance of that happening. Within 15 minutes United were reeling as Charles Wilson opened the account and by the half hour Clem Stephenson had shot Huddersfield into a two-goal lead. Sadly, the gulf between United and the first division side was all too apparent. Wilson added a third in the second half and Town cantered to an easy victory. But there were lessons to be learned and within the year United were striding towards the first division themselves. But for some time they, and the rest of the Football League, had to remain in awe of Huddersfield who, after defeating United, went on to become champions for the next three seasons.

TOWN TRIUMPH.

Story of Manchester United's Disaster.

TWO GREAT GOALS.

*Huddersfield T....3 *Manchester U....0*

[BY JACQUES.]

STRONG contrasts were to be noticed in the Cup-tie played at Old Trafford on Saturday on a dull grey afternoon, with a powerful breeze blowing from goal to goal, and before the greatest assembly of the public attracted in the ties of the day.

Each eleven had a left wing moulded on somewhat similar lines. Manchester United had M'Pherson and Lochhead. The inside man a clever dribbler, his partner gifted with speed. Huddersfield Town had Smith and Stephenson—the inside player an adept at footwork, and the outside man very fast.

Beyond all question the Huddersfield pair were the greater combination. For one thing they had the better understanding. M'Pherson did not co-operate with his partner. When he received his pass he ran hard ahead, and his one idea was a centre or a shot.

A Useful Move.

Smith not only ran fast but used brains, and his short, backward pass to Stephenson, made when the attempt at a centre was expected, always looked a dangerous move on the board. Stephenson yielded nothing to Lochhead in skill, and he was the greater schemer and the more forceful player of the two.

Huddersfield Town, then, were the stronger side so far as the left wing were concerned. Let us compare the two centre-forwards. Henderson, of Manchester United, was never an effective figure. He had little to do with the feeding of his outside men—Barson was largely left to that task, and did it well. He made but one shot of any note, and generally he seemed an industrious worker never getting there.

Charles Wilson was of a different type. He moved deftly, swept the ball out to either side of him, was quick to bring the ball to his boot and shoot, and very thrustful. There was little difference in the effectiveness of the opposing right wings, save that Walter had greater speed than Spence—a fact which he clearly demonstrated to the discomfiture of the United defence in the second half.

There was not a weak half-back on the field. Steele, despite an influenza cold—I believe it was left to him whether he was fit to play or no—acquitted himself well, and so did the others, with Barson the most powerful worker and the personality of the six.

Barson did all that man could do behind an ineffective forward line. He was as sound in attack as he was in defence, and ever in the thick of the fray with head and with foot.

He combined judgment with his strength. Very early in the game Barkas, by his great dash, ascertained supremacy over M'Pherson, and in the second half Wadsworth played a masterly game.

Athletic News, 4 February 1924

1925

AFTER JUST THREE years in the lower league United fought their way back into the first division. Almost from the start they were challenging, stringing seven wins together during the autumn of 1924 which immediately pushed them ahead of the pack. They did not always maintain the momentum, losing eight games and drawing another 11, but, by the end of the season, they were neatly sandwiched two points ahead of Derby County in third spot and two points behind champions Leicester City.

Promotion was virtually assured on Saturday, 25 April 1925 against Port Vale at Old Trafford, leaving Derby County with only the faintest mathematical possibility of overtaking them. The 40,000 Old Trafford crowd knew better and United were crowned there and then. It was a pulsating performance with Arthur Lochhead firing them into the lead after just three minutes. Spence hit a second in the 10th minute and United were well on their way to the first division. Smith and McPherson added a couple more in the second half and, as the final whistle blew, all that mattered was the result at Coventry, where Derby were struggling to stay in the race. Nobody left Old Trafford; the United players hovered anxiously around the sidelines while the crowd nervously awaited the tannoy announcement. When it came, there was as deafening a cheer as Old Trafford had ever heard. Derby had drawn 0–0 and only a United defeat in the final fixture and a huge Derby victory could alter the course of history. Clearly neither was going to happen. United were back where they belonged.

Heading the goalscoring list was Billy Henderson who had been transferred halfway through the season after scoring 14 goals in just 22 appearances. He had moved on to Preston North End to pay for the arrival of Albert Pape, surely one of United's strangest signings. United had telephoned his club, Clapton Orient, at 4pm on the Friday evening of 6 February 1925 to open negotiations. The following day Orient were due at Old Trafford for a league fixture and, when they arrived at 1pm, the club began discussions with the player himself. He quickly agreed terms and, having arrived to play against United, he suddenly found himself in their colours and lining up against Orient. His former team-mates were unaware that he was about to desert their ranks until they were inspecting the pitch an hour before kick-off. Pape, however, lasted only 18 games, despite scoring on his debut, and he too was on his way before the year was out. Arthur Lochhead, who hit 13 goals, was another who joined the transfer merry-go-round of 1925. He had been with United since 1921 when he joined them from Hearts but, the following season, after only five more appearances, he moved to Leicester City. It was a serious mistake by United as they watched him shoot Leicester into the runners-up spot during the 1928/29 season and score 105 goals in little over 300 appearances.

But most of the credit for United's

DERBY ONLY DRAW.

But Manchester United Make No Mistake.

RELEGATION UNCERTAINTY

THE LEAGUE.—Second Division.

Barnsley	1	*Chelsea	0
Halliwell.			
*Clapton Orient	1	Portsmouth	1
Shea.		Mackie.	
*Coventry City	0	Derby County	0
Fulham	2	*Crystal Palace	1
Edmunds, Wolfe.		Blakemore.	
*Leicester City	1	Bradford City	0
Carr.			
*Manchester U.	4	Port Vale	0
Lochhead, Spence, Smith, M'Pherson.			
*Oldham Ath.	4	Blackpool	1
Pilkington, Heaton, Gillespie, Wynne.		Bedford.	
*The Wednesday	5	Hull City	0
Trotter (2), Barrass, Marsden, Powell.			
*Southampton	1	Wolv'rhamt'n W.	1
Price.		Lees.	
*Stockport Coun.	1	Middlesbrough	1
Meads.		Williams	
*Stoke	0	South Shields	0

RESULTS TO DATE.

	Pld.	Won	Lost	Drn.	Goals For	Goals Agst.	Pts.
Leicester City	41	23	7	11	86	32	57
Manchester Utd.	41	23	8	10	57	23	56
Derby County	41	22	9	10	69	34	54
Portsmouth	41	14	9	18	53	50	46
Chelsea	41	15	11	15	49	36	45
Wolverhampton	40	19	15	6	54	50	44
Hull City	41	15	15	11	50	48	41
Port Vale	41	17	17	7	47	55	41
Southampton	40	11	11	18	35	36	40
South Shields	41	11	13	17	41	38	39
Clapton O.	41	14	16	11	42	42	39
Middlesbrough	41	10	12	19	36	43	39
Fulham	41	15	17	9	40	55	39
Bradford City	40	13	15	12	37	43	38
Wednesday	41	15	19	7	50	56	37
Stockport C.	41	13	17	11	37	53	37
Blackpool	41	14	19	8	63	59	36
Stoke	41	12	18	11	33	44	35
Barnsley	40	12	17	11	45	59	35
Oldham Ath.	41	12	18	11	34	51	35
Crystal Palace	41	12	19	10	38	53	34
Coventry City	41	11	21	9	45	81	31

Empire News, 26 April 1925

NEARING HARBOUR.

Manchester United Help Themselves Against Port Vale

Manchester United gave one of their most convincing displays against Port Vale yesterday, and their four goals victory did not flatter them in the least.

With promotion practically assured there were big scenes of enthusiasm at the finish from a crowd that must have numbered close on 40,000.

It was a great wind-up to what has been a memorable season, and though at times play was a trifle scrappy there were other times when some really good football was seen.

Particularly was this the case when Spence and Smith, the United right wing, were in action. Indeed, Spence played a very big part in the victory, and besides scoring once he was the indirect means of two other goals.

Lochhead was frequently prominent, and M'Pherson was in better trim than he has been for some weeks. There was not really a weak link in the line, but undoubtedly Spence and Smith were the stars.

Barson was a powerful figure in the half-back line, with Grimwood next, and further behind both Moore and Jones were sound and solid defenders.

Steward did his bit well, and his vis-a-vis, Brown, though he might have prevented the fourth goal, had little chance with the others.

Of the Vale backs, I liked Cooper, a youngster of 19 years, who should go far. Briscoe was as good as any of a rather overplayed half-back line, and St range the leading light amongst the forwards. Kirkham was not nearly so conspicuous as usual, and Lowe, at outside right, was the pick of the extreme men.

Two Quick Goals.

Though facing the breeze United opened so strongly that within ten minutes they were a couple of goals up, and might easily have been more.

The first was the outcome of a fine run and centre by Spence, who cut in and placed the ball so well that Lochhead had little difficulty in scoring.

A terrific drive by Smith whizzed past the Port Vale upright, and then M'Pherson put the ball across for Smith to return and Spence to head into the net.

As the half progressed the visitors improved, and Strange made two good attempts. Kirkham headed wide when he had a real chance of scoring.

A minute after the resumption United went further ahead. Again it was Spence who made the position, beating the back and centring low for Smith to place it out of Brown's reach.

A little later Smith had hard lines. With the goalkeeper out of position he hooked the ball against the base of the upright, and it rolled right along the goal-line and out.

At the other end Steward saved, and then came a great goal from M'Pherson, who, standing on the touchline, drove in a ball that quite baffled Brown.

The Vale made several efforts to break through, but generally the Manchester men held the upper hand, and were good winners at the end.

Most of the crowd waited on, and when the result of the Derby game came through there was wild enthusiasm. The United players remained on the field whilst the band played "Auld Lang Syne." Altogether a great day.

performance that season must go to the defence which conceded only 23 goals, a record which stood for many years. It was pretty much the same defence as had served the club since the beginning of the 1920s. Hilditch and Barson were still at the heart of it with Charlie Moore and Jack Silcock behind them. In goal was the reliable Alf Steward who finally succeeded John Mew in 1923. Between then and 1932 he was always the first name on the teamsheet, making 326 appearances and even finding time to do a little batting for Lancashire. The man he replaced, John Mew, was now nearing the end of his career, only donning the goalkeeper's jersey when Steward was injured. Mew, however, had played almost 200 games for the club, with most of those coming between 1919 and 1923. In 1920, he represented England against Ireland but left Old Trafford in 1926 for Barrow before coaching in Belgium and South America.

Mew makes an important save during his brief comeback in 1926.

1926

SUSPENSION OF FOOTBALL MANAGER

For the Remainder of the Season.

F.A. AND MANCHESTER UNITED.

Mr. J. A. Chapman, of the Manchester United Football Club, has been suspended by the F.A.

The following official notice was issued by Mr. Wall, secretary of the F.A., yesterday afternoon:—

"For improper conduct in his position as Secretary-Manager of the Manchester United Football Club, the Football Association have suspended Mr. J. A. Chapman from taking part in football or football management during the present season."

The F.A. Commission first met to inquire into certain affairs connected with the United club on September 20 at the Grand Hotel, Manchester. They later met at Sheffield a week later, where it was thought that they would announce their decision.

Mr. Chapman has been at Old Trafford for five years, having been signed on a five years' agreement when he came from Airdrieonians. The contract is due to expire in November.

When Mr. Chapman was engaged by United his salary was a four-figure one, and at that time he was one of the highest-paid managers in the football world.

Sporting Chronicle, 8 October 1926

MANCHESTER UNITED

Hilditch Appointed as Temporary Manager.

POPULAR PLAYER.

Sporting Chronicle, 9 October 1926

Clarence Hilditch leads out the team at White Hart Lane only months before he took over as player manager.

ON 20 SEPTEMBER 1926 a Football Association investigating committee under Frederick Wall met at the Grand Hotel in Manchester to begin an inquiry into the affairs of Manchester United. They continued their deliberations in Sheffield a week later and then met again in Manchester during the first week in October. Little news of the investigation leaked out, but then on Thursday, 7 October they announced to an astonished footballing public that United manager John Chapman was to be suspended from football. 'For improper conduct in his position as secretary-manager of the Manchester United Football Club,' read their short statement, 'the FA have suspended Mr J A Chapman from taking part in football or football management during the present season.'

Nothing further was added and no explanation was given. There was silence everywhere. Chapman packed his bags and quietly left, never to return. To this day, the truth remains a dark secret. His dismissal raised a few eyebrows, although, in those days of sober reporting, there was not even any speculation in the press as to what had happened.

In his place United sensibly appointed Clarence Hilditch as temporary player-manager. To date he remains the only player-manager in the club's history. Born near Northwich in Cheshire, Hilditch played amateur football with Witton Albion and Altrincham before signing for United in 1916. After the war, he became a regular first team choice and remained a permanent fixture in the half-back line for the next dozen years. He was a dependable player, popular with his colleagues and loyal to the club, remaining with United until 1932. He was never honoured by England, although he did play in the Victory International against Wales in 1919 and against South Africa in the 1920 Commonwealth internationals but neither game warranted a cap.

Hilditch took over at Old Trafford at a difficult time and, knowing that his appointment was always temporary, he could hardly stamp his own ideas on the club. All he could do was to make sure United ticked over smoothly until a replacement appeared. In the event, Hilditch was in the manager's seat only until the end of the season but crucially he kept United in the first division so that the new manager at least had a secure foundation to build for the future.

1927

CLARRIE HILDITCH was always only a temporary appointment and, after just seven months in the job, United handed Herbert Bamlett the onerous task of managing the club. No doubt impressed by the fact that Bamlett had taken Middlesbrough to the top of the second division and the brink of promotion, United saw him as the man to revive their fortunes. Prior to Middlesbrough, Bamlett had managed Oldham Athletic and Wigan Borough and, in his earlier days, he had also been a league referee. His greatest claim to fame was that he had refereed the 1915 Cup final between Burnley and Liverpool. In 1909, he had also been the man who called off the Burnley/Manchester United Cup tie when Burnley led 1–0 with just 18 minutes remaining. In the rearranged match United won and went on to capture the Cup. It might be said that United owed him some kind of favour for that decision!

Bamlett, however, had little influence on United's fortunes. He recruited strikers Henry Rowley and Tom Reid but, although both performed well, particularly Reid, they alone could bring little change. The season following Bamlett's appointment, United finished 18th in the league, narrowly avoiding the drop into the second division and, although they improved marginally the following season, they quickly slumped again and were relegated in 1931. Not surprisingly, that was also the year which marked the end of Bamlett's reign in the managerial chair.

UNITED'S FUTURE.

Mr. Bamlett's Task at Old Trafford.

Much interest has been aroused by the announcement that Mr. Herbert Bamlett has been appointed football manager of the Manchester United club. He will take up his new duties on Tuesday next, and the agreement entered into is one of two years.

Herbert Bamlett, writes H. P. R., has a big task in front of him, but given freedom of action I have not the least doubt that he will help to put the United once more on a sound footing. He is a man who has played the game, and his long experience should stand him in good stead now he is in charge of a club that, with a successful side, can attract an average attendance of about 40,000 for each home game.

It is, perhaps, as a referee more than a manager that I know him best.

He was one of the best conductors of a game that I ever dropped across and that he was not afraid of the home crowd as so many of the officials are to-day was shown when he stopped the English Cup-tie at Turf Moor between Burnley and Manchester United. Burnley on that occasion were leading and looked like winning. Mr. Bamlett, recognising that he made a mistake in ever allowing the game to start brought the match to an abrupt termination.

It was a little incident that will never be forgiven by Burnley people as the United won the replay and went on to annex the Cup. It was a bold step to take but nine out of ten would agree with Mr. Bamlett's action.

He is perhaps unfortunate in coming to Old Trafford when the team is on the down grade, but in my opinion there is little risk of relegation and he will find in the reserve eleven quite a host of young players who are certain next season to make quite a name in the game.

Mr. Bamlett, who has seen three years' service at Middlesbrough, has largely been responsible for building up the great side that appears certain to enter the First Division of the League.

Manchester Evening News, 2 April 1927

Herbert Bamlett as manager of Oldham. He came to Old Trafford with a good record, but could not improve matters at United.

1928

THE 1927/28 SEASON was hardly a campaign to remember, although it ended on a spectacular note as United thrashed Liverpool 6–1 to avoid relegation by the narrowest of margins.

As the season wound to its dramatic climax on Saturday, 4 May, any one of six teams could have been relegated. Sheffield Wednesday were propping up the league on 36 points with four teams above them, including United, on 37 and Spurs on 38. United probably did not fancy their chances of avoiding the big drop, although their visitors, Liverpool, were themselves only a couple of points better off despite being halfway up the table. Nevertheless, United had shown some plucky spirit towards the end of the season, winning four out of their previous six fixtures. They had slowly slipped down the table since the New Year and by March were third from bottom. But, in April, they strung together a couple of good results, beating Burnley and Bolton before losing to Bury and Sheffield United. They then beat Sunderland at Old Trafford, but still found themselves on 22 April at the foot of the table with just two games remaining.

In their penultimate fixture they beat Arsenal 1–0 at Highbury to move off the bottom and then faced Liverpool at Old Trafford, desperately needing a victory. Within 11 minutes their prayers were answered as Joe Spence shot them into the lead. Rawlings added two more quick goals before Liverpool replied and by the interval Spence had added another, giving United a surprising 4–1 lead. In the second half, Spence completed his hat trick before Hanson made it 6–1 to give them their biggest league win of the season. The 30,000 crowd could hardly believe their eyes but even then there was a nailbiting wait for confirmation that they had done enough. They had. Middlesbrough went down at Sunderland and were relegated along with Spurs. United's six goals had done their goal average no end of good. So tight was the log jam at the middle and end of the table that only seven points separated the bottom club from Derby County in fourth place.

Joe Spence's hat trick may well have saved United that day, as indeed he did on many occasions during their short sojourn in the first division. He was top scorer for the season with 24 goals in all, his best figures since his arrival from north-east amateur football in March 1919. A typical robust centre forward, he was immediately drafted into the first team and remained there until 1933, making a record 510 appearances and scoring a total of 168 goals.

Welsh international Tommy Jones, ever-reliable in defence.

THE MANCHESTER CLUBS.

Six Goals for Safety at Old Trafford.

It is wonderful what a team can accomplish when necessity knocks at the door. Requiring to defeat Liverpool, from whom they had secured only one point in the five meetings since their return from the Second Division, Manchester United found security by running up their biggest score of the season, and Liverpool retired from the pitch at Old Trafford bearing with great cheerfulness the burden of a 6—1 defeat. The first period was interesting, and Liverpool made the United fight for everything they got, and at any rate Riley, the tall South African goalkeeper, is probably still so much a South African as to care little whether any other Lancashire club (save that to which he has given allegiance) meets with disaster. He was beaten six times, once not without a degree of responsibility, but he gave a capital exhibition throughout. The United led 4—1 at half-time, and when they made it 5—1 four minutes after the restart the subsequent proceedings became at times farcical and often boring. Liverpool kept the ball rolling, but it was asking rather too much of human nature that they should work up a cup-tie spirit beneath a strong sun and possibly risk limbs in an effort to accomplish the wellnigh impossible task of getting four or five goals themselves just to send their opponents into the "wilderness."

As a matter of fact, the United were very worthy winners, and the disgruntled "supporter" who spoke of the new team that would be required next season could not, when challenged, point to a glaringly weak spot in the side as it played in this game. Rawlings led the forwards well and was a keen thruster, while Johnston and Hanson, his inside colleagues, provided progressive artistry that you might seek at Huddersfield and not always find. Thomas was not so good, but Spence scored three goals, all spectacular, and two of them the reward of prompt decision and faultless marksmanship. Mann and Wilson worked tremendously hard and earnestly until the battle was won, and young McLenahan worked to the end of an afternoon that should be one of happiest recollection for him. Moore was guilty of some uncertain clearances, but Jones gave a most polished display.

Manchester Guardian, 7 May 1928

THE SEASON'S BEST

Manchester United Learn a Vital Lesson and Score Six.

*Manchester United .... 6 Liverpool 1

Athletic News, 7 May 1928

FIGHTING TO SAFETY.

Manchester United Rout Blackburn Rovers in Thrilling Match.

Athletic News, 15 April 1929

1929

UNITED ENDED the 1928/29 season in rousing form with five wins and a draw in their final half-dozen fixtures. They had been beaten 6–1 at Derby on 30 March but replied with some creditable victories over the next few weeks. After a 1–0 win over relegation-doomed Bury, high-flyers Sunderland and Blackburn were both beaten 3–0. Next in line were the mighty Arsenal who were slammed 4–1 at Old Trafford, and then Everton, the previous season's champions, were soundly beaten 4–2 at Goodison. The season then ended in comparative calm with a goalless draw against Portsmouth.

Tom Reid (centre), a prolific forward whose 14 goals in 17 games at the end of 1928/29 transformed United's season.

It was an astonishing turnabout considering United had already lost 15 games before March was over and looked possible relegation candidates. The explanation could be found in Tom Reid, a freescoring centre forward, who had been signed from Liverpool during the early part of the year. He made just 17 appearances that season but still managed 14 goals. Reid was a Scot, born in Motherwell, who had begun his career with Clydebank. Liverpool signed him in 1926 and in 51 games over the next three years he scored 31 goals. But Liverpool had a surfeit of quality strikers and felt able to part with their centre forward when Herbert Bamlett made inquiries. Liverpool's loss turned out to be United's gain. He spent five seasons at Old Trafford, netting 67 goals in just 101 appearances before joining Oldham in March 1933. Against Blackburn, Arsenal and Everton Reid netted a couple of goals each game and it was largely thanks to him that United avoided the drop into division two.

But the credit should not go to Reid alone. He was ably assisted by James Hanson, a young Manchester lad who had been with the club since 1924. He began as understudy to centre forward Bill Henderson and did not win a regular place until the 1927/28 season when he netted 10 goals. The following season he struck 19 goals and established a lucrative partnership with Tom Reid. Unfortunately, just as he was developing into an outstanding striker, he was seriously injured on Christmas Day 1929 against Birmingham City. He never played again and Tom Reid was left to do battle alone up front.

1930

AS IF THE previous season had not been bad enough, the 1930/31 campaign was one of the worst United have ever experienced. It began disastrously and barely improved as time wore on. In their opening encounter they conceded four goals to Aston Villa, followed by three goals at Middlesbrough, while in their next three fixtures they were thrashed 6–2 at Chelsea, 6–0 by Huddersfield and 7–4 by Newcastle, both at Old Trafford. They had conceded 26 goals in five games with 17 of them coming at home. It was little wonder that Old Trafford's normally devoted support was rapidly waning. An enthusiastic 18,000 had watched the opening fixture but by the time Newcastle were running riot at Old Trafford, less than 11,000 faithful fans were in attendance.

There was much murmuring on the terraces and in September the Supporters' Club began to make uncharacteristic noises. Leaflets appeared and a five-point plan was put to the club. The supporters wanted a new manager, an improved scouting system, some signings, five shareholders co-opted to the board and money raised through a new share issue. They were serious and far-reaching demands, but, foolishly, the board ignored them. They even refused to meet with the Supporters' Club, arguing that they were an unofficial body not recognised by the club and unrepresentative of the bulk of supporters.

Yet the Supporters' Club spoke much sense and were only voicing the disenchantment of the terraces, the newspaper sports columns and even some of the players. Had results suddenly picked up or the board taken some action, everything might have been quietly forgotten. Instead, results continued to deteriorate. By the end of September they had lost all of their opening eight fixtures and were firmly anchored to the foot of the table. On 4 October they travelled across the city to Maine Road

The boycott never really came off; the organisers chose the wrong match for it.

UNITED CLUB BOYCOTT

Last Night's Decision

RESOLUTION TO STAY AWAY

At a public meeting of about 3,000 supporters of the Manchester United Football Club in the Hulme Town Hall last night it was decided by a large majority to boycott to-day's match between the United and the Arsenal, and a vote of "no confidence" in the Board of Management was passed. Except for one or two minor interruptions the meeting was carried through in an orderly manner. The Chairman (Mr. S. Masen) pointed out that the quarrel was with the management and not with the players.

Mr. Charlie Roberts, who seconded an unsuccessful resolution that the boycott be withdrawn, said the players had his deepest sympathy, and he blamed the management for the present position at Old Trafford. The management had created their own trouble, and they could not say they had never had warning.

Mr. Roberts's sympathies, however, were not with a boycott, which would not have public opinion behind it. He could not understand why the management called themselves business men, and yet were losing at least a large sum of money a week through lack of enterprise.

Mr. G. H. Greenhough, who convened the meeting, gave details of the domestic affairs of the club and quoted figures from balance-sheets. As a shareholder he was entitled to know where the money went, and the balance-sheet did not show that.

The directors of the club had refused to interview him.

Guardian, 18 October 1930

An END to MOB LAW!

Let Manchester UNITED Now PUSH ON With Their PLANS.

Athletic News, 20 October 1930

under a threat from the Supporters' Club that if the board did not react there would be a mass boycott of the Arsenal fixture on 18 October. The announcement caused headlines but the club refused to respond. So did the players as United lost 4–1. The following week they were beaten 5–1 at West Ham and the Supporters' Club immediately called a public meeting for the Friday evening of 17 October to discuss the mooted boycott.

The meeting was held at Hulme Town Hall and as many as 3,000 turned up, packing the aisles and squeezing into every available seat. There was anger; the club had stood on the brink of relegation almost every season since their return to division one, the board seemed disinclined to sign quality players, there were no star names in the team and money was being wasted as Old Trafford stood silent and empty. A resolution of 'no confidence' in the board was put to the meeting and unanimously agreed. Mr Greenhough, the secretary of the Supporters' Club, then moved a motion to boycott the following day's match. Charlie Roberts, the former captain and now a Supporters' Club nominee to be co-opted to the board, spoke against the boycott, arguing that they should be getting behind the players rather than deserting them. The argument is not with the players, he pleaded, but with the board. For once Roberts was unsuccessful and the meeting overwhelmingly voted to boycott the Arsenal game.

The visit of Cup-winners Arsenal was undoubtedly one of the attractions of the season and some newspapers spoke of a possible 50,000 gate. In the event only 23,000 made the effort, although even that was the highest attendance of the season. Heavy rain may well have discouraged some from making the trip and we shall never know precisely how many deliberately boycotted the fixture. The police had taken precautions with extra numbers on duty in case of trouble, but no attempts were made to dissuade fans from passing through the turnstiles. All the papers, of course, had been hostile to the boycott and later described it as a total failure. They had more difficulty in excusing the result. United lost 2–1 and the following week lost 4–1 at Portsmouth. The boycott may not have worked, but it was clear from the results that there was a serious problem, with nobody showing much inclination to resolve the crisis. They had now lost all 12 of their opening fixtures, scoring 14 goals and conceding 49. Needless to say, they were bottom of the table. Eventually Herbert Bamlett was fired, though not before it was too late, while the financial crisis which the Supporters' Club had foreseen tore the board apart and, for a second time, almost bankrupted United.

Charlie Roberts spoke out against the management of the club, saying they had created problems for themselves.

1931

CAN UNITED BEAT A LOW RECORD?

Points Lost in Game of Too Much Vigour.

*Blackburn Rovers..1 *Manchester United0*

Athletic News, 13 April 1931

UNITED BEGAN 1931 in as serious a predicament as they had ever encountered. They were bottom of the league, having won just two games with a mere seven points to their credit. Things barely improved in the months ahead, as they remained glued to the bottom of the division. Attendances had also slumped since the beginning of the campaign with little more than 10,000 turning up for each home fixture. By the end of the season, it had declined even further and on only one occasion, against Manchester City in February, did the attendance at Old Trafford exceed 10,000 during those latter months.

There was never any doubt that United would be relegated and the second division was beckoning long before the season was over. The only question was whether they would break all records. They did. In their final fixture they drew 4–4 with Middlesbrough at Old Trafford in front of a mere 3,900. There was an uncanny feeling inside the ground that afternoon, with empty terraces and shouts echoing around the rafters. The only jewel on display that day was Middlesbrough's goalscoring ace George Camsell who struck four goals. When United studied the statistics at the end of the crusade they made for depressing reading. They had lost 27 games, winning only seven

AT LOWEST EBB.

Record Equalled at Manchester.

CAMSELL BLOW.

**Manchester United4 Middlesbrough....4*
(Half-time: 2—3.)
By WANDERER.

IT is sad to relate that interest in the affairs of Manchester United is at the lowest ebb. Only 4,000 spectators saw the game with Middlesbrough, which rang down the curtain on a season that has been disastrous in more senses than one for the Old Trafford club.

It even terminated with them having their name written down in records, for, relegated with 22 points, they now share with Middlesbrough the unenviable distinction of going into lower circles with the lowest number of points since the League was extended.

Athletic News, 4 May 1931

and conceded a staggering 115 goals. They had just 22 points to their name and shared with Middlesbrough the distinction of being relegated with the lowest-ever number of points.

To offer excuses for their performance seems almost futile but they had suffered injuries, particularly in the early part of the season, which left their defence sadly depleted. Players like Frank Barson had departed, while others such as Jack Silcock, Clarence Hilditch and Alf Steward were now past their prime and the influx of new young players had found life at the bottom of the league too dispiriting to reproduce their potential. In the latter half of the campaign with the defence intact they did not leak anywhere near the number of goals they had earlier conceded. Indeed, from January until the end of the season, they conceded a fairly respectable 36 goals, with 10 of those coming in the last two games, compared with 79 before the New Year.

At the end of the season the board took the inevitable decision and sacked manager Herbert Bamlett. The boycott that had earlier demanded his sacking had finally realised one of its principal demands. Most of his four years in charge at Old Trafford had been spent trying to haul United off the bottom of the table with few successes worth mentioning. There was no immediate replacement – perhaps another sign of the board's paralysis – and secretary Walter Crickmer was asked to take over the reins. He was to be assisted by chief scout Louis Rocca, the man who, as long ago as 1902, had suggested that Newton Heath be renamed Manchester United. Both Crickmer and Rocca had given outstanding and lengthy service to the club, and continued to do so for many years, but as United plunged further into crisis they were not given the facilities to produce the necessary miracle.

Crickmer, a long-term work-horse behind the scenes, became temporary manager in 1931.

Scott Duncan welcomes his new Irish goalkeeper Tommy Breen in 1936, showing that he was not simply interested in signing players from Scotland.

1932

Scots Soccer Nursery.

NEW MANAGER'S HINT.

MR. SCOTT DUNCAN, Manchester United's new manager, must have been surprised at the warmth of the welcome that awaited him when he visited the city yesterday.

He takes up duties on August 1; this was merely a "look round" and an occasion for a chat with his new directors.

In an interview with a *Sporting Chronicle* representative, however, he outlined broadly his policy and plan of campaign.

"Before anything can be done," said Mr. Duncan, "I shall want to see United play. And I do not believe in condemning a player who has a bad game or two. I always give a player every chance of proving himself.

"In practice games, too, the United players will need to pull their full weight. By that I mean they will take the game seriously. It has always been my desire to see players give of their best every time. There can be no slacking in football to-day."

Mr. Duncan told me that he was well in touch with footballers in Scotland.

"If certain positions in the United team need strengthening I shall know where to go for my players," said Mr. Duncan.

"I have had all the 'probables' under observation," he declared.

Mr. Duncan has been manager of Cowdenbeath for about five years.

"The principle upon which I will work," Mr. Duncan said, "is to make football stars rather than buy them. I would rather build soundly and well, creating a good all-round average, than have an unbalanced side with two of the greatest football stars in the country.

"Great names are all right, but they do not make a team. Unless there is definite harmony between every department they are not worth while."

Sporting Chronicle, 15 July 1932

AFTER THE SACKING of Herbert Bamlett it took United almost 18 months to appoint a new manager. Finally, in July 1932, Scott Duncan took over the managerial chair with a salary of £800 per year. It was a bold appointment enthusiastically greeted by players, supporters and the press alike, especially as he promised an immediate input of fresh blood and a new nursery system to encourage the development of young local players.

Duncan was a former player who had once guested for United in a first world war game. During his playing career he had been with Dumbarton, Glasgow Rangers and Newcastle United and had the distinction of being one of the very few players ever to have played both for Rangers and Celtic, having turned out in a couple of friendlies for Celtic during the first world war when he was actually on the books of rivals Rangers. He was a shrewd man whose knowledge of the game quickly won him the support of his players and, in his familiar trilby, he soon became part of the Old Trafford furniture. Although he eventually became one of United's longest-serving managers, the club experienced mixed fortunes under him and, at the end of his five years, there was little to boast of in the way of honours.

There were also major changes on the administrative side, with James Gibson moving into the chairman's seat. United had never adequately filled the gap since the death of John Davies in 1927. Gibson, himself a successful entrepreneur with the clothing firm of Briggs, Jones and Gibson Ltd, arrived in the midst of yet another financial crisis. It was precisely as forecast by the boycotters of the previous year. Gates were still poor and, with Manchester suffering the effects of unemployment during the depression, they were unlikely to improve. Football had become a luxury few could afford.

As 1931 ended United were, once again, almost bankrupt. The bank refused any further credit and there was no money available to pay the players' wages. It was at this point that a second fairy godmother, this time James Gibson, stepped in and placed £2,000 at their disposal. Like Davies many years previously, he was prepared to provide more money and take on the club's liabilities if the board would reconstitute itself. By spring Gibson was president along with a new board whose members had promised cash injections when necessary. At the end of the year, with their new chairman, board, manager and players, United were hardly recognisable from the club that had ended 1931 with a 7–0 defeat at Wolves. Yet, despite all the promise and potential, results on the field still continued to elude them.

1933

CHRISTMAS IS NEVER an ideal time to be playing football and the highest scores somehow inevitably occur during the festive season. On 27 December 1930 Aston Villa slammed United 7–0 at Villa Park and the following year Wolves repeated that scoreline at Molineux. They were the highest defeats in United's history. Then, on 26 December 1933, Grimsby also managed to put seven past United, although the Reds did manage to score three themselves. It was little wonder the United players and supporters rarely looked forward to Christmas during the early 1930s.

Tommy Jones, Jack Mellor and Jack Silcock were all regular stars at the heart of the Manchester United defence in the early 1930s.

But at least United could console themselves with the fact that Grimsby were top of division two while they were lingering fifth from bottom. Grimsby were three up at half time and at one stage led 6–1. It was the most miserable season in United's history and they escaped relegation by the skin of their teeth. Away from home they conceded 52 goals as they tried out three different goalkeepers. In all, 38 players were used during the season.

United's makeshift defence was chopped and changed, with Tom Manley virtually the only regular. Manley was really an outside left but was equally effective in the half-back line and, with United's resources sadly depleted that season, he spent much of the campaign alongside centre half George Vose. Manley had joined United from nearby Northwich Victoria during the 1931/32 season and played 195 games for the club. He left Old Trafford shortly before war began, joining Brentford, but had played only three matches when the league season was brought to a halt. He returned to Old Trafford to play wartime football, but, when hostilities ended, he went back to Brentford where he continued playing until he hung up his boots in 1950. During his eight seasons at United he scored 41 goals, contributing 14 during 1935/36 when United won the second division championship. But his most important goal came at the end of the 1933/34 season when he hit an eighth-minute effort against Millwall at The Den to save United from a humiliating drop into division three north.

GRIMSBY GO SEVEN

SCORING POWER OF LEADERS

DOUBLE REVERSE FOR UNITED

Daily Dispatch, 27 December 1933

UNITED LIKELY TO LOSE AND GO DOWN

1934

United Survive!

THRILLING FIGHT FOR SAFETY WITH TEN MEN

***Millwall** .... 0 **Manchester United** 2*

Sunday Chronicle, 6 May 1934

ON THE SATURDAY morning of 5 May 1934 the Manchester United team travelled to Millwall painfully aware that nothing short of victory could save them from the third division north. They were facing one of the most crucial matches in their history with most pundits having already written off their chances of remaining in the second division. The *Manchester Evening News* reckoned they were doomed and called it 'the most heartbreaking season in the history of Manchester United'. They stood next to bottom on 32 points with Lincoln below them and already relegated, while Millwall were just above them on 33 points. If United won then Millwall would be relegated, making the United/Millwall clash something of an 1890s-style Test Match.

Millwall had drawn at Old Trafford earlier in the season and boasted a fairly useful home record for a club facing relegation. United on the other hand had not travelled well that season, losing 13 games away from their beloved Old Trafford. Nevertheless, as the season wound to its conclusion they had strung together a run that had seen them lose only one of their previous six matches. Much of this latter success had been due to four new signings made as the club desperately delved into the transfer market to dig themselves out of trouble. Bill McKay, a Scottish wing half, and full back John Griffiths had arrived from Bolton, while another half back, Robertson, came from Stoke and the one-time England international goalkeeper Jack Hacking was signed from Oldham Athletic. All four lined up against Millwall.

The clash attracted the biggest crowd of the day, with 35,000 squeezed into Millwall's tight enclosure at The Den. United showed just a couple of changes, with George Vose pulling on the number five shirt after an absence of two months and Hugh McLenahan and Tom Manley preferred up front. They were crucial changes that altered the course of United's history.

Millwall began with a flourish and for a time it looked as if the pundits might be right and United were bound for the third division, but then, with eight minutes gone and against the run of play, Manley fed a useful pass to Cape out on the left wing. The pint-sized winger seized his chance and, pushing the ball down the flank, chased it into open space before returning a centre for Manley to slam into the back of the net. It marked the turning point of the game as Millwall's spirit dissipated and United suddenly rediscovered their confidence. At half time the score remained 1–0 but, within two minutes of the restart, Cape neatly added another. There was no way back for Millwall and United clung comfortably to their lead. As the final whistle blew, United's travelling band of supporters roared their delight and more than 3,000 of them turned up at Central Station later that night to welcome their heroes home.

Left: Jack Hacking conceded just six goals in the last 10 games of 1933/34.
Right: Despite their poor recent record, the supporters felt confident for 1934/35.

1935

THE 1930S WERE a lean period for United. Although they won the second division championship in 1936 and were again promoted in 1938, there was little else to cheer. Nor was there much to admire on the field. Throughout the period they rarely boasted an international player, although there were one or two players of quality who in a better side might have won international recognition. One such player was George Vose who had arrived at Old Trafford in September 1932 from the Rugby League stronghold of St Helens. Vose was a centre half of undoubted quality. Tall, slim and agile, he could turn and control the ball in the tightest of situations. He was at Old Trafford for seven seasons and made more than 200 appearances before war brought his career to a premature halt. After the second world war he played briefly with Runcorn in the Cheshire League but by then he was well past his peak. Instead of the international caps which perhaps should have come his way, he had to be content with just one honour – a second division championship medal.

Above: Vose was one of United's few stars in the 1930s.

FULHAM'S GRIM BATTLE

BUT MANCHESTER PULLED OFF A FINE WIN

Manchester United 1, Fulham 0
(Last season, United (h) 1—0; (a) 1—3.)

Old Trafford has rarely seen a more grim battle than that which developed when Rowley scored a smashing goal for the United in the first half against Fulham.

The teams went "hammer-and-tongs" for each other, but Manchester maintained a tight grip and deservedly pulled off a victory, which keeps them right in the running for the leadership.

A tendency to kick blindly under pressure, and faulty combination, was the Londoners' failing. Arnold was dangerous, but Perry was well held by Vose, who gave a grand defensive display.

On the other hand, the United forwards showed rare spirit and understanding, and gave Tootill a worrying time.

The Finch-Arnold wing soon developed into a menace to the United defence, and lively Fulham attacks brought three corners. These were only cleared with difficulty.

Tootill was then nearly "swamped" in a furious United assault when Much, Bamford, and Cape all swarmed round the goal.

The Londoners' tricky forwards were being well held at this stage, in spite of Hammond's great work, and the United went ahead through Rowley, who scored with a crashing shot.

Manchester gave the Fulham defence a harrowing time after the interval. Tootill saved a "beauty" from Bamford

Fulham were too disjointed in their forward moves, though individually they played attractive football. Perry nearly scrambled the ball through in a dangerous melee, with Hall beaten, but could not count upon effective support at the critical moments

News of the World, 13 October 1935

Below: His quality play was vital in helping United to their second division championship.

1936

MANCHESTER UNITED PROMOTED

Thrilling Win at Bury

Daily Dispatch, 30 April 1936

Ground improvements were necessary following promotion in 1936.

UNITED DID NOT begin their fifth season of second division football with the look of champions. By mid-November they had already seen six defeats, losing four games in a row at one stage. By the end of the year, they had added a seventh defeat to their record and were hovering in the middle of the table. On 4 January they lost yet again, this time to Bradford City, but it was their final defeat that season. Yet why they should have been so dramatically transformed is difficult to fathom as they played much the same team throughout the campaign. Perhaps their success came from growing confidence and a few healthy scorelines. Manager Scott Duncan claimed they had been playing to a plan since the New Year, concentrating on two points at home and one point away. Whatever the reason, it seemed to work. By February they were beginning to climb slowly out of the doldrums, and by mid-March they had jumped to fourth place, just three points behind the leaders. By early April they were in second spot and Old Trafford was sensing the prospect of promotion.

The crucial game came on Wednesday, 29 April when United travelled the short distance to Bury with at least 20,000 supporters in tow. They had beaten Bury at Old Trafford on the previous Saturday and now needed to win to clinch promotion. It was not that difficult. They were three goals ahead within 30 minutes but then, understandably, they relaxed and, with two decisive strikes, Bury dramatically pulled the score back to 3–2. United were suddenly on the rack and defended desperately for the final 15 minutes but managed to hold out. Gigg Lane was invaded at the final whistle as United supporters swarmed across the pitch to carry their heroes shoulder-high towards the dressing rooms. The following Saturday United needed just one point at Hull to be crowned champions of the second division. It was duly achieved with a 1–1 draw.

It was United's home record which formed the backbone of their triumph. They had lost just two games at Old Trafford, and drawn only three, scoring 55 goals. Leading goalscorer was Henry Rowley, with 19 league goals, followed by Tommy Bamford with 16. Rowley had joined United from non-league Shrewsbury in 1928 and, although he began positively, he quickly lost confidence when United dropped into the second division. After just one game in division two he left Old Trafford, returning to first division football with Manchester City. Two years later he signed for Oldham and then in 1934, at the age of 30, he rejoined United to play some of the best football of his career. Goalscorers, however, need to be where the goals are and, as United again struggled in the first division, Rowley found opportunities all too rare. He played just 17 games that season before quitting football, but he had contributed 55 goals in 180 games for United.

United's captain for the season had been wing half Jimmy Brown, a close season buy from Burnley. Brown, a sturdy, dependable Scot, had played eight seasons with Burnley but found a new lease of life at Old Trafford under Scott Duncan. Although they were topsy-turvy years for the club, he made over 100 appearances and twice guided them to promotion before joining Bradford Park Avenue in February 1939.

1937

NO SOONER had United arrived on the first division scene than they were on their way back down again. It was as sudden as that. They opened their account with a draw at Wolves but by Christmas, with just three victories to their name, they were languishing in the relegation zone. It was a desperate time, with 31 players pulling on the red shirt as they searched for a solution to stem the growing crisis. A young Walter Winterbottom was given his opportunity, playing 23 games, but a spinal injury effectively put an end to his career the following season after just four more appearances. Nevertheless, the former schoolteacher took up coaching and, in 1946, was appointed England team manager, a post he held until 1963.

There were, however, a few highlights to what was generally a miserable season, notably the 68,796 gate that watched United beat prospective league champions Manchester City 3–2 at Old Trafford in September 1936. A further 64,000 saw City take their revenge four months later. Wing half Bert Whalley, who had been introduced to first team football the previous season, had an extended run during 1936/37 but played only a handful more games before he took up a coaching position that was to be crucial in the development of the Busby Babes. In all, he played only 39 times for United, although he made many more appearances during the war. But his role behind the scenes in later years can never be overstated and his death in the Munich disaster left United mourning a tragic loss.

RELEGATION ISSUES FURTHER COMPLICATED

Leeds Go To Bottom Place

MANCHESTER UNITED AND WEDNESDAY FIGHT

Last night's football served rather to further complicate than ease the First Division relegation problem. Manchester United drew at Sunderland, Leeds United surprisingly lost to Wolverhampton Wanderers, and Sheffield Wednesday brought off a coup over West Bromwich Albion, who, though sixth from the bottom, are now still vitally concerned in the relegation issue.

It now seems fairly certain that unless Leeds can win their last two matches, with a coincident slump on the part of their nearest rivals, United are doomed.

The problem as to who will accompany them into the Second Division appears to be between Manchester United and Wednesday, though the latter, with a match in hand, have a slightly better goal average. However, a falter on the part of others slightly higher up in the table might even sound their death knell.

The whole situation may not be solved until the very last day of the season, and then perhaps only on percentages.

Sporting Chronicle, 22 April 1937

Bert Whalley, who joined United on a free transfer from Stalybridge Celtic in 1934, gave the club over 20 years' dedicated service.

United's £3,000 for New Left Winger

A BOURNEMOUTH STAR PLAYING TO-MORROW

Manchester Evening News, 22 October 1937

1937

IN 1937 TWO PLAYERS were brought into the United ranks who in time would dramatically change the fortunes of the club. But, ironically, for the man who introduced them it was all too late.

Johnny Carey joined United from the Dublin club St James' Gate in November 1936. He was spotted by Louis Rocca who was on a spying mission to look at various other players. It was said that as soon as he cast eyes on Carey, playing only his third game, he immediately recommended him to manager Scott Duncan. Carey was duly signed for £250 and was drafted into the first team a year later making his debut against Southampton in September 1937 at the age of 18. He began life as an inside forward but, during the war, converted to right back and subsequently won fame and glory as one of Britain's most elegant defenders.

A month after Carey's introduction, Scott Duncan swooped on the third division club Bournemouth and signed another youngster by the name of Jack Rowley. The 19-year-old had joined Bournemouth only eight months previously from the Birmingham League but was already impressing after only 20-odd matches. The fee was £3,000, a not inconsiderable amount at the time, yet United did not baulk at the asking price and Rowley joined the Old Trafford staff on Friday, 22 October 1937. The following day he was on the left wing facing Sheffield Wednesday, though after a sprightly start he faded in the second half. For the next six weeks he had to be content with reserve football but then re-emerged as a centre forward, scoring four goals in United's 5–1 win over Swansea. Rowley was there to stay and over the next 18 years became one of the most prolific scorers in the club's history.

Just weeks after engaging two players who would eventually have such an impact, manager Scott Duncan resigned. On the field it had been a bleak start to the season. By the end of October they had lost six matches and any prospect of promotion seemed to have already faded. Whether Scott Duncan jumped or was pushed is irrelevant, the signs were clear enough and he left for East Anglia to take over the managerial chair at Southern League Ipswich. During his time at Old Trafford, United had not been altogether unsuccessful. They had won promotion after five years in the second division, although they had just as quickly returned. But Duncan's career had hardly been an overwhelming triumph. In truth, United were little more than a good second division side and Duncan was now paying the price for failure. A few days after his resignation United thrashed Chesterfield 7–1 and began a run which would carry them to promotion. But it had all come too late for the man who had promised much when he arrived in 1932 but had, in fact, delivered little.

The prolific-scoring Jack Rowley heads for goal in training.

1938

AFTER THE DISPIRITING opening to the 1937/38 season, which saw United lose six games before the end of October, they rolled up their sleeves and began a fruitful burst that brought only five more defeats that season. In only his second game Jack Rowley netted four goals and soon became the perfect foil for Tommy Bamford. By New Year's Day United were in contention and, timing their run with the perfection of a relay sprinter, they leaped into third spot as Easter approached.

It was always going to be a closely fought battle to see who would accompany Aston Villa into the first division, but nobody could have imagined it would be so dramatic. On the penultimate Saturday of the season the three leading contenders – Sheffield United, Coventry and Manchester United – all lost. Sheffield United had now completed their programme and were two points ahead of their rivals who were split by goal averages alone. All rested on the final fixture, with United at home to Bury and Coventry away to Stockport. Both United and Coventry had to win to have a chance of promotion instead of Sheffield United. It was that close. As it happened United won 2–0, while Coventry were held to a 1–1 draw thanks to a disputed penalty in the last minute. United's two goals were just enough to edge them ahead of the Yorkshiremen into the promotion-winning spot.

Besides Carey and Rowley, Stan Pearson was another youngster who was drafted into the first team following Scott Duncan's resignation. He made his debut in the 7–1 thrashing of Chesterfield and, although it took him a few years to secure a permanent spot in the team, he eventually played 345 games for United over the next 17 years. He was a stylish and powerful inside left whose positive running brought him 148 goals and helped his partner Jack Rowley to many more.

Manchester Clubs Exchange Positions

FOOTBALL'S FAREWELL YESTERDAY WAS ABOUT AS DRAMATIC AS IT COULD BE.

Champions a year ago, Manchester City were relegated to the Second Division, and they exchange status with Manchester United!

Sunday Chronicle, 8 May 1938

George Mutch challenges the Spurs keeper Taylor in a rare second division clash between two sides much more used to the top flight.

By the end of the season, United's team was markedly different from the one that had opened the campaign. George Mutch, for so long one of the few quality players at Old Trafford, had decided to try his luck elsewhere when Preston came in with a £5,000 bid. He had been with United since May 1934, when he arrived as an £800 buy from Arbroath. He was the leading scorer in his first season with 19 goals and went on to register 49 goals for United in 120 appearances. A season after leaving United he scored a last-minute penalty at Wembley to lift the Cup for Preston. Tom Jones and John Mellor also faded from the scene, with Jones departing for Scunthorpe while Mellor moved to Cardiff City. Jones, a defender, had joined United from Oswestry Town during the 1924/25 season and was first choice for a number of years until he left during the 1936/37 season after 200 appearances. His partner for so many years, John Mellor, made only a handful of appearances after 1933 and was on his way in 1936 after Grimsby Town had dished out a 6–2 lesson.

Football Carries On

Sunday Dispatch, 3 September 1939

Despite the efforts of the programme writers to concentrate on the importance of gaining two points, world events soon took precedence.

1939

Bill McKay was one of many professionals whose career was effectively ended by the onset of war. He had been a regular in the side for five years and would have gone on to greater things.

THERE MUST HAVE been apprehension on the terraces that final Saturday before war broke out. Everybody knew that Germany's deadline to pull out of Poland was only hours away and, equally, everybody recognised that Hitler would not retreat. Nor for that matter would the British government; an ultimatum had been issued and they would stand by it. But, for the moment, there was still time for leisure. United, who had ended the previous season in 14th place, were away to Charlton on what was the third match of the new football season. They had made a brightish start to their campaign with a 4–0 win against Grimsby at Old Trafford, followed by a midweek draw at Chelsea. But, at The Valley on a scorching Saturday afternoon, they were unluckily beaten 2–0.

At 11am the following morning, with the deadline passed and Hitler continuing to ignore demands for a withdrawal from Poland, Britain declared war on Germany. The next day the newspapers reported that all sport had been halted. It was hoped that it would only be temporary but, within two days, the League Management Committee met to cancel the league season; Saturday's results were now meaningless. Of course, nobody anticipated that it would be another seven years before league soccer reappeared, although football was played one way or another during the long and painful interim.

For United, like so many clubs, the war meant the loss of players. Some joined the forces immediately, others simply bided their time awaiting their call-up papers. For many, the war meant an end to promising careers. Others played much of their best football during the period, but it was all to little effect. So, when peace arrived, they were sadly beyond their best days.

The war was a watershed, with only a handful of players surviving the years to play in both pre-war and post-war football. Goalkeeper John Breedon, who had played 38 games for United prior to September 1939, continued between the posts for much of the war but found himself out of the reckoning once league soccer resumed and went off to manage Halifax Town. William Bryant was another who might have enjoyed more recognition. Prior to the outbreak of hostilities he had made 160 appearances for United following his transfer from Wolves. A dashing outside right, he scored 44 goals during that period but, although he regularly turned out between 1939 and 1945, he was not up to first division standards by 1946 and moved on to Bradford City. John Griffiths was another former Wolves player who arrived at Old Trafford via Bolton Wanderers, making 176 appearances prior to the war. A right back, he continued to play until 1944, but by the end of hostilities he had quit the game. Perhaps the most promising of all was Bill McKay, a sturdy Scottish half back who came to United via Hamilton Academicals and Bolton. He was one of four newcomers who had been signed in March 1934 as United faced the prospect of third division football. Over five years he played 184 games, scoring 15 goals, and although he turned out for the Reds during the war, he moved on to non-league football in 1946.

1940

THE WAR YEARS brought stringent hardships to United as well as to players and supporters. All leisure activities were disrupted, with football forced to take a back seat until peace returned. In place of the normal Football League a series of regional leagues was instituted so that teams would have to do less travelling, while players were permitted to guest for the club closest to their barracks. It led to some strange selections, with third division sides often fielding international stars while first division clubs scratched around for players. Every week brought forth a surprise line-up, with as many as 40 different players being used in a season. United themselves guested some outstanding players and, on one occasion in June 1940, fielded a forward line that included Manchester City's Irish international Peter Doherty and the Stoke City winger Stanley Matthews. Their side that day had nine players who were on the books of other clubs plus a centre half from a local junior team.

Although there were leagues, there was little competitive spirit and few prizes. There were even fewer spectators, with most of United's supporters absent fighting a war. Throughout the six years of hostilities United could rarely attract more than 4,000 to an average game and only local derbies ever pushed the attendance into five figures. Many of their fixtures were also played across the city at Maine Road as Old Trafford was severely damaged by bombing.

For the record, United won the Lancashire Cup in 1941, beating Burnley 1–0 in the final, and topped their regional league in 1941/42. In the 1944/45 season they reached the League North Cup final where they lost to Bolton. But sadly there was little else to boast about other than a few spectacular scorelines. New Brighton were hammered 13–1 in August 1941 and Wrexham were beaten 10–3 in the same year, while Burnley were thrashed 9–0 in April 1944.

More tragically, the club lost a number of players, including Ben Carpenter who had joined them from Burton Town shortly before the outbreak of war. He was killed in action while others like Johnny Hanlon and Allenby Chilton were wounded. It was an unhappy period for everyone, but when football officially kicked off again in August 1946 United were better equipped for the new season than anyone might have dared imagine.

Players were often hard to find during the war, as this cartoon reveals.

ENGLISH MATCHES

FOOTBALL LEAGUE WAR CUP.—SEMI-FINALS

Blackburn R. (0) **1** **Newcastle U.** (0) **0** 14,238
Clarke.

Fulham..........(0) **3** **West Ham U.** (3) **4** 32,799
Woodward, Rooke 2. Brown, own goal, Goulden, Foxall, Small.

REGIONAL LEAGUE MATCHES

SOUTH "C"

Arsenal..........(2) **5** **Southampton** (0) **0** 3,000
Crayston, Drake, Jones (L.) 2, Kirchen.

Charlton Ath. (2) **4** **Portsmouth** ....(0) **2** 500
Robinson 2, Welsh 2. Wilkinson, Anderson.

	HOME						AWAY					
					Goals					Goals		
	P	W	D	L	F	A	W	D	L	F	A	Pts
Tottenham	18	6	2	2	25	17	5	2	1	18	13	26
West Ham	16	6	2	0	22	7	4	1	3	30	19	23
Arsenal	18	6	2	2	26	14	3	3	2	15	12	23
Brentford	17	6	2	2	27	14	1	2	4	10	17	18
Millwall	17	5	1	3	25	15	1	4	3	9	14	17
Fulham	16	5	1	1	16	10	3	0	6	18	25	17
Charlton	16	4	2	2	25	20	2	1	5	11	15	15
Chelsea	18	3	1	[illegible]	18	25	1	2	7	15	28	11
Bo'ton	16	4	2	[illegible]	17	18	0	1	7	8	33	11
Portsmouth	18	2	3	4	12	16	1	0	8	14	29	9

SOUTH "D"

Aldershot Tn. (1) **3** **Crystal Palace** (1) **2** 1,500
Chalmers 2, Hagan. Owens, Dawes.

Brighton & H. (2) **2** **Watford**.........(0) **2** 500
Stephens 2. Dunscomb, Lewis (G.).

Norwich City (0) **1** **Southend Un.** (0) **3** 1,500
Little. Lewis, Bell, Robinson.

Q. P. R. ....(2) **5** **Bournemouth** (0) **0** 1,000
Mangnall 2, McEwan, McCarthy 2.

	HOME						AWAY					
					Goals					Goals		
	P	W	D	L	F	A	W	D	L	F	A	Pts
C. Palace	16	7	1	1	41	11	5	0	2	20	15	25
Q P R	18	7	1	1	26	12	3	2	4	12	16	23
Watford	17	6	3	0	39	10	1	3	4	10	17	20
Aldershot	17	6	1	2	23	13	1	2	5	14	31	17
Clapton O.	17	6	1	2	25	16	1	2	5	8	26	17
Southend U.	16	5	1	1	22	8	2	1	6	14	27	16
Norwich C.	16	6	1	1	23	13	0	3	5	8	18	16
Bournem'th	16	5	1	1	22	6	1	1	7	14	33	14
Reading	18	5	1	3	19	16	1	1	7	12	26	14
Brighton	17	1	4	3	16	18	0	0	9	11	47	6

WESTERN

Crewe Alex. ..(1) **3** **Chester**..........(1) **1** 400
Cobourne, Waring, Dyer. Yates.

Manchester U. (0) **0** **Everton**.........(0) **3** 6,000
Stevenson 3

New Brighton (0) **0** **Liverpool**....... (0) **0** 1,000

	HOME						AWAY					
					Goals					Goals		
	P	W	D	L	F	A	W	D	L	F	A	Pts
Stoke City	22	10	1	0	29	10	3	4	4	28	31	31
Liverpool	22	6	4	1	34	19	6	1	4	32	21	29
Everton	22	8	1	2	41	18	4	3	4	23	15	28
Man. Un.	22	9	0	2	46	16	5	0	6	28	25	28
Man. City	22	6	3	2	43	24	6	1	4	30	17	28
Wrexham	22	8	3	0	35	17	2	2	7	10	33	25
N. Brighton	22	7	2	2	35	15	3	1	7	20	37	23
Port Vale	22	7	0	4	34	25	3	2	6	18	31	22
Chester	22	5	3	3	26	20	2	2	7	14	31	19
Crewe A.	22	6	0	5	30	25	0	1	10	14	54	13
Stockport C.	22	4	[illegible]	[illegible]	23	25	0	2	9	22	54	11
Tranmere R.	22	2	2	7	26	40	0	1	10	15	53	7

News of the World, 2 June 1940

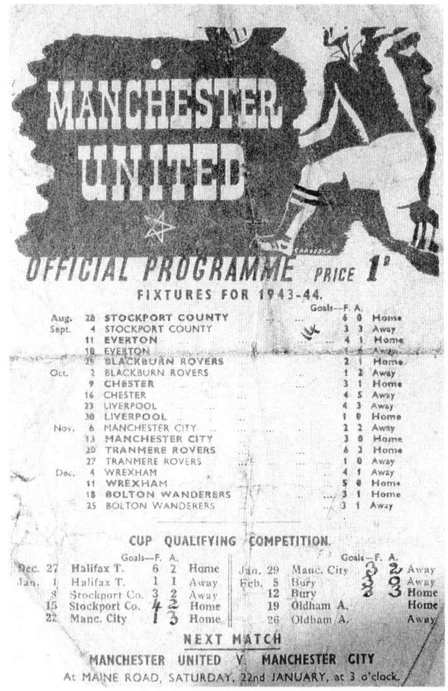

A wartime programme shows how local all the games were.

1941

OLD TRAFFORD was no longer the hubbub of excitement as match-day approached nor the theatre of spectacle on the day itself. Instead, it was an empty shell of a stadium where the wind could be heard grumbling through the stands and where the grass was beginning to seed on the terraces. But, on the night of Tuesday, 11 March 1941, there was a roar around Old Trafford, not from the crowds but from enemy bombs, as the Luftwaffe descended on the north-west with Trafford Park as one of its targets. The vast industrial estate, the home of the first British-built Model T Ford car, was now pouring out arms and ammunition for the war effort. It was severely damaged by enemy bombs. Not surprisingly, some fell short of their target and one landed on the Old Trafford ground itself, causing devastation. The main stand was virtually destroyed, a section of the terracing was ripped apart and the pitch was scorched by the blast.

If Old Trafford had been a sad sight the day before, it was a tragic picture the following morning as the United staff and players quietly surveyed the mayhem. There was little mention of it in the papers, as censorship restricted information on war damage, besides there were far more important matters than a few bombs on a football ground. Nevertheless, it was the end of football at Old Trafford until 1949. But, thanks to the generosity of Manchester City, United were given the use of Maine Road for their fixtures, although they did not return any favours, slamming City 7–1 a month later. Old Trafford's last game, on 8 March, had seen a 7–3 victory for United over Bury with Johnny Carey and Jack Rowley both hitting hat tricks.

By the end of the war, Old Trafford was in a dilapidated state, a shadow of its former self. The seeds on the terracing had turned to grass and a six-foot high bush had sprouted on the overgrown pitch. The ground resembled a disused factory site rather than the famous stadium that had hosted Cup finals and internationals. But there was no fear; once the war was over it soon returned to its former glory.

The rubble of Old Trafford after it had been bombed.

NIGHT RAIDERS IN THE NORTH-WEST

Attack on an Inland Area

STREAM OF 'PLANES

High-explosive and incendiary bombs were dropped by enemy aircraft during a fairly heavy attack on an inland area in North-west England last night. The raiders met fierce opposition from the anti-aircraft gun batteries. At times the concentration of gunfire was heavier than had been heard previously in the district.

The 'planes came over in procession and for a long period of the attack,' which ended before midnight, there was not a minute during which the drone of engines could not be heard. The earlier 'planes dropped some flares and incendiary bombs. A fire was started, but members of the fire brigade, assisted by the A.F.S., were speedily on the scene and brought the outbreak under control.

Later 'planes dropped some high-explosive bombs, but the barrage from the ground defences appeared to prevent the raiders from making a heavy concentrated attack.

FIRE SERVICES' GOOD WORK

High-explosive bombs caused some damage to business and private property in several districts, but the casualties were very few, although some people were killed. Swift combative measures on the part of fire-watchers resulted in the limitation of fires, and those which did break out were of a small nature and received prompt attention from firemen of the regular and auxiliary services and from fire squads which were on duty.

It was reported that a hospital and a sanatorium in an outlying district were struck by incendiary bombs and that slight fires broke out in both institutions.

Slight damage was done to dwelling-houses in one or two working-class districts and slight outbreaks of fire were reported from a football ground and a training institute. In another district a bomb fell in the yard of a school, but it did very little damage.

Guardian, 12 March 1941

1945

ALTHOUGH NOBODY could have guessed at the time, the arrival of Matt Busby was as momentous an event as any in the history of Manchester United. It ranked alongside the appointment of Ernest Mangnall, the signing of Billy Meredith and the timely intervention of J H Davies to save the club from bankruptcy. Not since 1911, when they last captured the league championship, had United claimed anything of note. They had won promotion from the second division a few times, but a club the size of United should never have been there in the first place.

Like so many important events, Busby's arrival passed almost unnoticed at the time. The *Manchester Evening News*, of course, reported it, although the paper devoted little coverage to football during the war. The hostilities were not quite over, but victory was certain and already plans were being confidently laid for the future. At least everybody knew that there would now be a future.

It was on Monday, 19 February 1945 that Company Sergeant-Major Instructor Matthew Busby was appointed manager of Manchester United, a post which had been officially vacant since the departure of Scott Duncan in 1937. Secretary Walter Crickmer had loyally stepped into the breach for a second time during those years, intelligently guiding the club through the final months of peacetime football and the difficult years of war.

At the time, Busby was still on the books of Liverpool, where he had been offered a five-year contract as assistant to manager George Kay once he had been demobilised. He was still in the army as an instructor at the Sandhurst Military Academy when he received a letter from Louis Rocca, the United scout, informing him of the managerial

February 1945. Sergeant-Major Instructor Matt Busby signs for Manchester United, watched over by secretary Walter Crickmer, to become the club's new manager and so ushered in a new era.

1945

Matt Busby Signs as United Manager

By A STAFF REPORTER

COMPANY SERGEANT-MAJOR INSTRUCTOR MATT BUSBY, Liverpool right half-back and Scotland captain, to-day signed an agreement to become manager of Manchester United when he is demobilised.

Only a few years ago Busby (now aged 34), who has proved himself one of the great half-backs of modern times, was the "forgotten man" of international football.

Attractive Player

His thousands of Manchester fans, remembering him as a stylish and attractive player when he turned out for Manchester City, unswervingly believed in his brilliance when Scotland's selectors seemed to have neglected and forgotten him.

And he justified their faith. After one pre-war international cap in 1934 he was ignored until the 1941-2 season, since when he has appeared for Scotland in eight games, several times as skipper.

In these games he has been outstanding, and to-day he made a name in Scottish football.

"Busby has had a number of offers, but he approached us himself as he particularly wanted to come back to Manchester," Mr. W. Crickmer, Manchester United Secretary, explained to-day. "He will build up the team and put it right where it belongs—at the top."

Busby, who played with Alex James when he was a boy, left Manchester City for Liverpool in 1936 at a fee of £8,000, and has been released from his appointment as Liverpool's post-war coach.

Manchester Evening News, 19 February 1945

vacancy at Old Trafford and their interest in meeting with him. Busby was keen to come to United and quickly arranged a meeting with chairman James Gibson and Walter Crickmer. The rest, as they say, is history.

Ironically, Busby's footballing career had begun as a 17-year-old with rivals Manchester City, where he played more than 200 games before joining Liverpool for £8,000 in February 1936. At Maine Road he was on the losing side in the 1933 Cup final when Dixie Dean destroyed City, but a year later he collected a winners' medal as City powered to victory over Portsmouth and two years later he was skipper of the side. At Anfield he combined with fellow Scots Tom Bradshaw and Jimmy McDougall to form one of the most elegant half-back lines in Liverpool's history. He played 125 games for the Merseysiders before war cut short his career and he enlisted with the 9th battalion of the King's regiment. Surprisingly, he won only one Scottish cap, although he might well have collected many more had war not disrupted his career at such an important phase. Nevertheless, he did represent his country on at least seven occasions in wartime internationals.

Busby was only 34 when he took over at Old Trafford but was, even then, much in demand. United and Liverpool were not the only clubs seeking his services; Reading, Ayr United and, later, Spurs were also in the hunt. But there was no doubt that Manchester was where Busby's heart lay. His arrival was to spark the fusion of two great forces.

Within a couple of seasons of his arrival, Busby had transformed United into title contenders. Over a period of 10 seasons, the Reds were only out of the top five once.

1946

IT WAS 'as you were' when football kicked off again after the second world war with a fixture list identical to that on the first day of the abortive 1939/40 season. But there were some things which were different – the crowds for a start. They flocked in their thousands everywhere to stand on sun-soaked terraces or pontificate from the stands. Stamford Bridge welcomed 61,000, there were 55,000 at Goodison, 53,000 at Roker Park and 50,000 at Molineux. Manchester United welcomed 41,000, but there was something else different for them – they were opening their league campaign at Maine Road and not Old Trafford. Until the War Damage Commission coughed up some money, bomb-wrecked Old Trafford remained empty and silent.

Of course, there was much else that was different. United fielded a team that was barely recognisable to those who had not enjoyed wartime football. In goal was Jack Crompton, an agile young keeper who had joined United in 1944 from local football after a spell as an amateur with Oldham Athletic. Ahead of him were Johnny Carey, maturing into one of the most elegant defenders in the land, and Bill McGlen, a dependable left back who soon switched to left half to make way for John Aston. The half-back line was composed of Welshman John Warner, the immortal Allenby Chilton who had made his debut for United the day before war broke out and that classic England left half, Henry Cockburn. It was as formidable a half-back line as that of Duckworth, Roberts and Bell which had steered United to such glory in the days of Edwardian gas-lamps. Up front there was Scottish international Jimmy Delaney, a recent snippet of a buy at £4,000 from Celtic, and Stan Pearson, rugged, energetic and scheming. Alongside him, Johnny Hanlon had briefly pulled on the number nine shirt though his moments of fame were short-lived. Jack Rowley at inside left – tall, powerful and as deadly as ever – served United for many more years while Charlie Mitten was now weaving circles down the left wing. It was an outstanding team which changed little over the next few years and, with Matt Busby and Jimmy Murphy firmly ensconced at the helm, it soon transformed United from the music-hall joke of pre-war football to giants of the post-war years.

LEAGUE I.

Attendance.
A. Villa ....(0) 0 Midsbro' (0) 1 50,000
Mannion.
Chelsea ....(2) 4 Bolton ..(2) 3 61,400
Spence 2. Lawton 2. Lofthouse 2. Forrest
Everton ......(0) 0 Brentfrd (1) 2 55,338
Wilkins McAloon
Huddersfield ..(1) 1 Blackpol (3) 3 14,378
Glazzard. Mortensen. Blair. Munro.
M'nchester U. (1) 2 Grimsby (0) 1 40,000
Mitten. Rowley McGowan.
Portsmouth ...(3) 3 Blckbrn (1) 1 31,000
Reid 2. *Crook Rogers
Preston ....(2) 3 Leeds U. (1) 2 25,000
McIntosh. Finney. Dougal. Grainger.
Sheffield U. ...(0) 0 Liverpol (0) 1 30,000
L. F. Carney
Stoke ....(1) 2 Charltn (1) 2 30,000
Ornston. Steele. Duffy Welsh.
Sunderland ...(2).3 Derby ....(1) 2 53,000
Burbanks. Whitelum 2. Stamps. Doherty.
Wolves ....(0) 6 Arsenal .(0) 1 50,845
Pye 3. Westcott 2. Mullen. Lewis
Half-time scores in parentheses.
*Put through own goal.

Sunday Dispatch, 1 September 1946

Post-war goalkeeper Jack Crompton. As safe a pair of hands as any in the club's history. He played his last game for United in 1955 – and kept a clean sheet against Huddersfield Town.

UNITED LUCKY TO SURVIVE

Close Passing Fault

MANCHESTER UNITED... 2 GRIMSBY TOWN 1

THIS will not do, Manchester United! For a team from whom so much has been expected, they began by nearly faltering against Grimsby Town. In fact, a minute from the end Grimsby had bad luck not to equalise when a shot from Johnson (J. W.) beat Crompton and struck the upright.

Sunday Chronicle, 1 September 1946

1947

United are still in honours race

MANCHESTER UNITED... 3 PORTSMOUTH....... 0

MANCHESTER UNITED are still putting up a great struggle in the championship race. They won as they pleased against Portsmouth, ;but they made it hard work for themselves ,n the second half.

They had sufficient chances before the interval to have made the game secure, but only one goal separated the teams, this by Morris after ten minutes. United, however, were put on their victory march soon after the interval with a goal by Mitten, and near the end Rowley got the third.

Sunday Chronicle, 18 May 1947

UNITED BEGAN the 1946/47 season in sparkling form with five successive victories, including a 5–0 thrashing of eventual champions Liverpool. The outcome of the league title, however, remained in doubt until the season's final game, played on 14 June. The worst winter on record had caused the postponement of scores of fixtures and the Football League was forced to extend the season well into June. Even the Derby had been decided before the championship.

United were always leading contenders along with Liverpool, Stoke City and Wolves, but, in hindsight, their chances evaporated when Liverpool took their revenge at Anfield with just three games to follow. United then drew at Preston but Liverpool kept marching on. In their penultimate fixture United comfortably beat Portsmouth, while Liverpool could only draw with Brentford, and once more the title race looked wide open. Liverpool, however, had two matches remaining while United had only one. Although they then won that fixture, trouncing Sheffield United 6–2, Liverpool went on to win both games and headed the league. Only Stoke could have caught the Merseysiders but, on 14 June, they surprisingly went down to Sheffield United and the table remained as it was. Liverpool were champions and Manchester United were runners-up.

It had been a brave campaign by Busby's new team, who struck 95 goals and boasted fewer defeats than anyone else. It boded well for the future. Jack Rowley was predictably top marksman with 26 league goals, followed by Stan Pearson with 19. The much-respected Bert Whalley decided, after 13 years at United, to hang up his boots at the end of the season and take on a coaching job with the club. He had joined them from Stalybridge Celtic in May 1934, making 30 league appearances before the outbreak of war. During the war his career blossomed and he became a regular choice at wing half. As a coach he was an instant success, guiding and motivating many of the youngsters who eventually formed the backbone of the future. Whalley would not normally have travelled on the fateful trip to Belgrade but, with Jimmy Murphy engaged on international duty as manager of Wales, he stepped into his place and was tragically killed. United owed much to Whalley whose own footballing career had been interrupted by war and whose coaching career was destroyed at Munich. He was one of the great unsung heroes of Old Trafford.

Bert Whalley (left) and Jimmy Murphy (with ball) coaching some of their young stars.

1948

THIS WAS WEMBLEY'S FINEST FINAL

Six-Goal Thriller

News of the World,
25 April 1948

THE *NEWS OF THE WORLD*'S description of the 1948 Cup final as 'Wembley's finest' was perhaps a slight exaggeration, although there is no doubting that it was one of the greatest finals of all time.

United arrived at Wembley taking as contorted and difficult a route as imaginable. In a memorable third round tie they beat Aston Villa 6–4 at Villa Park after being a goal down in 13 seconds. At half time United were leading 5–1, but Villa fought back to make it 5–4 before Stan Pearson netted a sixth for the Reds. They then faced league champions Liverpool for a home tie, but, with Manchester City also drawn at home, United were forced to look for alternative accommodation. They chose the home of Liverpool's rivals, Everton, and it proved a lucky choice as United won 3–0 in front of an admiring 74,000. In the next round they were again drawn at home, this time against Charlton Athletic, but, with Manchester City also drawn at home, United chose Leeds Road, Huddersfield as their venue and they comfortably beat the Londoners 2–0.

The quarter-finals brought a further home draw for United, but City had a home league fixture, so United travelled to Villa Park for their clash with Preston. They won 4–2 in front of another 74,000 crowd and then found themselves pitted against Derby County in the semi-final at Hillsborough. Stan Pearson hit a hat trick to add to the four goals he had already scored in United's Cup run as

Top: Up for the Cup – the way it used to be. United fans, dangerous weapons and all, in celebratory mood in Trafalgar Square.

Right: Nothing could stop United, not even Robinson in the Blackpool goal, seen here leaping to foil yet another United attack, as he was beaten four times in all.

they ran out 3–1 winners. United had faced first division opposition in every game and had been watched by an astonishing 300,000 in the process. After the final it was over 400,000 – an aggregate attendance which has probably never been bettered.

In the final United faced Stanley Matthews' Blackpool in what was as exciting a contest as anyone could recall. Having missed out on the championship to Arsenal, and with it the possibility of the double, United were determined to bring some silverware back to Manchester, but after 12 minutes it looked as if it might be Blackpool carrying the Cup north when Eddie Shimwell gave them the lead from the penalty spot. Fifteen minutes later United equalised as Jack Rowley outsprinted the Blackpool goalkeeper. But it was not for long, as Blackpool again took the lead when Hugh Kelly flicked on a Matthews free kick for Stan Mortensen to drive home. In the second half, United grimly struggled as Matthews and Mortensen desperately tried to unlock their defence. But skipper Carey was inspirational, calmly defending and then urging his forwards on as he unleashed sweeping passes upfield. In the 69th minute United's patient build-up paid off when Rowley headed home Johnny Morris's free kick to level the scores. Ten minutes later United were in the lead for the first time as John Anderson threaded a delightful ball between the Blackpool defence for Pearson to slam home. A roar, like a clap of thunder, reverberated around Wembley. Seven minutes later the Cup was secured for Manchester as John Anderson's chance shot soared gloriously into the back of the Blackpool net. United had won the Cup. It was 39 years to the day since Billy Meredith and company had last given United their only taste of Cup glory.

For Johnny Morris, the Wembley final was to mark the pinnacle of his United career. He played just 22 more games for the club before he was surprisingly transferred to Derby County after a dispute with manager Matt Busby. Troublesome or not, Busby demanded a British record fee of £24,500 for the curly-haired youngster. At Derby he won three England caps before he signed for Leicester, where he saw out his league days. A Radcliffe boy, spotted inevitably by Louis Rocca, Morris made his debut shortly after the resumption of league football. A spirited, skilful inside forward, he made 92 appearances for United and scored 35 goals.

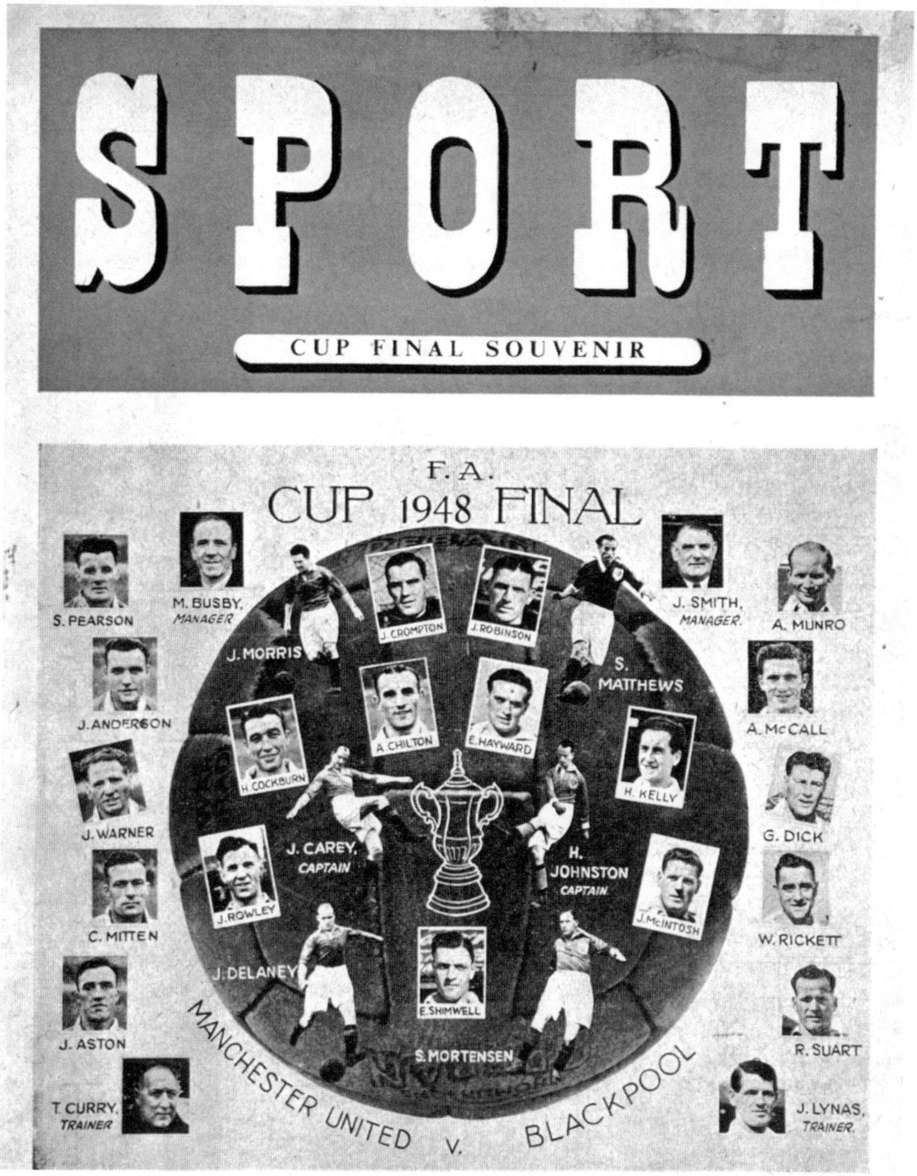

With Matthews and Mortensen lining up for the opposition, the 1948 Cup final promised to be one of Wembley's finest. Nobody was to be disappointed, except perhaps Matthews and Mortensen.

Skipper Johnny Carey captured the accolades for United's outstanding Cup triumph but, if one man should have been singled out, it was Stan Pearson whose eight goals in six matches had been a vital contribution. Pearson was a Salford lad who had joined United in 1937 making his debut immediately following Scott Duncan's resignation as United trounced Chesterfield 7–1. By the end of the war he had matured into a fine, stylish inside forward as capable of scoring goals as creating them. He was the perfect partner to Jack Rowley and registered 149 goals in 345 appearances before he left to join Bury in 1954. He would always be remembered as the man who fired United on their way to another Cup triumph.

1949

Who would have guessed that non-league Yeovil would attract more than 80,000 for their fifth round Cup clash with United? More predictable was Jack Rowley's five goals.

EVERYONE WANTED to see Yeovil, the greatest giant killers since the war, and, when they were drawn against Cup-holders Manchester United at Maine Road there was sure to be a crush for tickets. Yet nobody anticipated that little non-league Yeovil would attract 81,565 to watch them.

Yeovil had already dismissed second division Bury from the Cup, beating them 3–1 in the third round on their famous sloping pitch at the Huish. In the next round they were rewarded with a plum home tie – first division giants Sunderland, who arrived with England international Len Shackleton and a future England star Willie Watson. But the Wearsiders' pedigree did them little good as the 5,000–1 part-timers sneaked a 2–1 victory. Then, in the fifth round, they were drawn away from home against the mighty United.

The game was played on Saturday, 12 February with around 7,000 Yeovil fans, reckoned to be a third of the town's entire population, pouring into the city of Manchester. They arrived by train, car and coach. It was a game none of them was going to miss, even if it meant paying over the odds for tickets. The black market price was simply staggering, with 3s 6d uncovered seats exchanging hands for £2, while 5s and 7s 6d stand seats were fetching between three and five guineas. With 20 minutes to kick-off all Maine Road's gates had been firmly shut with thousands more locked outside. It was one of the biggest gates ever outside London. They could have filled Wembley stadium for this Cup tie.

Could Somerset's no-hopers achieve the impossible? The answer was 'no', and a resounding no. After just six minutes Jack Rowley hit United's first goal; by half time he had a hat trick and United held a 4–0 lead. Just because Yeovil had captured the public's imagination, United were not going to spare them any embarrassment. Another four goals went in during the second half and Yeovil's brave dream had turned into a nightmare. They lost 8–0: Rowley hit five and Ronnie Burke added two, while Charlie Mitten collected the other. Yet they had not been altogether disgraced. As the final whistle blew 81,565 fans cheered them from the field after a Cup tie that would always be remembered as the game everyone wanted to see.

Manchester United made it "Woevil" Town

By KEN WOLSTENHOLME

MANCHESTER UNITED .... 8 YEOVIL TOWN 0

MANCHESTER UNITED gave a perfect exhibition, and Yeovil Town were hopelessly outclassed, but they kept the promise of player-manager Alec Stocks—"Whatever happens, we'll play football."

They never ceased striving for a goal, and by the way they were playing at the end you would have thought they were on level terms, yet they never had a hope.

The Cupholders might have been giving a coaching exhibition.

They put on show every move in the game, and they executed them so perfectly that goals were bound to come.

But when they did come the United players refrained from indulging in the usual back slapping act.

The two outstanding men in the Yeovil side were centre-half Blizzard and goalkeeper Hall, who made three great saves, despite suffering a painful injury.

Not a man on the field deserved adverse criticism and although one-sided, it was a clean and sporting game.

Empire News, 13 February 1949

MANCHESTER UNITED WIN THEIR FIRST 'HOME' MATCH

Daily Graphic, 25 August 1949

1949

AFTER EIGHT YEARS' absence from bomb-wrecked Old Trafford, United finally returned home on Wednesday, 24 August to face Lancashire neighbours Bolton Wanderers for their opening home fixture of the new season. During those intervening years they had made Maine Road their base and had enjoyed considerable success, finishing as runners-up in the league two years in succession and winning the FA Cup in 1948. But, at last, it was time to go back to Old Trafford. Much of the damage to the pitch and stands had been repaired, although there was still some work to complete. There were even ambitious plans afoot to extend Old Trafford's capacity to 100,000 but they never materialised.

For most of the players Old Trafford was new territory. Few of them had played there before and, as they ran out to face Bolton on a breezy summer's day, it must have been almost like playing away from home. But Carey, Rowley and Pearson had experienced the famous roar of the Stretford End. Old Trafford must have been an exciting experience for a new generation of supporters as they joined the 42,000 fans who flocked down the Chester Road and across the Trafford Park Bridge. Manchester had almost forgotten what it was like to have football on the west side of the city, with bumper to bumper traffic jams and long queues which caused thousands to be late.

But it was all worth it as United ran out 3–0 winners, with Charlie Mitten striking their first Old Trafford goal for eight years. And what a roar the Stretford End gave him!

Left: Blitzed by German bombs, Old Trafford underwent drastic rebuilding during the post-war years.

Below: The ground was ready for action in August 1949, with Bolton Wanderers as the unlucky first victims.

1950

Mitten signs for Bogota—£40 a week

EVENING NEWS REPORTER

CHARLIE MITTEN, Manchester United outside-left, was to-day reported to have signed a two-year contract with the Sante Fe club in Bogota (Colombia) at £2,050 sterling a year, almost £40 a week.

But when his 29-year-old wife, Betty, at her home in Royston Road, Davyhulme, was told of the report, she declared : "I can't believe it. I still maintain he won't sign without first coming home and discussing it with me

"I am still going ahead with plans for a holiday at Scarborough in two weeks' time.

Manchester Evening News, 24 June 1950

UNITED FANS were astonished when they picked up their newspapers during the summer of 1950 to read that their long-time favourite, Charlie Mitten, had deserted them for an unknown Colombian team by the name of Santa Fe. But it was true; after 113 consecutive league appearances Mitten was off to play football in South America.

The Bogotá affair, as it became known, caused a sensation. Mitten was not the only one to be tempted abroad. Neil Franklin, the Stoke and England centre half, George Mountford, also of Stoke, and Billy Higgins of Everton all joined the exodus south. At one point, Henry Cockburn was rumoured to be considering an offer as well. It was money which tempted them. Mitten and all his other fellow professionals were earning a maximum wage of £12 a week and, at the age of 29, Mitten understandably wanted to secure his family's future after winning almost every honour in the English game, including a Cup-winners' medal, but, surprisingly, he had never been capped by England. He was promised a signing-on fee of £2,500 plus a salary of £2,500 a season and a win bonus of £35 a game plus £1,500 on completion of his contract. It was a considerable amount of money and many more league players were tempted before some of the adventurers returned home disillusioned.

Born in Burma, where his father was serving in the army, Mitten had joined United straight from school in 1936. He made numerous wartime appearances for United, Aston Villa and Tranmere Rovers before making his league debut for United against Grimsby as peacetime football resumed in August 1946. He was a fast, accomplished outside left, rated one of United's finest-ever players by Matt Busby, who made 161 appearances for United, scoring a creditable 61 goals.

Life in Bogotá, however, came to a quick end as his family craved for life back home. He was still officially a United player but, on his return, there was little chance they would continue with his services. Instead, he was fined

Charlie Mitten keeps United's hopes alive in the FA Cup semi-final against Wolves. But not for long; United lost the replay.

Charlie Mitten in a Cup tie against Preston at Maine Road before he disappeared to South America. He scored a goal to help United to a 4–1 triumph.

£250 by the FA and suspended for six months. Mitten was still young and fit enough to make a comeback and joined first division Fulham. He later became manager of Mansfield and in 1958 took over at Newcastle United.

UNITED'S "BABES" COOL, CONFIDENT

BY TOM JACKSON

Manchester Evening News, 24 November 1951

IT was a case of on with the old—and the new—at Anfield this afternoon, where Manchester United, seeking their first victory this month, included four reserves in their line-up against an unchanged Liverpool team.

For 18-year-old Irish boy Jackie Blanchflower and 21-year-old local Roger Byrne the occasion was particularly noteworthy. Both were making their entry into senior football, Blanchflower in place of Gibson at right-half and Byrne for Redman at left-back.

1951

The elegant Roger Byrne.

ON SATURDAY, 24 November United gave a debut to two youngsters who played a crucial role in the club's fortunes over the next seven years. It was the birth of the Busby Babes and Tom Jackson's piece in the *Manchester Evening News* was aptly headlined 'United's Babes Cool, Confident'. It was probably the first time the word 'Babes' was ever mentioned in association with United.

One of the 'Babes' was an 18-year-old half back from Belfast named Jackie Blanchflower, while the other was a 21-year-old defender called Roger Byrne. They turned out for United in a goalless draw at Anfield and won unstinting praise from the press. 'United's discoveries – debutantes Blanchflower and Byrne – were among the successes of the game', reported Kevin Wade in the *Sunday Chronicle*. He added that: 'Byrne played brilliantly at left back and Blanchflower was always in the picture with telling passes and first time tackling that did much to upset the smooth harmony between Payne and Liddell.'

Byrne had joined United in 1949 from local football and, within three years of making his debut, he became a permanent fixture in the England team. He eventually succeeded John Carey, not only at left back but as captain, and went on to make 277 appearances before he died at Munich. He was a fine attacking full back who could also score goals, netting 19 for his club, and even had a few early outings on the wing before he settled into defence. In his short international career he won 33 England caps and topped that with three league championships and a Cup final appearance. Without a doubt Byrne was one of the most outstanding defenders ever to wear an England shirt and he brought a command and calm to defending that has rarely been equalled.

Jackie Blanchflower never quite won the accolades of many of his Busby Babe contemporaries, nor of his more famous brother, the Tottenham and Northern Ireland captain Danny. Yet he made 116 appearances for United and represented his country on a dozen occasions. He survived Munich, but his injuries were so horrific as to put an end to his playing career. Blanchflower was the kind of player every manager likes to have in reserve. He could play anywhere and with equal ability and enthusiasm. In the 1957 Cup final he even deputised in goal after Ray Wood was injured. Yet he was probably more at home as a wing half or at inside right, and showed his goalscoring instinct by hitting 27 goals.

The introduction of Byrne and Blanchflower signalled the beginning of changes. United went on to win the league that season with many of the players who had formed the backbone of the side which had been so successful during the post-war years.

1952

SINCE THE WAR United had never been out of the top four. They had finished as runners-up on four occasions and the championship title was now long overdue. It finally arrived in 1952 and was never more deserved.

United had opened the year in second place, just a couple of points behind leaders Portsmouth who had already captured the title twice since the war. By February, they had moved into the top spot above Portsmouth and Arsenal, and stayed there for the remainder of the season. The title was virtually won with a midweek victory over Chelsea in the penultimate game of the season, but there was still a mathematical possibility of Arsenal overtaking them. And, by chance, the final fixture brought United face to face with their only challengers. United led Arsenal by two points and had such a superior goal average that Arsenal needed to win by seven goals at Old Trafford to steal the title. There was never any chance, although on the morning of the game Arsenal were apparently hellbent on achieving it. As it happened, there were seven goals but six of them came from United as they rounded off the season in championship style, trouncing the Gunners 6–1.

Jack Rowley netted another three goals to add to the 27 he had already scored while Stan Pearson grabbed a couple and Roger Byrne, playing out on the left wing, scored his seventh of the season. It had been an outstanding campaign and the post-war team had now deservedly carved their place in history. But, for many of them, it heralded the end of their careers. The team had been together for five years and it was time for new and younger blood.

Goalkeeper Jack Crompton had already been temporarily displaced by Reg Allen, but he made a brief comeback and remained on United's books until October 1956 when Ray Wood became first choice. Safe and sure, Crompton had joined United in 1944 and played a total of 211 games, with his finest moment coming during the 1948 Cup final. Two days before the match the giant

'LUCKY ARSENAL' LABEL IS DEAD

Manchester United ....6 Arsenal 1

SEVEN goals were needed from Arsenal to deprive Manchester United of the First Division Championship. There were seven, but the United hit six of them to clinch their season's great work. But bury that old "Lucky Arsenal" label after the injury hoodoo that has dogged the Cup finalists.

Sunday Dispatch, 27 April 1952

Arsenal finished with nine men. Outside-left Don Roper, with a knee bandaged limped off the field with four minutes to go, and after the first 25 minutes Arsenal were without centre-half Arthur Shaw, who sustained a suspected fracture of his left wrist as he took a powerful centre from Rowley in the stomach and fell down.

Shaw was the Wembley deputy in the event of Ray Daniel not having recovered from injury. So centre half and outside left are two big Wembley headaches for manager Tom Whittaker.

On the brighter side, left-back Lionel Smith came through the test, and surely centre-forward Holton will merit a place in the final team on this display.

Before Shaw retired United had settled any remote chance of being beaten by goal average when Rowley opened the score after eight minutes following one of Carey's long lobs.

There was danger to United in the way Holton moved over to the left wing to combine with Roper, but it looked suspiciously like another home goal when a Rowley shot hit the underside of the Arsenal bar and bounced down before Barnes cleared.

There were two goals in a minute just before half-time, Pearson having a shot deflected by a defender and then Rowley creating one of the most brilliant goals of the season. He dribbled round the defence, keeping the ball inches in play, and then squared to make Byrne a gift goal.

The Arsenal attack gradually became one of flashes by Holton and occasional rushes by Cox, who half-volleyed a Holton centre into goal one minute after Rowley had scored United's fourth

United combined superbly, but finished none too well. Then after 80 minutes Rowley scored from a penalty and Pearson ran on to crash in a Rowley centre in the last minute.

John Downie, an £18,000 record signing from Bradford Park Avenue in 1949, quickly repaid his valuation, scoring 11 goals in United's title-winning season, his best haul for the club. International honours, however, eluded him.

goalkeeper had been on the operating slab for the removal of an abscess on the spine but recovered sufficiently to pull off a save 11 minutes from time that many swear changed the course of the game. From United he went to Luton Town as trainer, but returned to Old Trafford to help out after the Munich disaster and even enjoyed a third spell at United under Tommy Docherty.

John Downie was also nearing the end of his Old Trafford days and made just another 22 appearances during the 1952–53 season. In all he played 115 times for the club and scored 36 goals following his transfer from Bradford Park Avenue in 1949. He had been bought to replace Johnny Morris and, although he had been a record buy, he proved such a valuable acquisition that, when he signed for Luton Town in the summer of 1953, United recouped most of their original outlay.

But new talent was also emerging to take the place of the post-war heroes. A young Roger Byrne made his debut at full back that season, while Johnny Berry joined the club from Birmingham City for £25,000. A determined little winger, Berry went on to make 273 appearances in a red shirt and win four England caps before injuries sustained at Munich brought his career to a premature halt.

It's all over. United are champions for the third time.

1952

AS LEAGUE CHAMPIONS United once more found themselves competing for the Charity Shield. This time their opponents were Cup-winners Newcastle United. It was a stirring early season encounter, which United won 4–2. Although United had captured the league title they were now, in truth, beyond their best. Similarly, Newcastle had seen better days, although both clubs quickly rebuilt and went on to win further honours before the 1950s were out – United claimed two more league titles and Newcastle added another FA Cup victory to their collection.

The youngsters who forged United's future were already arriving, and playing that day were Roger Byrne and Johnny Berry. But the clash of these two great northern teams marked the beginning of the end for Busby's famous post-war side. Jack Rowley pulled on the red shirt for the last time in early 1955 before moving to Plymouth as player-manager. He was one of the most prolific marksmen in United's history, scoring 208 goals in 422 appearances. He joined the club in October 1937 and won six England caps as well as league championship and Cup-winners' medals.

Henry Cockburn also departed, joining neighbours Bury in October 1954, after 275 appearances. A tenacious little half back, he was as strong and agile as any defender and, although only 5 feet 4 inches, he could outjump most forwards. Having joined United from local football, he made his league debut with the restart of soccer after the war and went on to win 13 England caps as well as a Cup-winners' and league championship medal.

Allenby Chilton also moved on after 16 years and almost 400 games at centre half. Tall, elegant and dependable, Chilton won a couple of England caps and skippered United late in his career.

Two great teams paint their "sunset" in glorious colour

Daily Dispatch, 25 September 1952

Jack Rowley was one of United's 'sunset' stars in their Charity Shield victory over Newcastle.

He made his debut the day before war broke out following his move from Seaham Colliery. During the war he was wounded in Normandy. But he recovered and returned to shape the backbone of United's defence. In 1955, he joined Grimsby Town as player-manager and helped them towards the third division north title.

One of his partners in defence, John Aston, also hung up his boots. He made his league debut with the resumption of peacetime football having joined the club in May 1937 and went on to make 282 appearances. He was a tough, no-nonsense full back never afraid to venture up field and have a crack at goal, scoring 30 times during his Old Trafford days. Aston was also the rock of the England defence and won 17 caps at left back. He played his final game for United in April 1954 before taking up scouting duties.

The team that had been built around Crompton, Carey, Aston, Chilton, Cockburn, Delaney, Downie, Rowley, Pearson and Mitten had been a prize-winning side. It may not have had the individual flair of the Billy Meredith–Charlie Roberts side of the Edwardian era, but it was solid and rugged with all-round ability. It was a difficult team to score against but one which could quickly switch from defence into attack. With its passing, United said farewell to an outstanding period in its history, but it was also opening a new chapter to an even greater epoch with a team that would combine all the finest qualities of United's two triumphant eras.

1953

When United signed Tommy Taylor they broke the bank. But what a goalscorer: 128 goals in 189 appearances for United. He maintained his incredible strike-rate at international level for England too after winning his first cap in 1953.

IT WAS THE day Stalin died. But, for Manchester United fans, the more important news was the signing of the Barnsley inside forward, Tommy Taylor. Over the next five years, Taylor set the country alight with his goalscoring feats and powered United towards two more league titles. He might have been expensive, but it was one of the best pieces of business Matt Busby ever concluded for the Reds.

It was said that 17 league clubs had put in an offer for the young man who was reluctant to leave his home town. But the Yorkshire club, wallowing at the bottom of the second division, had finally decided to cash in while they could. United were always favourites for his signature and Taylor made it abundantly clear as soon as Barnsley decided to sell that his preference was Old Trafford. It was the highest fee United had ever paid for a player, but it fell slightly short of the British record fee of £34,500 which Sheffield Wednesday had splashed out on the Notts County inside forward Jackie Sewell in March 1951. It was later revealed that, in fact, United had not paid £30,000, as reported, but £29,999, Busby being reluctant to burden the 21-year-old with a £30,000 tag.

Taylor had played just 44 games for Barnsley, but what attracted so much interest was the 26 goals he had netted. No one doubted that he could maintain that rate of scoring, even in first division football, and they were not disappointed for he struck 112 league goals in just 166 appearances for United. Taylor was the final piece in Busby's jigsaw – the marksman who would translate the efforts of those around him into goals. An unusually skilful attacker, as well as being robust and powerful, he brought a Continental touch to the English game and revelled in international football, scoring 11 goals in 14 European games for United and 16 for England in 19 appearances. His tragic death in the Munich air disaster was a bitter blow, not only to United but to his country as well, who have rarely seen his equivalent since.

Barnsley deals net £40,000

Daily Dispatch, 5 March 1953

1953

THOSE WHO SAW him play swear he was the finest wing half British football has ever produced. Busby, Charlton, Shankly, Billy Wright and Alf Ramsey have all testified to the brilliance of Duncan Edwards. When he died, still only 21 years old, he had already left a legacy that would survive the years.

Matt Busby had personally travelled to his home at Dudley just hours after his 16th birthday to talk with his parents and to formally secure his signature, such was the importance he placed on bringing Edwards to Old Trafford. And it was not long before the youngster was thrown into league football.

Edwards made his debut nine months after signing, on Saturday, 4 April 1953 at Old Trafford against Cardiff City. He was still only 16, but stood 5 feet $10\frac{1}{2}$ inches and weighed a mighty 12 stone 6 pounds. He had already made several appearances in the Central League, was a member of the youth team and had captained England Boys. He was the fifth teenager to pull on the United shirt that season, following bravely in the footsteps of Johnny Scott, Eddie Lewis, David Pegg and John Doherty. Not all made the grade, but there was never any doubt with Edwards. United may have been walloped 4–1 by Cardiff that Easter Saturday, but all the signs were that this youngster would be around for many more years. The season was virtually over and Edwards went back to the Central League when Henry Cockburn returned to fitness. However, he reappeared in October and hardly missed another game until his death, making 175 appearances and scoring 21 goals.

Edwards was the complete player – powerful, fast and just as capable of scoring goals as preventing them. He had a maturity way beyond his years. At 18, he was the youngest player ever to turn out for England and he had collected 18 caps by his death. No doubt, in time, he would have captained both United and England and would have still been in his early 30s when United captured the European Cup. Who knows what might have been had Edwards lived? It was a tragedy that his talents were never allowed to flower fully.

Right: Duncan Edwards was already a star at 16.

The most famous Babe and Busby discuss terms.

Edwards, 16, in United's first team

BY TOM JACKSON

DUNCAN EDWARDS, aged 16, reported at Manchester United's headquarters at Old Trafford to-day for duty as usual with the ground staff—and a few minutes later received the biggest news of his life.

He was told by Mr. Matt Busby, the United manager: "Go and get your football boots, son, you're playing for the first team against Cardiff City."

Though thrilled by the news Edwards took it calmly. He asked permission to 'phone his parents at Dudley, Worcestershire, and then raced a few hundred yards to give "Ma" Watson, the landlady who looks after him and several other Busby youngsters, the big tidings.

Mrs. Watson "the best landlady anyone could wish for," is used to her boy footballers making good.

Several of her 'teen-age "boarders," including Mark Jones, Jackie Blanchflower and David Pegg, have already made First Division grade, and when Duncan hustled around for his soccer togs she did her best to take things quietly. There was no fuss and no outward excitement.

Manchester Evening News, 4 April 1953

1953

ALL GREAT FOOTBALLING careers must draw to a close; the more dignified, the better. Some, finding the pace too tough, drop into the lower divisions and end their days in front of half-empty stadiums where the incessant barracking echoes around the terraces. And, when they finally hang up their boots, they disappear almost unnoticed. But that was not for Johnny Carey. When he went, he went at the top.

Carey had been considering his future as the season drew to a close and on the day of the final league match he gave notice. The United board repeatedly tried to dissuade him and even dreamed up a job on the staff. But he had made his decision and on Saturday, 23 May he announced that he was quitting.

He had enjoyed 17 seasons at Old Trafford, joining the club as an inside left in November 1936 for £250. He had played in nine different positions for United and in seven spots for Ireland, but it was as a right back that he made his mark. He may have been versatile but he was also one of the most elegant players in United's history. He was the ideal captain: rarely ruffled, always calm, and a fine example to the younger players around him. He was known as soccer's first gentleman, whose modesty was inversely proportionate to his talent. He played 344 games for United, scoring 18 goals, and captained them to league championship and FA Cup honours. He was Busby's eye and spirit on the field and was always the first name pencilled in on the weekly teamsheet. He made 29 appearances for Ireland between 1937 and 1953, captaining them on many occasions. In 1947 he skippered the Rest of Europe against Great Britain at Hampden and in 1949 he was Footballer of the Year. In that year he also led the Republic of Ireland to an historic victory over England at Goodison Park, the first time England had been beaten on English soil by any team other than the home countries.

Carey was astute enough to realise that United's post-war team was breaking up. In Roger Byrne United had already uncovered a full back who could proudly carry on where he was departing. He knew his days were numbered and initially welcomed United's promise of a coaching position, but, once word was out that he was looking for a backroom job, Blackburn Rovers swooped with an offer he could barely refuse and he left to become Rovers' manager. He later managed Everton, Leyton Orient and Nottingham Forest, but never with the success that he had led United.

Johnny Carey, who left United as one of the most popular players in the country.

Johnny Carey retiring

JOHNNY CAREY, Manchester United and Eire captain, and one of the greatest footballers of all time, to-day announced his retirement as a player.

He made the decision, he said, "because I don't feel capable of playing the United brand of soccer for another season." Carey added that his future is undecided, although he has been offered a position by Manchester United. "I hope to remain associated with the game that has been so good to me."

Carey was, of course, offered terms for next season. He has been thinking over his decision for several weeks, and the first to know what he intended to do was Mr. Matt Busby, the United manager, who was told by Johnny shortly before he left for his coaching tour in the United States.

In announcing his retirement the United captain said: "My 17 seasons at Old Trafford have been very happy ones, and my thanks are due to the directors, manager, secretary, players, trainers, and other staff for their help. The encouragement I got from our supporters and the Press have enabled me to get the most out of my ability. To them also my warmest thanks."

NINE POSITIONS

Carey, aged 34, has been one of the most versatile footballers in the game. He appeared in nine different positions for United and in seven positions for Ireland and Eire. Usually he appeared at right-half or right-back.

In 1948 Carey captained United in their Cup Final triumph over Blackpool, and another great honour came a year earlier when he led the Rest of Europe side against Great Britain.

Carey cost United £200 when they signed him from St. James's Gate (Eire) in 1936. In 1949 he was elected "Footballer of the Year" by the Football Writers' Association.

A tribute from Tom Jackson

SO Johnny Carey, the man who has always lived up to the title of "soccer's first gentleman" has played his last game for United.

Soccer will be indeed all the poorer without this modest, almost self-effacing Irishman who has proved such a wonderful inspiration to the team he has captained throughout all their great post-war years.

Manchester Evening News, 23 May 1953

1954

TERRIFIC STUFF BY THE BUSBY BOYS

Manchester Evening News, 27 April 1954

IN APRIL 1954 United's youngsters faced Wolverhampton Wanderers in the final of the Youth Cup. It was a repeat of the previous season's final when United had trounced Wolves 7–1 in the first leg at Old Trafford. They had then drawn the second leg, but captured the trophy 9–3 on aggregate. This time it was not quite so easy. The opening game at Old Trafford, in front of 18,000, was drawn 4–4 but at Molineux a David Pegg penalty gave United victory before 28,651 spectators. They went on to retain the Cup the following year, eventually winning it five years in succession.

United had already introduced many of the youth side into their league team. By the end of 1953, Duncan Edwards had become a regular choice while Jackie Blanchflower, Dennis Viollet, Colin Webster, Albert Scanlon, Mark Jones, David Pegg, Bill Whelan and Billy Foulkes were all experiencing, or about to experience, their first taste of league soccer. Besides them, Roger Byrne had firmly established himself as captain, even though he was still only 25, and new signing Tommy Taylor, at 21 years of age, had hit 22 league goals during the 1953/54 campaign and would score another 20 the following season. There was also winger Johnny Berry, a £25,000 signing from Birmingham at the start of the 1951/52 season, who had quickly made his mark.

Outside left David Pegg, moulded in the Tom Finney tradition of wingers, made his league debut in late 1952 but did not become a regular until 1955. Capped once by England, the Doncaster-born winger went on to play 148 times for United, scoring 28 goals before losing his life at Munich. The fair-haired Albert Scanlon fired his way into contention in 1954 and, over the next six years, scored 35 goals. He was another outside left, with a more brash style than Pegg that won him many admirers. Scanlon, the nephew of Charlie Mitten, survived the Munich crash, though he missed the remainder of the campaign through injury. He returned at the beginning of the following season and completed 127 games for United before joining Newcastle United for £18,000.

Another young half back, Mark Jones, was also beginning to challenge for a regular spot and, over the next few years, helped form one of the steadiest half-back lines in European soccer. After an early debut, he eventually secured the centre half shirt in 1955, making 120 appearances. He was on the fateful trip to Belgrade and played brilliantly against Red Star but sadly lost his life in the snow of Munich.

The stars of United's Youth Cup team against Wolves were two 16-year-olds born within days of each other who had yet to make their appearances in league football. One was Wilf McGuinness while the other was the nephew of Jackie Milburn – Bobby Charlton. Also challenging for a first-team place was Eddie Colman, another Babe who eventually partnered Edwards and Jones. Colman was only 21 when he died in the Munich disaster and there were those who regarded him as being potentially as outstanding a player as Edwards.

Of the team that so gloriously swept Wolves aside in 1954, eight went on to play league soccer for United and three of them perished at Munich.

FA Youth Cup winners 1954/55. Six would eventually turn out for the seniors.

Matt with just some of his famous Busby Babes.

1955

SIGNS THAT UNITED'S new young team were set for an assault on the league championship could be spotted as early as November 1955. An impressive 3–0 victory over the current league champions, Chelsea, at Old Trafford left United in second place and looking confident. The game marked a turning point in United's fortunes. The old post-war team had now disappeared and the young turks had stepped into their boots. In the *Empire News*, football reporter

EDWARDS THE MAN FOR WEMBLEY

by JAMES HARDY

MANCHESTER UTD. ..... 3 CHELSEA 0

STEP forward, Eddie Colman! And you, too, Duncan Edwards! Here we have two Manchester United wing half-backs, both now in the Army. They were the two youngest players on the field at Old Trafford, but how magnificently they played!

For 19-year-old Colman, who made his League debut at Bolton last week and was now appearing in League football at Old Trafford for the first time, it was simply wonderful.

He has a body-swerve which always gets opponents running the wrong way. He was opposed, in this instance, to England international Roy Bentley. But names mean nothing to Eddie. He gave a diamond-studded display in Manchester United's victory.

Duncan Edwards, also 19-years-old, on the opposite flank, was also at his best—he looks a certainty for the England team against Spain at Wembley, at the end of the month and some of his shooting was in the same category.

Empire News, 20 November 1955

Chelsea Fall To Taylor's Tricks

MANCHESTER UTD. 3, CHELSEA 0

News of the World, 20 November 1955

United in transition. The famous post-war champions with some new additions from the Busby Babes. They remained a formidable force.

James Hardy reckoned United looked championship material, while elsewhere in the paper there was a call for Duncan Edwards to be in the England team facing Spain at Wembley later that month. In the event, the advice was not heeded but within five months Edwards stepped out in an England shirt to face Scotland while still only 18.

Another England player, Tommy Taylor, hit two of the goals against Chelsea while a third England player, Roger Byrne, converted a penalty. Taylor's pair brought his total to 11 for the season and by the time the campaign was over he had netted 25 in just 33 appearances. In his first season at Old Trafford he had struck seven in 11 games and had followed that up with 22 in 35 matches the following season. In 1954/55 he claimed 20 in 30 games and, at the time of his death, had scored an astonishing 128 goals in 189 appearances for United.

Making his home debut that day against Chelsea was another Busby Babe, Eddie Colman. He had played his first game for United the previous week at Bolton and, although United lost 3–1, Busby kept faith in the young man. Colman did not disappoint him. He had joined United straight from school, turning professional in November 1953 and had played in three Youth Cup finals before making his league debut. Once in the first team, he was there to stay and went on to make 107 appearances before his death at Munich. He was a midfielder, built in the mould of a young Nobby Stiles, tenacious, sharp and determined, with an eye to attack as well as defence. His early death robbed United and the English game of a player years ahead in tactical awareness. With the tall, powerful Edwards by his side United could switch their half-back line from defence to attack with the slip of a ball. They were almost the perfect combination. That Colman had not been capped at the time of his death was a tragedy.

1956

MANCHESTER TEN YEARS'

FEW FOOTBALL WRITERS had predicted championship honours for United as the 1955/56 season kicked off. One or two rated them an exciting prospect but quibbled about so many youngsters and their lack of experience. Nor did the season begin in championship fashion: only three wins in the first eight fixtures. But from then on, it was plain sailing. They lost only four more games the entire season and were undefeated at Old Trafford. They shot to the top of the table in late October after just 15 games and, although they were briefly nudged back, by Christmas the battle was won. United were top and they never looked back, winning the title in glorious style with games to spare. Blackpool were runners-up trailing 11 points behind as United lost only once between 1 January and the end of the campaign. The title was officially secured on Saturday, 7 April when a post-war record crowd of 62,277 crammed into Old Trafford to watch them beat Blackpool 2–1. Over a period of 10 years, United had been out of the top four only twice and their latest championship had been won with a team whose average age was a mere 22.

Tommy Taylor, not unexpectedly, was top marksman with 25 league goals, while Dennis Viollet notched 20 of his own. Nobody else even reached double figures. There were some outstanding victories, including a 5–2 hammering of Newcastle and a double over the previous season's champions Chelsea. On Boxing Day, Charlton were walloped 5–1 at Old Trafford but, just to show that football really is a 'funny game', Charlton returned the compliment the

Top: United are feted at Manchester's Town Hall after winning the title.

Right: Champions again. Roger Byrne shows Old Trafford the league trophy.

UNITED CHAMPIONS: RUN OF SUCCESS

Sunday Dispatch, 8 April 1956

Watch Forest in tense struggle for promotion

By LINESMAN

MANCHESTER UNITED are again League champions—for the fourth time in their history and the second time since the war.

The gates were closed at Old Trafford yesterday half an hour before the start of their vital game with Blackpool, their only remaining challengers, and a new post-war record crowd there of 62,277 saw United recover from one down at half-time to win 2—1.

But the man who has planned their tactics, manager Matt Busby, was not present at the moment of success ; he was in Scotland attending a funeral.

What a wonderful run his boys have had in the ten years since the war. Here is their record of final positions in the First Division table:

2—2—2—4—2—1—8—4—5—1

Add to that a Cup Final win in 1947-48 and it clearly makes them the pre-eminent post-war club.

The average age of the present team is 22, with Roger Byrne, the left back, and John Berry, the outside right, the only two players left of the championship side of four years ago.

And United could stay on top for some time to come for most of their players are at the start of their careers.

The impeccable Dennis Viollet, whose 20 goals were a vital contribution to United's championship triumph. With a total of 178 goals in almost 300 games, Viollet rates as one of United's finest marksmen.

following day beating them 3–0. In the FA Cup there was another surprise as second division Bristol Rovers carried off their scalp with a 4–0 win. In recent years United's record in the competition left much to be desired, although that would soon change.

Dennis Viollet's 20 goals were a vital boost to the team, giving their attack an added thrust. A Manchester lad, he had made his debut in April 1953 but had to wait until the following season before he secured the number 10 shirt. But, once he had pulled it on, it rarely left his back. Viollet was a much-underrated marksman, yet his record speaks volumes. During the 1954/55 season he struck 21 goals, in 1956/57 he hit 25 goals while in 1959/60 he smashed the club record with 32 goals. In all he hit 20 goals or more in six successive seasons. When he left the club in January 1962 to join Stoke in a £25,000 deal, he had scored 178 goals in 291 appearances. He added another 59 goals at Stoke before he went off to the United States. Viollet was a lean and hungry goalscorer with a delicate touch and deceptive body swerve but, surprisingly, he won only two England caps. They say that goalscorers hunt better in pairs and in Viollet, Tommy Taylor had the perfect foil. Perhaps Viollet was a trifle unlucky to be toiling in the shadow of his more illustrious partner yet he remains one of the most prolific marksmen in United's history.

1956

Dennis Viollet hits United's eighth goal as they run out 10–0 winners.

UNITED'S CHAMPIONSHIP triumph entitled them to a crack at the European Cup, now in its second season. The competition, dreamed up by the French sporting newspaper *L'Equipe*, had been inaugurated the previous season, with Real Madrid as the first winners. Chelsea, the 1954/55 English league champions, had been invited to enter and were keen to accept but had been strongly dissuaded from taking part by the Football League, leaving Scottish champions Hibernian as Britain's only representatives. Matt Busby, however, was determined that the League would not bar his team from entering. They were the English champions and it was their privilege to compete with the best in Europe. Above all, Busby wanted to prove that United could match any team on the Continent. After some initial skirmishing, the Football League sensibly backed down and United were given the go-ahead, although a lack of floodlights at Old Trafford initially meant that their home games had to be played elsewhere. And, as when bomb damage had left United homeless, it was neighbours Manchester City who stepped in again to offer a helping hand.

And so, in late September 1956 as Britain rolled towards a crisis over the Suez Canal, United set off on their European travels with a trip to Brussels where they comfortably disposed of the Belgian champions Anderlecht. The second leg was even more of a formality, as United hammered their Belgian counterparts 10–0. At half-time they led 5–0, after Tommy Taylor had started the rout in the eighth minute. By the final whistle Taylor had scored a hat trick, while Dennis Viollet had struck four, Bill Whelan two and Johnny Berry one. It was a stunning performance that had the handful of footballing journalists who had bothered to attend reaching for the hyperbole. Even Jeff Mermans, the Anderlecht captain, could not hide his admiration when, in the *Manchester Evening News*, he called United world-beaters, rating them better than even the mighty Magyars, Honved. Sadly, most of the soccer press missed English football's first glimpse of European competition, reckoning domestic events far more important than United's flirtation with Continental football. But, by the end of United's first campaign, they had changed their mind.

Ten-goal United hailed as best in Europe

Manchester Evening News, 27 September 1956

WHAT BELGIUM'S MR. SOCCER THOUGHT ABOUT THE MATCH

United are world-beaters: No shame for us in defeat

By JEFF MERMANS,

Captain of Anderlecht and already a soccer legend in his native Belgium. In an interview with

TOM JACKSON

THERE is not a single excuse we can offer for our humiliating defeat. We gave of our best, but it was not just good enough against what must rate as one of the best club teams in the world.

News Chronicle, 27 September 1956

1957

AFTER THEIR RECORD 10-goal thrashing of Anderlecht, United then disposed of the German champions, Borussia Dortmund. That victory pitted them against Atlético Bilbao in a quarter-final that served up two of the most memorable matches United had ever experienced. The first leg was fought on a bitterly cold January day in the northern Spanish port of Bilbao where snow, sleet and mud greeted the English champions. It was clearly not to United's liking as they slumped to a three-goal deficit by half time. They had produced a catalogue of errors that matched their schoolboy age, but, in the second half, they retrieved the impending catastrophe as Taylor and Viollet brought some respectability to the scoreline. But it did not last long as Bilbao struck twice more to make it 5–2, only for Bill Whelan to score a dramatic late goal that gave United the faintest hope for the second leg. Yet no one in the United camp ever doubted that they could do it in the return match.

BEATEN UNITED CHEERED OFF
Three-goal rally scares Bilbao

News Chronicle, 17 January 1957

UNITED TOUCH THE TOP
The match of a generation

News Chronicle, 7 February 1957

The second leg beneath the glare of the Maine Road lights was watched by 70,000 enthralled fans. Even if Fleet Street had not stirred to the thrill of the European Cup, Manchester certainly had, with 75,598 having already cheered the victory over Borussia. By the end of this tie, Fleet Street had been rudely awoken by what experienced sportswriter Henry Rose described in the *Daily Express* as the 'Greatest Victory in Soccer History'. As half time approached, however, United had still not dented the Basques' stubborn defence. But, in the 42nd minute, a speculatiye Edwards shot cannoned off a defender and Dennis Viollet snapped up the opportunity. Shortly after half time Viollet hit another only for it to be disallowed, but a minute later Taylor pounced on a quickly-taken free kick and it was 2–0. The game was now level at five goals each. Had the away goal rule been operational at this time, United would have been through. As it was, they still needed one more goal to avoid a replay in Paris. And, with just five minutes remaining, Tommy Taylor ran the ball down the line, skipped past two defenders and slipped a pass for Johnny Berry to crash the ball into the back of the net. United had achieved the impossible.

The Busby Babes' greatest triumph. Some 70,000 saw them beat Bilbao 3–0.

In the *Daily Herald*, George Follows described it as the greatest football match he had ever seen, the greatest crowd he had ever heard and the greatest centre forward display he had ever known. Everyone agreed – it was Tommy Taylor's night. Against Jesus Garay, Europe's number one centre half, the curly-haired Taylor had wriggled and inspired one of the greatest comebacks in the club's history. Bilbao had been on a £200-a-man bonus to win the tie; Taylor and company had been on one of just £3.

1957

BY JANUARY of 1957 United were four points clear of the rest of the field and heading for their fifth league championship. There was never any doubt about who would win the title. The previous season's champions were so young that they could only improve and mature with each year and looked destined to be champions for the next five seasons. It was not until their 13th game, against Everton, that they suffered their first defeat, going down by a remarkable five goals to two at Old Trafford.

Once into the New Year, however, United stormed away from the pack, losing just three more games before the end of the campaign. Tottenham, Preston and Blackpool were their closest rivals but, by the time United had been crowned, they were eight points ahead of Spurs. The chasers had to concede the race well before the end of the season when a 4–0 victory at Old Trafford over Sunderland clinched yet another league championship for the Busby Babes. A crowd of 58,725 watched Billy Whelan hit a couple with Edwards and Taylor adding the rest. Surprisingly, Whelan ended the season as leading marksman with 26 league goals, followed by Taylor with 22 and Dennis Viollet with 16. In all, United had notched up an astonishing 103 goals, the first team to crack the 100 barrier in the division since the war. Added to this were 15 Cup and 24 European Cup goals, giving a grand total of 142 during the season. Tommy Taylor had scored 34 of these in 44 appearances, while Bill Whelan hit 33 and Dennis Viollet 25.

It was Billy Whelan's first full season in league soccer, yet his impact had been considerable. Born in Dublin, he came to Old Trafford from Home Farm in 1953, making his debut in March 1955. The following season he had just 13 outings at inside right, scoring four goals,

Above: Does Mrs Charlton know about this? Singer Elizabeth Larner swoons with Bobby, Tommy Taylor and Dennis Viollet.

Right: Billy Whelan nets the second for United against Manchester City, September 1956.

BUSBY BOYS

First leg of treble and the old look

MANCHESTER UNITED are Champions again. Yesterday they thrashed Sunderland 4—0 to clinch the first leg of the fantastic treble they are chasing, but more important than the win itself was the manner of its achievement.

GONE was the tired look about the Champions' play—BACK was the snap and bite. The crowd of close on 60,000 went home happy that their favourites would take the field on Thursday with a very good chance of entering the final of the European Cup.

Empire News, 21 April 1957

CHAMPIONS AGAIN

but finally displaced Blanchflower as the 1956/57 season kicked off. He won the first of his four Irish caps in 1956 and, when he died at Munich, he had made 96 appearances for United, scoring a remarkable 52 goals. Yet such was the reservoir of talent at Old Trafford that Busby could afford to leave him out of the side and, although he was in the squad that went to Belgrade, he never appeared against Red Star. He clearly had an eye for goal, coupled with the most deceptive body swerve, delicate ball skills and an ability to create goals as well as score them. Had he lived, who knows what heights Whelan might have reached.

Also among the goals was another youngster, by the name of Bobby Charlton, who had hit 12 in 17 appearances. The 18-year-old, a member of the club's FA Youth Cup-winning side, had made his debut standing in for Tommy Taylor against Charlton Athletic on 6 October, where he made an immediate impact with a couple of goals. But then he was the nephew of Jackie Milburn, scorer of over 170 league goals for Newcastle. Towards the end of the campaign, Charlton became a more established figure in the side, often displacing Bill Whelan, although he did not win a permanent spot until after Munich. Charlton travelled on that fateful flight, but crawled from the wreckage to become, in many ways, the saviour of the club, as he went on to record 708 first-class appearances for the Reds, scoring 223 goals.

1957 MURDER IN

UNITED'S EUROPEAN CUP semi-final brought them face to face with the mighty Real Madrid. Real, still a largely unknown quantity, had won the first European Cup the previous season when they had begun to stamp their flowing style on the football map of Europe. Britain had seen nothing of the Spanish glamour team, but, after playing United, Real made an indelible impression on British football fans.

The first leg was played on 12 April in the cauldron of Real's Bernabeu stadium roared on by 125,000 ecstatic fans. United went down 3–1, with Tommy Taylor snatching United's goal to give them a brief lifeline at 2–1. But it did not last long; within minutes Mateos had made it 3–1 and United's fate had been sealed. They had held Real goalless for a full hour but had finally succumbed to their irresistible skills.

Nevertheless, United continued to believe that they could retrieve the situation as they had against Atlético Bilbao, but in Real they had met a team whose growing confidence eventually swept them to five successive European Cup triumphs. They could match almost any United player with one of supreme quality. At centre forward there was the Argentinian maestro Alfredo Di Stefano, who fed voraciously off the wing work of the wiry little Frenchman Raymond Kopa. Alongside them were Rial, the stocky Gento and toreador Mateos, each capable of turning a half-chance into a goal. With a forward line like this, they hardly needed a defence yet in Zarraga, Marquitos and Muñoz they boasted as tough and stubborn a resistance as any in Europe. Would there ever be a finer club side? When the Hungarian Ferenc Puskas pulled on the famous white shirt a few seasons later, it showed they could improve yet more.

Real's arrival in Manchester gave Old Trafford its first European night under floodlights. Installed by the General Electric Company, the lights brought a new dimension and an exciting era to football, not only at United but wherever the game was played. There were 65,000 inside Old Trafford that spring evening to witness another glorious chapter in the history of the club.

Little else, however, went according to plan. By half time United were two goals behind and trailing 5–1 on aggregate: Kopa had burst through the United defence to gobble up a Di Stefano

United at the shrine v Real Madrid. Ray Wood saves from the incomparable Di Stefano.

MADRID

Manchester United—hacked and slashed—end 2 goals down in the European Cup

MADRID, Thursday.—Real Madrid got away with murder before 125,000 witnesses at the Santiago Bernabeau Stadium here today. They hacked, slashed, kicked and wrestled their way to a 3-1 victory in this European Cup semi-final first leg.

Daily Herald, 12 April 1957

OUR CHAMPIONS GO DOWN FIGHTING

Daily Mirror, 26 April 1957

Tommy Taylor, flanked by United fans at the Bernabeu, watches the Babes practise.

backheel and Mateos had converted a fierce Gento shot which Ray Wood could only parry. United must have known in their hearts that there was no comeback from such a deficit, yet Matt Busby's sides were not renowned for giving in easily and after the interval they reappeared, even more determined. Within 11 minutes Billy Whelan had snapped up a loose opportunity, giving United their long-awaited fillip. Wave after wave of red shirts stormed tirelesssly towards the Real goal, as tackles flashed and tempers flared. Time and again Alonso saved desperately from a rampant United forward line and only in the 85th minute did his guard deny him when a young Bobby Charlton levelled the scores. And that was how it remained. United were out of the European Cup, defeated by the finest side in world football.

1957

THERE ARE those who would argue that 1957 marked a zenith in the story of Manchester United Football Club. They might, in future years, go on to collect further league championships, FA Cups and even a European Cup, but in 1957 they stood on the brink of an unprecedented treble. Even after failing so magnificently against Real Madrid they still had every hope of achieving a domestic double of league and Cup, something which no other side in modern soccer history had accomplished.

United were odds-on favourites to beat Aston Villa at Wembley but, on a May day when the ground was gloriously bathed in sunshine, the chill of injustice would numb those who had gathered around TV sets expecting to witness a new epoch. It all happened in a flash. With just six minutes gone, Peter McParland, Villa's flying Irish winger, recklessly charged Ray Wood as the big goalkeeper, with ball in hands, was preparing to kick upfield. It was a nonsensical, pointless foul and it was a wonder McParland remained on the field.

Ray Wood lay motionless, McParland beside him. But at least the Villa man had only himself to blame for his injury. Wood's cheekbone had been shattered and minutes later he was stretchered off. Jackie Blanchflower pulled on his jersey, Edwards was pushed into the centre half spot and United had to make the best of it with only 10 men, as no substitutes were then allowed.

United fought heroically, winning the goalless first half on points. Wood reappeared briefly on the right wing shortly before half time but was little more than a passenger. In the second half, with their rhythm unsettled, and their shape distorted, United succumbed as McParland scored twice in the space of five minutes. And even one of those goals was strongly disputed as offside. It seemed that the gods were determined United would never claim the double. Yet Tommy Taylor managed to pull a goal back and, in a last-ditch effort, a dazed Wood returned to man the goal. But it was too late. United battled bravely for the final few minutes, at last showing some of the style and skill that had won them so many admirers. But sadly they had run out of time.

Heroic Jackie Blanchflower can only watch as McParland gives Villa the lead.

Stand-in goalkeeper Jackie Blanchflower was undoubtedly the hero of the hour, holding Villa's marauding forwards at bay; but for Ray Wood it was the pinnacle of his career, as he played just a score more games for United. The following year he was seriously injured at Munich and was out of action for the rest of that season. He returned to Old Trafford but, with Harry Gregg now firmly established between the posts, he could not regain the goalkeeper's jersey. He played just once more after Munich and then moved to Huddersfield Town in late 1958. He had joined United in December 1949 as an 18-year-old from Darlington, making his first appearance that season, but had to wait a couple more years before he became a regular choice. He was capped three times by England, played 205 games for United and had a career total of more than 450 league and cup games.

FRANK McGHEE says: The Babes have all it takes for the 'double' of the century

Daily Mirror, 4 May 1957

Below: A stunned Ray Wood receives treatment after colliding with McParland.

1958

UNITED TRAVELLED to Belgrade on a pea-souper of a Monday morning, little knowing that some of them would never see Manchester again. They were scheduled to play the Yugoslav champions Red Star in the second leg of the European Cup quarter-finals on the Wednesday afternoon, having already beaten them 2–1 back home.

United began brilliantly with Dennis Viollet scoring within 90 seconds as a lucky rebound fell his way. The great Yugoslav goalkeeper Vladimir Beria – everybody's favourite Continental keeper – could only watch in disgust. On the half hour, United took a further step towards the semi-finals when Charlton dispossessed Kostic close to the halfway line and began a loping run towards goal before firing a rocket of a shot that swept past Beria. Two minutes later the nephew of 'Wor Jackie' seized on a loose ball, made his way through a ruck of players, and hammered in United's third. It was now 5–1 on aggregate – surely that was enough. It was, but only just.

Two minutes into the second half, Red Star pulled one back. Another arrived from the penalty spot eight minutes later. Now it was all hands to the pump as Red Star unleashed all their power at United. Shot after shot peppered the United goal, with Gregg springing and lunging like a crazed cat. Yet he was always equal to it, bringing off his most spectacular feat when, with just four minutes remaining, he dashed from his goalline to take a threatening ball. But, in doing so, he stumbled and fell outside the penalty area. From the free kick Kostic bent the ball around a stranded Gregg and Red Star now needed only one more goal. For three minutes United held their breath as their hearts pumped and their pulses raced. It was close, mighty close, but at the final whistle they had hung on and were through to the last four.

For many of the football writers who reported the Red Star game, it was to be the final match report they would ever file. George Follows of the *Daily Herald* was one; he reckoned he had just seen the best football United had ever played; while Tom Jackson in the *Manchester Evening News* had, for possibly the only time in his career, the front page lead story. Neither returned from Belgrade and the football pages which had once sparkled with their prose were all the poorer for their deaths.

Manchester Evening News

27,653 TV & RADIO—PAGE 2 WEDNESDAY, FEBRUARY 5, 1958 PRICE 3d.

RED STAR v. UNITED RED DEVILS

United snatch 3-0 Cup lead

Manchester Evening News, 5 February 1958

Top: The final photograph. United line up against Red Star.

Bottom: The final practice at the Yugoslav Army Stadium.

1958

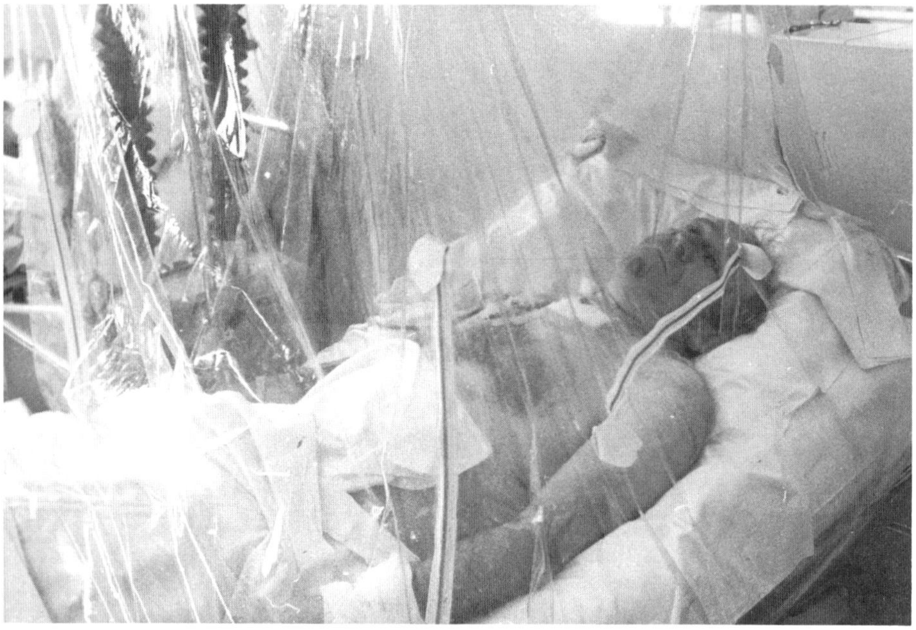

Above: For days Busby hovered between life and death.

LIKE THE ASSASSINATION of President Kennedy and a handful of other momentous world events, anyone old enough at the time can remember vividly where they were and precisely what they were doing when the horrific news came over on the radio that the plane carrying the Manchester United football team had crashed at Munich airport, killing many of those on board. It left the nation stunned, shocking even those who had never seen a football match, let alone Manchester United. It wasn't that United were just another football team – and heaven knows that would have been bad enough – but this team was the finest side British football had produced in decades.

There is little that can be said about the tragedy of Munich that has not already been well documented elsewhere. The chilling facts speak for themselves. United, returning from Belgrade where they had just drawn 3–3 with Red Star to secure a place in the semi-finals of the European Cup, had briefly stopped over in Munich to refuel when the weather deteriorated. Twice their twin-engined BEA Elizabethan aircraft attempted to take off only to fail. Shortly after 3pm, with the snow falling heavily, a third attempt was made. But, as the giant aircraft roared down the runway, the usual power that would lift it into the skies was missing. Flight Zulu Uniform – 609 crashed in the snow and slush 60 yards beyond the end of the runway, crossing a road before its port wing smashed into a house. The starboard side of the fuselage hit a wooden hut and the cockpit struck a tree while the wing and part of the tail were torn off.

Twenty-one lay dead in the immediate aftermath. Two others, including Duncan Edwards, would later add to that toll. Eight United players were among the victims. They were Roger Byrne, Tommy Taylor, Duncan Edwards, Eddie Colman, Mark Jones, Bill Whelan, Geoff Bent and David Pegg. United coach and former player Bert Whalley and trainer Tom Curry were also killed along with secretary Walter Crickmer. Edwards, although dragged alive from the wreckage, died in hospital two weeks later. Matt Busby hovered between life and death for a short while but pulled through. The bulk of his great side had been destroyed in a few moments.

Eight journalists also perished. They were Alf Clarke of the *Manchester Evening Chronicle*, Don Davies of the *Manchester Guardian*, George Follows of the *Daily Herald*, Tom Jackson of the *Manchester Evening News*, Archie Ledbrooke of the *Daily Mirror*, Henry Rose of the *Daily Express*, Eric Thompson of the *Daily Mail* and Frank Swift, the former Manchester City and England goalkeeper, of the *News of the World*. Two crew members also died along with two other passengers.

Although Johnny Berry and Jackie Blanchflower both survived, injuries took their toll and neither played football again. When United returned to Wembley a few months later there were only two players in the side from the previous season's final.

Daily Mirror FRI FEB 7 1958

2½d FORWARD WITH THE PEOPLE No. 16,843

SOCCER AIR TRAGEDY

Manchester United plane crashes

21 dead

AN Elizabethan airliner—on charter to Manchester United football team, the fabulous "Busby Babes," crashed on take-off at Munich Airport, Germany, yesterday, and plunged the world of Soccer into mourning.

Among the twenty-one dead were United stars Roger Byrne (captain), Tommy Taylor (centre forward), Mark Jones (centre half), Eddie Colman (right half), Billy Whelan (inside right), David Pegg (outside left), Geoff Bent (left back).

Also dead was ex-England goalkeeper and sportswriter Frank Swift. While in hospital last night fighting for his life, was manager Matt Busby, who gave his name to the team and made it one of the most famous in football.

Twenty-three of the 44 passengers survived.

Daily Mirror,
7 February 1958

The scene of carnage where 23, mostly young men, lost their lives.

1958

Assistant manager Jimmy Murphy (centre) with Munich survivor Bobby Charlton and new signing Ernie Taylor begin to pick up the pieces following the Munich air disaster, which had destroyed the magnificent Busby Babes.

IT IS IMPOSSIBLE to imagine the sentiment that must have swirled around Old Trafford the night United returned to the fray. The crowd was charged with emotion, the players distressed, and the public beyond Old Trafford willing United on to a seemingly impossible victory. Almost 60,000 pilgrims came to pay their respects, eyes tearful in the glare of the Old Trafford lights, senses numb, not really sure whether to cheer or cry; most did both.

United had been scheduled to play Sheffield Wednesday in the fifth round of the FA Cup on Saturday, 15 February, but, in the aftermath of Munich, the fixture was postponed until the following Wednesday evening. With so many dead and others injured, Jimmy Murphy's immediate problem had been to find enough players to represent the club. There were still many fine youngsters in the youth team who could be called upon but United also needed some experience. So Murphy, who had stepped into the breach while Busby still hovered between life and death in a Munich hospital, was forced to dip into the transfer market. Within days he signed the diminutive Ernie Taylor from Blackpool who, with a couple of Cup-winners' medals from his time at Blackpool and Newcastle, was as well versed in first division football as anybody. He was also an England international and, although he was now 33 years old, he still had plenty to offer a club like United in a dire situation. But Murphy also needed some flair and for that he was obliged to trade expensively. Just 75 minutes before United kicked off against Wednesday he signed Aston Villa's England Under-23 wing half Stan Crowther for £35,000. Crowther himself was little older than most of the remaining Babes and had only 50 league appearances to his credit, yet in his short spell at Villa he had impressed many with his vision and dash. However, Crowther was already Cup-tied, having appeared in the competition for Villa, but the FA generously waived that rule aside and, within an hour of putting pen to paper, the golden-haired Crowther was pulling on the red shirt of United.

'United Will Go On' read the front

UNITED WILL GO ON . . .

On 6th February, 1958 an aircraft returning from Belgrade crashed at Munich Airport. Of the twenty-one passengers who died twelve were players and officials of the Manchester United Football Club. Many others lie injured.

It is the sad duty of we who serve United to offer the bereaved our heartfelt sympathy and condolences. Here is a tragedy which will sadden us for years to come, but in this we are not alone. An unprecedented blow to British football has touched the hearts of millions and we express our deep gratitude to the many who have sent messages of sympathy and floral tributes. Wherever football is played United is mourned, but we rejoice that many of our party have been spared and wish them a speedy and complete recovery. Words are inadequate to describe our thanks and appreciation of the truly magnificent work of the surgeons and nurses of the Rechts der Isar Hospital at Munich. But for their superb skill and deep compassion our casualties must have been greater. To Professor Georg Maurer, Chief Surgeon, we offer our eternal gratitude.

Although we mourn our dead and grieve for our wounded we believe that great days are not done for us. The sympathy and encouragement of the football world and particularly of our supporters will justify and inspire us. The road back may be long and hard but with the memory of those who died at Munich, of their stirring achievements and wonderful sportsmanship ever with us, Manchester United will rise again.

H. P. HARDMAN, CHAIRMAN

NEW BABES RISE TO GREATNESS

By FRANK McGHEE

MATT BUSBY will be proud to call the new Manchester United "MY TEAM."

That is the highest compliment I can pay to the side built on the shattered framework of the famous Busby Babes which played so brilliantly, so bravely, so wonderfully at Old Trafford last night.

Their victory over Sheffield Wednesday in this fifth round Cup-tie was more than just another football win.

It was a memorial built with skill and courage to the men they mourn and the men who are still in hospital after the Munich disaster.

Busby can be proud of these eleven Cup heroes

Daily Mirror, 20 February 1958

Left: 'United Will Go On' was the brave and now famous message as they returned to action less than two weeks after Munich.

Next Home Match
1st DIVISION
United v NOTTS. FOREST
22 Feb. Kick-off 3-0 pm

Shirts Red — MANCHESTER UNITED — Knickers White

Youth International Match
ENGLAND v GERMANY
Wednesday, 12 March
Kick-off 7-30 pm

GREGG
FOULKES 2 — GREAVES 3
GOODWIN 4 — COPE 5 — CROWTHER 6
R WEBSTER 7 — TAYLOR 8 — DAWSON 9 — PEARSON 10 — BRENNAN 11 L

Referee:
A. Bond, London
Kick-off 7-30 pm

FOOTBALL GREEN PLEASE

Linesmen:
F. Wain, Bakewell
Red Flag
F. P. Clarke, Coventry
Yellow Flag

L FINNEY 11 — FROGGATT 10 — SHINER 9 — QUIXALL 8 — WILKINSON 7 R
O'DONNELL 6 — SWAN 5 — KAY 4
JOHNSON 3 — MARTIN 2
RYALLS

Team changes will be indicated by loudspeaker

Shirts Blue and White Stripes — SHEFFIELD WEDNESDAY — Knickers Black

Team changes will be indicated by loudspeaker

Above: No United names were printed on the teamsheet, just 11 blank spaces, as the line-up was uncertain right up to the kick-off.

cover of the match programme that evening, but on the centre pages 11 blank spaces had been left to fill in. As the names of the side were read out over the tannoy there was silence, although a cheer went up when the announcement was made that Crowther would be in the side. Gregg, Foulkes, Greaves, Goodwin, Cope, Crowther, Webster, Ernie Taylor, Dawson, Pearson and Brennan. It was a strange line-up, yet they did United proud.

Wednesday must have felt the entire world was willing United on and, under such pressure, it was hardly surprising that they lost. In the 27th minute young Shay Brennan, making his debut and converted from full back to winger, saw his corner fly into the net, albeit aided by the Wednesday keeper. In the 70th minute Brennan struck again as he seized on a rebound and, shortly before full time, Alex Dawson, with only a handful of league games to his credit, added a third to give United a 3–0 victory. Brennan had been the star of the show in what was the first of 355 appearances for the club. Dawson also went on to play first-team football with United for a number of years, along with others like Freddie Goodwin. United had won against all the odds. A new team had bravely taken the field and had ensured that United would indeed go on.

1958

AFTER THEIR HEROIC victory over Sheffield Wednesday in the fifth round of the Cup, United stormed on, conquering West Bromwich Albion in a quarter-final replay before meeting Fulham for a place at Wembley. In the first match at Villa Park, the two sides drew, but in the replay at Highbury, United swamped the Londoners 5–3 to clinch their place in the final.

The trip to Wembley was always going to be a sentimental journey for United, especially as Matt Busby had recovered sufficiently to promise his presence for the big occasion. The entire nation, except, no doubt, for a small enclave around Bolton, was willing a United victory, but on that warm May afternoon the young heroic hearts of United were sadly too inexperienced for the battle-hardened men of Bolton.

Dennis Viollet joined Busby in making a gallant return to the fray, pulling on his old number 10 shirt for only the third time since the Munich disaster. Yet, despite the national wave of sympathy that had swept United along throughout the traumatic months following Munich, the fairy tale was about to come to an abrupt and unhappy end. It was Nat Lofthouse, the Bolton and England centre forward, who shattered the dream when he pounced in the third minute to edge the Lancastrians ahead. United fought hard to retrieve the deficit but, in Bolton and particularly in the 32-year-old Lofthouse, they faced formidable opponents. At half time United remained a goal behind, but in truth they had hardly looked likely to reverse the position.

With just 10 minutes of the second half gone, however, there came the incident that would not only win the Cup for

Busby returns to take his place alongside Jimmy Murphy.

Lofthouse Wembley

HIS TWO GOALS WIN CUP FOR BOLTON

By BOB FERRIER

BOLTON WANDERERS ...2 MANCHESTER UNITED 0

MANCHESTER UNITED, after the most harrowing but remarkable season in any club's history, were outclassed in the Cup Final by a Bolton Wanderers team which put sentiment in its proper place and played solidly, and sometimes splendidly.

Sunday Dispatch, 4 May 1958

steals wonder of from the United

Bolton but would go down in the annals as one of the most controversial goals in Wembley's history. It came as goalkeeper Gregg leaped for a high ball almost on his goalline only to find Lofthouse charging into him and bustling both goalkeeper and ball over the line. The referee pointed decisively to the centre circle, while the United defenders looked on in disbelief that he had not whistled for an infringement on the goalkeeper. But the goal counted and United now had little chance of recovery. Even then the incident aroused considerable controversy, while today it is almost unimaginable that a goalkeeper could be bundled over his line without his opponent being severely reprimanded, let alone a goal being given. It seemed as if all the gods were pitted against United. They had lost the Cup final the previous season after Ray Wood had been heavily charged by Aston Villa's Peter McParland and now, just months after the tragedy of Munich, another final had been decided by questionable conduct and poor refereeing.

The charge that brought controversy and a goal. Lofthouse bundles Harry Gregg into the back of the net.

United twice came close to narrowing the gap as Charlton hit two thunderbolts, one striking the inside of the post, but that was as near as they ever came to wresting the lead from their opponents. At the end of the day, everyone accepted that Bolton were the better side and even Busby and Gregg magnanimously agreed that Lofthouse's charge had been fair. Gregg, who had survived the Munich disaster, was the most expensive goalkeeper in Britain at the time, having joined United from Doncaster Rovers for £23,500. Already a Northern Ireland international, he collected a total of 25 caps and made almost 250 appearances in the United goal.

After the horror of Munich the nation had wanted United to win the Cup, but it was not to be. Bolton's victory remained unpopular and the game would always be remembered for the moment Lofthouse bundled the giant Irish goalkeeper into the back of the net. When United returned to Manchester the following day, thousands lined the streets in an emotional welcome. It was almost as if they had won the Cup.

1958

Albert Quixall bids farewell to Hillsborough.

ALBERT QUIXALL was the glamour boy of English soccer when he signed for Manchester United. Young, handsome and with a quiff of golden hair, he cut a dashing and unmistakable figure across the football field. It was fitting that his services should cost a British record fee of £45,000, topping the previous record, paid by Spurs for Cliff Jones, by £10,000, although Quixall himself merely collected a £20 signing-on fee.

Quixall was a Yorkshire lad, born and bred, rising through the ranks of his home team Sheffield Wednesday. The 25-year-old had won two second division championship medals with the Owls, collected five England caps to add to his Under-23 and B honours, played almost 250 league games and scored 63 goals before his transfer. United needed an experienced inside forward who could steady and steer the youngsters around him. Although they had signed Ernie Taylor and Stan Crowther in the wake of the Munich disaster, both had offered short-term relief rather than long-term solutions. By the end of the year, Crowther had moved on to Chelsea after just 20 appearances while Taylor had joined Sunderland.

Quixall was a good investment, albeit an expensive one. He played for six seasons at Old Trafford, making 183 appearances and scoring 56 goals, before joining Oldham Athletic in September 1964. In the previous year he collected his only honour with United – an FA Cup-winners' medal – yet he remained a favourite with the Old Trafford crowd who always appreciated his flair and unorthodoxy. He brought excitement, forming a formidable inside forward partnership with Bobby Charlton, which rekindled memories of the Busby Babes.

SKY-HIGH QUIXALL GOES FOR £45,000

Daily Mirror, 19 September 1958

1959

Above: Ray Wood, who made the last of his 205 appearances for United in 1958/59, pulls off another save.

CHARLTON, SCANLON AND VIOLLET ARE ALL IN ENGLAND SCORING FORM

Century at Old Trafford for Busby's XI

Sunday Dispatch, 5 April 1959

THE POST-MUNICH United team was beginning to take shape by the end of 1958. Albert Quixall had arrived in a blaze of glory while little Ernie Taylor and Stan Crowther had moved elsewhere. Dennis Viollet and Albert Scanlon, both fully recovered from their injuries, had returned to the battle while Bobby Charlton was maturing into an outstanding inside forward. Harry Gregg, who had seized his opportunity in goal just prior to Munich, had now permanently displaced Ray Wood.

United began the 1958/59 season with mixed fortunes. By mid-November they had already lost eight matches and there seemed little prospect of them climbing up among the leaders, yet after a 6–3 hammering at Bolton they lost only three more league games the whole season. That defeat initiated a run of 12 matches which saw them collect 23 points out of 24. By February they were challenging for the title and, when they beat league leaders Wolves 2–1 at Old Trafford, they found themselves level on points with the leaders. With Wolves engaged in the FA Cup the following Saturday, United merely had to win at Highbury to edge two points ahead. But sadly, they lost 3–2 and never regained the initiative. Although they maintained the pressure, losing only two more games that season, Wolves never faltered and ran out champions six points ahead of United in second spot.

United had scored 103 league goals with Bobby Charlton hitting 29, one of the highest tallies in the club's history, while Albert Scanlon scored 16. Scanlon, the nephew of former United star Charlie Mitten, had made his first-team debut in November 1954. But, with so much talent at Old Trafford, it was not until shortly before Munich that he established himself as a regular. He was seriously injured at Munich but returned as the 1958/59 season got under way. Scanlon was a tenacious little winger who was always a thorn in the flesh of any opposing defence, and he played 127 games for the club before moving to Newcastle United in November 1960.

And so ended a dramatic 18 months in United's history. In the wake of Munich, few would have given the club much hope of first division survival, yet they were FA Cup finalists in 1958 and league runners-up in 1959. Their achievements said much for the spirit and determination of all involved in the club.

1960

Setters thrilled by Busby bid

MATT VISITS ALBION TODAY TO TALK £30,000 BUSINESS

Daily Mail, 6 January 1960

AT THE END of 1959 Wilf McGuinness tragically fractured a leg, an injury which eventually ended his playing career. And 1960 began no better, as United slumped to a 7–3 defeat at Newcastle. United had serious problems and there was only one solution: Busby had to dip into the transfer market to plug the gap left by McGuinness. The name of Ron Yeats was mentioned, but all inquiries were rebutted by Dundee United who were unwilling to part with their giant centre half. So instead, Busby turned to the unsettled West Bromwich Albion wing half, Maurice Setters. Setters had been on the transfer list since the beginning of the year and had already rejected offers from Everton and Manchester City after West Brom had agreed terms with both clubs. But, when United showed interest, there was not a moment's hesitation from the former England Youth captain and within 10 minutes of meeting Busby, Setters had duly signed for United at a fee of £30,000.

Tall, with short cropped hair and a mean stare, Setters was not the kind of man you looked at twice. He was as tough and aggressive a defender as United had seen since the days of Frank Barson. He had been bought to shore up a leaking defence and, by the end of the season, nobody could argue that it had not been money well spent. A Devon man, he began his career with Exeter City before signing for West Brom where he spent five years and won England Under-23 honours. He remained at Old Trafford for six seasons, playing 186 games and winning a Cup medal in 1963 and more Under-23 honours, before joining Stoke in a £30,000 deal in October 1964. Further moves took him to Coventry and Charlton and, after a total of more than 500 games, he embarked on a backroom career with Doncaster, Sheffield Wednesday and Rotherham.

Another recruit in 1960 was Noel Cantwell, the West Ham United full back who arrived in a £30,000 deal in November. Cantwell gave sterling service to the club, making 144 appearances, and captained the side in the 1963 Cup final. Born in Cork, he was first capped by Eire in 1953 and won a total of 36 caps over the next 14 years before taking up various coaching and managerial positions.

Maurice Setters – not the kind of man you look at twice – makes a strong challenge.

1961

Mirror Sport

£38,000 transfer

BUSBY DASHES TO SIGN HERD

Daily Mirror, 27 July 1961

Hot-shot David Herd strikes the ball at 72.5 mph to beat all rivals in a scientific experiment.

UNITED HAD BEEN tracking David Herd ever since 1951 when they had considered signing him from Stockport County. But they hesitated, and the young man moved to Arsenal. For two years Busby had been actively stalking his signature, but Arsenal were reluctant to part with their Scottish international. Busby had all but given up hope by the summer of 1961 when he put in a casual call to Highbury to ascertain the latest position. 'You can have him for £38,000,' came the reply and Busby was on the next train to London. Herd had turned down Arsenal's latest contract and had indicated to his club that he would like to move to United. The rest was a formality.

David Herd was the son of the former Manchester City player, Alec Herd, who had lined up alongside Matt Busby during the 1930s. Indeed, Alec and David Herd had themselves played together in a third division north game at the end of the 1950/51 season, creating something of a unique father and son record. Busby knew the family well and had always shown a special interest in his old colleague's son. By the time he arrived at United, however, he was 27 years old but had proved himself as fine a marksman as any in the Football League, having hit 97 goals in 166 appearances with the Gunners. By any standard that was a high ratio and, with Dennis Viollet nearing the end of his playing career, Busby saw him as an ideal partner for Bobby Charlton. The following season they were joined by Denis Law, and later by George Best, to provide an attack in which each player was capable of hitting 20 goals a season. Herd was sharp, aggressive and accurate, the kind of marksman who scores goals without any fuss. At United he was always overshadowed by his more illustrious team-mates but that should never hide the importance of his contribution, especially his 28 goals during the 1964/65 league championship season.

Herd made his United debut at the beginning of the 1961/62 campaign and was a regular throughout most of his Old Trafford career, eventually making way for Brian Kidd. In all he made 262 appearances and scored 144 goals, including two against Leicester that helped win the FA Cup in 1963. He arrived at United with five Scottish caps, for which he had to thank Busby who had personally persuaded the Scottish selectors to give him his first opportunity in 1958. Yet, surprisingly, he did not win any further international honours at Old Trafford. Seven years after his transfer from Arsenal he joined Stoke City and later wound up as manager of Lincoln.

1962

BUSBY HAD LONG been an admirer of Denis Law. From the days when the skinny, bandy-legged 16-year-old first pulled on a Huddersfield Town shirt, Busby had earmarked him as one for the future. Had circumstances been different, Law might have been a United player years earlier but Manchester City were quicker off the mark and Law ended up at Maine Road in March 1960 for a record £56,000. Keeping him at City, however, proved to be more difficult than anyone had imagined and, after one season, he moved to Italy, bringing a handsome profit to the club as he was the first British player to smash the £100,000 barrier. His stay at Torino turned out to be just as temporary and he might well have ended up at Juventus alongside another British export, John Charles, had Busby not intervened to bring the young Scottish international back home. Law had detested Italy with its disciplined, pressure-cooker atmosphere and

Mirror Sport

British transfer record goes

UNITED LAND LAW—AT £115,000

By BILL HOLDEN

MANCHESTER United yesterday signed Denis Law, Scottish international forward, from Torino for a fee of £115,000.

But Torino, who signed Law from Manchester City for a similar fee in June last year, receive only £75,000.

For they still owed City £40,000, and United had to hand City a cheque for that amount before Torino could clear the transfer with the Italian and English Football Associations.

When Torino signed Law, they paid a deposit on the fee and agreed to pay the remainder in instalments over a short period.

Afterwards, they claimed they could not meet the payments within the time limit.

The sum United are now giving for Law, 22—the son of an Aberdeen trawlerman—is a record payment by a British club.

It makes the player worth about £48 an ounce.

Previous highest fee was the £99,999 Spurs handed over to Milan to buy Jimmy Greaves.

Law, delighted at joining United, said: "It has always been my ambition to play for this club."

He has also won a £5 side-bet with Torino club-mate Joe Baker that he would be first to re-sign for a British club.

Baker, whom Arsenal hope to sign, will visit Highbury on Monday for a medical check-up and further discussions.

Daily Mirror, 13 July 1962

Left: Ironing out the final details. Law and Busby meet in Lausanne to settle the record transfer deal from Torino.

Right: With 236 goals in almost 400 appearances, Law would become one of the most prolific marksmen in the club's history.

reluctance to allow him to play for his beloved Scotland. He couldn't come home soon enough. The fee was £115,000 – a British record – but as time proved, it was one of the bargains of the decade.

Law turned out to be one of Busby's most inspired signings, bringing a dash of excitement and artistry to Old Trafford that had not been seen since the pre-Munich days. He quickly developed a rapport with the fans that brought them flocking to the Stretford End where old-timers would liken him to Billy Meredith. And, on occasions, he could be just as belligerent as the toothpick-chewing Edwardian, turning down contracts, demanding more money and getting himself into trouble with referees. But the fans always loved him, revelling in his delicate touches and razor-sharp reflexes. When he sensationally moved back to Maine Road in July 1972 on a free transfer, the similarity with Meredith was haunting. And nobody, especially at Old Trafford, will ever forget his final footballing act – the cheeky backheel that sentenced United to second division football. In truth, he was probably more like City's other favourite son, Peter Doherty – skin and bones that belied an unnatural skill and power – than the enigmatic Meredith.

Law remained at Old Trafford for 10 years, scoring 236 goals in almost 400 appearances to make him one of the most prolific marksmen in United's history. In 44 FA Cup appearances he netted an astonishing 34 goals, while in 33 European ties his tally was 28. His career total of 41 Cup goals still stands as a record. In one of the most daunting forward lines ever in English football, he not only converted the craftsmanship of Best and Charlton into goals but dodged, weaved and feinted to create as many himself. During the 1963/64 season he hit 46 goals, and a season later, as they clinched the league title, he was there with 39 goals.

In the 1963 Cup final against Leicester City he produced one of his most outstanding performances as he struck the first goal which set United on their way to victory. In 1964 he was European Player of the Year and, when he retired 10 years later, he had accumulated 55 Scottish caps and a record 30 goals for his country. He had made his international debut in 1958 at the age of 18 as Scotland's youngest-ever player and donned the Scottish shirt for the final time 16 years later in 1974. Sadly, he was absent through injury for United's greatest triumph when they won the European Cup; but even if he could not be present in body, he was there in spirit. Few players in the history of United have won the hearts of the fans as Law did, nor carved their skills with such artistry; his name will forever rank alongside Old Trafford's all-time favourites.

1963

Crerand going–£55,000

By DON HARDISTY

SCOTLAND and Celtic right-half Pat Crerand will join Manchester United this week.

The clubs have agreed terms — about £55,000. Only Crerand's consent is needed, a mere formality.

The Crerand fee will not be a record for a wing half, except in Scotland. Everton's £60,000 to Sheffield Wednesday for Tony Kay set a British high a month ago.

Crerand asked for a move six days ago, when he was dropped for the second consecutive match.

PAT CRERAND

United will undoubtedly have to unload some of their huge stockpile of wing-halves.

The men in possesion, club skipper Maurice Setters and Nobby Stiles, already have a constant challenge from Irish international Jimmy Nicholson and Nobby Lawton.

Manager Matt Busby has tried permutations from all four in the past two seasons.

But wing-half has remained his most persistent headache. Crerand has the experience, the temperament and the football to cure it.

Daily Mail, 4 February 1963

HAVING CONTINUED the process of rebuilding the post-Munich team with the purchase of Law, Herd and Setters, Busby took a further step six months later with the valuable acquisition of Pat Crerand. The Glasgow-born Crerand arrived at Old Trafford from Celtic five years to the day after the Munich disaster. The fee was £56,000 but Crerand was worth every penny, quickly establishing himself as an elegant midfielder whose long, delightful passes had many a defence scurrying in retreat. After six years at Parkhead, Crerand had decided it was time to try football south of the border and there had been a clear understanding between Busby and Celtic that if he should ever become available then United would have first option. It was a chance readily seized by Busby.

Within a few months of his arrival, the Scottish international helped United towards a famous Cup triumph and, two years later, towards the league title. Subsequently, he collected a second league championship medal with United as well as a European Cup-winners' medal. On top of that, there were 16 Scottish caps and a reputation as a likeable but tough wing half. Crerand remained a first-team player until 1971 when he joined the coaching staff. He later became assistant manager under fellow Scot Tommy Docherty, but, after numerous disagreements, he grabbed the opportunity to manage Northampton Town in 1976. He played 392 games for United, scoring 15 goals, and was a regular for most of his nine seasons in the Football League. An aggressive player, he was always liable to display his anger with a little too much venom, causing more than a few embarrassing moments for the club and manager. Nevertheless, his combative instincts were crucial in controlling the midfield and providing the necessary edge all successful teams require. He remained a firm favourite with the Old Trafford fans.

Pat Crerand brought both elegance and aggression to the United midfield.

1963

UNITED'S CUP TRIUMPH – only the third in their history – opened with a 5–0 thrashing of Huddersfield Town in early March. The competition had been long delayed by an atrocious winter which seemed to linger forever, causing the cancellation of hundreds of fixtures. It meant that United's march to Wembley was completed in a little over eight weeks. Having beaten Huddersfield, they then disposed of Aston Villa, Chelsea and Coventry before meeting Southampton in the semi-final at Villa Park in late April. Although the mid-table second division side put up a stubborn fight, United had the edge and sneaked a 1–0 victory in a dour game to give them a barely deserved trip to Wembley.

The galloping ghost inspires Busby's Boys to Wembley glory

IT'S UNITED AT LAST

News of the World, 28 May 1963

Fans given star value for record £89,000

By FRANK BUTLER

Attendance 100,000
Receipts £89,000

Man Utd 3 Leicester 1

Law (29 min.) *Keyworth*
Herd (57, 85) *(80 min.)*

THE class and individuality of one player, Denis Law, the £115,000 Aberdonian inside-left, won the Cup for Manchester United. A 30-minute spell of speed and wizardry in the first-half knocked all the breath out of Leicester City.

Their opponents in the final were Leicester City, fourth in the first division and 18 points ahead of United, who ended the season a disappointing 19th, just three points ahead of relegated neighbours Manchester City. For once, United found themselves as underdogs facing a Leicester side with one of the best defensive records in the first division, inspired by England goalkeeper Gordon Banks. But an outstanding United team was now beginning to take shape. Law had arrived to kick the season off and Pat Crerand had pulled on the number four shirt in February to provide the midfield with some much-needed bite. Their Cup run had begun to give them some confidence and, although results were still generally dismal, their Wembley victory provided the motivation to take them to dizzy heights over the next few years.

It was the day United at last began to mature into a fine side. Suddenly all the confidence was brimming and the skills that had been quietly fermenting all season were now bubbling. On the day, United were by far the superior side, inspired by Denis Law who displayed all his masterly skills and dash as he repaid some of the outlay that had made him

Crerand and Quixall try out some expensive headgear after winning the FA Cup.

Britain's most costly player. It was a performance to cherish as he strutted and feinted, sprinted and darted, shuffled and bamboozled an awestruck Leicester defence.

It took just 30 minutes for United to register their authority as Paddy Crerand lashed in an inch-perfect cross for Law to swivel and meet it with a thump, 1–0. 'I can still see that pass coming towards me,' he later recalled. With United continuing to dominate, David Herd put them further ahead 12 minutes into the second half as he tapped in the easiest of chances, after Giles and Charlton had split the Leicester defence asunder. With 10 minutes remaining Leicester pulled a goal back but, almost immediately, Law headed against the upright and five minutes later Herd sealed their victory with his second of the afternoon. The Cup was coming back to Old Trafford after an absence of 15 years.

The triumvirate of Law, Charlton and Crerand had torn Leicester's iron wall defence apart, smashing through it as if it were mere tissue. As Munich survivors Bill Foulkes and Bobby Charlton stepped up to collect their winners' medals, they could do so knowing proudly that their performance had done justice to the memory of their former colleagues. Busby was on the verge of creating another outstanding team, but one man who did not appear to figure in his plans was Johnny Giles. The Cup final marked his farewell appearance and, during the close season, he was transferred to Leeds United for £37,500. He had made 114 appearances since joining United as a 17-year-old from Home Farm. But Giles had the last laugh as he powered Leeds towards a galaxy of honours.

This time Gordon Banks manages to deprive Law of a goal, but the striker set United on the way after 30 minutes.

1963

GEORGE BEST has probably captured more back page headlines than any other post-war British footballer. And, no doubt, he has hit the front page more times than anyone else as well, yet his first headline passed almost unnoticed. When the *Manchester Evening News* heralded his debut, they could never have guessed that it was to be the first of many, perhaps too many, George Best stories. Best stole the back pages from the word go. Even on his debut on Saturday, 14 September 1963 the *Manchester Evening News* lavished praise on the young 17-year-old right winger: 'Boy Best Flashes in Red Attack' ran the headline that evening. United fielded two 17-year-olds that day in the 1–0 win over West Brom at Old Trafford. Between them, George Best and David Sadler went on to make 800 appearances for United over the next 11 years and brought a heap of honours to Old Trafford.

Best arrived at United at the age of 15 but returned, homesick, to Belfast almost immediately, only to be dragged back to Manchester by Matt Busby. This was one prize Busby was not going to lose. Fifteen games after his league debut, Best was in the Northern Ireland team winning the first of his 37 Irish caps. He was an instant success. United were runners-up and FA Cup semi-finalists in

A shy, teenage Best, yet to feel at home in Manchester.

Boy Best flashes in Red attack

Manchester Evening News, 14 September 1963

his first season. The next year they were champions and six glorious years of success were beginning. Best won two championship medals, a European Cup-winners' medal and was voted European Player of the Year as well as Footballer of the Year. Against Benfica in the European Cup final he produced a dazzling performance that almost single-handedly won United the European Cup. In 466 appearances he scored 178 goals, he was the league's top scorer in 1968 and on five occasions netted more than 20 goals a season for United.

Best had everything. He was fast, skilful and dangerous. He could delight, he could tantalise; he could win games on his own or equally he could wander anonymously up and down the right wing. Sometimes he did both, suddenly snapping into action for a few seconds to destroy the opposition and then retire to reflect on his glory.

Best was a journalist's dream. Young, handsome, single, rich, fashionable and, above all, talented, he was the first of a new breed of superstar footballers. While the Tom Finneys and Stanley Matthews of the 1950s had hogged the back pages, Best shot football on to the front pages. He was photographed with girls, photographed in sports cars, snapped in clubs and snapped at boutiques. He was as much a part of the Swinging Sixties as the Beatles, Twiggy or Andy Warhol. But it all took its toll. The pressures on his time mounted, there was no stability to his life and he began to drink. He began to turn up late for training, sometimes reeking of vodka, having spent late evenings in clubs where he was seen with glamorous girls on his arms. After United's European Cup success, and with results declining, Best's extra-curricular activities began to be questioned. His casual approach and seeming lack of commitment became a barrier between himself and a number of players. There were dressing room rifts, while the retirement of Matt Busby, his father-figure, left him isolated in a changing Old Trafford. Yet the club was always lenient. Frank O'Farrell, finally exasperated by his nonsense, placed him on the transfer list, but Busby intervened. Best repeatedly walked out on United, only to be persuaded back. In the end, he played his last game on New Year's Day 1974 as United lost 3–0 to Queen's Park Rangers. A few days later, he failed to turn up for training and United ripped up his contract. He subsequently joined a succession of clubs including Stockport, Fulham, Hibernian and Bournemouth as well as playing in America and Ireland. Like a mercenary he followed the money.

Best was a genius but, like so many geniuses, could not temper his own life. His was a wayward talent. Yet none of this should detract from the excitement he generated. Those who saw him in full flight, particularly in his early years, will never forget the dash, the cheek and the invention.

Best, with only a spaniel for company, in digs that would suit Hilda Ogden.

1964

TO REACH THE semi-finals of the FA Cup for the third consecutive year United had to wage an epic duel with second division Sunderland that went to three memorable contests. Second division promotion challengers Sunderland proved no easy match, even though United themselves were battling for the first division title.

In the first encounter at Old Trafford, United found themselves trailing 3–1 with only four minutes remaining. But, just as they seemed to be bowing out of the competition, up popped Bobby Charlton to breathe new life into them as he slammed home a George Best corner. It was 3–2 and the minutes were ticking away. Surely United could not score again? They could, because nobody had yet realised the potential of the young man wearing the number 11 shirt. There he was, George Best, almost on the stroke of full time, to hit United's equaliser. The crowd of 63,000 gasped. Outplayed and outmanœuvred by the second division side, United had somehow, by luck or whatever, pulled back from the brink of defeat. They had hardly earned it and few gave them much hope at Roker Park, where 68,000 Geordies were confidently baying for United's scalp.

Law celebrates one of his three goals. Performances like this made him European Player of the Year in 1964.

United great again

LAW'S FURIES BREAK DEADLOCK

By BRIAN JAMES

Man. Utd....5 Sunderland...1

MANCHESTER United, the team that limply trailed its talent through a two-match trial and survived by a miracle, suddenly became great again last night.

Daily Mail, 10 March 1964

The replay took much the same pattern as the first game, with Sunderland, spurred on by their vociferous supporters, storming ahead shortly before half time only for Law to equalise 20 minutes later. It stayed like that until the 90 minutes were up, but, within 30 seconds of kicking off into extra time, United were behind again. The sound of the Blaydon Races roared from the terraces as Roker Park anticipated a famous Wearside victory. But, with the referee's whistle almost poised at his lips, Bobby Charlton appeared yet again to save the day, heading a seemingly harmless cross low into the goal and tantalisingly out of Montgomery's reach. United had escaped again.

A third clash was necessary and five days later the two teams faced each other once more. This time the venue was Leeds Road, Huddersfield and 55,000 travelled to see it, giving an aggregate attendance of 185,000 for the three games. United, having stuttered through the previous two battles, returned to their glorious winning ways, demonstrating the gulf between the top of the first and second divisions. But it was not before Sunderland had again taken the lead, as they broke the deadlock minutes into the second half. But, 60 seconds later, Law leaped at a Herd shot that had rebounded off a bunch of defenders and it was 1–1. Minutes later Chisnall made it 2–1, putting the Reds into the lead for the first time in the three contests. United were now rampant and, in the 51st minute Law, converted a penalty and then completed his hat trick 10 minutes later. The game had dramatically swung in United's favour and the plucky second divisioners had more than met their match. David Herd completed the rout in the 66th minute as he burst down the left, leaving two defenders stumbling before he crashed the ball in from the narrowest of angles.

United had won 5–1, scoring all their goals in the space of 15 minutes. It was little wonder the *Daily Mail* reckoned them 'Great Again'. Unfortunately, all the hard work came undone in the semi-final as they faced an attractive West Ham side led by Bobby Moore. United were well and truly beaten, losing 3–1, but could at least be content to see West Ham go on to win the trophy and then collect the European Cup-Winners' Cup the following season.

1964

PORTUGUESE BOUNCE UNITED OUT OF EUROCUP: 6-4 TOTAL

From DON HARDISTY
Lisbon, Wednesday

Sporting, Lisbon 5 Manchester Utd. 0
Sporting win 6-4 on aggregate

Daily Mail, 19 March 1964

IT WAS THE same night as Cassius Clay captured the World Heavyweight boxing title from Sonny Liston. United had returned to the European fray after an absence of five years, thanks to their FA Cup victory over Leicester. But it was a challenge which lasted scarcely fewer rounds than Sonny Liston as the FA Cup-winners went out to a surprise defeat by Sporting Lisbon of Portugal.

United had begun their return to European competition with a comprehensive victory over the Dutch Cup-winners Willem II of Tilburg, beating them 6–1 at Old Trafford after a 1–1 draw in Holland. The next round brought United face to face with the holders Tottenham Hotspur. Spurs won the first leg 2–0, but, with Dave Mackay breaking his leg after only eight minutes of the return tie, United roared on to a 4–1 win.

Sporting Lisbon, however, proved to be a different proposition, although after the first leg at Old Trafford, it seemed very likely that there would be a semi-final involving the Reds. United won 4–1, with Denis Law hitting a hat trick. On paper it looked a comfortable enough margin of victory that would safely see them through to the final four, but closer examination revealed the cracks that soon became all too apparent. Two of Law's goals came from penalties and the Busby Boys lacked what the *Daily Herald* called the 'killer touch'. Chances galore went begging while Dave Gaskell in the United goal was the quiet hero. Those with a canny eye might have anticipated disaster.

Denis Law scores the first of his three goals at Old Trafford.

What should have been a virtual walk-over turned instead into a nightmare. In the return leg at Lisbon, United were five goals down inside an hour and, although they managed to contain the Portuguese in the final half hour, they could not score themselves and so went out 6–4 on aggregate. It was a dire performance from United, who looked lethargic and exhausted; their only excuse, perhaps, was that the game came just days after their defeat by West Ham in the FA Cup semi-final. United were also chasing the league title and, as the season wound towards its fixture-crammed conclusion, the pressure proved too much.

Busby was furious, accusing them of letting down not just the club but the city and English football as well. In the dressing room he ranted and raved, threatening to drop players and fine them, but relented as United returned to their winning ways a few days later in the league. It had been United's most humiliating experience in Europe.

The Portuguese players angrily contest the referee's decision.

1965

Ugly scenes at Hillsborough as tempers flare between two of the most formidable sides in the league.

UNITED'S FOURTH consecutive appearance in an FA Cup semi-final should have been a proud occasion for the club. Instead, it turned into a squalid nightmare. Leeds United were their opponents and the combative Yorkshire side were beginning to earn a reputation for unstinting aggression while United, with players like Law, Crerand, Setters and Foulkes in their line-up, could just as easily mix it if necessary. And against Leeds it was often necessary.

The first battle, for that was the most apt description, took place at Hillsborough before a full house of 65,000. It soon became known as the X-certificate semi-final as players stood nose to nose, swapping punches and tugging on shirts. Law and Jack Charlton wrestled before they were torn apart, Law's shirt almost ripped off his back. It was the most ill-tempered semi-final in years and one which did neither club any credit.

Roy Peskett in the *Daily Mail* pinpointed the blame, beginning with the two managers, Don Revie and Matt Busby, for allowing their teams to get out of hand. Also on the carpet were the two captains, Bobby Collins and Denis Law, for not checking their players on the field; and finally referee Dick Windle did not escape criticism for his generous attitude – he booked only two players when five ought to have been sent off.

With neither defence willing to concede the merest inch the match petered out into a goalless draw. Four days later, at Nottingham, they faced each other again with the Football Association keeping faith in referee Windle and holding its breath. Fortunately tempers remained just short of bursting point in what was another tense encounter, but at least the public were saved the ugly antics of the previous contest. A last-minute goal by Leeds settled the debate, but, as the teams left the field, referee Windle was felled by an overexcited United fan. The culprit was speedily apprehended but Windle lay dazed for some moments and the episode hit the front pages the next morning. The incident may not have been directly the fault of either side but some blame had to be attached to the clubs. When players were fighting on the field it was hardly surprising if fans took up the cause on their behalf and in a similar fashion.

Cup ref may be dropped

By BRIAN JAMES

REFEREE DICK WINDLE may be taken off Wednesday's F.A. Cup semi-final replay between Manchester United and Leeds though neither club will complain officially about his handling of Saturday's maul at Sheffield.

The F.A. may take action today on their own initiative. Many F.A. Council members and officials watched the Chesterfield referee handle the game, which has been labelled the most ill-tempered semi-final in recent years.

Daily Mail, 29 March 1965

1965

IT HAD BEEN eight long years since United last won the league championship, when the Busby Babes of Tommy Taylor, Duncan Edwards and Roger Byrne had so majestically stormed away with the title. But with an FA Cup semi-final and the runners-up spot in the first division under their belts from the previous season, United began the 1964/65 campaign with more than a smattering of optimism.

Eight consecutive victories in the autumn, including a 7–0 hiding of Aston Villa, put them among the challengers and, as the New Year arrived, United were in third spot, with Leeds topping the table, followed by Chelsea. Only a couple of points separated all three, while the rest of the league trailed woefully behind. It remained much the same for the rest of the winter, with Chelsea finally losing ground as United trounced them

Irish international Shay Brennan gets the better of Arsenal's Frank McLintock.

Manchester United champs..

'CRIPPLED' LAW THE HERO WITH TWO GOALS

Manchester United 3, Arsenal 1

MANCHESTER UNITED are champions again. That five-word sentence manager Matt Busby has waited seven years to read became a fact at 9.10 p.m. last night with the final whistle of Old Trafford's last home game.

Daily Mirror, 27 April 1965

Goalmouth action from the championship-clinching game against Arsenal.

4–0 at Old Trafford in early March. By 5pm on the final Saturday of the season Leeds headed the table with 60 points but had only one fixture remaining while United, just a point behind them, had two to play. Leeds had already beaten United in a fierce FA Cup semi-final and in seven days' time were to face Liverpool at Wembley. The pressure was mounting on them and on the Monday evening they travelled to Birmingham for their final match. Meanwhile, United entertained Arsenal at Old Trafford.

If Leeds drew or lost and United won, then the Reds would be champions but if Leeds won, then the championship would go to the final game when United travelled to Aston Villa. United fielded a full international XI that night against Arsenal with four English, three Scottish, three Irish and one Northern Irish cap, while the Gunners boasted a mere seven internationals. All evening the scores from Birmingham were relayed over the loudspeaker. Leeds were being beaten, now they were pulling back, now they had equalised. Meanwhile, United were marching to a comfortable victory, perhaps inspired by the tannoy announcements. As the final whistle sounded, the players waited. United had won 3–1 and Leeds were drawing 3–3 – had Don Revie's team squeezed a winning goal? There might even have been one or two in the 51,000 crowd who remembered a similar occasion in 1911, when the United players mingled anxiously around the touchline awaiting the score from Liverpool to tell them that they had won the title.

Now, half a century later, history was repeating itself. At last the score came over. You could have heard a pin drop. Birmingham City 3, Leeds United 3. The Reds were champions. Had United needed to win their final fixture they doubtless would have done so. As it was, with the title wrapped up, they lost 2–1 at Villa and finished up champions on goal average.

Denis Law headed the goalscoring list with 28 league goals, followed by David Herd with 20. But others deserved to be mentioned. David Gaskell and Pat Dunne had shared the goalkeeping task between them while Tony Dunne and Shay Brennan mounted an effective rearguard action that conceded only 13 goals at Old Trafford. Brennan, underrated and often undersung, played 355 games for United after making his debut against Sheffield Wednesday immediately following the Munich disaster and collected 19 Irish caps. Tony Dunne was another who gave loyal and uncomplaining service, with 529 appearances over 13 seasons, before he joined Bolton Wanderers in July 1973. Another Irishman, he was capped 32 times by the Republic, mostly partnering his United colleague. Between them they made almost 900 appearances in the heart of the United defence and seemed inseparable for the best part of 10 seasons. It was as fine a full-back duo as United had ever known.

1966

UNITED! THE GREATEST OF THEM ALL

Daily Herald, 9 March 1966

UNITED WERE BACK in the European Cup after an absence of nine years. When they last appeared, Real Madrid reigned supreme over Europe. But, the Spaniards had handed their crown over to the Eagles of Lisbon, Benfica. The free-flowing football that had been the hallmark of those glorious European nights had now been replaced by iron-tight defences.

United began their sortie on the Continent with a trip to Helsinki, where they scraped a narrow win before slamming their opponents 6–0 at Old Trafford. In the next round, they the East German champions ASK Vorwaerts 2–0 in East Berlin and then added another three at home to give them a handsome 5–1 victory on aggregate.

United were now into the quarter-finals where they drew the Portuguese champions, Benfica. On their last encounter with Portuguese representatives, Sporting Lisbon, they had been shamefully eliminated. Benfica had already captured the trophy twice and been losing finalists on two occasions within the last five years.

A little over 64,000 were locked into Old Trafford for a sizzling first leg. United attacked from the whistle with Charlton instantly stamping his authority on the game, yet on the half hour it was Benfica who stunned the huge audience as Augusto headed home Eusebio's curling cross. By half time, however, United had retrieved the deficit as Herd slammed Best's through pass beyond the grasping Pereira and Law flashed at a Charlton centre to make it 2–1.

Fifteen minutes after the interval, Foulkes headed a Cantwell free kick into the net to make it 3–1 and Old Trafford erupted in anticipation of a famous victory. Eusebio tore at the United defence to create a second goal and almost a third. It had been a hard-fought victory but few believed that a one-goal lead would be enough in Lisbon, where Benfica remained undefeated in 19 European fixtures.

Their encounter before 90,000 in the Stadium of Light began with Eusebio being awarded the European Footballer of the Year trophy. Yet, after just 12 minutes, he might have handed it over to 19-year-old George Best who had already added two more goals to United's slender lead. Shortly after half time, Best weaved his magical way through the Benfica defence once more to set up John Connelly. The Portuguese pulled a goal back as Shay Brennan sliced through his own net but United, now rampant, added two more through Crerand and Charlton to end the night 5–1 winners. They had also seen two goals disallowed.

The 90,000 crowd had been silenced by United's mesmerising performance. Surely, here was a team worthy of succeeding Benfica and Real Madrid as European champions. Sadly it was not to be. Against Partisan Belgrade in the semi-final they lost 2–0 in Yugoslavia. Nevertheless, 62,500 turned up at Old Trafford hopeful that United might pull back the deficit but it was an impossible task. They finally scored after 73 minutes to give their supporters some hope but it was too late. Partisan's stubborn defence was methodically organised and chances were few and far between. Yet nobody could take away from United that glorious 90 minutes in Lisbon when the Reds had played the finest football seen in Europe since the heyday of Real Madrid.

Best scores United's second in one of the club's best-ever performances.

United sweep to their title

West Ham .... 1 Manchester Utd 6

Observer, 7 May 1967

1967

WHAT BETTER WAY to clinch the title than in outstanding style. That was the United of the 1960s. In their penultimate game of the 1966/67 season, United travelled to Upton Park and turned on a display of soccer artistry that had the critics stretching for their dictionaries. West Ham were three goals behind in the first 10 minutes and by full time were themselves watching in awe as United lifted the title with a 6–1 victory. The *Sunday Express* reckoned the first 30 minutes were as fine a display of football as witnessed since the war. Others thought it comparable with anything the Busby Babes could have produced. Matt Busby was a proud man – 'my greatest hour', he told one newspaper.

United had been title contenders from the start, even though they had lost six games by the end of 1966. But once the second part of the season was under way they slipped into overdrive and did not lose another game. They were two points ahead of Liverpool on New Year's Day and, although the Merseysiders clambered over them in February, United edged their way back to the top in early March and remained there. By the end of the season they were four points clear of Nottingham Forest, whose late burst had shot them into the runners-up spot.

Law celebrates winning the championship, while Best looks on. It was United's seventh title.

1967

Denis Law's two goals against West Ham helped him to a season's total of 23 league goals to add to the two he had scored in the FA Cup. During the early stages of the season John Connelly waved goodbye to Old Trafford after 112 appearances and 35 goals, joining Lancashire neighbours Blackburn Rovers for £40,000. The pint-sized winger had arrived at United as a £56,000 buy in the summer of 1964 from Burnley, where he had won league championship and FA Cup runners-up medals. At Old Trafford he added a second championship medal to his collection as well as another 10 England caps to the 10 he had already won at Turf Moor.

It was the emergence of John Aston who made Connelly's role superfluous. A home-grown product, young John Aston was the son of John Aston senior, who had been such an outstanding servant to the club during the post-war period. Young John had emerged through the club's youth team, making his first-team debut in April 1965 and going on to make 164 appearances in a red shirt before a broken leg virtually ended his United career. He left Old Trafford in July 1972, joining Luton Town and later Mansfield and Blackburn.

Below: Connelly's performances for United on the wing were so good as to revive his England career.

Above: A tricky winger, Aston was at his peak when a broken leg in 1968/69 halted his progress and he could never again hold a regular place.

1968

MANCHESTER—UNITED!

Odds on Busby or Mercer

News of the World, 5 May 1968

AT THE BEGINNING of January, United found themselves at the top of the league, three points clear of Liverpool. But a 2–0 defeat at Coventry on 16 March marked the beginning of the end of their reign as champions. Manchester City nudged fractionally ahead of them and, for the remainder of the season, it was a contest between United, Leeds, Liverpool and City. It was as tight a race for the title as had been seen in years with each week throwing up a different leader. With three games remaining United crashed to a surprise 6–3 defeat at West Brom and, although they recovered the following week with a 6–0 hammering of Newcastle, the game at West Brom had virtually sealed their fate. All finally rested on the last game of the season. City topped the table on goal average and travelled to Newcastle while second-placed United were at home to Sunderland. The championship was no longer in their own hands; even if they won they would have to rely on City failing to collect two points. But no matter what, the championship was coming back to Manchester.

On paper United appeared to have the easier game, but when Sunderland moved into a two-goal lead, it was clear that United's title challenge was falling apart. Best pulled a goal back shortly before half time and, although they pressed for an equaliser, it was a rugged confrontation that left football a poor loser. In the end United lost 2–1 while City swept to the championship with an inspired 4–3 victory at Newcastle. Even if United had beaten Sunderland it would have made no difference. United's challenge for the European Cup had taken its toll. However, by the end of the month they had forgotten their domestic disappointment as they became the first English club to capture Europe's major trophy.

George Best topped the goalscoring list with 28 league goals followed by Charlton and Kidd with 15 each. It was Brian Kidd's first season in league football and he would round it off by scoring against Benfica at Wembley. Brought in as a temporary replacement for David Herd, he showed such maturity that he hung on to his first-team place for seven seasons, eventually joining Arsenal in 1974 for £110,000 after 255 games for United.

Left: United offer their services to Colin Cowdrey to help regain the Ashes. He declined and England failed.

Below: Brian Kidd had his best season for United in 1967/68 but it was not enough for them to win the title. He won two caps for England in 1970.

1968

EUROPEAN CUP semi-finalists on three occasions, Manchester United finally went one better and reached the final – the first English club to do so – in 1968. Busby had welded together a fine team of talents, combining the rare skills of Best, Charlton and Law with the defensive qualities of Crerand, Foulkes and Stiles. It was a team that had twice captured the league championship, won the FA Cup, reached five consecutive FA Cup semi-finals, three European semi-finals and had twice been runners-up in the league. They were as exciting and as innovative a team as Britain had seen since the Busby Babes. Only one prize had eluded them – the European Cup.

They began their march on Europe at Old Trafford with what appeared a comparatively easy task against the part-timers from Malta, Hibernians. But if their first-leg victory of 4–0 sounded comfortable, it was far from it. Hibernians battled all the way and back home on their sun-baked bumpy pitch held United to a goalless draw. In the next round, United travelled once more to Yugoslavia and held out for a 0–0 draw against Sarajevo before scraping home 2–1 in a rugged and aggressive return leg at Old Trafford. Law and Stiles were both absent, which was probably just as well given the tactics of Sarajevo which led to the dismissal of Prljaca.

The unknown Polish champions Gornik Zabrze arrived in Manchester for the quarter-finals and put up stiff resistance, holding United to a single goal until the final minute when Brian Kidd backheeled Jimmy Ryan's speculative shot beyond the Gornik keeper to make it 2–0. They needed that second

Daily Mail, 16 May 1968

United storm into final

Real Madrid...3 Manchester United...3

United win 4—3 on aggregate

MANCHESTER United, for whom the European Cup had become a crusade of the spirit rather than just a Soccer competition, tonight reached the final at last.

United had tried to beat Real Madrid by the quality of their defence, and had felt the cold breath of failure at their necks when the Spaniards scored three goals in 12 minutes of the first half.

Pirri scores for Real Madrid but United win the tie on aggregate and go through to meet Benfica in the European Cup final – the first English club to reach this stage.

First blood to United as Best blasts them into the lead.

goal, as Gornik came close to ousting United in the return leg, played in a snow blizzard in front of 100,000 noisy Poles. United were forced back on to the defensive for much of the game but managed to hold the Poles at bay to reach their fourth semi-final.

And who should they face? None other than their old foe Real Madrid who were now, sadly, a shadow of the side that had so frustrated them back in 1957. But the romance of Real lived on and 63,000 packed into Old Trafford to see the present Spanish stars. Only Gento remained of the great Real side that had so dominated Europe in the first five years of the competition, but other new young players had arrived such as Pirri, Grosso and Sanchis who threatened to shatter the dreams of United.

In the first leg at Old Trafford, United toiled long and hard for scant reward. At the end of the evening a single goal – to United – separated the famous sides, leaving all to play for in the return tie. If Real's name spelled romance, then the presence of United was equally spellbinding as 120,000 Spaniards came to wonder in the magnificent Bernabeu stadium. They were not disappointed, as the two old rivals served up a dish their predecessors would have envied.

Within 40 minutes United were trailing 2–1 on aggregate, as first Pirri and then the galloping Gento put the Spaniards in the driving seat. Minutes later, United were back in contention as Zocco turned the ball into his own net only for Amancio to strike a third on the interval. United's spirit might have evaporated at that moment but, closeted in their dressing room, Busby reminded them that it was only 3–2 on aggregate and one more goal would win the tie. His pep-talk worked and in the second half United produced as resilient a performance as they had ever displayed. With just 20 minutes remaining, and with Real showing more ruggedness than was worthy of their reputation, David Sadler sidefooted a neat goal and then Bill Foulkes, the only survivor of the Madrid encounter in 1957, fittingly scored the equaliser. Foulkes had been at Old Trafford since 1949, making his debut in late 1952. When he finally retired in 1969 to join the backroom staff, the rugged defender had made an astonishing 679 appearances. United's 3–3 draw with Real had earned them a Wembley final against their other European adversaries, Benfica. There was one more moment of glory awaiting Foulkes.

1968

IT HAD LONG been Busby's dream to bring the European Cup to Old Trafford. Ever since the day when the Football League had tried to veto United's entry into the competition, he had longed for the moment when his team would lift the trophy. The tragedy at Munich had made him all the more determined as he set about rebuilding a side not just to win domestic honours but capable of becoming the greatest side in Europe. The European Cup had become United's holy grail. Now, as they lined up against Benfica at Wembley, he was within a whisker of his dream.

Benfica, finalists on four previous occasions and twice winners of the trophy, had been the most exhilarating side in European football for five years. Inspired by the aristocratic Eusebio, they had marched across the Continent delighting everyone with their delicate one-touch football. If ever a side could beat United it was Benfica and yet just two years previously United had destroyed the Eagles of Lisbon 5–1 on their own ground. If United could beat them once, they could do it again, Busby reminded them.

As United took the field at Wembley, they did so with one major handicap – there was no Denis Law. The fearless Scot was lying in a Manchester hospital recovering from a knee operation. Many feared his absence might be the difference between the two sides, but on the night United played as if the wily Scot was among them.

Top: United's proudest moment. Shay Brennan and Bobby Charlton parade the silverware after they have clinched the European Cup 4–1.

Right: Birthday boy Brian Kidd's header puts United into an unassailable 3–1 lead in extra time.

Busby dream comes true at long last

THE football might of Benfica, indeed of Portugal itself, was brought low by Manchester United at Wembley last night. In the presence of 100,000 frenzied spectators who had paid heaven knows what prices for admission. United won 4-1 after extra time and, for the first time in the 13 years of the competition, the European Champions' Cup has come to England. Better still to Lancashire. And, perhaps best of all to Manchester United.

Guardian, 30 May 1968

After a dour goalless first period, the game suddenly came ablaze in the second half as Charlton glided David Sadler's cross into the net. Wembley erupted but not for long as Benfica piled on the pressure to find an equaliser. Ten minutes from the end, with the United fans in full cry, Benfica levelled the score through Graca. They might even have clinched the tie with just minutes remaining as Eusebio twice broke free only to see Stepney save miraculously. It seemed as if Benfica had played all their cards and had still failed to find a winning hand.

Extra time marked the turning point. A long clearance, almost from the kick-off, by Stepney was headed on to Best and the mercurial winger who had been battered and bruised all evening began a sprint that ended with a trail of bemused defenders and the ball in the back of the net. It was young George at his most brilliant. A couple of minutes later Brian Kidd celebrated his 19th birthday as he headed United's third, and five minutes after that Charlton gave them an unassailable 4–1 lead.

Busby's dream had been realised. After 10 years it was a fitting tribute to those who had died at Munich and it was little wonder that the manager should share in the team's glory that evening. They had done it for him as much as for anyone and Wembley had rarely seen such emotional scenes. Best had skipped and danced his way around the broad acres of Wembley to the delight of millions watching throughout Europe, while Charlton had masterminded Benfica's downfall with his two killer goals. In defence Bill Foulkes had resolutely battled as if his very life depended upon it.

If any player should have been singled out it was Alex Stepney whose match-winning saves denied Eusebio and Benfica another European Cup. Stepney had arrived at Old Trafford via Tooting and Mitcham, Millwall and Chelsea. He made just one appearance at Chelsea before manager Tommy Docherty sold him to United for £55,000. Four years later he was in the England squad for the 1970 World Cup and, although he was never chosen, he did win one England cap in 1968. In all, he played 535 times for United, winning an FA Cup-winners' medal and a league championship medal as well as his European Cup honour. He also won a second division championship medal playing with a United team managed by the man who had once discarded him – Tommy Docherty.

An athletic crack at goal from David Sadler fails to add to the score in the Wembley final.

1968

UNITED'S EUROPEAN CUP victory entitled them to a crack at the prestigious World Club Championship against the South American champions, Estudiantes of Argentina. The game was played on a two-leg basis, but the opening contest in Buenos Aires turned into a savage clash that made the recent Cup semi-final battle with Leeds United look like a Sunday afternoon garden party. The *Mirror*'s headline, 'The Night They Spat On Sportsmanship', was an accurate reflection of the match.

As early as the first minute, Denis Law had his hair pulled, yet that was nothing compared with what was to follow. For 90 minutes the United players were buffeted, kicked, spat at and abused. Bobby Charlton needed stitches in a shin wound after being lashed at and, in the 14th minute, Nobby Stiles was head-butted, opening a gash over his left eye. But he battled on, the hero of the hour, turning his back on assaults and brutal kicks until the final minutes when he remonstrated with a linesman who had flagged him offside. The referee pointed firmly to the dressing room and Stiles, who had been labelled an 'assassin' by the local press, marched off to the jeers of the Buenos Aires fans.

Stiles was the one player the Argentinians feared most. His brand of combative football and ability to hold the ball under pressure was always likely to upset their rhythm. He had joined United as a schoolboy in 1957 and made his debut at the age of 18 in 1960. Fourteen years later, when he moved to Preston he could boast a World Cup-winners' medal, a European Cup-winners' medal, two league championship medals and 28 England caps. Although he played 363 games for United, a terrier in the midfield, he will always be remembered for his toothless grin the day England won the World Cup.

'Estudiantes were set on treachery, provocation and violence'

THE NIGHT THEY SPAT

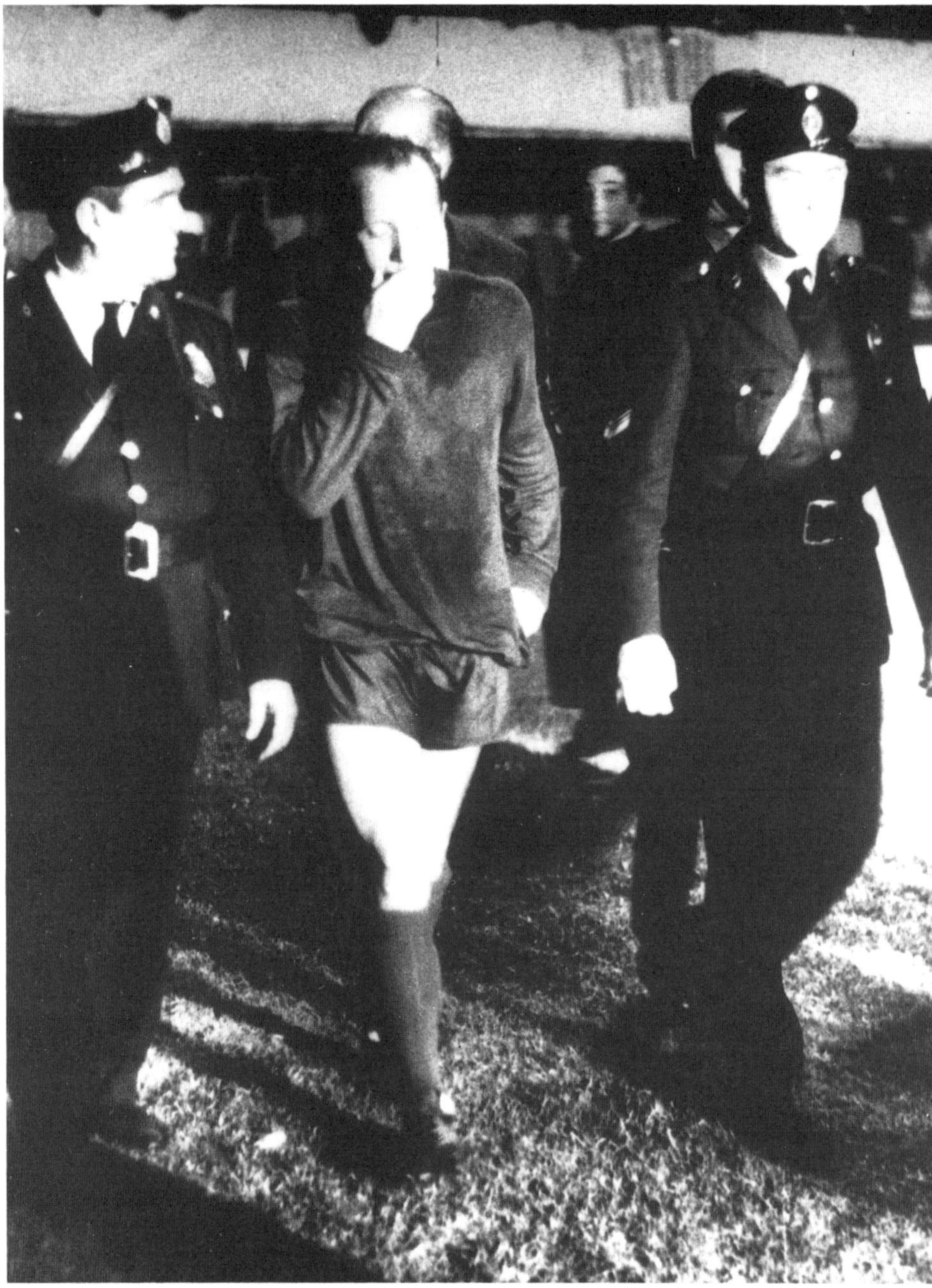

The unluckiest victim . .

Ten minutes from the end of a match that was a travesty of Soccer . . . United wing half Nobby Stiles has an escort of two Argentine policemen as he is ordered off for disputing a linesman's decision. All through he had stayed cool while he was butted, struck and kicked. It was a butt that opened a gash over his left eye in the fourteenth minute.

N SPORTSMANSHIP

Daily Mirror, 27 September 1968

Top: The battle of Old Trafford. A shame-faced Jose Medina receives his marching orders along with George Best.

Bottom: Willie Morgan smashes in United's late equaliser, but it wasn't enough.

United eventually lost the first leg by a single goal and lined up for the return at Old Trafford with tension simmering below the surface. For much of the second leg there was nail-biting excitement as United fought to find an equaliser in front of a packed crowd. Stiles had been banned from the return tie and Law had limped off early after an accidental clash but it did little to improve the tactics of the Argentinians who hustled, harried and frustrated United off their free-flowing football.

As early as the sixth minute the Argentinians had shot ahead as Madero found Veron on the far post with his curling free kick. That put them in the driving seat until the final 10 minutes when the strain and pressure finally exploded. First Best flashed his Irish temper at Medina after the Argentinian had again caught him and the referee had little alternative but to order both men off the field. Then, with just three minutes remaining, Willie Morgan snapped at Crerand's free kick to level the scores and, on the stroke of full time, Brian Kidd slammed home Morgan's cross for what everybody thought was the winning goal. But the Yugoslav referee had already blown for full time. Perhaps it was just as well. A third game might not have been a pleasant sight with the tension running so high.

United had just about had enough of Estudiantes and, although Busby promised he would play the South Americans again if United ever won the European Cup, there were few who relished the prospect. Fleet Street saw little point in the competition: Celtic had been mauled the previous year and now United had been subjected to the same brand of Latin brutality. The future of the World Club Championship was in serious doubt and indeed when Liverpool were asked to enter, having won the European Cup in 1977, they politely declined.

1969

IN CAPTURING the European Cup, Matt Busby had achieved his lifelong ambition and it came as little surprise, six months later, when he announced his retirement. A press conference had been called at Old Trafford and, although there had been some speculation in the papers about Busby's future, journalists arrived expecting the announcement of another major signing. Instead they

Time to go. Busby announces his retirement as manager after 23 years to a packed press conference.

Busby: who can follow a living legend?

By GEOFFREY GREEN, Football Correspondent

There was a certain ironic timing about the announcement yesterday of Sir Matt Busby's resignation at the end of the season as team manager of Manchester United and his change of role to that of general manager.

It came on the very day that Sir Alf Ramsey, the national manager, in the absence of Moore, appointed Bobby Charlton as captain of England on the eve of the match against Rumania at Wembley—the first United man to lead England on the field during all Busby's glittering 23-year reign at Old Trafford.

That is the way that things go and Charlton, having been telephoned by Busby himself with his decision at the England headquarters, in London, was quick to comment. "I was stunned when I first heard the news" he said. "But Sir Matt deserves a rest. It is obviously a great blow to players like myself, Billy Foulkes, Shay Brennan and Nobby Stiles who have been with him all our playing life. But I'm glad to know we shall not be losing him all that much. As general manager we shall obviously be in touch with him all the while."

To this Stiles, also of the England party, added: "I did not think this moment would ever come. A friend? He has been more like a father to me. But we shall not be losing him"

Uppermost in everyone's mind now will be the question of a successor. It will not be a position easy to fill or, more important, easy for the chosen one to support. Busby has become a living legend, the longest serving manager with the same club in the modern game, a man who has taken his club to every conceivable summit, bar that of World Club Champions.

The Times, 15 January 1969

heard a short statement from secretary Les Olive announcing Busby's impending departure. He would relinquish his coaching activities at the end of the season and assume the position of general manager. The board had tried to dissuade him, but recognised that at 58 years of age the duties of managing Manchester United were onerous and tiring. The search was now on for a new manager but Jimmy Murphy, just one year younger than Busby, would not be considered.

Busby had been at United for 23 years, during which time he had won five league championships, two FA Cups and the European Cup. He had built three outstanding teams from the Carey, Pearson, Rowley side of the 1940s to the Edwards, Byrne, Taylor team of the 1950s to the Law, Best, Charlton side of the 1960s. Each had been dedicated to exciting, attacking football, though always backed by a skilful midfield and combative defence. His finest buy? Busby reckoned it was Jimmy 'brittle bones' Delaney – a £4,000 signing from Celtic who, after six years at Old Trafford, returned north of the border to Aberdeen for £3,000. And his favourite player? Too difficult to say, although he always maintained that Edwards and Best were probably the chief contenders.

Following United's famous European victory, Busby was knighted, adding to the CBE he had already been awarded after Munich, and was later appointed a director of the club. Although he

The final farewell – or so it seemed at the time – as Busby salutes the crowd.

returned to the managerial chair a year later, following the sacking of Wilf McGuinness, it was only a brief sojourn until he had steered the team away from relegation and a new manager had been appointed.

United and Busby will always be synonymous. He was the man who created a great club, giving it honours, pride and power. Few managers in the history of the game have rivalled his expertise and achievements and no man has ever contributed more to the making of United than Sir Matt Busby. But how do you replace a legend? That was the club's immediate task.

1969

New manager Wilf McGuinness lays down the rules – but not for long.

WITH THE RETIREMENT of Busby, the race was on to find a replacement. Assistant manager Jimmy Murphy had been discounted because of his age, although in hindsight he may have proved a wise choice. Speculation threw up many notable names, with Don Revie, Jimmy Adamson, Jock Stein and Dave Sexton among those mentioned. But the favourite from the beginning was always Wilf McGuinness. Doubtless, he was also Busby's choice and on 9 April 1969 United announced to the world that the former player would succeed Sir Matt as manager, although he was not immediately given that title. Instead, he would be coach with full responsibility for team selection and the day-to-day running of the club, while Busby became general manager in charge of the overall policy concerning players. In effect Busby was there as a father figure to offer advice, but in reality he was a shadow that inhibited the new young manager.

At 31 McGuinness was the youngest manager in the first division. He had joined United as a 16-year-old from Mount Carmel school in Blackley and had first worn a United shirt in a reserve fixture at West Brom in March 1955. Six months later he made his first-team debut against Wolves but had to wait a few more years to secure the left half position. Even then, he was not always a regular choice, although he had represented England at every level from schoolboy to full international. At the time of Munich, McGuinness was recovering from a cartilage operation and consequently did not make the fated journey. As soon as he was fit again, however, he was quickly drafted into the side, although he was passed over in favour of Stan Crowther for the 1958 Cup final. He made 39 league appearances the following season but then broke a leg in a Central League match in December 1959 and was forced to retire at the early age of 22. Rather than lose his talents, United recruited him to their backroom staff as assistant trainer with the reserves and shortly after that, the FA appointed him trainer of the England Youth team. Sir Alf Ramsey also utilised his abilities, making him a training assistant during preparations for the 1966 World Cup.

McGuinness, however, faced an uphill task at Old Trafford. United had ended the season in mid-table and the outstanding side of Best, Law and Charlton was well past its peak. Replacing players of their calibre and creating as exciting a team was, in truth, impossible. Expectations were far too high and inevitably McGuinness was not able to deliver the honours Old Trafford had grown accustomed to.

Room made at the top for McGuinness

Guardian, 10 April 1969

Manchester United depleted and disappointed

The Times, 24 April 1969

1969

AFTER THEIR historic European Cup triumph United returned to the competition as favourites to lift the trophy for a second successive year. They began with a leg-stretching 10–2 aggregate victory over the gallant Irishmen of Waterford that brought seven goals from maestro Denis Law and then returned to Anderlecht, the scene of their first-ever European contest. On that occasion United had slammed 12 goals past the Brussels side, but 11 years later the Belgians had learned a thing or two about European competition and held United to a more respectable scoreline, going out 4–3 on aggregate. In the quarter-finals, United easily disposed of Rapid Vienna thanks to the wing magic of Best and Morgan who set up a semi-final clash with the Italian champions, AC Milan.

United journeyed to Milan for the first leg, where they faced not just one of the toughest sides on the Continent but 80,000 flag-waving Milanese fans in the San Siro stadium. It was a terrifying experience and after 48 minutes United were trailing 2–0. With 15 minutes remaining, it was made worse when young Scottish defender John Fitzpatrick was ordered off for kicking Milan's Swedish-born winger, Kurt Hamrin. But United hung on to keep the score down to two goals and at least had a faint hope for the second leg. But the prospect of putting three goals past one of the tightest defences in Europe was never a reality.

At Old Trafford Milan put up the shutters, defending stoutly and relying on the occasional quick breakaway. If not attractive, it was a resolute performance by the Italians who held out for 70 minutes until Best and Charlton combined to find a key to unlock their defence. The last 20 minutes were frenetic as United piled on the pressure and it seemed as if the equaliser had come as Pat Crerand chipped a delicate ball into the box and in the scramble that followed the ball looked to have crossed the line. But the referee would hear none of it and United's final hope had died.

Television later revealed that the ball had crossed the line and even the Italian newspapers were honest enough to admit that Milan had been lucky to escape a play-off. Unfortunately the referee's decision led to unruly scenes as the Stretford End unleashed its anger. Abuse and, more depressingly, missiles were hurled on the field and play was held up while calm was restored. But the fans' behaviour had more of an effect than they imagined. Once play resumed, United lost their rhythm. The drive and pace that had been injected by Charlton's goal had evaporated. Milan were through to the final and United's short reign as European champions was over.

AC Milan put up the shutters and hold out to win 2–1 on aggregate.

1970

AWAY TO LOWER division opposition in the FA Cup is always a daunting prospect. The pitfalls are all too obvious for the aristocrats who, naturally enough, are expected to come away with a handsome victory. Pride is at stake, while for the minnows there is nothing to lose and only glory to gain. In the past United had stumbled embarrassingly on lower division grounds and when they drew fourth division Northampton Town out of the hat for a fifth round FA Cup tie there must have been more than a few jangling nerves. But for once, the natural order of life turned out as it should, thanks primarily to the genius of George Best.

It was Best's first game following a month's suspension and he chose it to give one of his most remarkable exhibitions, netting six goals in United's 8–2 victory. There are those who claim it was his finest performance, matched only by his displays against Benfica. United began uncertainly and might well have been behind before Best headed United's opener in the 20th minute. A minute later he added a second and the score remained at 2–0 until moments after the interval when he popped up again to claim his hat trick. In the second half United ran riot; Best jinked, dodged and feinted, scoring three more times and also set up Brian Kidd's second goal with a dazzling run that left Northampton's defence in dizzy tatters. Yet it might have been such a different story had Northampton's early opportunities run their way or had they converted a second half penalty. As it was they had to be content with two late consolation goals and a performance by their opponents they could tell their grandchildren about in the years to come. The next day Best was the toast of Fleet Street as the pundits waxed lyrically over his superlative skills.

Georgie the six-goal genius

Observer, 8 February 1970

Six-goal George Best turning the Northampton defence inside out.

United recall Sir Matt to halt the slide

Wilf McGuinness, Manchester United's chief coach since April, 1969, and subsequently team manager, has been reduced to the ranks as trainer of United's Central League side. Sir Matt Busby has been recalled from the comparative peace and security of general manager to take charge of the team again. It will be quite like old times for everyone, except McGuinness.

On the basis that only the successful can survive in football management, the news from Old Trafford will come as no surprise. United finished a comparatively modest eighth in the League table last season; this season they have achieved little of any significance or character.

At the moment they are eighteenth and their defeat by Aston Villa, of the Third Division, in the Football League Cup semifinals probably was the last straw which broke the back of the United board's patience. Victory itself might have done no more than provide a stay of McGuinness's execution.

Guardian,
30 December 1970

1970

Wilf McGuinness at the beginning of his last month in charge: tired legs and dressing room squabbles finally led to his downfall in December 1970.

UNITED WERE accustomed to success. For more than 20 years Busby had served them a rich diet of honours and excitement. The fans had come to expect too much and when Wilf McGuinness failed to deliver any silverware a scapegoat had to be found. He had been in the job a mere 18 months and, although they had reached two League Cup semi-finals and an FA Cup semi-final, the outcome had ended in disappointment. At any other club such achievements might have been rewarded but at United second best was simply not good enough. The 1970/71 season had begun disastrously and by the end of November United had chalked up a mere five victories and were languishing in the relegation zone. There were also dressing room squabbles, which McGuinness seemed unable to handle. A place in the League Cup final had looked a certainty when United drew Aston Villa, but a 1–1 draw at Old Trafford threw that prospect into doubt. United lost the second leg 2–1 shortly before Christmas and, although it sparked off some speculation about his future, the board felt obliged to give guarantees about his job security. Perhaps they simply wanted him to have a happy Christmas, because on the evening of 28 December the board made up its mind: McGuinness had to go.

The decision leaked out the following day, yet it was all too easy to blame McGuinness. The United side that had captured the European Cup was already past its best in 1968 and by 1970 was surviving on tired legs and cunning rather than stamina and skill. Replacing the likes of Law, Stiles and Crerand was an impossible task and there was much dissension behind the scenes. Best was creating difficulties and McGuinness was not the man to handle him, while other players seemed to resent McGuinness's appointment and failed to contribute 100 per cent effort.

On reflection, McGuinness was perhaps still too close to the players and too young to have made the traumatic transition from player to manager. Meanwhile, Busby was always in the background, the man the players could go running to if they felt cheated and the man who still appeared to pull the strings. Rifts were inevitable. It had been a daring appointment in an attempt to maintain the smooth running of the club and perhaps with more time McGuinness might have squeezed the best out of his squad. As it was, they looked destined for the second division and drastic action was taken. McGuinness, much to his credit, agreed to return to his old job while Busby once more stepped into the breach. And it seemed to work: the dressing room arguments faded and results picked up. By the end of the season United had climbed into eighth position and were ready to consider another manager.

1971

THE PRESS HAD six months to speculate on McGuinness's successor. The usual names were thrown into the ring – Don Revie, Jock Stein, Dave Sexton, Ian Greaves, Don Howe and Frank O'Farrell all figured in the frame. Frank O'Farrell was the favourite and when his appointment was announced on Tuesday, 9 June 1971 there was general accord that the board had chosen the right man. Not only had O'Farrell proved himself in the lower ranks by taking Torquay from the fourth to the third division, but he had just seen his Leicester City side promoted to the first division playing a brand of attractive open football that had won much praise. O'Farrell was also older and seemed a man capable of handling the more excitable and awkward members of the squad, with even George Best agreeing that he was the players' choice. And, as O'Farrell took over, Busby was edged out of his way with the board welcoming him to their ranks as a director.

In many ways O'Farrell was a younger version of Busby – quiet, genial and courteous, not the kind of man to stand for any nonsense or allow players to get carried away by their own self-importance. In his playing days he had been an attacking wing half with Preston and West Ham, making over 300 appearances in 10 seasons and winning nine Irish caps. It had not been a particularly distinguished career, but since taking up the reins of football management he had impressed many with his thoughtful ways and enthusiasm for new ideas. Now he had to prove himself to the most demanding supporters in football – the fans of Manchester United.

MANCHESTER UNITED APPOINT O'FARRELL: BUSBY DIRECTOR

By DENIS LOWE

FRANK O'FARRELL, the shrewd and genial Irishman who has guided Leicester City back into the First Division, is Sir Matt Busby's successor as manager of Manchester United.

O'Farrell, 42, a former West Ham and Preston half-back, will take over one of the top posts in British football on July 1. Sir Matt, who has been in charge at Old Trafford since 1945, will then retire from all managerial posts and join United's board directors.

The appointment, which ends weeks of speculation in which the names of personalities such as Celtic's Jock Stein and Chelsea's Dave Sexton were linked with the post, was announced by Sir Matt last night after day-long discussions with O'Farrell and the Leicester board.

Sir Matt said later: "Frank O'Farrell has accepted the position of team manager. Our chairman, Louis Edwards, and I met him for discussions early today and, after meeting the Leicester board, Frank telephoned to confirm that he would be coming to Old Trafford.

Daily Telegraph, 9 June 1971

Welcome to Old Trafford. Sir Matt Busby introduces Frank O'Farrell to his new home, but the great man's presence was to cause him problems.

1972

DURING HIS TENURE at Old Trafford Frank O'Farrell made just a handful of signings. Only one lasted much beyond his stay in office. That was Martin Buchan, a £135,000 purchase from Aberdeen. Buchan was O'Farrell's first buy, coming eight months after he had been in the job. The Scot was a strong, accomplished defender who would have found his way into any league side. By the age of 20 he was captaining Aberdeen in the Scottish Cup final but after 133 games for the Dons, O'Farrell swooped to bring the young man south. At Old Trafford he had an immediate impact, reinforcing United's leaky defence and gave 12 seasons' outstanding service, making 455 appearances and skippering the side to the 1977 FA Cup triumph. He left United to join Oldham Athletic in 1983 but retired after one season at Boundary Park. He was capped 34 times by Scotland and was just one of six Scottish internationals to line up at Old Trafford under Tommy Docherty.

Less fortunate signings by Frank O'Farrell included Ted MacDougall, a £200,000 buy from Bournemouth. Although he was a third division player MacDougall had netted 103 goals in 146 games for Bournemouth. His signing was something of a gamble – and a hasty one at that – with many arguing that he would not be able to score goals in the first division. It was true, MacDougall laboured at Old Trafford and when Docherty arrived he was quickly dispensed with, joining West Ham United after just 18 appearances and five goals. He fared little better at Upton Park, hitting five goals in 24 matches before he moved on to Norwich, where he enjoyed considerably more success, scoring 51 goals in 112 appearances.

Martin Buchan on his debut. A £135,000 buy from Aberdeen, he would go on to make over 450 appearances.

Wyn Davies was another O'Farrell striker who failed to make an impact at Old Trafford and who moved on with the arrival of Docherty. But at least Davies had a strong pedigree, having scored goals prolifically with Wrexham, Bolton and Newcastle. He joined United from Manchester City but in 15 appearances managed only four goals. O'Farrell's other major purchase was Ian Storey-Moore, the £180,000 Nottingham Forest winger. He managed 39 league appearances before injury put paid to a promising career. Three players, costing £450,000 between them, had made just 62 appearances.

UNITED BOSS SWOOPS FOR BUCHAN

By BOB RUSSELL

MANCHESTER UNITED manager Frank O'Farrell last night clinched the £135,000 transfer of Scottish international defender Martin Buchan, 22, from Aberdeen.

The deal—O'Farrell's first major signing since he took over at Old Trafford last summer—was a record for a transfer from a Scottish club.

Daily Mirror, 29 February 1972

1972

FRANK O'FARRELL lasted just 18 months in the cauldron of Old Trafford. In that time he had held United in eighth spot and taken them to the quarter-finals of the FA Cup. He had spent money bringing in Ted MacDougall, Ian Storey-Moore, Wyn Davies and Martin Buchan. He had also introduced the tenacious little Sammy McIlroy to first team football and although McIlroy eventually made almost 400 appearances, it was still not good enough. Perhaps worst of all, O'Farrell had faced up to the continuing problem of George Best. At the beginning of December 1972 he lost patience with the wayward genius, first dropping him and then placing him on the transfer list at an asking price of £300,000. It was the end of a long list of steps that had been taken by the manager following Best's regular disappearing acts. A week later Busby met with Best to iron out the problems and dramatically announced that Best was now off the transfer list. O'Farrell quietly fumed, claiming that he had never been consulted.

Top: George: The way we shall probably remember him – surrounded by female admirers.

Right: George: Best forgotten.

Below: George – not at his Best after being sacked.

George Best and O'Farrell sacked by United

By TREVOR BATES and JOHN WILLIAMS

CRISIS-RIDDEN Manchester United yesterday sacked their manager, Frank O'Farrell, and his two assistants, and said their truant Irish star, George Best, would never play for the club again.

But when United's directors drew up the part of the statement dealing with Best, they did not know he had already sent them a letter announcing that he would never play football again.

United, whose history and victories have spread their name far outside the game, are seeking a " top manager " to replace O'Farrell and save the club from relegation.

Sir Matt Busby, manager of United in their years of triumph, will not return to the job, though he is a director of the club.

O'Farrell, 45, with 3½ years of his contract to run, will get about £42,000 in severance pay.

The two men sacked with him, Malcolm Musgrove (assistant manager) and John Aston (chief scout), do not have contracts but the club say they will " see them right."

Daily Telegraph, 20 December 1972

Confusion was now seeping into United's affairs at an alarming rate. It was clear that O'Farrell and Best were incompatible, yet to the fans Best remained the one player who could spark and flatter and the rift between him and O'Farrell did not win the latter any friends. The crisis at Old Trafford quickly became public knowledge and the focus of much back-page reporting. O'Farrell was said to be on the brink of resigning, while an article in the *Manchester Evening News* supporting O'Farrell led to its author being banned from travelling with the team.

The final straw came on 16 December when United travelled to bottom-of-the-table Crystal Palace and were thrashed 5–0. It was the club's most humiliating defeat in recent years and the knives were out for sharpening. The problem could no doubt have been resolved constructively but instead the directors chose drastic action. Three days later O'Farrell and his assistant Malcolm Musgrove were called to a board meeting and were sacked along with chief scout John Aston. But, perhaps even more dramatically, George Best was given his marching orders as well. He was back on the transfer list and would not play for the club again, announced the board. Ironically, Best had that very day written a letter informing the club that he no longer wished to play for them. It was the night of the long knives, although Old Trafford had not yet seen the last of George Best.

There were three criticisms generally levelled at O'Farrell. It was felt that he had failed to arrest the problem of Best. Bobby Charlton, for one, had long felt that the manager should have tackled the problem earlier. Instead, it had been left to drift with only meagre measures being taken. Meanwhile Best's wayward attitude had caused ill-feeling and resentment among many of the players. The dressing room atmosphere was clearly unhealthy. Secondly, it was felt that O'Farrell, while making some signings, had dipped into the market too late and for the wrong players. What was needed was a midfield man and a centre half. Players such as Alan Ball and Paul Reaney had all been available and considered, but O'Farrell had failed to grasp the opportunity. Finally, O'Farrell was considered aloof. He had arrived at Old Trafford with the reputation of being a tracksuit manager yet the day-to-day coaching of the players had been left to his assistant Malcolm Musgrove. 'He came as a stranger and went as a stranger,' said Denis Law.

In hindsight some of the accusations seem harsh. Best was uncontrollable and drinking heavily and no one could have tempered his wayward activities. The decision to sack him was almost certainly the best course of action and O'Farrell's decision to transfer-list him should have received more support from the board. Perhaps with more time and with Best out of the way O'Farrell might have reversed the fortunes of the club. Busby's presence was also a continuing intimidation and the latter's decision to reinstate Best placed O'Farrell in an impossible position. The whole episode had been one of the most shameful in the club's history, but at least United could now start afresh.

1972

AS THE UNITED players trooped dejectedly off the field following their 5–0 defeat at Crystal Palace, Tommy Docherty, sitting in the directors' box, was casually asked by Matt Busby if he might be interested in becoming United's next manager should something occur within the next week or so. A fortnight later, after Frank O'Farrell's hasty departure, the Doc had been officially installed in British football's toughest job. There was never any doubt that Docherty was the man United wanted and all newspaper speculation centred around the extrovert Scot.

At the time Docherty was managing the Scottish national team and already carried the remnants of a stormy managerial career which had taken him from overnight success at Chelsea to mediocre days at Aston Villa, Queen's Park Rangers, Rotherham and Oporto. Prior to that he had been a bulldozer of a wing half with Preston, Arsenal and Chelsea and had won 25 Scottish caps. Controversy followed him wherever he went, but as Scotland's manager he seemed to have settled and was welding together a team of outstanding talents that included United's Denis Law and Willie Morgan. Both testified to Docherty's change of character.

On Wednesday, 30 December 1972 Tommy Docherty blazed into Old Trafford and within moments his bubbling, abrasive personality had taken charge. The back-biting and sniping that had accompanied the latter days of O'Farrell were quickly swept aside and a new optimism was flushed to the surface. Docherty was made for United and in particular for the fans. He was an outstanding communicator who understood their demands and ambitions and wanted success for them more than for anyone. Docherty's personality was as big as Old Trafford, filling every nook and cranny. Although it finally resulted in problems, at least everyone knew who was in charge. There was never any possibility that players, former managers or directors would deter him from his plans. With money to spend and 50,000 paying customers at each home match, Docherty set out on his own glory trail. It took him to the depths and to the peaks before it all blew up in his face. But at least it was exciting.

IT'S DOC'S JOB!

United will name him as boss soon

TOMMY DOCHERTY, manager of Scotland, will have full control of trouble-shattered Manchester United within the next fortnight.

Paddy Crerand, temporarily in charge of United's first team following the sackings of manager Frank O'Farrell and assistant Malcolm Musgrove, will become the Doc's deputy.

Daily Mirror, 31 December 1972

The charismatic Tommy Docherty discusses United's problems with temporary manager Pat Crerand a few days before he was officially confirmed as Frank O'Farrell's replacement in the toughest job in football. However, the solutions did not come easily.

1973

'MAC FOR MAC' was the speculative headline in the *Daily Mirror* of 2 January. The report suggested that United's unhappy striker Ted MacDougall was about to move to London with Lou Macari the Celtic star taking his place at Old Trafford. It turned out to be uncannily prophetic. A fortnight later Macari was a United player and by the end of February MacDougall had gone to West Ham. The same paper also reported a meeting between George Best and new manager Docherty, fuelling speculation that Best might be about to return to Old Trafford. It didn't happen immediately but it was the first step in George's eventual rehabilitation.

Lou Macari celebrates his debut goal against West Ham, the club he later managed.

Lou Macari, the Celtic and Scotland striker, had been expected to sign for Liverpool, but United had shown more than a passing interest in the 23-year-old. However, Liverpool appeared to have pipped them to the post when he arrived at Anfield for talks with the Liverpool manager Bill Shankly. Terms were agreed with Celtic, and Macari promised to give his decision the following morning but in the meantime sat back to watch Liverpool beat Burnley 3–0 in an FA Cup replay. Two of the goals were scored by John Toshack, the man he was expected to succeed, and the next morning the deal was dramatically called off. Tommy Docherty needed no further prompting and within hours Macari had signed for United at a fee of £200,000.

Although the little Scot scored on his debut against West Ham, he took time to settle. The following season United were relegated, with Macari scoring just one goal. His talents began to shine through as United stormed to the top of the second division. During his 12 seasons at Old Trafford he made 373 appearances, netting almost 100 goals. He personified Docherty's approach to football – busy, Scottish and adventurous – and was a clear favourite with the Stretford Enders. Macari had been born in Edinburgh of Italian parents and had joined Celtic as a teenager. In his seven years at Parkhead he won two Scottish championship medals and two Scottish Cup-winners' medals but managed only one honour south of the border – a Cup-winners' medal in 1977. In all, he was capped 24 times by Scotland.

In the space of just one month at Old Trafford Docherty spent about £500,000, bringing in Arsenal's George Graham, Alex Forsyth of Partick Thistle, Jim Holton from Shrewsbury, Mick Martin from Bohemians and Lou Macari. Docherty now had six of his former Scotland team at Old Trafford as he set about building a tartan army south of the border. Further signings followed over the next few months, including Stewart Houston who came in December 1973 from Brentford for £55,000. In just three months Tommy Docherty had managed to sign as many players as Busby, McGuinness and O'Farrell had in the previous six and a half years.

PALACE ARE POISED AS TED PREPARES TO GO

By CHRIS HARRIGAN

TED MacDOUGALL would like a move to London if Manchester United officially decide today to place him on the transfer list.

And that will interest Crystal Palace, who were just pipped for his signature by former United boss Frank O'Farrell three months ago.

I understand that Palace will be watching closely this afternoon to see whether United's directors agree to put their £220,000 striker up for sale.

Last night MacDougall, still shocked over his sudden rejection at Old Trafford, told me: "If I've got to leave United I'd love a move to London."

Tommy Docherty, meanwhile, may soon move for Lou Macari, the talented young Celtic and Scotland striker. The United boss went to Glasgow yesterday, but with Celtic's game off because of 'flu, he saw Rangers beat Partick 1—0.

Daily Mirror, 2 January 1973

1973

SATURDAY, 28 APRIL 1973 marked the end of a romance; Bobby Charlton made his final league appearance in a red shirt. For 20 years Charlton and United had strode the world, from the bone-hard pitches of the southern hemisphere to the mud baths of Lancashire; from the ramshackle stadiums of the Third World to the multi-tiered fantasies of Spain and Italy. Wherever he went, Charlton was a hero. The whole world could speak at least two words of English – Borby Scharltun. But the romance had to come to an end sometime, even Bobby Charlton could not go on indefinitely.

The legend had joined United as a teenager, though given his north-east background and his famous uncle – Jackie Milburn – it was a wonder he was ever allowed to escape Geordie land. Newcastle, Sunderland, Middlesbrough – how did they ever let him out of their sights? His first taste of big-time football was with United's youth team. Three years in succession he helped them win the Youth Cup and was thrown into an early league baptism when he deputised for Tommy Taylor against Charlton Athletic in October 1956. He scored two goals that day and so began a sequence that brought him 247 goals in 751 appearances for United.

By 1958 Charlton had firmly established himself in the inside right position and made the ill-fated journey to Belgrade. He scrambled from the wreckage, dazed but unharmed, to find himself one of the few Babes still alive. For a 20-year-old it must have been a shattering experience to lose so many friends, yet

Top: Bobby Charlton in action during his last game for United.

Below: The press swarm round Charlton as he leaves the pitch.

HAVE A NICE ONE BOBBY!

The Mirror message to Britain's greatest sports ambassador as he plays his last League match

IF the Soccer fans will forgive the expression, it doesn't matter a damn who wins today's clash between Chelsea and Manchester United.

They should save their cheers for the man of the match. That's Bobby Charlton—even if he plays a stinker.

Favourite

Because today is the day that Soccer's favourite son hangs up his boots. Bobby is pictured on the right arriving in London yesterday for his 751st game for United—and his last.

Daily Mirror, 28 April 1973

he was mature enough to seize the new responsibility that had been so unkindly thrust on his young shoulders. Along with Foulkes, Gregg and Viollet, he was one of the few remaining links with the famous Busby Babes and it fell to him to carry United through this most daunting period of their history. He struggled back within weeks and spurred them to a sentimental trip to Wembley. It may have ended in disappointment, but he came back later to gain his winners' medal. More importantly, he returned to lead his team-mates up the steps, after he himself had scored two goals, to collect the European Cup. It was a moment of shared gladness and sadness between Busby and Charlton, the final link with the famous Babes. In the meantime he had won two league championship honours to place alongside the one he won in 1957, as well as the prized European Player of the Year award and the Footballer of the Year honour.

As an international he was first chosen to represent England against Scotland in 1958. His final appearance in an England shirt came 12 years later against West Germany in the 1970 World Cup. He won 106 caps, scoring 49 international goals and gained a World Cup-winners' medal in 1966. Charlton remains possibly the most honoured player in British football.

After Old Trafford Charlton moved 30 miles up the M6 to manage second division Preston North End, but it was an affair that never worked. He played another 38 league games with them but could not stop the Deepdale club from sliding into division three. He quit; and, although he had another brief fling, this time with Wigan Athletic, he returned to Old Trafford as a director.

His blistering shot, the shimmy of the hips, the powerful sprint, would never be seen again on a football field. It was fitting that his final appearance at Old Trafford should draw almost 60,000 fans. Five days later he pulled on the red shirt for the final time as he ran out against Chelsea at Stamford Bridge. It was no more than his due that the *Daily Mirror* should have devoted its front page to the occasion.

1974

LIFE CAN BE full of cruel ironies. And for United fans, none came crueller than Denis Law's cheeky backheeler that sentenced them to life in division two. Discarded by Tommy Docherty on a free transfer and never even informed, Law had joined his former club Manchester City, only to end his playing career by scoring the goal that relegated the club where he had found so much glory.

United had escaped relegation by a whisker the previous year but, with Tommy Docherty having cleared the decks at Old Trafford, better was expected the following season. Charlton, Law and Dunne all departed in favour of younger men. Docherty had made sound purchases in the shape of Holton, Macari and Forsyth but the team still spluttered and stumbled. By Christmas they had won only four games and as the New Year celebrations died down they found themselves third from bottom. Best had returned briefly to help resolve the growing crisis, but had in fact only compounded the problem. Following United's 3–0 defeat at QPR on New Year's Day he disappeared for the umpteenth time, but on this occasion never returned. It made little difference, however. By the end of the month United were next to bottom and in early February struck a new low as they found themselves propping up the rest of the first division. And yet, even in that position, they could still attract 60,000 to Old Trafford. For the remainder of the spring Norwich and United vied for bottom spot with Birmingham hovering anxiously above them.

The climax finally came on Saturday, 27 April when Manchester City visited Old Trafford. United simply had to win to avoid relegation and hope that Norwich in bottom place might defeat Birmingham. With eight minutes remaining the score at Old Trafford stood at 0–0 when a loose ball spun and bobbled tantalisingly in the United penalty box. It needed just the simplest of touches and who should be there to provide it but Denis Law, playing at Old Trafford for the first time since his rejection. He simply backheeled the ball past a grovelling Stepney and walked quietly away. No jumping for joy, no celebration. Old Trafford was stunned. It was Law's final league goal. He retired, as planned, a few days later but admitted to spending the most heartbreaking weekend of his life after his death blow.

Law's last sad word

ERIC TODD describes the scenes at Old Trafford

Guardian, 29 April 1974

United fans give Denis Law a scarf. So long a favourite with the Stretford End, his last act in league football was to score the goal that relegated United.

It was also Law's final kick in league football and a couple of minutes later he was sensibly substituted. But hardly had his replacement had time to break sweat when hundreds shamefully invaded the pitch. The teams were taken off but it did little to quell the invasion and eventually the referee had to abandon proceedings. It had all ended in tragedy, with Denis Law, rather like Brutus, plunging the dagger ceremoniously into an old colleague. United were relegated and their fans disgraced. For the first time in over 35 years, Manchester United were a Second Division side.

United fans invade the pitch as the Reds go down to division two.

1975

ON A WARM Saturday in mid-August the Manchester United team coach turned slowly into Brisbane Road, London E10. For most of its occupants this was new territory – the home of Leyton Orient Football Club. It was a ground United had not played on for many years but, more importantly, it was their first game in the second division since they had beaten Bury 2–0 on 7 May 1938. On most Saturdays Leyton Orient could attract little over 10,000 to their hotch-potch of a ground, yet the prospect of the Red Devils in the East End almost doubled their usual gate.

Rarely can a team have played in the second division and attracted such crowds. Week after week Old Trafford boasted the largest gate of any fixture in the country, even though the opposition hardly seemed to warrant the attention. Crowds of over 45,000 came to see York City, Fulham and Oldham Athletic, while towards the end of the season, as the smell of promotion loomed, gates topped 55,000. Even away from home United were filling grounds across the land and their appearance in the second division must have brought a sudden and welcome windfall to football's minnows. The crowds came not just because of United's name and glamorous past, but because they were leading the promotion race with a brand of fast, exciting football that had caught the imagination.

At last Tommy Docherty was piecing together as attractive a side as United had seen since 1968. He had learned from his earlier mistake of dictating tactics to them and now simply told them to go out and play their natural game. It worked and United led the division from the start. By January they were four points clear of Sunderland and the gap gradually widened as the spring progressed; five points by February, seven points by March. In the end the title was clinched on Saturday, 5 April with a 1–0 win at Southampton – and there were still three more games to play.

It was United's home record which had dictated their title win: only one game was lost at Old Trafford, 45 goals scored and 12 conceded. Sadly, however, one of the mainstays of that defence, Jim Holton, broke a leg against Sheffield

'Six foot two, eyes of blue,
Big Jim Holton's after you.'
So sang the Stretford End.

MANCHESTER UNITED are back in the First Division after just one season away from the top bracket. One point at Southampton would have been enough — they got two with a Lou Macari goal in the 76th minute.

Macari's goal came only a minute he had been booked for not standing 10 yards away from a free kick. Earlier Channon missed a penalty for Saints.

Sunday Telegraph, 6 April 1975

Willie Morgan resists Alan Mullery's attempt at an arm lock as United beat Fulham 2–1.

Wednesday in early December and never played first-team football again at Old Trafford. In a pre-season friendly against Red Star the following season he reappeared only to twist his knee in the pre-match kick-about and then, a few weeks later in an outing with the reserves, he tragically broke his leg yet again. It marked the end of his United career and he was transferred to Sunderland later that year. Holton had been one of Docherty's first signings, joining the club as an unknown from Shrewsbury Town. He played 69 games in the middle of the United defence and made 15 appearances for Scotland. 'Six foot two, eyes of blue, Big Jim Holton's after you,' chanted the Stretford End at the man who quickly became their favourite. Another loss at the end of the campaign was Willie Morgan, for so long a fixture in the midfield. He had arrived at Old Trafford from Burnley in 1968 and returned there after United's promotion. He had played 291 games and although he scored only 33 goals he had provided dozens more for Macari, Law, Best and Pearson.

If the Stretford End lost a couple of favourites, then it gained others. Towards the end of their victory campaign Tommy Docherty descended on Merseyside to pinch Tranmere's Steve Coppell. Pinch was the word because Bill Shankly, then helping Tranmere Rovers out, had tipped off Liverpool about the young winger but was ignored. So instead he gave Docherty a call. Coppell signed for £40,000 and was drafted into the first team almost immediately. A university graduate, Coppell made almost 400 appearances for the club, as well as winning 42 England caps, before a knee injury ended his career in October 1983 at the early age of 29. Another inspired Docherty purchase was Gerry Daly who joined United from the Irish club Bohemians in April 1973. Daly was a bustling midfielder, providing many of the goals that helped United to promotion. He eventually left Old Trafford in March 1977 after a series of rows with the manager and joined Derby County for £175,000. Six months later, he was joined by his old sparring partner when Docherty was appointed the new boss at the Baseball Ground.

Steve Coppell attacks down the right wing yet again.

1976

FA CUP FINAL AT WEMBLEY

Manchester United ....0 Southampton 1

The latter-day Saints

Sunday Times, 2 May 1976

Doc did not order this

IT WAS a final that never really caught fire, but it left Manchester United with the taste of ashes. Two or three weeks ago the double of the League championship and the FA Cup was a feasible target. Now they have nothing tangible to show for all those months of inspired and adventurous football, for a long string of performances that represented the most exhilarating flourish of the English season. What had seemed an irresistible surge has stuttered, and died like a racing car that runs out of fuel a few yards short of the chequered flag.

To say all this is not to belittle the positive achievement of Southampton, whose victory owed as much to the soundness of their technique as to the firmness of their will. The entire team played with an honesty and boldness of purpose that reflected the values of their Geordie manager, Lawrie McMenemy, one of the most appealing and forthright spirits in the game. They deserved to win and it will be right and natural if their memories of yesterday afternoon at Wembley glow in a way that no neutral's ever could.

Yet for those of us who are obliged to be objective, this final and its result had more to do with jobs well done than with grand gestures accomplished; more to do with conscientiousness than inspiration, with efficiency than with glory. Thus the defensive covering of Steele and Blyth, and the ceaseless harrying by Gilchrist, did at least as much for the winners as the long, telling passes of McCalliog and the forward probings of Channon and Osgood; and the stifling of Manchester United's vaunted threat along the wings (which led to the substitution of McCreery for Hill) could be considered as decisive as that late, beautifully executed and unmistakably fatal blow by Stokes.

Southampton won the Cup because they did a first-class job of work on the day. Manchester United lost because their capacity to do much more deserted them when they needed it most. Even in my hospital ward 40 miles from Wembley the intensity of their misery, mercilessly revealed by television cameras, was physically painful.

So Tommy Docherty, who has still to scale a major peak in his extraordinary career as a manager, finds himself back at base camp yet again. If there is any justice, Manchester United will surely dominate one or other of football's high places next season.

Hugh McIlvanney

Sunday Times, 2 May 1976

FOOTBALL CAN BE a cruel game. In early April United fans were savouring a possible league and Cup double, but within the space of a couple of weeks their dreams were suddenly shattered. On the morning United beat Derby County in the FA Cup semi-final to reach Wembley, they stood just one point behind league leaders QPR, but with a game in hand. In their first season back in division one United looked set to steal the title from under the noses of Liverpool, Derby and Leeds. But in April their double-fronted challenge fell apart. United lost three of their final six fixtures and ended up in third place, four points behind the eventual champions Liverpool. But if they had lost the league, there was still the possibility of the Cup.

In the final United faced second division challengers Southampton – surely it was a mere formality for the first division outfit? Before the game Tommy Docherty uttered just one word – Sunderland – to remind them that the big guns can come unstuck even at Wembley. Yet nobody really thought United would falter against the 5–1 underdogs. In retrospect, the pundits should have heeded the signs. United were tired and dispirited after their depressing run-in while Southampton manager Lawrie McMenemy had quietly built a well-organised side around the attacking flair of Mick Channon and Peter Osgood. On the day United failed to sparkle. Macari, Gordon Hill, Stuart Pearson and Sammy McIlroy all failed to reproduce the dash and flair that had taken them to within a whisker of the league title. Only Martin Buchan looked the part as he battled to inspire his jaded troops; but it was no use. In truth it was a poor match which failed to come to life until Southampton's late effort when, with only eight minutes remaining and with United clearly

The tears would be short-lived. A year later they would be back to celebrate and the disappointment of Southampton could be forgotten.

watching the clock in anticipation of extra time, Bobby Stokes stole in to hit Southampton's winner. It was little more than they deserved.

Gerry Daly demonstrates a new dance to Southampton's Paul Gilchrist, who refuses to join in.

Yet United's end-of-season demise should not hide the creditable achievement of Tommy Docherty's young side. They had returned to the first division and with their polished attacking play had offered a challenge that had taken many by surprise. Prior to their defeat at Ipswich on 10 April they had played 45 league and cup games and had lost only seven. But in the end their own success turned out to be their undoing as they were forced to play six matches in 19 days. It all proved too much and, like so many sides before and since, they faltered at the final hurdle. The Cup had been as unpredictable as ever.

In the Final analysis it's a Lawrie hijack

Observer, 2 May 1976

1977

Jimmy Greenhoff's rebound destroys Liverpool dreams of a treble and gives United the FA Cup.

'WE'LL BE BACK' sang the United fans in 1976 as they trooped dejectedly out of the old stadium and down Wembley Way. And, sure enough, 12 months later they returned, this time to make amends for their lacklustre display of the previous year. Their opponents now were not a middle-of-the-table second division outfit but the league champions and European Cup finalists, Liverpool, and United found themselves rated underdogs with the bookmakers.

United had reached Wembley with victories over Walsall, QPR, Southampton, Aston Villa and Leeds United. It had been as difficult a passage as imaginable, with their return clash against Southampton going to a replay. But having overcome so many difficult hurdles, it seemed United's name might already be inscribed on the trophy. Liverpool, having just clinched the league title, now faced two cup finals in five days as they followed up their Wembley appearance with a gruelling trip to Rome where they faced Borussia Moenchengladbach in the European Cup final.

The final turned out to be a dismal climax to the season and, save for a five-minute spell in the second half, Liverpool were always the better team. But Cup finals are about scoring goals and in that short spell between the 50th and 55th minute United scored two goals to Liverpool's one – but it was enough. The game's first goal came from Stuart Pearson, lurking as dangerously as ever

JUST 5 MINUTES OF PURE MAGIC

by JAMES MOSSOP

THE STEALTHY goal burglars of Manchester United brought their guile to Wembley's Jubilee Final and went away with the most famous piece of silver of them all, the F.A. Cup,

I hope the Soccer chroniclers record more than the statistics. These are briefly concerned with a magical five-minute spell in the second half when Stuart Pearson and Jimmy Greenhoff always lurking with the intention of ransacking Liverpool's treble dream, scored goals either side of one by Jimmy Case.

British boost

Here was a game of such grandeur, so memorable for its sportsmanship and grace, that British football can proudly reflect that the occasion was stage-managed to perfection.

Most of all I cherish the sportsmanship. The teams applauded each other at the end. Liverpool cruelly disappointed, burried their unhappiness and sought out the United man who severly damaged his ankle two weeks ago, Stewart Houston, to shake his hand.

And curly-haired, baby-faced Arthur Albiston, the 19-year-old Scot who took his place, had to be prised out of Houston's arms before he could collect his medal from the Duchess of Kent. Afterwards, in the noisy dressing-room party, Albiston tried to press his winners' medal upon Houston but the man on crutches would not hear of such generosity.

Sunday Express, 22 May 1977

Not many grab Tommy Smith's shirt and live to tell the tale. But Pearson did.

Mrs Greenhoff must have been proud of her two lads as they celebrated their triumph over Liverpool.

in the penalty box. Seizing on a ball from Jimmy Greenhoff, he instinctively found space and shot low under Ray Clemence's body to open United's account. But the cheers from the United fans perched high on the terraces were short-lived, as two minutes later Jimmy Case sent a ferocious shot into the top left-hand corner of United's net to level matters. Suddenly Wembley had come to life. There was even more to celebrate three minutes on, as Lou Macari swung a foot at the ball as it bobbled tantalisingly in the penalty area. It was a wild shot but as luck would have it the ball rebounded off a surprised Jimmy Greenhoff and soared into the Liverpool net. United were ahead. Liverpool, as ever, pressed forward but the Cup had already been won and now they would have to drag their tired limbs halfway across Europe to make amends.

Not many players can claim to have made their FA Cup debut in a Wembley final but it was a distinction which fell to the 19-year-old Arthur Albiston who stepped in to replace the injured Stewart Houston. Albiston performed admirably and went on to give many years' service to United, making 436 appearances for them as well as winning 14 caps for Scotland. The two Greenhoff brothers, Jimmy and Brian, also shone and between them played almost 400 games for the club.

Tommy Docherty had won his first major trophy at United and not surprisingly he gloried in the moment, balancing the lid of the FA Cup on his head and joining in the Wembley lap of honour. It was his privilege. He was the toast of the Stretford End and most of Manchester. Little did he know, however, that it was his last game in charge of United. Within weeks the smiles turned to tears.

1977

THE FA CUP barely had time to be given its place of honour in the United boardroom when the club found its good name splattered across the headlines. Tommy Docherty had been having an affair with the wife of the club's physiotherapist, Laurie Brown, and the full story was splashed across the front pages of every tabloid. It was not particularly dignified and sparked off predictable speculation that it might mean the end of Docherty's career at United.

Docherty had announced that he was leaving his wife, and setting up home with Mary Brown ('the woman I love'). He was hardly the first man to leave his wife and the affair had been known in footballing circles for some time. But it was embarrassing for United, especially as it involved another of their employees. Nevertheless, United immediately quashed any suggestion that they might sack Docherty. The story rumbled on for a fortnight and seemed almost on the point of disappearing when United suddenly rekindled the flame. Following an emergency board meeting at Louis Edwards' home, it was decided that Docherty must go. According to the club statement he was 'in breach of the terms of his contract'. Docherty was shattered; 'I have been punished for falling in love,' he told the press.

Had United held fire, the story would almost certainly have died within the week, so why did they choose to dismiss him? Undoubtedly the club was in a difficult position. Either Laurie Brown or Docherty had to go and to sack Brown after he had lost his wife seemed particularly harsh on someone who was an innocent victim of events. Perhaps at the

Tommy Docherty chewing the cud with Mary Brown after their affair became public knowledge.

Mary Brown

Punished for love affair, says Soccer boss as 'moral code' United tell him: You're sacked

Mrs Docherty

CLUB WIVES OUST DOC

Who will take over at Old Trafford? Back Page

By John Roberts and James Price

TOMMY DOCHERTY hit out bitterly last night after being sacked as manager of Manchester United, one of the top jobs in football.

Directors' wives at the club, which is proud of its family image, helped force him out. They acted from shock and embarrassment over his love affair.

The United women put pressure on the board following Docherty's announcement two weeks ago that he is setting up home with Mary Brown, wife of the club's physiotherapist.

Docherty, 49, who recently shook hands on a new four-year contract worth £100,000, after United won the F.A. Cup in May said: "I've been punished for falling in love. This is the most shattering experience of my football life.

Daily Express, 5 July 1977

root of their decision was a general disapproval of Docherty. After a shaky start that had seen United relegated, he had brought about an exciting transformation. The team had finished third and sixth in consecutive seasons as well as winning the Cup, yet there was much grumbling about Docherty's style of management. There were accusations about Cup final tickets, his attitude to certain players and there would later be a messy court case between Willie Morgan and Docherty. Docherty may well have been the kind of manager the Stretford Enders identified with, but his ways were hardly the kind of style expected by those in charge of the club.

Nevertheless, Docherty had made some shrewd purchases. The combination of Steve Coppell and the former Millwall winger Gordon Hill had brought a new breadth and pace to the United attack; while Stewart Houston, Gerry Daly and the powerful Stuart Pearson had all proved effective buys.

Docherty was probably his own worst enemy. He had voluntarily announced his marital problems to the press, although it would have all filtered out in time. Yet there is no doubt that he was developing a young, exciting team which may have gone on to achieve championship honours. But his crusading zeal was accompanied by a devil-may-care attitude that in the end sowed the seeds of his own undoing.

1977

Dave Sexton: calm, quiet and pensive. A far cry from Tommy Doc, he brought a new approach to United.

IN PLACE OF the flamboyant Tommy Docherty, United opted for the phlegmatic Dave Sexton as their new manager. Although he was always high on everyone's list it seemed, at the time, that Sexton was destined for Highbury rather than Old Trafford. Arsenal claimed he had already given his word to them but the sudden prospect of a job at Old Trafford was clearly too tempting. Docherty's dismissal also coincided with the dramatic resignation of Don Revie as the England manager, and it was hardly surprising that more than a few journalists reckoned the former Leeds man was bound for United. But it turned out not to be the case, with Revie opting instead for a lucrative pay-off in the Middle East.

Sexton joined United on Thursday, 14 July claiming that he had needed just 20 seconds to mull over United's £20,000 a year offer. A former inside forward with Luton, West Ham, Brighton and Crystal Palace, the 47-year-old Sexton had until recently been pulling the strings at QPR. He had also managed Leyton Orient and had been on the coaching staff at Arsenal before taking over as manager of Chelsea in 1967. And the man he had succeeded on that occasion was none other than the man who had given Sexton his first coaching job at Chelsea – Tommy Docherty. Under Sexton Chelsea won the FA Cup in 1970 and the European Cup-Winners' Cup in the following year, but his reign ended unhappily in 1974 with the sack. However, his dismissal took him a few miles up the road to QPR where he guided the unglamorous West London club to within a point of the league championship. There was no doubt that Sexton had a proven track record and it seemed he might be the man to steer United towards the title.

The quietly spoken Sexton was a complete contrast to Docherty. Calm, reserved and thoughtful, he was hardly the man to lash out at players or hype his side in TV interviews. If Docherty was a Stretford Ender then Sexton was an executive box supporter. Not for him any raucous dressing room celebrations or running around Wembley with the Cup – not that he had much opportunity of either while at United – but more likely a quiet dinner with his family at the local restaurant. The excitement of Docherty's final years was replaced with hard work, stern but fair discipline, and a less adventurous approach on the field. He was in many ways not dissimilar to Frank O'Farrell and although he tasted some success, he failed to bring any silverware back to Manchester. And in the end that was the undoing of the schoolmasterly Sexton.

In just 30 seconds, Old Trafford gets its new boss

Sexton: I'll be a winner

Daily Express, 15 July 1977

1978

Joe Jordan about to damage Southampton's David Peach.

THE LEEDS UNITED and Scotland striker Joe Jordan was rated among the most dangerous attackers in European football. Both Liverpool and Ajax had been tracking the 26-year-old and both had made substantial offers for his services. Jordan was keen to try Continental football but when United stepped in with a record offer of £350,000 he took little persuading to make Old Trafford his new home.

Jordan had joined Leeds from Morton seven years previously for £15,000, and in 139 full appearances scored 35 goals for the Elland Road club, winning a championship medal in 1974 as well as appearing in two European finals. Jordan was a powerful striker and although his goal tally may not have been as prolific as many others he was a goal provider of genuine quality. His strength was unmatched and in the penalty area he was a fearsome opponent, climbing high above defenders and able to fend off challenges with seeming ease. He had four seasons at Old Trafford before he finally fulfilled his long-held desire to play in European football, when he joined AC Milan in the summer of 1981 for the knockdown price of £175,000. He later played with Verona and then returned to Britain, joining Southampton before ending his career as player-manager at Bristol City.

Jordan was always a favourite at Old Trafford, scoring 41 goals in 125 appearances. He cut an exciting figure with his powered running and volatile temperament. In an international career that spanned almost 10 years he was capped 52 times. A few weeks later, Jordan was joined at his new club by another famous Leeds United Scot, Gordon McQueen. McQueen cost just under £500,000, but became the mainstay of the United defence over the next eight seasons, making 228 appearances. Tall, agile and strong, he made 30 appearances for Scotland before joining the Hong Kong club Seiko as injury had dogged the latter part of his Old Trafford career.

Jordan was Sexton's first major signing but his arrival heralded the end of the road for Stuart Pearson. A £200,000 Tommy Docherty import from Hull City, Pearson was now surplus to requirements and played only a handful more games for United before joining West Ham in September 1979. Capped 15 times by England, he played 178 games for United during his five-year stay, scoring 66 goals.

JORDAN SIGNS

By JIM RODGER

MANCHESTER UNITED manager Dave Sexton will today sign Joe Jordan, Leeds United's Scottish international striker, for £350,000.

Daily Mirror, 6 January 1978

1979

UNITED'S ROAD to Wembley had hardly been an easy route. They had faced and overcome three London clubs as well as plucky little Colchester United and then Liverpool in a replayed semi-final. And now at Wembley they met their fourth London side – Arsenal.

On league form there was little to separate the famous clubs, but United knew from their previous two Cup final appearances that league positions counted for little. It was the first time they had ever faced each other at Wembley and it turned out to be an occasion no one would ever forget, although for the first 86 minutes it looked as if it was destined to be one of the most

Lou Macari, with an acrobatic overhead kick, shoots for goal.

HAS THERE EVER BEEN A FINAL LIKE THIS!

ARSENAL (2) 3 MANCHESTER UTD (0) 2

Talbot (scored in 12 min 2 sec) **McQueen (86 min 20 sec)**
Stapleton (43 min 28 sec) **McIlroy(88 min 15 sec)**
Sunderland (89 min 10 sec)

Attendance: 100,000 Receipts: £500,000

SOCKS TUMBLING around his ankles, the sweat of effort darkening his shirt, Liam Brady stood in the centre of Wembley's vast stage and took his share of the applause at the end of a Cup Final that will be written into history because of its sensational climax.

Sunday Express, 13 May 1979

Sammy McIlroy skips past Arsenal's Steve Walford to level the scores at 2–2 with minutes to go.

disappointing Wembley finals in years and one which few would wish to recall.

Then suddenly, in the 86th minute, the game burst into life. At that stage United were trailing 2–0 after Brian Talbot had edged Arsenal ahead as early as the 12th minute. Frank Stapleton, then leading the Gunners' attack, added a second shortly before half time and the North Londoners were coasting to victory. United, not surprisingly, looked dispirited and jaded as the full-time whistle loomed, but they refused to concede defeat. Big Joe Jordan, battling tirelessly and winning everything in the air, and his former Leeds team-mate Gordon McQueen never gave up the fight. Fittingly, it was McQueen himself who dramatically revived the game when he thrust out a long left leg to send the ball scooting past Pat Jennings in the Arsenal goal.

Arsenal fans, already celebrating a Cup victory, were suddenly silenced while on the pitch panic set in among the players. With the old stadium still creeking from the celebrations and Arsenal looking rattled, Sammy McIlroy picked up a ball on the edge of the penalty area and weaved his way into the box before stroking it into the Arsenal net. It was unbelievable; United were back on level terms with less than 90 seconds remaining. Yet it was not to be. Almost on the stroke of full time, Liam Brady, who had already set up two Arsenal strikes, contrived to create a third when he slipped a pass to Graham Rix who centred for Alan Sunderland to slam home. In the cauldron of bursting hearts and racing blood United had let slip their concentration just as their minds were turning to extra time. There was no way back now and for the second time in the 1970s United had to be content with losers' medals. But what a finale they had given us.

1979

WILKINS, YORATH & GREENHOFF SET FOR £1½m MOVES

By DONALD SAUNDERS

DESPITE increasing anxiety about the spiralling cost of transfers during the most extravagant close-season in League history, another £1,500,000 will be handed over or promised today, if three more proposed big deals are clinched.

Daily Telegraph, 15 August 1979

Ray Wilkins on his debut. At £825,000, he was the club's most expensive signing.

MONTHS OF SPECULATION and negotiation were finally concluded on Tuesday, 14 August 1979 when the Chelsea and England midfielder Ray Wilkins signed for United. It was a club record fee of £825,000 which proved to be money well spent.

Wilkins had been linked with numerous clubs since his decision to quit Chelsea, but the London club had been determined to hang on to their precious commodity. United's overtures were initially rejected, but Wilkins was equally determined that his future should lie at Old Trafford and eventually Chelsea were forced to concede.

It was Dave Sexton himself who had originally signed the 15-year-old Wilkins for Chelsea, and with Sexton now incumbent at Old Trafford it was hardly surprising that he should wish to have his protégé join him. At Stamford Bridge Wilkins had skippered Chelsea to promotion and won 24 England caps. He was talked of as a future England captain and with the larger stage of Old Trafford to display his talents it was not long before he was leading both his club and his country. He took time to settle at United, but once his authority was established he became the cog around which the team turned. He was calm, decisive and full of running, the kind of skipper who leads from the front; and with his long, raking passes he added a refined touch to United's football. He went on to make 190 appearances for the club before being transferred, many would say prematurely, to AC Milan for £1.5 million in May 1984. At United he added another 38 caps to his name and collected an FA Cup-winners' medal as United trounced Brighton in a memorable Cup final replay.

IT'S A DEAL!

United's swoop lands Wilkins

Daily Star, 15 August 1979

1980

IT MUST HAVE come as a shock to United supporters to turn on their television sets one January evening and find their own club accused on Granada Television's 'World In Action' programme of corrupt and fraudulent practices. Not only was Granada a Manchester-based company, but the programme normally dealt in exposing shady deals and naming guilty men in high places. Suddenly, however, the spotlight had been switched from the usual arena of government and business to football. The following morning United's name, and in particular that of chairman Louis Edwards, was splashed across every front page, accused of crooked business activities.

The programme had alleged that Louis Edwards, who also ran a meat trading company, had not only won favours through some questionable transactions in the meat business but had also been involved in share dealing at United which had produced substantial profits for himself. The programme, which had taken almost a year to compile, also claimed that a special fund existed at Old Trafford to bribe the parents of schoolboy players.

The footballing authorities and the police began immediate investigations. Questions were tabled in the House of Commons and there was speculation that the club might even be thrown out of the league. But, before the claims could be fully examined by anyone, the 65-year-old Edwards suddenly died of a heart attack. His son, Martin, who assumed his mantle as chairman of the club, was in no doubt that Granada's allegations had killed his father. The death of Louis Edwards brought an immediate end to any further police inquiries and the story quietly disappeared from the newspapers. From time to time, however, various journalists have attempted to resurrect the claims, but none has ever succeeded in reawakening much interest.

Louis Edwards had been a director of the club since 1958, having been introduced to United circles by Matt Busby. By 1965 he was not only chairman but had also acquired the bulk of the shares. Louis Edwards' legacy can be seen everywhere at Old Trafford: the stadium improvements, the development association, the executive boxes all carry the stamp of Edwards, who as chairman authorised these many initiatives.

Accused chairman says: My conscience is clear

SOCCER BOSS IN PROBE

Daily Express, 29 January 1980

Louis Edwards on a happier occasion. But he would soon be refuting allegations made against him by a television programme.

CITY MPs CALL FOR PROBE INTO UNITED

Manchester Evening News, 29 January 1980

1980

ON SATURDAY, 5 APRIL 1980, 57,000 streamed out of Old Trafford convinced that United were at last on the verge of their first league title in 13 years. United had just beaten league leaders Liverpool 2–1 and, with six fixtures remaining, were now snapping at the heels of Bob Paisley's team. What the fans had just witnessed was a colossal struggle between the two best sides in the country and, although Liverpool had the chances to win the game, luck suddenly seemed to be turning United's way.

United had tracked Liverpool throughout the season. In January they lay just two points adrift and had even pulled level in February. But as spring broke the gap widened until 5 April, when United resuscitated their title dreams and began a last-effort push for the championship. It was Jimmy Greenhoff, playing his first game of the season after a pelvic injury, who resurrected United's title chances as he headed them into a 2–1 lead. Dalglish had put Liverpool ahead early in the first half but Mickey Thomas had snatched an equaliser before Greenhoff delivered his knockout blow.

The following Saturday, with Liverpool Cup-bound, United closed the gap even further; and then on 19 April, as the Merseysiders dropped a point at Anfield, a United victory over Norwich brought the clubs neck and neck, though United had played one game more. In the end that one game and Liverpool's unassailable goal difference were crucial. United now had only three games remaining but could manage just two victories, going down 2–0 in their final fixture at Leeds. In the event it did not matter as Liverpool had already wrapped up the title by then. A United victory over Leeds, however, would at least have left them level, with the title still going Liverpool's way on goal difference.

Nevertheless Dave Sexton had come within a whisker of the championship and closer than anyone since Busby. It augured well for the future although, as their goal tally clearly demonstrated, United still lacked an outstanding individual goalscorer. Joe Jordan topped the list with 13 league goals followed by Lou Macari with nine. Not since George Best in 1967 had anyone scored more than 20 league goals in a season and indeed it would be another eight years before anyone equalled his achievement.

Sinking a titanic team

Observer, 6 April 1980

Jimmy Greenhoff celebrates the winner against Liverpool.

After two-hour United board meeting..

SEXTON SACKED

MANCHESTER United last night sacked manager Dave Sexton and his assistant Tommy Cavanagh.

By BOB RUSSELL

After a two-hour meeting of the six-man United board of directors Sexton emerged tight-lipped and drove off in his club car; refusing to make even one word of comment.

Daily Mirror, 1 May 1981

1981

AFTER WINNING seven games in a row to wind up the season in eighth place, 12 points adrift of champions Aston Villa, it came as something of a shock to read that manager Dave Sexton had suddenly been sacked. Prior to his end-of-season winning streak United had laboured, usually in mid-table, and rumour had been rife that his days were numbered. Still, everyone reckoned seven successive victories were more than enough to stave off dismissal. But on Thursday, 30 April, a short statement by the club announced that 'the team's performance had failed to live up to the high standards of football entertainment expected of Manchester United'. Along with Sexton, assistant Tommy Cavanagh was also shown the door, although both were compensated.

After four years at the helm Sexton had failed to win one trophy. Since his appointment following the sacking of Tommy Docherty during the 1977 close season, United had finished respectively tenth, ninth, second and eighth in the first division and had lost to Arsenal in the 1979 Cup final. That was the sum of their achievements and it was not good enough for United.

Sexton out. Following seven successive wins, with a goal tally of 10–2, Sexton was sacked by the United board for failing to live up to their high expectations.

Sexton had bought expensively, four times breaking the club's record transfer deal in bringing Joe Jordan, Gordon McQueen, Ray Wilkins and Gary Birtles to Old Trafford. While three of those highly-priced purchases had proved sound investments, the signing of Birtles was a disaster. A £1.25 million buy from Nottingham Forest, Birtles had scored only once in his first 28 games for United and this despite having netted 32 goals in 87 league games at Nottingham Forest. Eventually he made 63 appearances for United, scoring just 12 goals before United sold him back to Forest in September 1982 for the knockdown price of £300,000. Two years' service had cost United a little under £1 million, plus wages.

Although Birtles was still on United's books when Sexton was sacked there can be little doubt he was a key factor in Sexton's dismissal. Sexton had spent £3.5 million on new players but had recouped only £1.5 million on departures, giving a net loss of £2 million. Had Sexton's expenditure produced results, then he might have survived. But United's new commercial budgeting could not withstand both a deficit and a low league position. Perhaps Sexton was also too similar to Frank O'Farrell. Quiet, thoughtful and sometimes overly reserved, he had failed to develop a close rapport with the players even though he was recognised as an outstanding coach. However, it was not long before he was back in business, with Coventry City anxious to secure his services.

1981

WHEN DAVE SEXTON was dismissed United already had clear ideas as to who his successor should be. Two men topped their list and United were confident that one of them would be managing the club within a few weeks. Approaches were initially made to the Southampton manager, Lawrie McMenemy, who had built a highly successful side at The Dell with minimum resources. It was McMenemy who had masterminded United's downfall at Wembley when Southampton were still a second division side and, although they had won little else, Southampton had always been spoken of as a well managed club. McMenemy gave due consideration to United's offer, but at the end of the day declined.

Next on the list was the Ipswich manager, Bobby Robson, another man who had created success out of meagre resources by careful buying and nurturing of home-grown players. But again Robson refused as Ipswich clung desperately to their treasure. Ron Saunders, manager of league champions Aston Villa, was next in line, but with the challenge of the European Cup at Villa Park, he too rejected United's tempting offer. There was gloom at Old Trafford. Nobody, it seemed, wanted to take on the awesome and precarious responsibility of running Britain's largest and most demanding club. Everyone was mindful that four managers had been sacked in the wake of Matt Busby's success. But there was one man who would leap at the opportunity. He was the West Bromwich Albion manager, Ron Atkinson.

Atkinson in many ways resembled a previous incumbent, Tommy Docherty. Loud, brash and decisive, he was a players' man, preferring free-flowing football rather than the over-instructed, dossier coaching approach of others. He had wide experience of league football, having skippered Oxford United from the obscurity of the Southern League to the second division and had then managed Kettering Town and Cambridge United. He had taken the latter from the lower reaches of the fourth division to the top of the third before being tempted by West Brom. At The Hawthorns he had nurtured a side that had finished fourth in the table and without any of the massive spending that later became his hallmark.

The 42-year-old Atkinson was formally appointed as United's new manager at the beginning of June. West Brom tried unsuccessfully to hold on to their man but the glamour of managing United was far too attractive an offer for Atkinson to refuse. After what had been a dour spell under Sexton, the new manager aimed to bring some of the excitement back to Old Trafford. He spent heavily and, although it paid dividends with three Wembley finals and a return to European football, the coveted league championship continued to elude United.

Ron Atkinson for United

RON ATKINSON is the new manager of Manchester United! All that remains is the official announcement that will come in the next fortnight, writes JOE MELLING.

United will go through the formality of an official approach to West Bromwich although the Midlands club have already made it plain they would vigorously resist the move.

But, I believe, that if it comes to an impasse Atkinson would resign from The Hawthorns rather than give up the challenge of restoring United's entertainment image.

United chairman Martin Edwards will have succeeded at the fourth time of asking since his controversial sacking of Dave Sexton. Lawrie McMenemy, Bobby Robson, and Ron Saunders have all turned down the Old Trafford hot seat.

One factor holding up endorsement of the deal is the absence of West Bromwich chairman Bert Millichip, who is with the England party and not due to return until after Saturday's World Cup game in Hungary.

Atkinson, ironicallv has been offered a new four-vear contract at West Bromwich to run from the start of next season. I understand he has not signed the agreement.

Daily Express, 1 June 1981

The flamboyant, bejewelled Ron Atkinson ponders how he can bring the league title to Old Trafford. But, like others before him, it was to elude his grasp.

1981

A QUICK LOOK at his playing staff convinced new manager Ron Atkinson that United were not going to win any championships with the squad at his disposal. New players were needed including a defender, a goalscorer and couple of midfielders. The first to sign was John Gidman, the former Aston Villa and Everton full back, who joined the club in a deal that took Mickey Thomas to Goodison. Welsh international Thomas had been at Old Trafford since November 1978 when United paid Wrexham £300,000 for his services. After 110 games and 15 goals, however, Atkinson decided he was no longer needed and the tenacious little winger who had appeared in the Wembley final against Arsenal was on his way. Gidman was a strong, attacking full back whose Old Trafford career was plagued by injury, although he returned to help United destroy Everton's dream of three trophies as they captured the FA Cup in 1985.

Atkinson's other priority was to find a goalscorer. Joe Jordan was itching to leave and join the exodus of British stars to the Continent. Even before arriving at Old Trafford he had intimated his desire to play on the Continent and in the summer of 1981 AC Milan stepped in with a £175,000 bid. Jordan had made 125 appearances for the club, scoring a creditable 41 goals, and his aggressive, forceful play was well suited to Italian soccer. In his place Atkinson looked to Frank Stapleton, the strong, powerful Arsenal striker who had been on United's books as a teenager but who left to join the Gunners as a 17-year-old. Now, the man they once had for nothing was costing them £1 million. At Highbury, Stapleton had netted just over 100 goals in 300 appearances, including one that helped defeat United in the 1979 FA Cup final. Born in Dublin, Stapleton was an experienced Irish international who eventually won more than 60 international caps. He left United in the summer of 1987 to join the Dutch champions Ajax.

Frank Stapleton scored 60 goals in 223 league appearances for United and set up many more for his team-mates. He was one of the most complete strikers in the first division.

Stapleton set to join United–for £1.1m

The Times, 21 August 1981

1981

AFTER SIGNING Everton's John Gidman and Arsenal's Frank Stapleton, Atkinson plunged into the transfer market to find a couple of midfielders. He began by returning to his former club West Bromwich Albion where he spent around £600,000 on Manchester-born Remi Moses. The 20-year-old Moses was a lifelong United supporter who jumped at the idea of returning home. In his three seasons at The Hawthorns, Atkinson had developed the Moss Side boy into a tough, ball-winning midfielder. To complement Moses' aggression, however, Atkinson now needed someone with creative ability in the middle of the field. But who to sign? Glenn Hoddle, Mark Lawrenson and Trevor Francis had all been the subject of unsuccessful inquiries. The answer was staring him in the face – his former number seven at The Hawthorns, Bryan Robson. West Brom, however, were reluctant to part with him, although they always knew that they were fighting a losing battle. Moses was allowed to make the move to Old Trafford while the haggling over Robson's price began. In the end West Brom settled for £1.5 million and duly received a fat cheque of just over £2 million for

Remi Moses about to come on for his debut against Swansea City.

United agree to pay a record fee of £2m for Robson and Moses

Bryan Robson became Britain's most expensive footballer last night—with a glowing tribute from his new manager and a stinging rebuke from his old one. The 24-year-old England midfield player is joining Manchester United for £1.5 million—£50,000 more than Wolverhampton Wanderers paid for Andy Gray, the previous record signing.

Robson will probably sign today, although the United manager, Ron Atkinson, is toying with the idea of signing him at Old Trafford on Saturday when United play Wolves.

Mr Atkinson said: "It's a hefty price, but one I consider to be realistic. Bryan is the best midfield player in the country. He can serve Manchester United for the next 10 years—six of them in midfield and four at the back. I have wanted him since I took over at Old Trafford".

Ronnie Allen, Mr Atkinson's successor at West Bromwich said: "Robson has been a pale shadow of his former self. He has been no use to anyone. Something had to be sorted out because we would not go on living with this problem. I am glad that it is all over. I want players who want to play for West Bromwich Albion"

Robson said: "It's a fantastic move for me and a relief. I am sure it will be of benefit toevery-one concerned."

His move comes a fortnight after Remi Moses joined United from West Bromwich.

Moses is valued at £500,000 in the package, which is topped by £400,000 vat and levies.

The two signings follow United's £900,000 purchase of Frank Stapleton from Arsenal and means that Mr Atkinson must sell to recover some of the outlay. He said: "It is inevitable that when new players come into a club others will leave."

Robson is expected to make his first appearance in next Wednesday's League Cup tie at Tottenham. His first league match for United will be on Saturday week at Maine Road against Manchester City.

The Albion board met yesterday morning after the Uefa Cup dismissal by Zurich Grasshoppers and decided that Robson could leave. Mr Allen said: "This has been very unsettling all round but at least now we can concentrate on playing football". And of the fee for Moses, he said: "When you consider that it was to have gone to a tribunal—with a figure of £300,000 being quoted—we feel we have done well to get that extra £200,000".

Robson's arrival puts a question against the Old Trafford future of another England midfield man, Ray Wilkins.

The Times, 2 October 1981

the pair. It was the biggest transfer deal in British soccer history, though it also raised the likelihood that Atkinson would be forced to sell in order to finance his dealings.

Robson had joined West Brom as a raw 15-year-old directly from school in the north-east, making his debut three years later in April 1975. During the 1976/77 season he broke his leg three times, but whereas others might have opted for a less precarious occupation, Robson returned on each occasion with even more determination. When he arrived at The Hawthorns he had been a skinny scrag of a lad standing just 5 feet 2 inches and weighing little more than 7 stone. But what he lacked in physical power he more than made up for in persistence and single-mindedness. A diet of raw eggs and Guinness also helped! By the time he arrived at Old Trafford he had already been capped a dozen times by England. Before long he was leading both his country and his new club and by 1990 had won over 80 international caps.

Injuries continued to dog him but, as before, he would quickly return, shrugging off pain and plunging into the tackle with little thought for the consequences. Robson was without a doubt one of the club's best signings since the days of Busby when Denis Law arrived in 1962. A gifted, creative midfielder, he had all the aggression of a defender; fast and enthusiastic, he regularly notched up a dozen or so goals each season as he stole into the area. And, just as likely, he would be found on the goalline as United defended. In Bryan Robson United had found the perfect midfielder, even though they had been obliged to pay a price for his talents.

A young Bryan Robson shoots for goal soon after joining United in a record £1.5 million transfer.

1982

Robert Armstrong—Brighton 0, Manchester United 1

The young influence

Guardian, 26 April 1982

Sixteen-year-old Norman Whiteside comes on for his debut.

WITH 12 MINUTES remaining and the scores deadlocked at 0–0, Ron Atkinson gambled on throwing a 16-year-old apprentice into the fray. It was 24 April 1982 and United were away to Brighton. Mike Duxbury, who had failed to prise open the Albion defence, was pulled off and onto the field stepped a giant of a teenager – Norman Whiteside. If Duncan Edwards had been a powerhouse at 16, then here was another springing from the same youth-team breeding ground. Within minutes of Whiteside's appearance Ray Wilkins had won the game for United with his first goal in two years. Whiteside, although contributing little to the scoreline, clearly impressed the commentators who all fancied the look and strength of Atkinson's latest discovery. Playing alongside him was another teenager, Scott McGarvey who, unfortunately, would enjoy little of the success that came Whiteside's way.

Whiteside, on the other hand, went from strength to strength, initially as a striker and later in the midfield. At the end of the season and after just two first-team appearances he was a surprise choice for the Northern Ireland World Cup squad. He played in all five games in Spain as Northern Ireland bravely battled their way through to the quarter-finals. He was the youngest player ever to appear in the World Cup finals and his mature, spirited performances won him countless admirers. The following season he was a regular in the United team, becoming the youngest ever scorer in a Milk Cup final and then weeks later crowned that distinction by becoming the youngest player ever to score in an FA Cup final. It was his goal which won United the Cup.

It had been a glorious start to his career. Unfortunately it did not always follow the same pattern. Popular with the Stretford Enders, he was deeply disliked by fans elsewhere as he tore at opponents, sometimes fairly, sometimes a little too eagerly. He was also dogged by injury and, like George Best before him, found that fame and youth do not always mix easily. Alex Ferguson eventually placed him on the transfer list but there were few inquiries and he was left to fight for his place in an increasingly talented squad. Finally, he was transferred to Everton during the summer of 1989 for a fee of £600,000. He had played well over 200 games for United, scoring more than 60 goals, and had picked up 36 caps.

Whiteside shields the ball from the attentions of the Brighton players.

BUZBY BOY

Ron's £300,000 call to Beardsley

from STEVE DELANEY in Vancouver

RON ATKINSON last night landed 21-year-old striker Peter Beardsley on a 7,000-mile telephone link between Spain and Vancouver.

Daily Star, 21 August 1982

1982

At first, everything fitted fine for Beardsley at Old Trafford.

ALL CLUBS MAKE mistakes when they plunge into the transfer market. And it can be acutely embarrassing when expensive players fail to live up to their promise (as in the case of Garry Birtles) or when they leave only to realise their true potential elsewhere. Players fail for a variety of reasons such as competition for places, inability to strike up a rapport with the manager or simply because they develop at different stages of their careers. George Best and Denis Law were stars by the age of 17 whereas others like Sammy McIlroy seemed to improve with age.

During the 1970s a teenage Frank Stapleton had been on United's books, but had failed to impress manager Tommy Docherty and was released, only to return a few years later at a cost of £1 million. He had proved to be an expensive mistake. The 1980s, however, brought an even more embarrassing error after Ron Atkinson had signed the promising Peter Beardsley for £300,000.

The Newcastle-born Beardsley began his career with Carlisle United where he was closely scrutinised by the bigger clubs. But nobody was prepared to offer Carlisle's asking price and the gifted youngster was eventually sold to Vancouver Whitecaps for £250,000. He might almost have been forgotten had United not played a couple of games in Vancouver and found themselves on the wrong end of two Beardslcy goals in a 3–1 defeat. Atkinson was impressed and maintained contact with the Vancouver manager and former United player, Johnny Giles. In August 1983, with his search for an experienced attacker breaking down – both Kevin Keegan and Andy Gray had been lined up – Atkinson decided to opt instead for youth and potential. A quick phone call set up the deal and the 21-year-old Peter Beardsley joined United for £300,000, with a further £200,000 to be paid if, as Giles expected, he ever won an England cap.

As everyone knows Beardsley never made the grade at Old Trafford, appearing for just 45 minutes against Bournemouth in the Milk Cup before being replaced by Norman Whiteside. It was altogether an unhappy experience and Beardsley was allowed to slip away, initially returning to Vancouver Whitecaps for £250,000 before winding up at Newcastle where he matured into a world-class player. By the summer of 1987, with more than a dozen England caps to his credit, half the first division were battling for his signature. By now the asking price had risen to £2 million, several times what United had bought and sold him for, and it was United's biggest rivals Liverpool who snapped up the maturing England striker. Atkinson should have trusted to his initial instincts.

1983

UNITED'S RECORD in the League Cup had never been impressive. Since first entering the competition in 1960 they had never progressed to the final and for many years had even shunned the new trophy, although their reappearance in 1969 seemed to herald a gathering interest as they reached successive semi-finals. But it was not until 1983 that United finally clambered over the last hurdle to reach Wembley and by this time the League Cup had been renamed the Milk Cup.

They reached the final stage of the tournament with victories in the earlier rounds over Bournemouth and Bradford City before facing tougher opponents in the later stages. In the fourth round Southampton were beaten 2–0 at Old Trafford and then Nottingham Forest were hammered 4–0 before they faced Arsenal in the two-leg semi-final. United virtually booked their ticket to Wembley with a 4–2 win at Highbury as Coppell scored twice. And it was the former Tranmere player again who was on target at Old Trafford as United eased into the final with a 2–1 victory in the return leg. Having dispatched such tough competition United might have expected easier opponents at Wembley. Instead, they faced Liverpool, who after years of neglecting the competition themselves were now making a habit of winning it and were appearing in their fourth final in six years.

United were also making a habit of visiting Wembley – this was their fifth appearance in eight years; before the year was out they would be back three times. But it was a sadly depleted United team which marched out at Wembley behind manager Ron Atkinson. Bryan Robson sat gloomily on the touchline nursing torn ankle ligaments, while John Gidman and Martin Buchan were also spectators.

Yet, after just 12 minutes, United gave Liverpool the fright of their lives when the precocious Norman Whiteside, playing at Wembley for the first time, swept them into the lead and wrote himself into the history books as the youngest scorer in a League Cup final. Hardly had the cheers died away, though, before United suddenly had to reorganise as Kevin Moran joined the injured on the sidelines. Minutes later Gordon McQueen pulled a hamstring and, with Lou Macari already on for Moran, United had used their only substitute. McQueen was pushed up front and Frank Stapleton dropped back to strengthen the defence. It was an uncomfortable, makeshift arrangement and it was probably inevitable that Liverpool would equalise, although when they did United were just beginning to think they might hold out. But Alan Kennedy's 75th-minute swerving shot caught Gary Bailey unsighted and the United goalkeeper could only grope blindly as the ball spun into the net.

In extra time United caved in, as their crippled line-up wilted under the strain. Whelan, with a stinging curling shot, made it 2–1 and as the match petered out United's weary defence were lucky not to concede three or four goals. In the dying minutes, however, Liverpool's victory was soured when Bruce Grobbelaar raced 35 yards out of goal to upend the crippled McQueen as he broke behind the Liverpool defence. It was a needless and cruel challenge and the Liverpool goalkeeper could count himself lucky to remain on the pitch.

Bruce Grobbelaar fouls an already-injured Gordon McQueen just before the end of extra time.

Brave United gored in Paisley's corrida of power

Guardian, 28 March 1983

Mike Duxbury, a United stalwart throughout the 1980s, challenges Kenny Dalglish for the ball.

United had put up an heroic struggle, grappling against the odds as their injured army limped through the battle. Arnold Muhren in midfield had regularly shown his elegant Dutch skills but they alone were not enough. Signed from Ipswich in the summer of 1982 Muhren, the first Dutchman to play for United, made 92 appearances before injury forced him out of the English league. United's fans, massed on the terraces, could be proud of their side and, although they did not know it, they would be back within two months with an outstanding triumph to celebrate and Muhren would again be there to play his part.

1983

TWO MONTHS AFTER losing to Liverpool in the Milk Cup final, United and their supporters were back at Wembley. This time it was the FA Cup final and United were determined they would not walk away empty handed.

Their opponents were bottom of the league Brighton who had just been relegated to the second division. On paper it looked an easy proposition but, although it eventually turned out that way, it took United two games to prove their superiority after they had almost lost the Cup in the dying seconds of their first drawn game.

United had reached Wembley the hard way with all but one of their games against first division clubs. They began at Old Trafford against West Ham, winning 2–0, and then travelled to Luton where they picked up a similar victory. In the fifth round they were again drawn away and, although Derby defended doggedly, Norman Whiteside's goal was enough to give them a home tie against Everton. As ever the Merseysiders proved stubborn opponents, with Frank Stapleton's last-minute goal the only difference between the two famous Cup fighters in a sizzling quarter-final. As if they had not had a difficult enough route to the last four, United then drew the toughest opponents, Arsenal, leaving Sheffield Wednesday and Brighton to battle out the other tie.

Top: Bryan Robson scores his second goal in the replayed final.

Bottom: Dutch master Arnold Muhren completes the rout from the penalty spot.

UNITED BY A LANDSLIDE!

Daily Star, 27 May 1983

United had already beaten Arsenal in the Milk Cup semi-finals that season, but there was always the sure knowledge that Arsenal would be looking for revenge. And when Tony Woodcock shot them into a first-half lead, it seemed the Gunners might be Wembley-bound. But in the second half Ashley Grimes combined with Bryan Robson to set up United's equaliser and then Whiteside volleyed home the winner.

Daily Mail, 27 May 1983

Brighton ......(0) 0 Manchester Utd ......(3) 4

ATT: 92,000. RECEIPTS: £640,000

REFEREE: MR ALF GREY

Robson 25 and 43 mins
Whiteside 29 Muhren (pen) 62

Happy birthday

United's heroes give Sir Matt the perfect present

MANCHESTER United celebrated the 74th birthday of the man who made them famous with a Wembley victory of historic magnitude.

Not for 80 years, and never in this noble stadium, has the FA Cup been won by four clear, crushing unanswerable goals.

Sir Matt Busby, father of the greatest United team of all, sat among their directors content that Ron Atkinson has begun the creation of a side to compare with his tragic Babes.

Overwhelming

United's red army of supporters turned briefly away from the slaughter of Brighton's Seagulls to sing 'Happy birthday, Sir Matt'. No football man could have wished for a better present. The new United delivered the Cup in the overwhelming style we had expected of them on Saturday.

It was as if Busby's club had waited the five intervening days for the perfect occasion on which to ratify the expanding quality of Atkinson's team.

The extra-time dramatics of the first drawn game gave way to the emotional jubilation of a replay which restored form and order to the 1983 final.

Right: The players celebrate after winning the FA Cup by the biggest margin at Wembley.

It was a strange twist of fate that Brighton's dismal league season should end at Wembley. Relegated or not, they were out to make the most of it, arriving at Wembley by helicopter, and then took a first-half lead, even though their skipper Steve Foster was absent through suspension. United had similar problems with Remi Moses also suspended while an injured Steve Coppell watched from the touchline. Coppell's number 11 shirt had been handed to Alan Davies, a young Manchester lad with only two appearances behind him.

A goal down at half time United hardly needed reminding during the interval that underdogs Southampton had denied them in 1976. Whatever else Ron Atkinson said in the dressing room, they reappeared in a more determined mood and within 10 minutes Frank Stapleton had pulled them level. United were now in command and in the 74th minute Ray Wilkins struck one of his rare goals that fully deserved to win the Cup itself. With just minutes remaining it seemed as if Wilkins' goal would be sufficient when from a corner Brighton undeservedly equalised. United could have kicked themselves as they lined up for another 30 minutes. However, extra time produced no further goals although in the last minute Brighton's Gordon Smith, racing alone in the six-yard box with only Gary Bailey to beat, fluffed his moment of glory. United heaved a sigh of relief and prepared for the replay.

Thursday, 26 May was Matt Busby's 74th birthday and what better way to celebrate than to present him with the FA Cup. Steve Foster was now back in the Brighton line-up but, surprisingly, his presence failed to provide Brighton with that extra fillip. Instead, United, as originally anticipated, strolled to a comfortable victory. Halfway through the first half two goals in a four-minute spell from Bryan Robson and Norman Whiteside set United's victory in motion. Whiteside had now chalked up another record by becoming the youngest-ever scorer in an FA Cup final. On the stroke of half time Robson added a third and there was little doubt where the Cup was destined. In the second half Gary Stevens wrestled Bryan Robson to the floor in the penalty area but, instead of stepping up to take the spot kick himself, the skipper magnanimously handed the ball to Dutchman Arnold Muhren. United had won by four goals to nil, the biggest-ever winning margin in a Wembley Cup final and the highest victory for 80 years. That night Matt Busby celebrated his birthday in fitting style as United gained their first trophy in six years.

1984

Robert Maxwell's disappointment over United was in some way compensated when his club Oxford United won the Milk Cup in 1986.

THE FINANCIAL AFFAIRS of Manchester United had already been strewn across the front pages once before, in 1980, when Louis Edwards had been accused by a television programme of shady dealings. Now, four years later, United's finances hit the headlines again, this time because newspaper proprietor Robert Maxwell wanted to buy the club.

Maxwell, the millionaire publisher-owner of Pergamon Press and Mirror Group Newspapers, had made a shock £10 million bid to buy out Martin Edwards and his family. Maxwell already owned one football club – third division Oxford United, which he had acquired for just £130,000 – but he now had ambitions to run Britain's biggest club. The Edwards family held 70 per cent of the club's shares, with Martin holding just over 50 per cent and his brother Roger holding a further 20 per cent. It was a tempting offer, although many fans could hardly believe that anyone, no matter what the offer, would ever consider selling a club like Manchester United.

Edwards was clearly interested and secret discussions between the two men were arranged. It was later alleged that no price was ever suggested by Maxwell, but the £10 million sale tag attached by the press was clearly not too far from the mark. As talks and speculation continued, so the pressure on Edwards not to sell became intense. A consortium of angry Manchester businessmen was even formed, promising to match any bid by Maxwell. Eventually, the whisper from Edwards was that £15 million, £15 a share, would secure United. But Maxwell was unwilling to pay that price and let it be known that his £10 million bid was on a take-it-or-leave-it basis. Edwards would not take it and on Valentine's Day the offer was withdrawn.

But United had come within a whisker of being sold and may today have been under the rule of one of the most influential businessmen in Britain. Maxwell, however, did not stop at United. Later that year his family was in charge at Derby County and then in 1987 he tried to buy Elton John's Watford, only to be thwarted when the Football Association stepped in and called a halt to anyone owning more than one football club. Edwards, however, had wavered and signalled that he might be open to the right offer in future.

Mirror Sport
Maxwell moves for the big one
£10 MILLION TO BUY UNITED

Mirror Sport on Friday

We said it first . . now Maxwell admits he wants to own United

Daily Mirror, 8 February 1984

1984

Robson had a triumphant game against Maradona and Schuster of Barcelona.

Night of glory for Robson

Maradona's men rocked by United

THOUSANDS of adoring fans last night carried Bryan Robson shoulder high from the scene of Manchester United's finest hour under Ron Atkinson's management.

Daily Mail, 22 March 1984

WHEN BARCELONA arrived at Old Trafford for the second leg of their Cup-Winners' Cup quarter-final with a two-goal lead, few gave United much chance of survival. Yet, that evening, United gave one of their finest displays in European soccer, which brought memories flooding back of their encounter with another Spanish team, Bilbao, in 1957.

United had lost the first tie 2–0 in front of 90,000 fanatical Spanish supporters in the daunting Nou Camp stadium, after Graeme Hogg had put into his own net and Rojo had scored a second almost on the stroke of full time. Yet a two-goal deficit did not deter United, nor the 58,000 who turned up at Old Trafford paying a record £200,000 in gate receipts.

With $10 million Argentinian Diego Maradona and West German international Schuster in their ranks, Barcelona were one of the most awesome sides in European football. Yet at Old Trafford they were humiliated as Bryan Robson proved himself the equal of any player in the world. It was Robson himself who began the rout as he seized on a Whiteside flick from a Wilkins corner halfway through the first half to give United the lead. With the second half minutes old it was Robson again who brought the aggregate scores level as he tapped in a stinging Wilkins shot that was only half saved. A minute later Albiston streaked down the left wing and crossed to Whiteside who headed down for Frank Stapleton to slam in. United now led 3–2 on aggregate and, although the Spaniards gathered their wits and bombarded the United goal for the final quarter of an hour, they could not find the key to unlock United's back four. Every man had played his part but as the final whistle blew it was Bryan Robson who was carried shoulder-high as hundreds invaded the pitch.

United's outstanding victory had Fleet Street purring with delight and there were visions of another European campaign to match those of the Busby Babes and the European Cup-winning side of 1968. Dukla Prague, Spartak Varna and now Barcelona had fallen prey to Robson and his men. Next in line was Europe's other glamour team – Juventus. Now it was Frenchman Platini, Pole Zbigniew Boniek and Italians Paolo Rossi, Dino Zoff and Gentile who drew the crowds. But this time there was no Bryan Robson, Arnold Muhren or Ray Wilkins, and United were sadly doomed from the start. Graeme Hogg again had the misfortune to put into his own net and although United equalised through Alan Davies they faced a mountain to climb in Turin. Although the previously suspended Wilkins returned for the second leg, Juventus swept into an early lead amid the firecrackers and smokebombs of the Stadio Communale. Norman Whiteside, coming on as substitute, struck an equaliser and it was not until the dying seconds that Paolo Rossi hit the goal that put Juventus into the final. It had been a brave fight by United and the British press reflected everyone's pride in them. Even without the backbone of their midfield they had continued to peg away and with a little more luck might have clung on for a draw and a replay.

The titanic victory over Barcelona was Ron Atkinson's proudest moment at Old Trafford, but with a ban on British clubs in Europe only a year away it was the last memorable European occasion for some years.

1984

THE SIGNING OF Gordon Strachan led to an unexpected international tug-of-war as United and FC Cologne almost came to blows over which club had secured his signature. The Aberdeen midfielder had looked set to move abroad until United came in with a late offer which the 27-year-old found too tempting. Cologne claimed that he had already signed for them and that they had a piece of paper to prove it. And so the wrangle went on. It more than suited Aberdeen, and their manager Alex Ferguson, as a transfer to a West German club would have meant a fixed ceiling price whereas United were offering substantially more. Atkinson had attempted to sign Strachan earlier in the season only to meet with a polite refusal, but once word of Strachan's interest in moving became public Atkinson made his bid

Fiery Scot Gordon Strachan battles with Liverpool's Sammy Lee and Ronnie Whelan during the first FA Cup semi-final between the two old rivals in 1985. He won a Scottish Cup medal and an FA Cup medal in successive seasons.

United wrap up Strachan

GORDON STRACHAN signed a post-dated four-year contract with Manchester United yesterday.

United manager Ron Atkinson gets the player he called 'a Steve Coppell with tricks,' having spent less than half the fee he is getting from Milan for Ray Wilkins.

Strachan will get £120,000 a year, while Aberdeen collect £600,000 instead of the £350,000 they would have got had their star player gone to West Germany.

An international tug-of-war for Strachan ended less than 24 hours earlier when Cologne vice-president Karl-Heinz Thielen was told his document bearing the player's signature was worthless.

'At no time did Aberdeen

By PETER JOHNSON

give Strachan permission to speak to Cologne and they did not consider the agreement valid,' said United chairman Martin Edwards.

Ambition

Aberdeen manager Alex Ferguson said : 'At the time, Gordon had fallen out with me and went ahead and signed the paper without seeking advice.'

Strachan, 27, said after yesterday's negotiations : 'It had been my ambition to play on the Continent for the last two years. I never even thought of coming to England, but United appeared at the last moment and you just don't turn down a chance like that.'

Strachan plays his last game in Scotland in the Scottish Cup Final against Celtic on Saturday week.

Meanwhile, Wilkins concluded eight hours of hard bargaining late last night to confirm his transfer to Milan for £1·4 million. He ended up with a contract worth a total of £700,000 over three years. He returns to Italy for a medical on June 25 and then a formal signing.

Luther Blissett welcomed Wilkins to Milan then said : 'I don't regret coming to Italy, but I've had enough of the place. I shan't join Manchester United, I just want to go back to Watford.'

Daily Mail, 10 May 1984

for the tenacious, flame-haired international. The deal eventually went through, with United paying Aberdeen £600,000 and Strachan £120,000 a year.

By coincidence, the deal was settled the same day as United lost Ray Wilkins to AC Milan in a move that temporarily swelled the United coffers by £1.4 million. Not only had United found a quick replacement but they had made a profit as well. Strachan had been an integral part of the Aberdeen machine that had broken the Glasgow monopoly. He had joined the Dons from Dundee in November 1977, winning his first Scottish cap in 1980 and arrived at Old Trafford with more than two dozen in his suitcase. His tireless talent soon flourished on his new stage and was only interrupted by the arrival of Alex Ferguson at Old Trafford. The two men were known not to be bosom pals and the new manager's arrival eventually initiated an inevitable move. It was Leeds United who were finally successful in persuading him to join their blossoming squad at Elland Road in March 1989. Strachan had played 160 league games for United, scoring 33 goals.

1985

UNITED FACED as difficult a task as any Cup finalists when they lined up against league champions and European Cup-Winners' Cup holders Everton at Wembley. The Merseysiders, having won their European trophy three days earlier, were now chasing a unique treble and only United stood in their way. Eight years previously Everton's neighbours, Liverpool, had also appeared in a Cup final against United in a similar situation. On that occasion United had ended Liverpool's dream of three trophies but could they also thwart Everton?

United's road to Wembley had begun exactly as it had 12 months previously – against Bournemouth, where they had suffered a humiliating early exit. This time at least they were drawn at home and, in front of 32,000, took suitable revenge with a 3–0 win. In the fourth round Coventry City were beaten 2–1 at Old Trafford, which was followed by a 2–0 win over Blackburn in the fifth round. West Ham were the victims in the quarter-finals, losing 4–2 at Old Trafford. United then faced Liverpool in a stirring semi-final at Goodison Park. A fortnight before the semi-final United had beaten the Merseysiders at Anfield, but blocking their path to Wembley proved considerably more difficult.

With United leading 1–0 and with only seconds remaining the Merseysiders levelled the score to force extra time. Then again, with United leading 2–1 thanks to Frank Stapleton, Liverpool again stole an equaliser on the stroke of full time. That meant a replay at Maine Road four days later. When Paul McGrath headed into his own net after 40 minutes, it looked as if the pendulum was swinging in Liverpool's favour. But United refused to lose heart and Bryan Robson burst through the Liverpool defence to slam home a much-deserved equaliser. Then with 12 minutes remaining, Mark Hughes brushed aside a phalanx of challenges to make it 2–1. This time Liverpool could find no way back and United were at Wembley.

Everton, with a handsome league triumph behind them and a majestic display that had won them the European Cup-Winners' Cup, began as favourites. At least United for once had a surplus of players to choose from. Alan Brazil, a £700,000 signing from Tottenham the previous season, was one of the unlucky men to be left out along with young Graeme Hogg. United had come a long way since their first Cup final appearance in 1909 and were now taking the

Referee Peter Willis points to the touchline as the United players protest. But Kevin Moran had to go and the Reds were down to 10 men.

Sunday Times, 14 May 1985

United's ten

Above: The United bench jumps for joy at Whiteside's winner.

Below: Tough Irish defender Kevin Moran shields the ball from Paul Bracewell.

field for their 10th final with five victories to their credit. Only two other clubs had ever appeared on more occasions and nine of United's appearances had come since the second world war, making them one of post-war football's most successful Cup sides. But Everton began determined to add a third trophy to their season's collection.

A tough, stylish outfit, managed by Howard Kendall, Everton set about their task brusquely and probably shaded the first half on points. And the second half might well have gone their way too, had Kevin Moran not upended Peter Reid with a clumsy but unintentional foul. The lightweight Reid spun through the air and by the time he had landed referee Peter Willis had decided that it was a sending-off offence. Moran was staggered and, although the Everton players appealed for leniency, Willis was resolute: Moran had to go. He was the first player to be sent off in a Cup final. Moran, a Sexton purchase in early 1978, had quickly established himself in the first team. A tough, resilient defender, he was prone to head injuries and it became a common sight to see Moran chasing around the field with blood gushing from his forehead.

With United now down to 10 men the odds had swung dramatically in Everton's favour, but what nobody had anticipated is that 10 men often fight with the spirit of 11 or more. United were suddenly quicker to the ball, challenging and hustling in midfield, and by full time looked the smarter bet. Everton, after their week's exertions in Rotterdam, were looking jaded and weary as they turned around for extra time. But still no goals arrived. Then, just as it looked as if a replay was beckoning, Norman Whiteside burst down the right and, as he twisted towards the penalty area, struck a left-footed shot when he had been expected to cross the ball. His shot spun sharply beyond Neville Southall's stretching arms and into the bottom corner of the net. It was sufficient to win the Cup. Just as United had shattered Liverpool's dream of a treble in 1977, so they now broke the hearts of another Merseyside club.

lash Everton's dream

1985

United are on course to equal Tottenham's League record

By Stuart Jones
Football Correspondent

Manchester City	0
Manchester United	3

Pity the players of West Bromwich Albion, Southampton and Luton Town. They are the next three set of first division troops who will be sent in against Manchester United. They will be armed with careful plans, a spiri of determination, and even a drop or two of optimism. So, presumably, was the Light Brigade.

Between them West Bromwich, Southampton and Luton have so far collected 15 points, nine fewer than United, in three times as a many fixtures. The odds must be, therefore, that Ron Atinson's side will at least equal Tottenham Hotspur's 25-year-old league record of opening with 11 successive victories.

The Times,
16 September 1985

THE 1985/86 SEASON began in devastating style with 10 successive victories and a 15-game unbeaten run before United suffered their first defeat. It was the best sequence in the club's history, but sadly fell just short of Tottenham's record 11 wins from the start of a season. The press drooled over their performances ('a frightening exhibition' waxed one reporter) and the crowds flocked to watch. By early November United were 10 points clear at the top of the table, with 41 points from 15 games, and looked to be well on the way to their first championship since 1967. But, just as suddenly, it all fell apart. By the end of the year they had suffered four defeats and Liverpool, who knocked them out of the Milk Cup in late November, were snapping at their heels.

Injuries began to take their toll. John Gidman had broken a leg, Gordon Strachan had dislocated a shoulder and the lively young Danish winger Jesper Olsen was also on the injured bench and then Bryan Robson joined them with a pulled hamstring. The slide continued; West Ham put them out of the FA Cup in the fifth round at Old Trafford, Bryan Robson was sent off and Stretford End favourite Mark Hughes was being lined up for a transfer to Barcelona. The season could not come to its conclusion quick enough and, by the time it did, United had slipped to fourth place, well behind champions Liverpool. What had begun with so much promise ended merely in disappointment.

Bryan Robson is helped off having dislocated his shoulder in March 1986. The season which had started so well for United stuttered to a halt as injuries took their toll. With Robson out, the Reds won only four of their last 14 games and the title slipped away. It was the most frustrating campaign of recent years.

1986

IN HIS SHORT CAREER at Old Trafford Mark Hughes had caught the eye of a number of European clubs including Juventus, Inter-Milan and Barcelona, who were all said to be preparing bids for the young striker. United seemed resigned to losing him and banking the large fee rather than making efforts to persuade him to remain. Eventually it was Barcelona, managed by Englishman Terry Venables, who tempted United to part with their Welshman, but his transfer led to considerable resentment among United fans who had taken 'Sparky' to their hearts.

In three seasons Hughes had made only 110 appearances but his 47 goals had caught the eye of European commentators. He had made his debut as a teenager in October 1983 but had to wait until the following season before he firmly established himself in the first team. In that second season he scored 24 goals in league and cup matches as well as collecting an FA Cup-winners' medal and a handful of international caps. The following year proved leaner as he lost form, no doubt plagued by transfer talk, as well as finding himself more closely marked, and he managed just 18 goals in 45 appearances. United's stirring start to the season slowly evaporated as transfer speculation increased and although it cannot wholly be blamed for their transformation, it certainly did not help their title prospects.

PARTING SHOT

Daily Mirror, 20 March 1986

Hughes tangles with Ruud Gullit soon after joining Barcelona.

There was always a feeling that Hughes was half-hearted about leaving Manchester and would have stayed had Ron Atkinson and the club made sterner efforts to persuade him that Old Trafford was his natural home. Whatever the discussions between Hughes and United, he finally signed for Barcelona in May 1986 for £2 million. Yet, no sooner had he put pen to paper than there was talk of Venables quitting the Spanish giants. In the event that did not happen for a further year and, when it did, it had far-reaching repercussions for the former United player. At Nou Camp, the Welsh international linked up with the England striker Gary Lineker and, although the partnership promised much, the goals never materialised. Within three years Venables, Lineker and Hughes all left Barcelona and returned to England.

1986

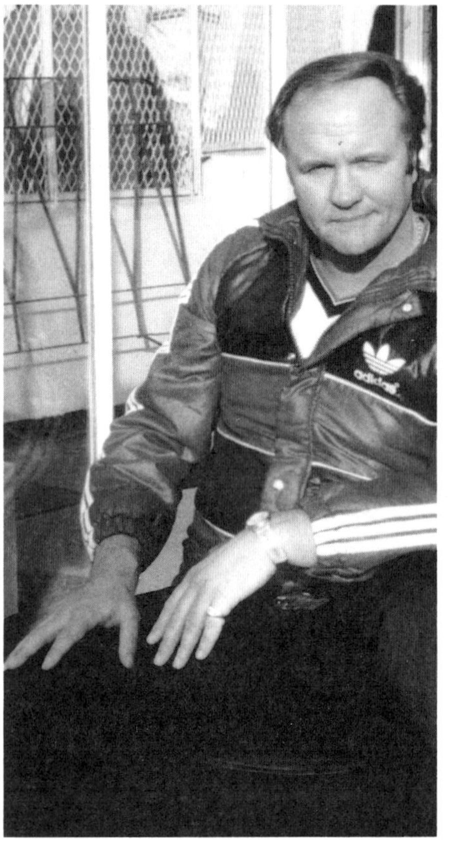

The pressure shows on Ron Atkinson's face as United's form slumped. Cup-winners and title challengers in 1985, in 1986 it all went wrong.

United plump for Ferguson as Atkinson's reign ends

Stephen Bierley reports on the latest change of manager at Old Trafford

MARTIN EDWARDS, Manchester United's chief executive, travelled north yesterday and persuaded Alex Ferguson of Aberdeen to become the next manager at Old Trafford. Archie Knox, Ferguson's co-manager at Aberdeen, will join him, but not until Aberdeen have appointed a replacement manager. It was a busy day for Edwards, who had earlier sacked Ron Atkinson after an emergency board meeting.

Ferguson has been top of United's unofficial future managers' list for some time. He has had remarkable success at Pittodrie, and impressed Edwards during the dealings which saw Gordon Strachan leave Aberdeen for United in 1984

Sitting in his hotel room in Santa Fe, New Mexico, this summer during Scotland's build-up for the World Cup in Mexico, Ferguson stressed he felt he was too young at 44 to become the permanent manager of the national team: "I would like one really big job first, either in England or on the Continent."

Ferguson was well aware that Atkinson was under contract at Old Trafford, but his obvious ambition was to manage United. By the time the World Cup was over it was an open secret.

Atkinson's death knell sounded at The Dell on Tuesday evening after a 4-1 defeat' but it had been a long time ringing. With United, the best supported club in the land, unable to break free from the bottom of the First Division, the fans began to vote with their feet. Atkinson's time was short and yesterday, on a bright, autumnal morning, he was swept away with the falling leaves.

He arrived at the club's training ground denying his job was in danger, but a little later called together his players to tell them he was leaving. The first edition of the Manchester Evening News carried his rallying call on the back page — "We can bounce back" — while the stop press beneath read "Atkinson sacked." It was the headline all Manchester had been expecting.

The crowd against Coventry last Saturday was down to 36,000, while more than 10,000 fewer had watched United draw with Southampton in the Littlewood's Cup a few days before. This drop in support, more than any other factor, hastened Atkinson's departure. The club's overheads are huge, and the directors' dividends were in danger.

The irony of Atkinson's sacking is that the seeds of his downfall were sown at the time of his greatest success. He took over from Dave Sexton in June 1981 via Whitney Town, Kettering, Cambridge United and West Bromwich Albion. At West Brom he constructed an entertaining, attacking team and it was this commitment to attack that caught Edward's eye, even if Atkinson was fourth choice.

United won the FA Cup in 1983 and 1985, and then the following season won 13 and drew two of their first 15 League matches, playing a blend of glorious football that had Old Trafford positively purring.

It seemed the Championship, last won in 1967, was about to be snatched from the Liverpool mafia. But the purring was abruptly halted as the cat leapt smartly out of the bag. Bryan Robson was injured. Hamstrings twanged a mournful tune — each week, it seemed, another player limped off clutching his leg — and United were spavined.

The ground began to shift beneath Atkinson's feet and United supporters, understandably frustrated, were further angered when Mark Hughes was transferred to Barcelona.

This season began with Edwards stating there was no money available for transfers. The dreaded vote of confidence followed and it became clear that if the return of Robson did not change matters the inevitable would happen. Yesterday it did.

Victories over Southampton and Sheffield Wednesday in the League gave brief but false hope, while events off the field were turning the club's social litmus paper redder than red: players fined for a drinking session in Amsterdam; Olsen and Moses involved in a training ground punch-up. Atkinson denied the latter, digging himself deeper and deeper into the ground as the facts leaked out.

Atkinson might take some comfort from the fact, Sir Matt Busby excepted, that he has outlasted all other post-war managers.

Since he took charge, United have finished third twice and fourth on three occasions. So near. Coupled with his Cup success, Atkinson could hardly be branded a failure, yet he has never been wholly liked in Manchester. Perhaps his Liverpool background was never quite forgiven, even if he was brought up in the West Midlands.

But whatever his public image, in private Atkinson was deeply ambitious and fiercely committed to United. For a few glorious weeks — from October 17 to the first week of November of last year — he luxuriated amidst the burning glow of success at the top of the First Division. Manchester United stretched themselves to the limit but the championship race, as Liverpool repeat ad nauseum, is a marathon, not a sprint. The Reds pulled up lame, and Atkinson was left clutching the bandages. He will, you suspect, not be out of work for long.

ALEX FERGUSON (left) is one of the select band of British managers to have taken his club to a major European honour. As well as that European Cup winners' Cup success, Aberdeen have won three League championships, four Scottish Cups and one League Cup since he took over in 1978.

He became assistant to Jock Stein as Scotland's team manager and took over control on Stein's death.

In 1983, he was on the verge of taking over at Rangers, but eventually turned it down.

Both as a player and a manager, there has been an abrasive side to Ferguson. He was an aggressive centre-forward with St Mirren and Rangers, and his first managerial appointment (apart from a very short stay at East Stirling), again with St Mirren, ended at an acrimonious industrial tribunal.

Ferguson had long resisted signing a contract with Aberdeen, but finally did so at the start of this season.

Ferguson was on a basic salary of £50,000 at Pittodrie. Two years ago, with bonuses, he received £120,000,

Guardian, 7 November 1986

THE GLITTERING OPENING to the 1985/86 season had ended in eventual humiliation for United and, as the 1986/87 season opened, Atkinson must have known that this was his final chance for glory. He had already survived Old Trafford longer than any other post-Busby manager yet had still failed to bring the league championship home. But the new campaign could hardly have kicked off to a worse start as United lost their opening three fixtures. After nine matches they had only one victory and four draws to their name. By the beginning of November they were fourth from bottom with only 13 points from 13 games, whereas a year previously they had topped the league with 41 points from 15 matches and stood 10 points clear of the field. As far as the pundits were concerned, United's league challenge was already over.

On 4 November United travelled to Southampton to replay a third round Littlewoods Cup game. The first match had been a dour goalless draw at Old Trafford and much depended on the outcome of their replay. But, when United went down 4–1, it was clear that Atkinson's days were numbered. They were out of two competitions and the season was barely under way. All that remained was the FA Cup and, with United relying so heavily on ticket sales to finance their transfer deals, there was little hope of bumper receipts for the season. The knives were out, speculation was rife and two days later the inevitable happened.

In the end Atkinson failed because his brash, anarchic style hardly suited the boardroom clientele, while his penchant for gold bracelets, champagne and a suntan won him few admirers on the Stretford End. As with Tommy Docherty, you either loved him or hated him. As long as United were winning he would survive, but as soon as they started

losing he discovered he had few friends. He could, however, boast two FA Cup triumphs and an appearance in the Milk Cup final, while in the league United had finished third, third, fourth, fourth and fourth in his five seasons in charge. It was hardly a poor record, yet there remained a feeling that United had let slip a glorious opportunity the previous season when they were playing such stirring football.

Atkinson had also spent heavily – more than £8 million – bringing players such as Gidman, Stapleton, Moses, Robson, McGrath, Beardsley, Brazil, Olsen, Strachan, Turner, Barnes, Davenport and the two Gibsons to Old Trafford while recouping almost £6 million on sales, more than half of which was received for Wilkins and Hughes alone. It was perhaps the loss of those two which did more to damage his relationship with the fans than anything else. Neither should have been allowed to depart, especially Hughes who was developing into such an exciting prospect. Indiscipline was also rampant,

Alex Ferguson came to Old Trafford determined to bring order and success to the club.

with the club's name more than once splashed across the front pages. There were rumours of heavy drinking among the players, and the set-to between Moses and Olsen which Atkinson had dealt with disgracefully was yet another nail in the coffin.

At least on this occasion there was no painful delay before a new manager was announced. After sacking Atkinson in the morning, chairman Martin Edwards flew to Aberdeen by lunchtime to finalise the appointment of Alex Ferguson. There seems little doubt that some discussions had already taken place and by the late afternoon Edwards was able to announce that the Aberdeen manager was the new man in charge at Old Trafford. It was an intelligent appointment. The workaholic Ferguson had transformed Aberdeen into a major force in Scottish football, winning three league titles, four Scottish Cups and the European Cup-Winners' Cup. A strict disciplinarian, Ferguson was an articulate and thoughtful tactician who had built a powerful side at Pittodrie on scant resources. He had an outstanding CV; all he had to do now was transfer his Scottish success to England.

How the golden days gradually lost their shine

SOCCER COMMENT

David Lacey

MANCHESTER UNITED are playing at Oxford tomorrow, which is an ironic coincidence, because Ron Atkinson's fate was surely sealed at the Manor Ground, where he spent the bulk of his playing career, in January. Not by the result mark you — United won 3-1 — but by the realisation that afternoon that the club were about to begin the process of selling Mark Hughes to Barcelona after an offer they could not refuse.

Manchester United had led the First Division for six months but they lost their next fixture, at home to Nottingham Forest, 3-2 and after being beaten 2-1 at West Ham a fortnight later lost the leadership for good. In that game they also lost Bryan Robson.

The team, the manager, the captain and the striker who at one stage had seemed the man most likely to get crucial goals in the championship struggle were never the same again. Only a repetition of Manchester United's inspired run last autumn would have kept Atkinson in his job beyond Christmas. s things have turned out he has survived Bonfire Night by less than a day — appropriate timing for a manager known to some sections of the media as "Flash."

He has gone not just because of bad results and certainly not because United seriously fear relegation — although it did happen 12 years ago, and in their present injury-stricken state the team is no better now than it was then. No, Atkinson and United have parted company after five-and-a-bit years because the chairman, Martin Edwards, could see no hope of an improvement under his stewardship.

In fact, Edwards gave Atkinson what amounted to a public warning earlier this season. While gilding a radio interview with the usual words of support for a manager in trouble, he did point out that if Atkinson failed to get things right on the field then it was the chief executive's job to do that was necessary to improve the situation.

Manchester United have not won the League championship since 1967. So long as they were signing outstanding players and producing entertaining football, this did not matter too much; the biggest crowds in the League still flocked to Old Trafford from all over the country.

The selling of Hughes, who was never that keen to play in Spain, was no doubt conditioned by Old Trafford's keenness to maintain a healthy cash flow in the face of the English clubs' indefinite ban from the European competitions following the Brussels tragedy.

Nevertheless it meant that United could no longer be regarded as one of the leading plutocracies of world football.

Atkinson could not be blamed for this situation.

However, he proceeded to spend the Hughes money on players who, while they might be important cogs among big wheels, were never going to attract coachloads from Plymouth on their own account. Poor bargains, erratic team selection and an increasing tendency towards safe options have combined to unseat the Sun King from his throne.

Atkinson has also paid the price of loyalty to Mick Brown, his assistant at West Bromwich Albion, who continued to hold the post at Old Trafford when it was obvious that something other than the basic disciplines was needed to inspire the players.

United managers are in trouble once the team becomes ordinary. Dave Sexton's side had just won seven matches in a row when a posse of Press cars screeching into the Old Trafford forecourt in April 1981 told him that his time had run out. Sexton had built a consistent, competent Manchester United team, but the gates were falling.

In their choice of Alex Ferguson as Atkinson's successor United have remained true to the Old Trafford management pendulum which for more than 15 years has swung between roundhead and cavalier in a regular arc.

Frank O'Farrell gave way to Tommy Docherty, who gave way to love. Sexton, a quiet, unassuming figure, was succeeded by Atkinson, who liked wearing gold, led from the front, was always able to give the press a tasty headline and, in short, seemed just the man the club needed.

However, the Manchester supporters never took to him as they had taken to Docherty, discerning the difference between a likeable rogue and a pleasant but at times distant showman. The strange thing is that some time ago Atkinson, no fool and realising that the goid bracelets, cufflinks and whatever were in danger of bringing him derision, made a conscious effort to tone himself down.

He has not glittered for a long time now, and with the dulling of his image the light seemed to go out of his management. In his last few months at Old Trafford he has been the man he was as a player: a hard worker and even harder to stop once his mind was made up, but rarely showing the inspiration that makes the difference between effort and genius. It is to his credit that, given a very average playing background, he made it so far as a manager.

The most important player in his managerial career has been Bryan Robson, both at West Bromwich and Manchester United. Had Robson stayed fit so much might have been different. In the end i all comes down to players. Ask Bobby Robson.

Since Matt Busby retired in May, 1970 after 25 years in the job, the roll-call of United managers is: Wilfred McGuinness (sacked, December 1970); Sir Matt Busby (filling in until June 1971); Frank O'Farrell (sacked, December 1972); Tommy Docherty (sacked, July 1977); and Dave Sexton (sacked, April 1981). Ron Atkinson was appointed in June 1981, and in his five seasons United have finished third, third, fourth, fourth, and fourth again in the championship, and won the FA Cup in 1983 and 1985.

Atkinson's main dealings on the transfer market with United were as follows:

BOUGHT: Bryan Robson (from WBA) for £1.5 million; Frank Stapleton (Arsenal), £900,000; Jesper Olsen (Ajax), £800,000; Terry Gibson (Coventry), £600,000; Remi Moses (WBA), £600,000; Alan Brazil (Tottenham), £600,000; Peter Davenport (Nottm Forest), £570,000; Gordon Strachan (Aberdeen), £500,000; Colin Gibson (Aston Villa), £275,000; Chris Turner (Sunderland), £275,000; John Gidman (Everton), £250,000; John Sivebaek (Vejle), £250,000; Paul McGrath (St Patrick's), £100,000; Mark Higgins (Compensation), £60,000; Peter Barnes (Coventry), £50,000; Arthur Graham (Leeds), £45,000; Joe Hanrahan (University Coll, Dublin), £30,000. **TOTAL:** £7.4 million.

SOLD: Mark Hughes (to Barcelona) for £2 million; Ray Wilkins (AC Milan) £1.5 million; Garry Birtles (Nottm Forest) £350,000; Ashley Grimes (Coventry) £350,000; Sammy McIlroy (Stoke) £250,000; Alan Brazil (Coventry) £250,000; Mickey Thomas (Everton) £200,000; Scott McGarvey (Portsmouth) £100,000; Stephen Pears (Middlesbrough), £70,000; Alan Davies (Newcastle), £60,000. **TOTAL:** £5.3 million.

Guardian, 7 November 1986

1987

McClair is going to United

By DAVID WALKER

MANCHESTER UNITED have clinched the signing of Celtic striker Brian McClair.

McClair telephoned United manager Alex Ferguson from his Marbella holiday home to give him his decision.

But Ferguson is resigned to failing in his bid to bring the striking partnership of McClair and Barcelona's Mark Hughes to Old Trafford. The £2 million it would cost to clinch Hughes's return has killed the deal.

Daily Mail, 13 June 1987

IT WAS EIGHT MONTHS before Ferguson stepped into the transfer market. He sized up his squad and, after a season that had seen them finish in 11th place – their worst position since the relegation year 1974 – he decided that new troops were urgently called for. Top of the wanted list was a first-class striker and an experienced defender.

Peter Davenport, a Ron Atkinson purchase, had never really settled to reproduce his Nottingham Forest goalscoring form and, with Mark Hughes still in Spain, the battle-worn Frank Stapleton was at times fighting a lone campaign up front. Davenport, although initially given a vote of confidence by Ferguson, was eventually allowed to move to Middlesbrough in 1988. Ferguson's search for a target man took him back to Scotland, and in particular to Glasgow, where he signed the 23-year-old Celtic striker, Brian McClair. On the same day, Ferguson made it a double deal when he also secured the services of the England and Arsenal full back Viv Anderson. McClair, with 35 goals in his final season at Parkhead, was a bargain at £850,000 while the vastly experienced Anderson, with over two dozen England caps to his credit, cost a mere £250,000. It was a good day's shopping.

Brian McClair scored 24 goals in his first league season.

Viv Anderson, a great attacking full back, on the ball.

Above: The sparks fly as Mark Hughes volleys towards the Spurs goal. The spectacular striker was guaranteed an ecstatic welcome on his return to Old Trafford. Hughes and McClair scored over half United's goals in 1988/89.

1988

MARKED

● MANCHESTER UNITED have clinched Mark Hughes' £1.5 million return to Old Trafford.

● The move will be officially announced next week, even though Juventus have launched a late bid for the Barcelona striker.

Daily Mirror, 11 June 1988

SINCE LEAVING Old Trafford in the summer of 1986 for the Spanish giants Barcelona, Mark Hughes had had an unhappy time. Signed by the Barcelona manager Terry Venables for £2 million, he partnered the England striker Gary Lineker but the alliance had never really flourished. The young Welshman had been homesick and had never settled in the city. The dismissal of Venables heralded the end of his Spanish sojourn, with new manager Johan Cruyff immediately loaning him to West German champions Bayern Munich. At least in Munich's Olympic stadium the busy Welsh attacker regained his confidence and once more began to reflect his £2 million price tag. Hughes was clearly surplus to Barcelona's requirements and, although Bayern coveted their new striker and were keen to engage him permanently, they could hardly compete with United either emotionally or financially. Hughes was longing to return to Old Trafford and similarly the Stretford End was ready to welcome him back with open arms. And so, in June 1988, the inevitable happened, with Hughes re-signing at £1.5 million for the club he loved, ending what he described as 'a three-year nightmare'.

Happy return

● MARK HUGHES yesterday completed his £1.8 million move from Barcelona back to Manchester United.

● The 24-year-old Welsh international striker signed a five-year contract at Old Trafford and said:

● "I have enjoyed my time abroad but I am delighted to be back.

● "It was only the thought of playing for Manchester United again that brought me back to England."

● Hughes is looking forward to linking up with Brian McClair in United's attack next season.

● "I have not seen very much of Brian but what I have seen has been very impressive," he added.

● Hughes left Old Trafford two years ago in a £1.8 million move to Spain.

● But he played much of last season on loan at Bayern Munich.

Daily Mirror, 25 June 1988

Determination on the face of Hughes, delighted to be back with United after two years at Barcelona.

1989

ALEX FERGUSON'S second full season in charge was a grave disappointment. Out of the FA Cup and the Littlewoods Cup at early stages, they eventually wound up in 11th place in the league after their promising challenge petered out. Gates had fallen by the end of the season and an ominous slow hand-clap could be heard around Old Trafford. It had been four years since United last brought any silverware home. The rush of youngsters into the side had helped revive exciting memories but in the end had proved ineffective. To win back the fans and give them something to cheer Ferguson decided on further rebuilding. Viv Anderson, Brian McClair, Steve Bruce, Jim Leighton, Mark Hughes and Mal Donaghy had already cost him a gigantic outlay of £4.6 million. Further purchases were necessary if United were to compete with the other big-money clubs such as Liverpool, Everton, Arsenal and Spurs. And, with Manchester City now back in the first division, it was doubly important that United should attract support.

Top of United's list was Neil Webb, the talented Nottingham Forest and England midfielder. Out of contract at Forest, Webb was a free agent and he took little persuading to join his England colleague Bryan Robson at Old Trafford. The fee, set by a tribunal, was £1.5 million. Webb was an exciting attacking midfielder who had averaged a goal in every three games with Forest, and whose speciality was to steal into the penalty area, rather like Bryan Robson, lending an extra dimension to the strike force. He had begun his career at

Lancashire lad Mike Phelan and England star Neil Webb are welcomed to Old Trafford by Alex Ferguson, giving a big boost to the midfield.

MANCHESTER UNITED manager Alex Ferguson put a smile back on the face of a depressed Old Trafford yesterday as he completed the signings of Nottingham Forest's Neil Webb and Norwich's Mike Phelan.

Fergie gets his men!

And it might have been a spectacular hat-trick. Only hours earlier, Ferguson flew back from Copenhagen after making an offer still being considered by giant Swedish defender Glenn Hysen.

The powerful 28-year-old Hysen, out of contract with Fiorentina, talked late into the night with Ferguson and chief executive Martin Edwards.

Hysen, who will be in England on Monday for talks with both United and Spurs, said: "I must see what kind of money Fiorentina are prepared to pay me.

"But the football and the astmosphere of the game in England is a big attraction for me."

Webb and Phelan's fees seem certain to be set by tribunal.

Daily Mirror, 16 June 1989

Reading before signing for Portsmouth in 1982. Three years later he joined Brian Clough for £250,000 and had collected 18 England caps before arriving at Old Trafford. Webb was the second of Ferguson's big summer buys, the first being Mike Phelan, the 26-year-old Norwich City captain who cost £750,000. A Lancashire lad, Phelan had joined Norwich from Burnley four seasons previously for £45,000 and, in joining United, rejected tempting offers from Everton, Spurs and Nottingham Forest.

The massive outlay inevitably meant the end of the line for a number of players. Norman Whiteside, for so long a favourite with the Stretford Enders, moved on to Everton in a £600,000 deal after a number of months on the transfer list and an unhappy season, while Paul McGrath was involved in a £400,000 transfer to Aston Villa. Both men had given long service to the club, though sometimes they had provided more aggression than elegance in midfield.

Robson and Webb had already built up a good rapport in the England midfield. Sadly, their first season together at United was plagued by injuries.

1989

AFTER ROBERT MAXWELL'S attempt in 1984 to buy United there were two opposing schools of thought about the future. One suggested that Martin Edwards, having been tempted by Maxwell's offer, had merely postponed what was now an inevitable decision to sell. The other school of thought reckoned Maxwell's failure to acquire the club had slammed the door on any future deal and that Edwards had realised just how dear the club was to his and the fans' hearts.

Throughout the summer of 1989 consistent rumours circulated in Manchester that Edwards was about to sell. Yet little attention was paid to them by the press, particularly as they were heavily denied and it was not the first time such rumours had floated to the surface. It therefore came as a complete surprise when, on the eve of a new football season, the story broke that United had been sensationally sold. At first, there was no clear indication who the buyer was, but most supposed it was United's Lebanese director Amer Al Midani, though David Murray, the owner of Glasgow Rangers, was another possibility. Within the day, however, it was revealed that the purchaser was the hitherto unknown Michael Knighton, a property developer based in the Isle of Man. Knighton, at one time on the books of Coventry City until a thigh injury ended his career, was said to have offered £20 a share. As chief shareholder with 50.5 per cent of United's total shares, Martin Edwards stood to gain £10 million from the shares which his father Louis had bought for £20,000.

Knighton duly breezed into Old Trafford as the new season kicked off with a home fixture against Arsenal and paraded before the Stretford End, showing one or two tricks of his own with the ball. The Stretford Enders loved it,

Why I sold my United — Edwards

By David Meek

MILLIONAIRE property tycoon Michael Knighton is the new owner of Manchester United.

United supremo Martin Edwards quit as chairman today in a sensational £30m sell-out — and told me he did it for the good of the club.

"I believe that what I'm doing can only be for the long-term benefit of Manchester United," he said.

The takeover will net the Edwards family a £10m fortune — and could turn at least three other directors into millionaires.

Mr Knighton, 37, today promised to invest a massive amount of money into the club.

He is offering £20m for the 1m shares in United — and has pledged up to £10m for immediate ground development, including a new cantilever stand at the Stretford End.

And he says cash is available for new players.

The new chief said: "There will be no massive changes. I am here to learn and the infrastructure will remain the same. I want time to come up for breath and take stock.

"Martin will stay as vice-chairman and as chief executive."

Mr Edwards, 44, said: "I very much welcome Michael Knighton's proposed involvement and look forward to working with him.

"I admire his vision and commitment. The additional financial resources he will bring with him mean that the plans to redevelop the Stretford End can at last be translated into reality."

Mr Knighton plans to bring in some of his own directors, and there could be a boardroom upheaval as the present directors decide whether to take the money and go.

There will be a particular problem for Amer Midani, the wealthy Lebanese director who has always nursed a dream of his own to buy the club one day.

David Murray, chairman of Glasgow Rangers and a neighbour of Knighton's in the Isle of Man, said today he was "in no way involved" in the offer for Manchester United.

Mr Knighton is believed to have raised his takeover cash by selling property holdings in Edinburgh.

He is an Isle of Man tax exile who made his money in Edinburgh and comes originally from Derbyshire.

He is a football fanatic but has no United links. But as a schoolboy player he once attracted the attention of Manchester City.

He later joined Coventry City but his career was cut short by injury.

The worry for fans is that he is also a property developer and Old Trafford lies on the edge of a £1,000m redevelopment in Trafford Park.

Supporters must also question the timing of the Edwards sell-out just a day before the new season.

But the club has been treading water lately, with the championship still looking as far away as ever.

Manchester Evening News, 18 August 1989

especially when United went on to beat the league champions 4–1. Within a couple of days, however, further questions were being asked about Mr Knighton. On Thursday, 24 August the *Manchester Evening News* exclusively revealed that Michael Knighton was not the only one involved in the deal and it was reported that a hotel would be built at the back of the Stretford End.

When Knighton's two backers and the Citicorp bank pulled out of the deal, the sale of United was suddenly in jeopardy and the fans were left wondering what was going on. United also seemed to be affected as they slumped to three defeats, culminating in a 5–1 hammering at Maine Road. In the meantime Knighton found other backers and shortly before his deadline was able to find sufficient cash to make the obligatory £20 per share offer to every shareholder. It meant a potential outlay of £20 million for the new owners of United, MK Trafford Holdings.

The press continued to voice its suspicions about Mr Knighton, with the *Daily Mirror*, whose publisher Robert Maxwell had himself once been on the verge of purchasing the club, leading the attack. But it was the *Manchester Evening News* which usually got it right and which should be applauded for its numerous exclusives. Nobody was quite sure where the money was coming from, with Knighton said to be hawking the deal around his City friends. There was even a legal battle when Martin Edwards took Knighton to court for a breach of confidentiality. It was all very messy.

Days before the deadline it was clear that Knighton was in difficulties and it came as no surprise that with hours to go he should pull out, 'in the interests of United', as he put it. He and his stockbrokers maintained that he had in fact secured a deal with a number of financial institutions, but for the sake of the club had instead decided to tear up his contract with Martin Edwards. The pay-off was a seat on the board of directors.

Not everyone was happy with the arrangement, but it has to be said that even fewer would have been happy had the deal gone through. There was criticism from the Bank of England Takeover Panel about the way the bid had been organised as well. When it was all concluded, Edwards was quoted as saying that he still wanted to sell United but would not discuss the subject 'until the end of the season'. Nevertheless it hardly stopped tongues wagging, nor the newspapers speculating. From time to time there were reports of secret negotiations or talks to finalise a deal. Even a pop star – Phil Collins – was said to be on the verge of buying the club but there was nothing official. United, and particularly Martin Edwards, had been greatly embarrassed by the whole affair which had seen United's name strewn across the front pages with the most speculative, and often inaccurate, headlines. Somewhere there was a lesson to be learned for the club.

Ferguson and Michael Knighton together – but it wasn't to be. The Knighton deal collapsed in acrimony.

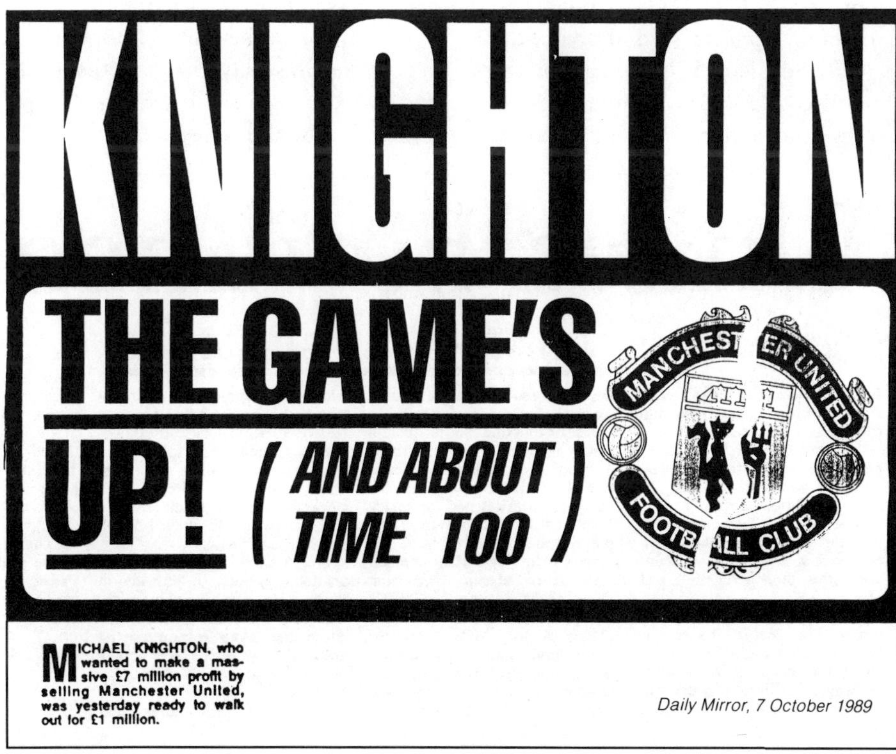

KNIGHTON

THE GAME'S UP! (AND ABOUT TIME TOO)

MICHAEL KNIGHTON, who wanted to make a massive £7 million profit by selling Manchester United, was yesterday ready to walk out for £1 million.

Daily Mirror, 7 October 1989

1989

Paul Ince finally got his wish to join United after much delay.

AFTER THE HEFTY summer signings of Michael Phelan and Neil Webb, United plunged into the transfer market yet again with a double deal that brought Middlesbrough's Gary Pallister and West Ham's Paul Ince to Old Trafford. Pallister was the first to sign, joining the club for a British record fee of £2.4 million, while Paul Ince arrived for a little over £1 million. West Ham's asking price for Ince had initially been £2 million, but the 21-year-old midfielder failed an Old Trafford medical and the deal was called off at the last moment. Two weeks later it was resurrected when an independent medical report said that his pelvic injury was not quite so serious as initially assumed. But it was enough for West Ham to drop the price and for manager Alex Ferguson to take the gamble.

The 24-year-old Pallister had come to prominence a couple of seasons previously, when Middlesbrough won promotion from the second division. His powerful displays in the back four had been the backbone of Middlesbrough's success and had resulted in a welter of inquiries from first division clubs, as well as a call from the England manager Bobby Robson. By the time he joined United he had collected a couple of England caps and was clearly being earmarked for a long international career.

Paul Ince, on the other hand, had not yet worked his way through the ranks and was still an England Under-21 international, though his displays in the West Ham midfield had shown sufficient maturity to make his graduation to the full England team more than likely. Ferguson had been forced into the market to seek a quick replacement for Neil Webb, who had been seriously injured while playing for England before the season had barely begun. He had made just a couple of appearances for United and would clearly be sidelined for most of the rest of the season, at best. Ince was the obvious replacement but a week later Ferguson swooped into the transfer

United buy Ince for £2m

JOE LOVEJOY on a record signing at Old Trafford

PAUL INCE, who has spent the summer agitating for a move from West Ham to Manchester United, finally got his way last night, when Alex Ferguson agreed to buy him for a club record fee of £2m.

The transfer will be a disappointment to Tottenham, who had also hoped to sign the 21-year-old midfield player.

Ince said that he would never play for West Ham again when they sacked John Lyall as manager after their relegation last May.

He relented when Lyall's successor, Lou Macari, called his bluff, but alienated management and supporters alike with a stunt in which he was pictured in United strip, and his departure became not so much a question of whether as when.

Macari dropped him for the 2-0 victory at home to Bradford City on Tuesday, explaining that speculation about his future had affected his form. Ince watched the match from the stand, but abuse from supporters caused him to leave the ground early. West Ham immediately signed Martin Allen from Queen's Park Rangers for £660,000 to replace him.

Ince, capped by England at Under-21 level, came to prominence last season, when he was the outstanding member of a side destined for the Second Division. His transfer was completed too late for him to be available for United's match at Derby this afternoon, leaving his new team's followers to wonder where he will be accommodated by a club already well stocked for midfield men after the £2.25m acquisition of Neil Webb and Michael Phelan.

Ince, who is expected to make his debut at home to Norwich on Wednesday, can also play in defence, but his arrival invites speculation that Bryan Robson may be given the sweeper's role many would like to see him filling for England.

United's record outlay had stood at £1.5m, a sum they had paid three times — for Robson, Webb and Mark Hughes. Further expensive forays into the transfer market can be expected, with Ferguson, who has spent £9m in his three years in charge at Old Trafford, eager to use the £10m pledged by Michael Knighton, the club's new owner, to assemble a team good enough to challenge for the championship.

The next arrival could be Gary Pallister, Middlesbrough's England centre-half, who is the subject of another £2m offer.

Independent, 26 August 1989

Danny Wallace, the exciting Southampton winger, was the last of Ferguson's five big summer signings.

market yet again. This time he spent £1.1 million on Danny Wallace, the 25-year-old Southampton midfielder who was bought to provide some width to the United attack.

The purchase of Ince, Pallister and Wallace brought Ferguson's spending at Old Trafford to an astonishing £12 million, although he had also recouped £4 million in the sale of players. Into the squad since his arrival had come Viv Anderson, Brian McClair, Steve Bruce, Lee Sharpe, Jim Leighton, Mark Hughes, Mal Donaghy, Michael Phelan, Neil Webb, Gary Pallister, Danny Wallace and Paul Ince. An entire team had been bought while almost an entire team, the legacy of Ron Atkinson's reign, had been sold. Peter Barnes, Mark Higgins, Terry Gibson, John Sivebaek, Graeme Hogg, Chris Turner, Peter Davenport, Jesper Olsen, Liam O'Brien, Paul McGrath and Norman Whiteside had all departed. It had been a massive clear-out. Ferguson now had his own players around him and there was no one else to blame if success did not come United's way.

Record signing Gary Pallister heads clear. After an uncertain start, he became United's most consistent player in 1989/90, fully justifying his £2.4 million transfer.

1990

UNITED'S SEASON began and ended on a high note; it was a pity about what happened in between. Their campaign kicked off to a glorious start with a sparkling display as United ran league champions Arsenal ragged. United won 4–1 and there were high hopes that the championship might at last be on its way to Old Trafford. But, after just a handful of games, Neil Webb was injured and United's season began to turn sour. At the final count they had escaped the drop by just five points.

It was their most miserable league season for years, which brought into question the future of manager Alex Ferguson. In the end, his position may well have been saved by a magnificent Cup run which began at Nottingham Forest. Few would have put money on United to overcome Forest, but that was precisely what they did thanks to substitute Mark Robins' goal. In the fourth round, they faced fourth division Hereford, who might have been giantkillers of the past but they were certainly not giant-killers of the present as Clayton Blackmore's goal settled the tie.

In the fifth round, United were drawn away again, this time to second division Newcastle. Although the Geordies put up a tough fight, United won the day with a 3–2 victory. In the quarter-final, they were drawn away yet again, though only a short hop across the Pennines to Sheffield United. The second division high-fliers gave United a fright, but

MY FINEST HOUR!

Fergie's gamble pays off

ALEX FERGUSON ended his personal season of torment with a pot of precious silver and then declared: "This is the greatest day of my life."

Daily Mirror, 18 May 1990

Lee Martin strikes home the winner. It was only his second goal for the club, but he will never score a more important one in his career.

Replay hero Les Sealey leaps bravely for the ball.

Brian McClair's first-half strike was enough to put United into the semi-finals, where they faced neighbours Oldham Athletic who had already reached one Wembley final. Oldham gave United as hard a battle as any side all season with the first game ending in an exciting 3–3 draw. Three days later, at Maine Road, Mark Robins was again the man to seal United's fate as he pounced in extra time to send the Reds into the final.

United's Wembley opponents, Crystal Palace, had finished the season with the same number of points as United and had even managed a 2–1 win at Old Trafford earlier in the season, as well as the scalp of Liverpool on their way to the final. It was always going to be a tight contest, although the bookies reckoned United to be the likely winners. Palace, however, managed by former Old Trafford favourite Steve Coppell, swept into an early lead and it took a thundering header from Bryan Robson to level the scores. At half time there was little to choose between the two sides. After an hour, however, the ball took a kindly deflection in the penalty area for United, landing at the feet of the unmarked Mark Hughes, who promptly thumped it into the back of the net. That goal brought a swift response from Steve Coppell, who sent on substitute Ian Wright. With almost his first touch, Wright scored a memorable individual goal which forced extra time. In the first period Ian Wright volleyed in beyond Jim Leighton from a superb cross to edge Palace ahead. With seven minutes remaining Palace still led and just as the terraces began to hail a London victory Mark Hughes appeared to save United's embarrassment.

Five days later, the two teams lined up at Wembley once more, but this time there was a significant difference. Scottish international goalkeeper Jim Leighton had been dropped and was replaced by Les Sealey who had made just two appearances for United during the season while on loan from Luton. It was a brave decision by Ferguson to drop a goalkeeper who had shared days with him at Aberdeen, Scotland and Old Trafford. But it paid off, with Sealey flinging himself expertly to save from a Palace free kick early in the first half and, despite some rough treatment from the Palace attack, he performed like a player who had manned the United goal all season.

If the first contest between these two evenly-matched sides had been as exciting a Wembley final as anyone could remember, then the second was a great disappointment, with Palace's spoiling tactics leaving their mark and stirring United into a spirited performance. United were always the better side and it was inevitable that they would score. Their goal, a well-hit drive by Lee Martin, arrived on the hour and was enough to give United the Cup – their seventh – equalling Aston Villa and Tottenham's record. It was also a personal triumph for captain Robson who became the first man to climb the Wembley steps three times to receive the battered old trophy. A season that at one time had seemed destined for disaster had finished in glory, giving rise to a resurgence of optimism for 1990/91.

Cup hero hands medal to axed Leighton

Daily Mirror, 18 May 1990

1991

ENGLISH CLUBS HAD been banned from European competition since the appalling disaster at the Heysel stadium in 1985. But in 1990, after a five year ban, English clubs were at least readmitted into Europe. And United, as holders of the FA Cup, qualified for the European Cup-Winners' Cup.

United had only ever won one European trophy and that was the greatest prize of all, the European Cup. However in the 1990/91 season they were to add a second European trophy to their collection and would prove that they had a fine team in the making.

They began their assault back in September 1990 with a home leg against the Hungarians Pecsi Munkas and in front of 26,411 enjoyed a comparatively easy 2–0 win. The second leg presented few problems either, with the only goal of the game coming from Brian McClair. In the next round, instead of a feared 1,000 mile trip to some outpost in Eastern Europe, United faced the prospect of a 30 mile trek down the motorway to Wrexham. Almost 30,000 turned up at Old Trafford for the first leg with United powering into a 3–0 lead to make the second leg a mere formality. United duly won 2–0 and were through to the last eight without having conceded a goal.

In the quarter-finals United faced the somewhat unglamorous French side Montpellier. United stormed into an early lead and looked set for a bumper evening but the French eventually put up some stubborn resistance and sneaked away from Old Trafford with a 1–1 draw. But in France it was a different tale with Montpellier forced to abandon their defensive tactics, leaving enough space for United to come away with a 2–0 win. United had the luck of the draw in the semi-finals, avoiding Juventus and Barcelona, and instead faced a tie against Legia

Joy for Steve Bruce (no 4) after putting United ahead, McClair, Blackmore and Sharpe move in to congratluate the goal-scorer.. The goal was later credited to Mark Hughes, who had helped the ball into the net.

Warsaw. What's more the first game was in Poland where United won by a comfortable three goals to one. The second leg, without any pressures, hardly brought the best out of United as they sauntered to a 1–1 draw in front of 44,000. United were into only their second-ever European final.

After such an easy trip to the final it was sobering to discover that their opponents in Rotterdam would be one of the biggest clubs in European football, Barcelona. A huge contingent travelled from Manchester, desperate to see United end their 23-year drought. But for Mark Hughes it would be a particularly special occasion. The United midfielder had been with Barcelona between 1986 and 1988, before the Spanish giants offloaded him to Bayern Munich. Hughes had a point to prove and in one of his finest performances inspired United to an historic victory. In the first 45 minutes United enjoyed the best of the play but went into the dressing-room with no goal to show for their efforts. Then 23 minutes into the second half Hughes was fouled on the edge of the box. Robson floated the free kick, Steve Bruce rose to head the ball goalwards and Mark Hughes was left with the fairly simple task of bundling the ball over the line. Seven minutes later Hughes latched on to a delightful through ball from Bryan Robson, neatly rounded the goalkeeper, and drilled the ball into the back of the net to make it 2-0. Even then there was to be a late scare with Ronald Koeman pulling one back for Barcelona in the 79th minute. For the next 10 minutes there was panic as the Spanish side unleashed everything at United. But the Reds held out and with the final whistle were able to celebrate another famous triumph in Europe.

BARCELONA 1
MAN UNITED 2

The two men who were responsible for the goals, Mark Hughes (with cup) and Steve Bruce, celebrate United's European victory.

Hughes double delight

ALEX FERGUSON made history, Mark Hughes kept to the script and they sang Land of Hope and Glory as 25,000 deliriously happy Manchester United fans celebrated English football's glittering return to European competition.

A thousand flashbulbs lit the night air over Rotterdam as United's army of followers took their treasured pictures of Bryan Robson lifting the Cup Winners' Cup and United's lap of honour.

Daily Mirror, 16 May 1991

FERGIE'S NIGHT OF EURO TRIUMPH

1992

Right:
Brian McClair celebrates his goal with Paul Ince and Mark Hughes.

Opposite:
Gary Pallister with the Rumbelows League Cup.

IN 1991 UNITED had battled their way into the League Cup final, trouncing the eventual champions, runners-up and fourth placed sides on the way. It had been a magnificent run. But in the final they were drawn against second division Sheffield Wednesday and who wouldn't have put money on United to give Ron Atkinson's side the same treatment.

But Atkinson had remembered a thing or two about United from his days at Old Trafford. The result was that Wednesday pulled off the surprise of the season. Thirty years in the League Cup and they had still not lifted the trophy. It seemed to be something of an unlucky competition for United. They had twice appeared in the final, only to lose. The question now was whether they could make this season third time lucky.

The competition began easily enough with a home tie against Cambridge United. A young Ryan Giggs was given his first taste of League Cup football that evening, coming on as a substitute for Neil Webb, even managing to get his name on the scoresheet. It was a good omen. Giggs, still with only a handful of games to his name was looking like an exciting prospect. In the second leg with little danger of losing by more than three goals United were quite happy with a draw at Cambridge. Round two brought slightly stiffer opposition against a useful looking Portsmouth side who later that season would come within a whisker of reaching the FA Cup final. But in October they offered few problems for United, going down 3-1 at Old Trafford. Local rivals Oldham were the next visitors but again presented no worries. McClair opened the scoring and United's new Soviet winger Andrei Kanchelskis, signed from Shakhtyor Donetsk in May 1991 for £650,000, completed the formalities. United were into the last eight but faced a tough task with an away game at Leeds. The previous season United had faced Leeds in the semi-final, and now the Yorkshire side were out for revenge. What's more United were also facing Leeds three times in one week with a league fixture, an FA Cup match and the League Cup semi-final. Leeds were also serious championship contenders but, in a battle royal at Elland Road, it was the reds of Lancashire and United who ran out winners by three goals to one, thanks to Blackmore, Kanchelskis and young Ryan Giggs again.

New signings Peter Schmeichel and Paul Parker..

A new United side was now taking shape, showing a number of changes from the previous year. The tall Danish goalkeeper Peter Schmeichel had taken over from Les Sealey while big signing Paul Parker had been added to the lineup along with Kanchelskis and

McClair's blast keeps boss in line for double

BRIAN McCLAIR sent United's passionate army of fans into ecstacy with a Wembley winner.

Sun, 13 April 1992

Giggs. United were beginning to look a formidable team.

In the semi-final United faced second division promotion hopefuls Middlesbrough. There were no goals at Ayresome Park but at Old Trafford in a fiercely contested battle United found that luck was on their side as they sneaked through to the final. This time it seemed United's name might well be written on the trophy.

In the final Brian Clough's Nottingham Forest were the opposition, four times winners of the trophy and six times finalists – just about as tough a proposition as you could imagine. And at Wembley they lived up to their reputation in a lively, entertaining contest. In the end it was the brilliance of new boy Ryan Giggs which settled the tie. Running at a scampering Forest defence he slid a perfect pass in the direction of Brian McClair for the only goal of the game.

United had clinched the League Cup at last. In the last three years they had won the FA Cup, the European Cup-Winners' Cup and the League Cup. There was now only one more trophy to lift.

HOW THEY RATED

THE Sun's man in the Midlands PETER WHITE runs the rule over the Manchester United and Nottingham Forest players in yesterday's Rumbelows Cup showdown.

FOREST

MARRIOTT
ONLY eighth senior match but one he won't want to remember. 6

CHARLES
LASTED 22 minutes before recurrence of hamstring trouble forced him off. 6

WILLIAMS
FOUND it hard to fill Stuart Pearce's boots and partly to blame for McClair's winning goal. 5

WALKER
FOREST skipper had work cut out to contain McClair but produced a fine display. 7

WASSALL
KEPT tight rein on Hughes and produced a superb saving tackle on Ince. 7

KEANE
RAN tirelessly but must have rued missing an early scoring chance. 7

CROSBY
DANGEROUS at times, but showed frustration when booked for throwing ball away. 6

GEMMILL
VERY disappointing. Failed to reproduce exiting form of ZDS final. 5

CLOUGH
HAD plenty of space in midfield, but never had enough options on. 7

SHERINGHAM
HE struggled to keep pace with the game and failed to convert his one chance. 5

BLACK
BECAME far too isolated on left, and did little better when he moved inside. 5

LAWS
ABLE sub and kept Forest's hopes alive with a goal-line clearance from McClair. 6

UNITED

SCHMEICHEL
HAD a quiet afternoon, but made a vital save late on from Clough. 6

PARKER
HE always had winger Black under control to cut out one of Forest's big threats. 6

IRWIN
HAD to be on his toes to contain Crosby, and occasionally had to call for Phelan's help. 6

BRUCE
PLAYED captain's role. Rarely in trouble against Forest's lightweight attack. 7

PHELAN
DESTROYED so many promising Forest build-ups yet still found time to go forward. 8

PALLISTER
THE PFA Player of the Year showed why he is held in such high esteem. 7

KANCHELSKIS
DIDN'T see enough of the ball, but still managed to get in several telling crosses. 6

INCE
WORKED tirelessly to ensure United always held the upper hand in midfield. 7

McCLAIR
HIS 23rd goal of season capped an impressive display from the hard-working Scot. 7

HUGHES
ALWAYS created problems, but never had a chance to get on the scoresheet. 6

GIGGS
SHOWED why he's so highly regarded, displaying excellent skills down either wing. 7

SHARPE
LITTLE time to make impact after coming on as 75th minute sub for Kanchelskis. 6

1993

UNITED MAY HAVE won the FA Cup, the League Cup and even the European Cup-Winners' Cup in recent years, but since 1967 they had not won the one trophy that really mattered – the League championship. Twenty-six years without the title was a long time. They had come close in those years, and never more close than the previous season when they faltered at the final hurdle to finish as runners-up. But with the experience of that soul-destroying campaign now behind them and a bitter lesson learned United began the 1992/93 season determined to add the title to their growing list of honours.

Champions!

Fergie: The greatest moment of my life

Daily Express, 4 May 1993

This season however their assault on the title would have one significant difference - Eric Cantona.

The tall, athletic Frenchman had been a member of the Leeds side that had pipped United to the title the previous season. United manager Alex Ferguson had been on the look out for a strong man upfront since the serious injury to Dion Dublin and in mid-November had a record £3.5 million

Manchester United, FA Premier League Champions 1992/93

Ferguson signs Cantona for £1.2m

The Independent, 27 November 1992

bid for Sheffield Wednesday's David Hirst turned down. Then later that month in an off-chance conversation with the Leeds manager Howard Wilkinson about another player, he was told that Cantona was available. Ferguson could barely believe what he was hearing and within hours Cantona was on his way to Old Trafford, a bargain at £1.2 million.

Cantona was the final piece in the Ferguson jigsaw. He was not just a goalscorer but a goalmaker as well, a man with impressive skills, an entertainer in the old style, and a player who could win a game with one spectacular move. But United also had another bonus, the improving displays of young Ryan Giggs. Giggs had made his debut for United in March 1991 and had only become a permanent fixture in the side during the 1991/92 season. It was always clear that he had precocious skills but with every game he seemed to be improving, never afraid to show off his awesome repertoire. And with Eric Cantona alongside him his talents would truly blossom during the season.

United had made a shaky start to their campaign, still suffering the traumas of the previous season. During the autumn they had gone seven games without a win, hardly the form of title challengers. The side seemed to lack inspiration. But then along came Cantona making his league debut in the derby against Manchester City, as a substitute. United won and were firmly back on the winning trail. Cantona was also on the goal trail, claiming his first goal for the club against Chelsea. He was soon hitting a goal every game and by the beginning of January United topped the table for the first time that season. After that there was no stopping them. There were still some scares en route but on 2 May United were acclaimed champions of the Premier League as Oldham won at Aston Villa. The following evening Old Trafford celebrated as it had rarely celebrated before when Blackburn Rovers were the unfortunate visitors. United won 3–1 in a display of entertainment that had everyone on their feet. After 26 years United were champions again.

VERDICT ON OLD TRAFFORD'S CHAMPIONSHIP

ALEX FERGUSON: "It has been hard work to win the Premier League but it has all paid off. This is a difficult club to manage. There's a lot of pressure involved in the job. The standards are high here. We've set our own standards now with this triumph and we mustn't let those standards drop."

MARTIN EDWARDS: "I'm especially pleased for Alex. It's true to say that he has enjoyed the unswerving support of every member of our staff.

"For so long we've waited to repay our supporters for their tremendous loyalty. At last we can say we've done that, but I would ask them in return to stay off the pitch when the trophy is presented and leave the limelight to the players."

SIR MATT BUSBY: "I'm over the moon, as they say these days, and I mean that — the English League is still the hardest in the world to win. This team has exciting qualities and character after losing its way a third through the season. We've finished strongly and tomorrow will be one of the most memorable nights Old Trafford has ever known."

WILF McGUINNESS: "Alex has been under a lot of pressure. He has coped with that pressure and though he has made mistakes I think he's now on the verge of setting up what we'll look back on and call the Fergie dynasty to match the Busby dynasty."

PADDY CRERAND: "I'll be able to give back some of the stick they've given us during this long wait. This is going to be the start of something big."

GEORGE BEST: "Manchester United are one of the biggest names in football and that they haven't won it for so long is phenomenal. But now they've done it and the icing on the cake is that they are in the European Cup again. And the future looks terrific. They have a great crop of youngsters coming through and that should ensure continued success from now on."

BRYAN ROBSON: "It's been a long time and now no-one can throw that 26-year gap in the faces of the young players. Now we can go forward and hopefully dominate English football for the next 10 years like Liverpool did. We have a new foundation to build on. We have a young team, backed by a powerful youth set-up.

"I'm delighted for the fans and for myself at this late stage of my career. It's been an ambition to be a champion for 12 years and more. It's a great day for the boss."

STEVE BRUCE: "It was a great disappointment to lose out last year. Unless you experience something like that you can't grasp just how shattering it is. I have been at the club for six years and the championship has always been the ultimate one. This is the one we've always wanted and it'll take some time to sink in. "We were supposed to be trying to relax today because we have a match tomorrow, but you can kiss that game goodbye. The party's already begun and the people of Manchester can look foward to a great 24 hours."

MARK HUGHES: "We've had so many years of disappointment, particularly last year, and I hope that this will make up for it all. It was a tremendous performance by Oldham to do it for us. I was jumping up and down throughout their match. I knew when they went ahead they would make it difficult for Villa."

HOWARD WILKINSON: "Last season they showed their potential and this season they've proved they're the best team in England without a doubt. Alex has shown that despite what some people have said about him he's the right man for the job."

William Johnson

Daily Telegraph, 3 May 1993

New signing Eric Cantona watches from the stands at Highbury (top) as his new team win 1–0, and (above) in his first Premier League match, as substitute in the home derby against Manchester City which United won 2–1.

1994

Double de

The death of Sir Matt Busby on Thursday, 20 January stunned not only the city of Manchester but the whole footballing world. Busby was a legend, almost a part of British life. His death was front-page news. Even the television news led with it. Busby who was 84 years of age had been ill for some time. Manchester went into mourning. At Old Trafford flags flew at half mast and when United played Everton a few days later the biggest crowd of the season bowed their heads in silence to the memory of a great man, the man who had created the modern Manchester United. His funeral cortège weaved its way through the streets of Old Trafford, snaking past the stadium half-destroyed by German bombs when he took over in 1945 and which he had turned into one of the finest grounds in Britain.

Busby had created three outstanding United sides. There had

Tributes to the late Sir Matt Busby outside Old Trafford.

Manchester unites in farewell to Sir Matt

By Nigel Bunyan

THOUSANDS of soccer fans stood eight-deep outside Old Trafford yesterday to pay their last respects to Sir Matt Busby as his funeral cortege made a three-mile journey to the Manchester United stadium.

Many brushed away tears as the hearse bearing the former manager's mahogany coffin halted opposite the Munich Clock on Sir Matt Busby Way.

Officially, the clock is dedicated to the memory of those players, officials and journalists who died in the 1958 air disaster.

But, since Sir Matt's death a week ago aged 84, it has become strewn with flowers, scarves and favours in memory of the man who survived the crash after twice receiving the Last Rites and went on to make Manchester United one of the world's most successful clubs.

As the 14-car cortege came in sight, the driving rain stopped and supporters fell silent — leaving only the sound of the hooves of the two police horses, their riders in ceremonial uniform, that flanked the lead car.

Daily Telegraph, 28 January 1994

ight for United

Sunday Times, 15 May 1994

been the post war team that had been runners-up four times before finally clinching the title in 1952 to add to their 1948 FA Cup triumph. His second great team had been the Busby Babes, winners of two championships in the mid-1950s before they were so cruelly destroyed at Munich. Busby himself had hovered between life and death but had survived to make an emotional return to Wembley to watch his new side go down to Bolton Wanderers. And then there was his third great side, the team that captured two championships in the 1960s and went on to win the European Cup for their manager in 1968.

In May 1993 Busby had been present at Old Trafford, all smiles, as United lifted the championship. There could be only one fitting memorial to Busby and that was for the current side to go out and win the double, the one honour that had escaped Busby. United led the Premiership from start to finish. By Christmas they were so far ahead that the bookmakers even refused to take bets. But towards the end of the season they faltered slightly, dropping points as the pressures began to mount. United were in pursuit not just of the double but of the treble. They reached the Coca-Cola Cup final in March and took on Aston Villa at Wembley but went down 1–3. In the League luck suddenly seemed to desert them with the dismissals of Peter Schmeichel and Eric Cantona. But in a Wembley FA Cup semi-final, a goal down to Oldham and 90 minutes already showing on the clock, Mark Hughes poked a toe at an impossible chance and the ball zoomed into the back of the net. United's luck had turned. A few days later Oldham were comprehensively beaten in the replay and United were at Wembley for the fourth time that season. In the league Blackburn's challenge, which had brought them to within striking distance of United, suddenly petered out while United with impressive victories over Wimbledon, Manchester City, Leeds, Ipswich and Southampton reasserted their authority and were crowned champions.

In the FA Cup final United faced Chelsea, the side that had twice beaten them that season. But there would be no third victory for the Londoners. Chelsea may have held their own for an hour but suddenly two dramatic penalties within six minutes, expertly taken by Eric Cantona, and the game was all over. Hughes and McClair added numbers three and four. United had won the double, only the fourth team this century to achieve the honour. The Wembley crowd fittingly remembered Sir Matt, chanting his name in honour of the double.

Wembley celebrations after completing the Double.

PICTURE CREDITS

The publishers would like to thank the following for permission to reproduce copyright material:
Allsport: 199 top; Associated Press: 136, 140, 144; Associated Sports Photography: 207 bottom; Colorsport: 24, 32, 36, 40, 55 left and right, 64, 71, 77 left, 87 102 right, 105, 112 top, 118, 119, 121, 126, 129, 137, 138 bottom, 147, 161, 165, 170, 180, 196, 197, 198 right, 208, 210 top and bottom, 211, 212, 213 top and bottom, 214, 215: Joe Glanville: 100 top; The Hulton Picture Company: 53, 67, 68, 79, 82, 90 top, 94 bottom, 98, 102 left, 109, 139 right, 142 bottom, 143, 153, 154 bottom, 158, top, 172, 179, 182 top and bottom, 189; The Illustrated London News: 35 top; Joe Laskowski/Swifts Programmes: 80, 83 left, 84 left and right, 93 right; Manchester Evening News: 116, 134; Manchester United Football Club: 25, 47 top and bottom, 51, 100 bottom; Mirror Colour Print: 23 top, 26, 42, 43, 44, 48, 49, 61 top and bottom, 62, 63, 72, 74, 86, 89, 93 left, 96, 97, 104 top and bottom, 108, 111, 131, 132 top and bottom; Popperfoto: 90 bottom, 99, 106, 107, 110 113 top and bottom, 114, 114-115, 120, 124, 142 top, 154 top, 156, 193 bottom; G E Roberts/A Seabright: 52; P. Robsinson 162; Sport & General: 187; Syndication Inernational: 81, 88, 122, 123, 128, 133, 135, 141, 145 top and bottom, 146, 149, 150, 151, 152, 154 centre, 157, 158 bottom, 163 top, 164, 167 bottom, 168, 171, 174, 175, 177, 181, 183, 186 top and bottom, 188, 190, 193 top, 194, 201; Bob Thomas Sports Photography: 92 top, 117 top and bottom, 125, 130, 148, 163 bottom, 173, 176, 178, 184, 185, 192, 195, 198 left, 199 bottom, 200, 203, 204, 205 left and right, 206, 207 top; Tom Tyrrell, 85, 95, 138 top, 139 left; Vintage Magazines: 34, 38.

Special thanks goes to David Price and Ralph Mortimer to allowing us to reproduce their material and to Tom Tyrrell for this advice and assistance.

SHARP